the Tudor Kitchen

the Tudor Kitchen

What the Tudors ate & drank

TERRY BREVERTON

AMBERLEY

First published 2015
This edition published 2017

Amberley Publishing
The Hill, Stroud
Gloucestershire, GL5 4EP

www.amberley-books.com

British Library Cataloguing in Publication Data.
A catalogue record for this book is available from the British Library.

ISBN 978 1 4456 6040 0 (paperback)

Typesetting and Origination by Amberley Publishing.
Printed in the UK.

Contents

Introduction

Good husband and housewife, now chiefly be glad
Things handsome to have, as they ought to be had,
They both do provide against Christmas do come,
To welcome their neighbour, good cheer to have some;

Good bread and good drink, a good fire in the hall,
Brawn pudding and souse, and good mustard withal.
Beef, mutton, and pork, shred pies of the best,
Pig, veal, goose, and capon, and turkey well dressed;

Cheese, apples, and nuts, jolly carols to hear,
As then in the country is counted good cheer.
What cost to good husband is any of this,
Good household provision only it is;
Of other the like I do leave out a many,
That costeth the husbandman never a penny.

Thomas Tusser, *Five Hundred Points of Good Husbandry* (1557)

Did you ever wonder what the Tudors ate and drank? This book gives us an overview of the very fabric of Tudor life, for both rich and poor. The age saw an amazing variety of new dishes, many of which have been taken from contemporary sources for this cookbook. As well as giving us interesting and useful recipes, the book tells us to forget popcorn – when being entertained by Shakespeare's plays, theatregoers enjoyed vast quantities of oysters, crabs, cockles, mussels, periwinkles and whelks, as well as walnuts, hazelnuts, raisins, plums, cherries, dried figs, peaches, elderberry and blackberry pies and sturgeon steaks. Among the Tudor court's food purchases, in just one year, we count 8,200 sheep, 2,330 deer and 53 wild boar, plus thousands of birds such as peacock, heron, capon, teal, gull, shoveler, quail, pheasant, swan and cygnet.

Part 1 of the book explains how the Tudors farmed their animals and cereals, with the majority of the population having a monotonous diet with very little meat or fish. The first three chapters describe Tudor farming, food and drink, and the differences between diets and the classes. The fourth chapter informs us about the great kitchens such as Hampton Court and the fifth tells us of royal feasts and etiquette, and helps us understand how Henry VIII went from a thirty-two-inch waist aged thirty, to a fifty-four-inch waist aged fifty-five.

Part 2 gives us around five hundred recipes of the times, which can be tried by curious or enterprising readers. There are some astonishing combinations of flavours, and Tudor cuisine is something we are only now coming to appreciate. Of course, these surviving recipes were predominantly for the middle and upper classes. Many have been updated to give modern measures and ingredients, and all can be replicated and/or modernised. Some of the recipes date from the fifteenth century, and a few from just after the Tudor dynasty, but all were consumed during the Tudor age of 1485 to 1603. The Tudor idea of 'courses' is different to our own, but I have attempted to place them as starters, main courses, side dishes, sweet courses, snacks, preserves and sauces, although there is an overlap among categories. There is also a chapter on dishes that could appear disgusting to today's reader but are nevertheless interesting and entertaining.

In many cases the original recipe has been given with its source, and explanatory notes have been added to elucidate any text. The Tudor dynasty saw the first printed cookery book, followed by many others, but they were used as aide-memoires by professional cooks, so they do not have accurate quantities of ingredients. I have sometimes tried to indicate quantities, and used a mixture of decimal and pre-decimal measurements, as the over-sixties (including myself) are far more acquainted with the latter. However, many of the dishes are for the reader to experiment with, as no cooking times or quantities were given. England's greatest dynasty oversaw not only a Renaissance in the arts, but in cuisine, to which this book hopefully attests.

Part 1

The Tudor Diet

1

Tudor Farming

England and Wales were predominantly rural and agricultural, and at the beginning of the sixteenth century very few English towns had more than a few thousand people. Most of the population lived in small villages and made their living from farming. Production of food was the main economic activity, and the most important event of the year was the harvest, but harvests were especially bad in 1554–6 (during Mary I's brief reign) and 1594–7. London was vastly larger than any other English city, with a population of over 50,000 in the early sixteenth century. Only a very small proportion of the population lived in urban areas, and in 1520 the only cities outside London with over 7,000 inhabitants were Exeter, Bristol, Salisbury, Norwich, York and Newcastle. Those with over 4,000 people were Oxford, Gloucester, Colchester, Worcester, Coventry, Lynn, Yarmouth and Shrewsbury. Although the overall population doubled in the sixteenth century to about 4 million people, settlements other than London remained small.

A major effect of the twofold rise in population was a general increase in prices, especially of food. During the sixteenth century food prices rose fivefold, while prices of industrial manufactures only doubled. Rising food prices hurt both those on fixed incomes and those without enough land to supply their own needs. However, owners of large farms were able to take advantage of rising prices, and by increasing efficiency began to maximise profits. The introduction of new crops, and their periodic rotation, increased the long-term fertility of fields. Each year tenants might cultivate only two-thirds of the land, letting the other third lie 'fallow' so it could recover its fertility. Manor lands were thus farmed using the 'three-field system', with one field devoted to winter crops, another to summer crops, and a third lying fallow each year. Alternatively one field was used for grain, one for hay and a third left fallow, which was often sown with a legume which would be ploughed under to enrich the soil with nitrogen. Agricultural innovation increased productivity per acre, and the reclamation of marginal land through channelling marshes and draining fenland brought more land into productive use. A wealthy landowning middle class emerged, focussed upon gaining more estates by marriage into other such families.

The four most popular grains cultivated were wheat, barley, rye and oats. Wheat was most valued because it had the gluten content necessary to make better bread. All four could be sown in autumn for harvest the following summer. However, this 'winter crop' could be lost to an icy winter or a storm-ridden spring, so to ensure a harvest farmers would plant a second crop in the spring. This crop would not produce as much as it had not had as much time to grow, but was necessary security. The grain was planted as soon as the primitive wooden ploughs could scratch the soft ground, usually in March, and would be harvested in early autumn.

Grains were threshed in an open area of a covered barn, where a special wooden floor was set up. Flails were used to beat the stalks, causing them to shed their grain. The straw was then removed for fodder, bedding, roofing and the like, and the grain was scooped up with a wide, shallow winnowing basket. By tossing the grain into the air and fanning it, the lighter chaff (inedible husks) blew away until only the heavier grain remained. The heaviest grain fell closest to the winnower and was placed in dry storage to plant next season. Most of the grain was now dried in a kiln and taken in sacks to the local windmill or watermill to be ground into flour. Flax and hemp were also grown as important fibre crops, planting in March or April and harvesting in July. The common use of cotton in fabrics was to await its first industrial spinning in England in 1730, so wool was also used along with hemp and flax, with the very richest wearing flannel and silks.

Around 90 per cent of the population lived in rural farming communities, earning most of their income from livestock or arable farming. Most labourers either rented a cottage and were paid wages by the farmer, or received a cottage in return for working for the farmer. He then grew his own food while his wife also worked to survive and afford children. A farm labourer was paid 6*d* a day and a loaf cost 2*d*, but some villages had communal ovens where the women could make their own bread more cheaply. Labourers rose at dawn and generally went to bed at sunset. The only light in the cottage came from the fire or from rush lights, home-made candles made from reeds dipped in animal fat, which gave off very little light and a terrible odour. The upper classes could afford wax candles, but there was always a danger of a fire breaking out. Pottage, usually meat-free for the poor, was the usual breakfast. By the Elizabethan Statute of Artificers, labourers worked between 5 a.m. and

7 or 8 p.m. between March to September, and from dawn to dusk between September and March.

By 1600, around 800 markets in England gave access to a variety of foods. Country residents regularly purchased food at small markets and fairs, while city-dwellers usually shopped at markets held once a week. Account books kept for a London household in 1612 record weekly purchases of meats, poultry, wines, cooking fats, and flour and spices. In London, as in other cities, each market sold particular goods such as herbs, cheese or freshwater fish. Other items were bought from large regional fairs where vendors sold dry goods, livestock and grains. Provisioning London required a network of sixteen markets. Billingsgate sold grain transported from Thames Valley river ports and from the Baltic, salt from France, onions and roots, imported oranges and fruit, freshwater and saltwater fish and shellfish. By 1546, Leadenhall market vendors included crops from Essex; corn and cattle from Middlesex; and fruit, vegetables and hops from Kent. It is still a general food market, while Smithfield Market is a meat market which was formerly a live cattle market.

FARMING AND ENCLOSURE

Hedges only came into use as boundaries in the later Middle Ages, as strip cultivation gave way to larger enclosures. Hedges required yearly maintenance, pruning, training, and clearing of the ditches that ran alongside them, and this was generally carried out in February. Orchards existed, but were generally associated with large estates or monasteries. Under Henry VIII, the monasteries were closed and the great landowners who bought their estates began to keep great flocks of sheep to make immense profits in Europe. They needed to enclose their land with hedges and fences to stop their valuable sheep wandering, and threw poor people out of their houses, destroying villages. They now needed fewer labourers with the switch from crops to sheep, and the dispossessed vagrants were forced to wander through the country and into towns trying to find work to survive. Many were forced to live by robbery and violence to survive.

The 'enclosures' took over fields which had previously been leased to tenants or which had been used as common grazing land. English *champaign*, extensive, open land, had been commonly enclosed as pastureland for sheep from the fourteenth to the sixteenth century, as populations had declined owing to plagues and war. Foreign demand for English wool helped encourage increased production, and the wool industry was thought to be more profitable for landowners who had large decaying farmlands. Enclosure grew quickly in the reign of Henry VII (1485–1509), as common rights over land were thrown out by landowners. Only a small proportion of English land was enclosed, but the social effects were magnified because enclosure was concentrated in a few areas, especially the Midlands. The previously used open-field system had not been suitable for fencing off, and production, whether of crops or sheep, was on a smaller scale. Enclosure enabled the selective breeding of animals and cultivation of bigger crops.

However, Tudor authorities were nervous about a breakdown in social order. Lack of income made one a pauper, and if one lost one's home as well, that person became a vagrant, to be treated as a criminal. From Henry VII's reign onwards, Parliament began passing Acts to stop enclosure, to limit its effects, or at least to fine those responsible. The first such law was in 1489, and over the next 150 years, there were eleven more Acts of Parliament and eight commissions of enquiry on the subject. The people made efforts to remove old enclosures, and much legislation of the 1530s and 1540s concerns this problem. Former tenants, impatient for legislation to reclaim pasture for tillage, who were illegally destroying enclosures, began to group together. Kett's Rebellion in Norfolk in 1549, in the reign of Edward VI, was only put down with the use of German and Italian mercenaries. Agrarian revolts swept all over the nation, and other revolts occurred periodically throughout the century. The transition from the English 'village era' to the 'town era' was accelerated by enclosures. This new and extra concentration of available labour in the towns, desperate for work, enabled real growth in Tudor manufacturing and associated retail, banking and other service industries.

TUDOR ANIMALS

Cattle

All farm animals were far smaller than modern breeds, and a full-grown ox reached a size scarcely larger than today's calf. The average weight of a cow was around 350 pounds, compared to 1,200–1,300 pounds today. Cattle in Tudor times were agricultural work-horses, pulling carts and teamed up to pull ploughs and harrows. Farmers did not keep big herds of these working animals, either for their milk or beef, because neither was used on a regular basis in the diet of the masses. Beef was very much a rich man's dish, while milk was rarely imbibed. Working oxen, usually castrated males, were kept to pull ploughs, harrows and other farming tools. These oxen were very distinctive from today's cattle, built to pull a plough, with great shoulders and horns. Smaller farms may have shared a team of oxen. A team of two oxen and their ploughman could probably plough an acre in a day, and many Tudor fields were roughly this size. A few breeding cows were kept, and any excess milk from these was made into butter and cheese, and a small amount for the very young, very old and sick to drink. Cattle need much more space and attention than sheep, and unlike sheep have to be sheltered and fed in winter months, so were generally slaughtered for meat and leather before the onset of winter. Cattle horn was heated and shaped to make spoons and drinking vessels, and spices were kept in hollow horns with linen, dipped in melted beeswax, as a cover. From these small multipurpose cattle, we have bred two very distinct and much larger types. Generally, beef cattle are bred for their shape and quality of meat, and dairy cattle are bred for their milk production.

Sheep
Larger landowners began to enclose fields so they could breed larger and larger flocks of sheep. Wool was the main export from Britain, bringing in fortunes for those with large flocks. Like cattle, sheep were much smaller than today, but selective breeding had begun to give bigger sheep and thereby larger wool yields. The average weight rose from around 28 pounds in 1500 to 46 pounds in 1600, but today's ewes are 100–200 pounds and a champion ram can now weigh 1,200–1,600 pounds.

Sheep needed little care the year round, producing wool, milk, more sheep and eventually meat. It was important that they were marked, with notches on the ear and/or a splotch of dye on the back, since grazing land for sheep was often used in common. As they were so small, the fleece of a sheep often weighed less than two ounces. Wool was the material that everyone wore, and the quality of English wool was famous all over the known world. It was exported to the Lowlands, where it was spun and woven into very fine cloth and imported back to England. Sheep did not need the top quality grazing of the cattle, and were hardy enough to stay out all year round, being often brought lower down to more sheltered land in winter. A shepherd could tend a large flock, and a ewe will have one or two lambs each year, increasing the flock. The Tudors used more sheep's milk than cow's milk, and it was made into butter and cheese, forming a large part of the ordinary persons' diet.

'Sheep turned grass into wool' to provide the raw material for the woollen cloth-weaving industry, which was by far the most dominant component of the Tudor economy. For this reason, the growing of sheep for wool was not just a matter for farmers, but integral to the governance and economic health of the nation. In Tudor times, it was said that 'half the wealth of England rides on the back of the sheep'. The rise in prosperity owing to sheep, along with little civil disturbance, made the Tudor era far more settled than that of the Plantagenets. The Tudor period saw the first fundamental changes in agricultural practice, hastened by Henry VIII's Dissolution of the Monasteries and the break-up of their huge estates.

Early enclosures of arable land into sheep-walks turned many cottagers into 'landless vagabonds', but the countryside also became 'thickly dotted with the solid, well-proportioned homes of the middle-class husbandmen.' In 1516, Sir Thomas More in *Utopia* complained: 'your sheep that were wont to be so meek and tame, and so small eaters, now, as I hear say, be become so great devourers and so wild, that they eat up, and swallow down the very men themselves. They consume, destroy, and devour whole fields, houses and cities.' However, intensive sheep-farming also brought a new era of prosperity to the countryside. The yeoman-farmer prospered, and by 1600, more than 20 per cent had actually become freeholders. Many were literate enough to take advantage of the advice given by a new breed of agricultural writers, such as Thomas Tusser (1520–84), with his instructional poem *Five hundred points of Good Husbandry* (1573).

Although most commercial production of wool now comes from descendants of Spanish merino sheep, England produced Europe's finest wools during the Middle Ages. In fact, Spanish wools were then among the worst in Europe and were used in the production of the very cheapest fabrics. There were two principal types of sheep in England, a small sheep producing short wool, and a larger sheep producing long wool. The short-woolled sheep was a breed used on poor pastures, hills, moors and downs. Its wool was prepared by 'carding', using teasels to comb, disentangle and mix fibres together to produce a continuous web or sliver. It was then processed to make cloth, i.e. textiles of heavy texture thickened by 'fulling'. Fulling is the process of cleansing, scouring and milling the wool to make it thicker. The long-woolled sheep was found in rich grasslands, marshes and fens. Its wool was prepared for use by 'combing', and was used for lighter worsteds and serges, materials which were not usually fulled. Three breeds accounted for most wool production in the Middle Ages, the Ryeland, Cotswold and Lincoln. Ryeland was the most famous of short-woolled breeds, grown in the country between the Severn and the marches of Wales and was largely responsible for the 'Lemster ore', centred upon Leominster, the 'golden fleece of England'. However, the bulk of the fine wool exported came from the long-woolled Cotswolds and Lincolns.

Pigs

Pigs were the third major type of livestock, again far smaller than today's breeds. Sows were bred in December or January and would deliver their piglets in March or April. Piglets stayed in the farmyard with their mothers until about August, when they were considered strong enough to be driven out to forage in the woods. Even very poor families could usually afford to raise a pig themselves, since pigs forage so well and cost little to feed. The salted meat and offal from a December butchering would have to last the whole winter. The Tudor pig was nearer to the wild boar in looks, and the Tamworth, a long bodied, ginger pig is about the closest we have in looks to the Tudor pig.

Unlike other farm animals, the pig does not need a field and acres of grassland to survive. The peasant's pig would have been kept in a small enclosure behind his cottage, known as a *hogbog*. It was used by farmers and peasants alike to house both pigs and poultry. Pigs occupied the ground space while poultry had a raised hen house, with the design saving both space and danger to the hens at night. Pigs were an incredibly useful animal to keep, and a Tudor peasant would often receive a young pig in the spring as part of his wages. Not only did the pig eat any food leftovers, but pigs enjoy human waste. On one side of the pigsty was the 'midden' or human toilet, with a gentle slope into the pig quarters. The pig cleared the human waste, took nutrition from it, and made more manure. This then went onto the compost heap, which when well rotted, was put on the Tudor garden to help vegetables grow. However, a pig needed more food than just leftovers, and peasants had rights to take their animals onto common land to graze or into the landowner's woodland in late summer/early autumn. 'Pannage' is the ancient practice to fatten pigs before slaughter and salting for the winter, and was useful in that pigs ate green acorns and beech mast (nuts) which are poisonous to cattle and horses. There is still a 'Pannage Season' of 60 days in the New Forest. The pigs grazed on the undergrowth of plants, keeping the land clear of unusable plants so all the goodness in the soil could be used by the trees, and they also added richness to the soil by manuring it. Late autumn was the traditional time for killing pigs, as they were well grown so there was no point trying to feed them over winter, except for breeding sows and boar.

Horses

In Britain all our nine native breeds are classified as ponies, which despite being strong as riding animals, are not built to pull ploughs. The breeds are the New Forest, Dartmoor, Exmoor, Welsh Mountain, Fell, Dales, Highlands, Shetland and Connemara. Thus oxen were preferred as farm animals. All the heavy horse breeds came from the continent, with France and Belgium supplying horses for knights, built to carry enormous weights. Only the very rich kept these great horses for work on their farms. A team of horses could work faster than a team of oxen, but were far more expensive, needing better grazing to keep in good condition to work, requiring better shelters and feeding in the winter, and they could not work on steep slopes or heavy ground.

Geese, Doves, Chickens, Peacocks, Swans and Turkeys

The landowner and gentry would keep geese, to be eaten at feasts. The gentry would have had dovecots in their courtyards, as a great delicacy was 'squab', or young dove. Many people would have kept chickens with their pigs, not to be eaten until the end of their natural lives. They were needed for eggs and for pest control in gardens. Many wild birds also found their way into the cooking cauldrons. The wealthy ate pheasant and grouse, while the poor might trap songbirds to make into a pie.

There is an extant list of the dishes served at Henry IV's coronation feast in 1399. The menu includes eagle, heron, crane, bittern, force-fed castrated cockerels (*capoun de haut grece*), curlew, pullet, 'small birds', quail, partridge and egret (*Potage Dyvers* 1430). From 1200 onwards, peacocks were the most expensive birds available and the celebration feast of choice for the rich, but by the end of the sixteenth century, peacocks had fallen out of fashion and had been replaced by swans. Swans were a common Christmas dish on the rich man's table in 1500, and on Christmas Day 1512, in the Duke of Northumberland's household, five swans were dished up for dinner. Randle Home, around 1640, gave us a menu for 'A Christmas Days Feast' demonstrating that swan was still the preferred bird into Stuart times.

The First Course. Oysters; A Collar of Brawn; Stewed Broth of Mutton and Marrowbones; A Grand Sallet; A Potage of Capons; A Breast of Veal in stuffado; Boiled Partridges; A Chine or Surloin of Beef roasted; Mince Pyes; A Jegote of Mutton with Anchovis Sauce; A made dish of Sweet breads; A Swan roast; A Pastie of Venison; A Kid with a Pudding in his Belly; A stake Pye; A Haunch of Venison roasted; A Turkey roast, stuck with Clove; A made Dish of Chickens in puff Paste; 2 Geese roast, one larded; 3 Capons, one larded; A Custard.

The Second Course. Oranges and Lemons; A young Lamb or Kid; 4 Rabbits, two larded; A Pigg sauced with Tongue; Ducks, some larded; A made Dish in puff paste; Bolonia Sausages; Anchovis; Mushrooms; Cavieare; Pickled Oysters, in a Dish; Teales, some larded; A Gammon of Westphalia Bacon; Plovers, some larded; A Tart in puff paste; Preserved Fruit and Pippins; A Dish of Larks; Neats Tongues; Sturgeon, and Anchovis, and Jellies.'

In the 1560s the Duke of Northumberland's household menu contained not only a roast swan, but a goose and even a 'turkie'. Although expensive, Queen Elizabeth decreed that every household in England should eat goose as part of their Christmas Feast in 1588, as it was the first meal she enjoyed after the defeat of the Spanish Armada. Over half of the population lived at subsistence level, so it is hard to comprehend her order being carried out. Goose, chicken, turkey and swan were boiled, not roasted, and usually served with celery sauce.

A young trader named William Strickland, who sailed to the New World with the Venetian explorer Sebastian Cabot, turned up in his home town of Bristol in 1526 with six turkeys, which he sold for two pence each, the earliest known appearance of a turkey on these shores. Turkey is documented as being in London markets by the 1540s, but it was thought of as invalid food rather than Christmas fare at first. Turkey soon joined the long roll call of different meats adorning the Christmas tables of the wealthy. Toward the end of the age, turkey was beginning to replace peacock and swan as the centrepiece of feasts. Across Europe, Charles Dickens' *A Christmas Carol* created the breakthrough for the turkey in 1843. Scrooge gifted a Christmas turkey to the Cratchit family, making the bird a fashionable feast for the masses. The British royal family needed, as usual, time to catch on. They ate their first 'Christmas turkey' in 1851, replacing the traditional swan.

The guinea fowl is in the same taxonomic family as turkeys and chickens, *Galliformes*, but native to sub-Saharan Africa. They were reintroduced to Europe in the fifteenth century – 'collecting exotic animals was a hobby of Renaissance princes and the wealthy, and guinea fowl appeared in their royal parks and private menageries.' The Mamluk Sultanate, which controlled Egypt and modern-day Israel and Lebanon, served as a supplier. The Mamluks were ethnically Turkish, most coming from the Caucasus, and the birds became known as *galinias turcicas* or 'Turkish chickens', but were sometimes also known as 'Indian chickens'. As transatlantic trade developed in the sixteenth century, North American turkeys were confused with guinea fowl. Turkeys are native to the Americas, but the Europeans first encountering them thought that they looked like a kind of guinea fowl. Confusingly, guinea fowl were also called turkey fowl, because Europeans received most of their guinea fowl imported via Turkey. Consequently, the English used 'turkey cock' or 'cocks of *Inde*,' and the French word *'poules d'Inde'* to distinguish the new turkey. The Dutch call the turkey 'bird of Calicut' (Calcutta), but confusingly in Malaya it is a 'Dutch chicken'. The Japanese and Korean call it the 'seven-faced bird' and in Thai and Urdu it is the 'elephant chicken' or 'elephant trunk chicken.' In its homeland, the Blackfoot and Cree simply call it 'big bird', while in the Iranian Farsi language, the turkey is the onomatopoeic *booghalamoon*.

Rabbits

Rabbits accompanied the Normans across the English Channel, primarily as a source of food for the occupational armies. As the Norman forces settled in the area between Bury St. Edmunds and Thetford, the rabbits found the sandy soil ideal for making burrows. The sand, blown in from the coastal areas, covered areas left largely barren from overgrazing. These areas were soon home to large warrens, areas of land set aside from the Middle Ages onwards for rabbit husbandry. Rabbits were imported into England around 1200 from Spain, and they were delicate creatures that needed to be nurtured and protected to survive in the English climate. They were also valuable livestock, prized for both their meat and their skins, and guarded by the lord and his warrener.

From these early times, warren lodges were built out on the lonely warrens to accommodate the warrener, also sometimes doubling as a hunting lodge. The monasteries kept rabbits in *cunicularia,* which may have closely resembled hutches or pens, rather than the open enclosures with specialized structures which the domestic warren became. Such an enclosure was called a *cony-garth* (rabbit-yard), or sometimes *conegar, coneygree* or a *bury,* from burrow. The most characteristic structure of the *cony-garth* is the pillow mound. These were pillow-like, oblong mounds with flat tops, sometimes arranged like the letter E, or into more extensive, interconnected rows. Often these were provided with pre-built, stone-lined tunnels. The preferred orientation was on a gentle slope, with the arms extending downhill, to facilitate drainage. The soil needed to be soft, to accommodate further burrowing.

To keep the rabbits from escaping, domestic warrens were often provided with a fairly substantive moat. A pale, or fence, was provided to exclude predators and poaching. The rarity of rabbits meant that their meat was prized as a delicacy, while their fur was used for trimming clothes. In the thirteenth century one rabbit was worth more than a workman's daily wage. It was not until the eighteenth century that rabbits began to be seen as a food for the poor, since by then they were ubiquitous in the wild. Rabbit pelt was used extensively in the hat-making industry until the early twentieth century. During the nineteenth century, hat-makers used mercury as a binding element for the pelt. Since the liquid metal is absorbed through the skin into the bloodstream, it settled in the nervous system, resulting in nerve disorders, giving us the phrase 'mad as a hatter.'

Fish

Henry VII gave his permission and helped pay his 'well-beloved John Cabot … to seeke out, discover and finde whatsoever isles, countries, regions or provinces … which before this time have been unknown to all Christians.' Cabot's ship, the 50-ton *Mathew,* sailed from Bristol with a crew of eighteen in 1497. The crew would normally have been around ten men, but extra mariners were needed on such a long trip. She carried enough food for eight months, and a *Mathew* replica can be seen in Bristol Docks. After a month at sea, Cabot landed and took the area of 'new found land' in the name of King Henry VII. Like Columbus (who never reached the American mainland), Cabot mistakenly believed that he had reached Asia, but instead Cabot had found one of the northern capes of Newfoundland. His voyage was the first European encounter with the mainland of North America since the Vikings of the eleventh century. Cabot's sailors were able to catch huge numbers of cod simply by dipping baskets into the water, and the news almost immediately saw English ships sailing for the great fisheries called the Grand Banks. Cabot was rewarded with the sum of £10 by the king, for discovering a new island 'off the coast of China.' Cabot was also given a pension of £20 a year. Cod was salted and brought back in great abundance to Tudor England.

On certain days by law people had to eat fish instead of meat. At first this was for religious reasons, but Henry VII passed laws to enforce the eating of fish, and thereby support the fishing industry. Those who lived near the sea could often eat fresh fish like herrings or mackerel, otherwise the norm was dried or salted fish. Farmed fisheries declined with the Dissolution of the Monasteries, with not only fish ponds but fish weirs being neglected. Whale meat was fairly common and cheap, owing to the plentiful supply of whales in the North Sea, each of which could feed hundreds of people. It was typically served boiled or very well roasted on a Friday, as whales, like porpoises and dolphins were classified as fish. Friday was a meat-free day, but for centuries the church had allowed Barnacle Geese to be eaten on a Friday. No one had seen the nest of the migrating geese and it was believed that they emerged from barnacles, so were thus regarded as fish. Not until 1597 were their nests found on Novaya Zemlya in the Arctic Ocean by William Barents' expedition. Until they were hunted to extinction for their fur, and to be roasted or stewed, beaver were also accounted as fish. Delicacies such as porpoise meat, stewed otter and grilled beaver tail were served at banquets, interpreted as meatless alternatives for Lent.

TUDOR VEGETABLES

Until recently it was thought that the people in Tudor times were vitamin deficient and hardly ate vegetables and fruit. Certainly scurvy existed, but the poor man's diet included root vegetables and scavenged fruits and nuts. With the nobles, vegetables and fruits, unless imported, hardly featured in their household accounts as they had their own gardens. On the other hand, the purchase of porpoises, venison and the like would be accounted for. In season, intricate layered salads were popular in richer households, and Henry VIII employed a Flemish gardener to grow salad vegetables for his table.

Yeoman farmers' wives grew vegetables, herbs and also flowers for eating. The variety of vegetables grown included leeks, lettuce, garlic, peas, parsnips, skirrets (like parsnips), collards and kale (types of cabbage), lentils, turnips, broad beans, onions, spinach, carrots, beets, radishes and even globe artichokes and asparagus. People ate the leaves of beetroot plants rather than the roots. Vegetables were often not eaten to accompany meat as nowadays, but would be used by the farmer's wife to make a nourishing pottage which consisted of peas, milk, egg yolks, breadcrumbs and parsley which would be flavoured with ginger. Early carrots were not orange, but black, yellow, purple or white. They had been introduced into southern Europe around the twelfth century. Orange carrots were being grown by the sixteenth century and they first became popular in England during Elizabeth's reign.

A new vegetable from western Asia reached England in the sixteenth century, called cauliflower, from the Latin *caulis* (cabbage) and flower. The cauliflower was cultivated in Italy in the sixteenth century from where it made its way to France and then the rest of Europe and Britain. It seems to have been first introduced into England from Cyprus, and it is mentioned by Lyte, in 1586, under the name of 'Cyprus coleworts.' In John Gerard's *Herball, or Generall Historie of Plantes*, first published in 1597, we read in his chapter on coleworts: 'ColeFlorie, or after some Coliflorie, hath many large leaves sleightly endented about the edges, of a whitish greene colour, narrower and sharper pointed then Cabbage: in the middest of which leaves riseth up a great white head of hard flowers closely thrust together, with a roote full of strings: in other partes like unto the Colewoorts.' The picture of a cauliflower which accompanies Gerard's text shows a plant with a much smaller flower head relative to the volume of leaves than occurs in a modern cauliflower. Commercial cultivation in England began in 1619.

Kidney beans are native to South America, and were common in England by the mid-sixteenth century. Runner beans are native to Central America and were discovered by Europeans in the sixteenth century, being first grown in England in the seventeenth century, but imported before then. Brussel sprouts were developed in Belgium from the thirteenth century and became popular across most of Europe in the sixteenth century. Broccoli was grown in Europe in the sixteenth century but was rare in England. Henry VIII ensured that he had the 'new' globe artichokes growing in his gardens. Potatoes were brought to England in the 1580s but at first few English people ate them, whereas sweet potatoes featured fairly prominently after their discovery.

TUDOR FRUITS

Common fruits were apples, strawberries, redcurrants, blackcurrants, pears, plums, gages, damsons, cherries, blackberries and raspberries. The rich could afford exotic fruits such as pomegranates, peaches, grapes, oranges, melons, lemons and walnuts. Apricots, peaches and nectarines all started to be grown in England during the time of Henry VIII, who imported both the fruit and a trained gardener from France to look after them. The king is known to have loved globe artichokes, strawberries, cherries, quince marmalade and orange pies. In 1534 his household bought an orange strainer, a sign that the luxury fruit was available at court. Damsons and grapes were brought from the gardens at Richmond Palace to Hampton Court. Henry VIII wanted a wider variety of fruit, and instructed his fruiterer, Richard Harris, to travel to France and the Low Countries to bring back grafts of different apples, pears and cherries. Harris introduced amongst others the Golden Rennette apple. Henry's gardeners introduced apricots to Britain, planting espaliered trees at the garden of Nonsuch in Surrey.

Harris laid down the first large commercial orchard at Teynham in Kent, 'the chiefe mother of all the orchards for all those kinds of fruit.' Kent became the 'garden of England', growing all the above fruits, and including nectarines, quinces, melons, pomegranates, oranges and lemons. Sweet oranges were imported from Portugal, their original name being *Portingal*. These were a great improvement on those formerly available, which resembled the Seville or bitter oranges used in marmalade, and whose principle value was as a flavouring for sauces. Almonds and dried fruits had been imported into England during the Middle Ages, and with the emergence of a wealthy merchant class, imports increased greatly.

Pomegranates were known in Europe in the Middle Ages and they were mentioned by Shakespeare. Pomegranate is believed to be a corruption of the Old French words *pome garnete*, seed apple. Catherine of Aragon's emblem of the pomegranate can be seen on an altar cloth made by Catherine, in St Peter's Church, Winchcombe, Gloucestershire. Queen Mary was to later display the pomegranate as her badge in memory of her mother Catherine. Following each of his six marriages, Henry ordered that the new emblems and badges of his latest wife replace those of his previous one in his palaces. Pictures of his wives were also destroyed. Courtiers tried to keep up with the king's demands, but Sir Richard Clement, owner of Ightham Mote, somehow failed. One of Henry's favourite servants, Clement officiated at the wedding with Anne Boleyn. At his mansion near Sevenoaks, one will still find the Tudor Rose and pomegranate of Aragon, in the stained glass of the Great Hall and the barrel-vaulted roof of the New Chapel. Glass was terrifically expensive, and it is to be assumed that Henry never paid Clement's mansion a visit.

Bananas were known in the sixteenth century, but the first recorded sale of bananas in England was not until 1633. Figs were also introduced to England in the sixteenth century. Gooseberries are native to Europe and Western Asia. They were first mentioned in England in the sixteenth century when they were grown as a medicine. The name gooseberry may simply be 'goose berry' because they were eaten with goose or it may be a corruption of the Dutch word *kruisbes*, which means 'cross berry'. Peaches were grown in England by the late sixteenth century but they were rare and expensive until the twentieth century. Pineapples originally grew in South America and were discovered in 1493. However during the sixteenth and seventeenth centuries pineapples were very expensive as they had to be imported.

England saw the first 'love apple' when tomatoes came to England from Mexico. Tomatoes originated from the Andes in South America, where they grow wild in what is now Peru, Bolivia, Chile and Ecuador. They were first cultivated by the Aztecs and Incas as early as 700 CE. The English word 'tomato' comes from the Aztec *tomatl*. Tomatoes first arrived in Europe in the sixteenth century, although how they arrived here is unclear. The first cultivated tomatoes were yellow and cherry-sized, earning them the name golden apples: *pommes d'or* in French; *pomi d'oro* in Italian; and *goldapfel* in German. The Italian for tomatoes today is *pomodoro*. The French were convinced tomatoes had aphrodisiac properties and began calling them *pommes d'amour* or 'love apples'. Soon after the tomato's arrival in Europe, it was also known as the 'Peruvian apple'.

Tomatoes were originally grown in Britain and the rest of Europe as ornamental climbers and were cultivated for their decorative leaves and fruit. The first known British tomato grower was Patrick Bellow in 1554. However, the Elizabethans thought the bright red colour of tomatoes was a danger signal and the fruit poisonous. Popular sixteenth-century English herbalists, such as John Gerard knew that Spaniards and Italians ate tomatoes, but nevertheless wrote that the plant was 'of ranke and stinking savour'. Botanically, the tomato is a fruit, and cucumbers, squash, green beans and walnuts are all fruits as well. The confusion between 'fruit' and 'vegetable' arises because of the differences in usage between scientists and cooks. True fruits are developed from the ovary in the base of the flower, and contain the seeds of the plant (although modern cultivated forms may be seedless). Blueberries, raspberries, and oranges are true fruits, but so are many kinds of nut. Some plants such as the strawberry have a soft part which supports the seeds and is also called a 'fruit', although it is not developed from the ovary. Incidentally, the strawberry used in Tudor recipes is the wild strawberry, not the huge cultivated varieties we see today. It has a far, far better taste.

As far as cooking is concerned, some things which are strictly fruits, such as tomatoes or bean pods, may be called 'vegetables' because they are used in savoury rather than sweet cooking. The term 'vegetable' is more generally used of other edible parts of plants, such as cabbage leaves, celery stalks, and potato tubers, which are not strictly the fruit of the plant from which they come. Occasionally the term 'fruit' may be used to refer to a part of a plant which is not a fruit, but which is used in sweet cooking, for instance rhubarb. Paul Hentzner, in his *Journey into England* (1598), describes the sale of fruit as snacks in 'entertainments' such as bull and bear-baiting:

There is still another place, built in the form of a theatre, which serves for the baiting of bulls and bears; they are fastened behind, and then worried by great English bull-dogs, but not without great risk to the dogs, from the horns of the one and the teeth of the other; and it sometimes happens that they are killed upon the spot; fresh ones are immediately supplied in the places of those that are wounded or tired. To this entertainment there often follows that of whipping a blinded bear, which is performed by five or six men, standing circularly with whips, which they exercise upon him without any mercy, as he cannot escape from them because of his chain; he defends himself with all his force and skill, throwing down all who come within his reach and are not active enough to get out of it, and tearing the whips out of their hands and breaking them. At these spectacles, and everywhere else, the English are constantly smoking tobacco; and in this manner – they have pipes on purpose made of clay, into the farther end of which they put the herb, so dry that it may be rubbed into powder, and putting fire to it, they draw the smoke into their mouths, which they puff out again through their nostrils like funnels, along with it plenty of phlegm and defluxion from the head. In these theatres, fruits, such as apples, pears, and nuts, according to the season, are carried about to be sold, as well as ale and wine.

2

Tudor Food

Trade and industry flourished in the sixteenth century, making England more prosperous and improving the standard of living of the upper and middle classes. However, the lower classes did not benefit because of rising prices and did not always have enough food. There were no widespread famines, but localised bad harvests caused great distress. The most widespread hardships came with poor harvests in 1555–7 and 1596–8. In towns the price of staple foods was fixed by law, and in hard times bakers reduced the size of a loaf of bread in response. A series of bad harvests in the 1590s caused more widespread starvation and poverty. The success of the wool trading industry had decreased attention on agriculture, resulting in further starvation of the lower classes. Cumbria, the most isolated part of England, suffered a six-year famine beginning in 1594. Diseases and natural disasters also sometimes contributed to the scarce food supply.

The poor generally ate 'white meats', a euphemism for meals which contained little meat, consisting primarily of dishes using milk, cheese, butter, eggs, breads and pottages (broths). Peasants ate the coarsest bread with their pottage, a thick soup in which onions, cabbage and beans were boiled up with herbs and, perhaps thickened with oats, and a little pork or bacon added. Anything available or in season would be added, and the dish had existed since man had first made cooking pots that could withstand heat. In Tudor times, it was still the main part of an ordinary person's diet. Occasionally meat bones or fish would be added when available. Vegetables such as peas and beans were often dried to be used over the winter, until early spring produce such as nettle tips, ground elder and spring greens could be eaten.

For the poor, bread made from expensive wheat was a rarity. Usually it was coarse, gritty and made from barley or rye, but in hard times a mixture of beans, oats or acorns would be used to give the essential carbohydrates to be able to work. The poor family's diet was sometimes supplemented with locally caught fish, rabbits or birds, but taking any larger game was poaching and punishments were severe. Even taking fish, rabbits and birds was not allowed over many estates. All classes ate fish, because the law required that fish be consumed on Fridays and Saturdays, and other meats laid aside. Poorer people still had meat, but not the wide variety of the rich. They might eat chickens which they could rear themselves, but only at the end of their useful lives, and mutton from the local market when they had the money. They were encouraged to shoot rooks and crows because these birds destroyed crops and damaged the roof thatch on cottages and barns. Farm labourers were sometimes given *coloppes*, slices of bacon.

Bread was a major part of the diet of all classes and was very different from the bread we eat now. William Harrison, in his *Description of England* (1577), described bread: 'The bread throughout the land is made of such grain as the soil yields: nevertheless the gentility commonly provide themselves sufficiently of wheat for their own tables, while their household and poor neighbours, in some shires, are enforced to content themselves with rye or barley; yea, and in time of dearth, many with bread made either of bran, peas, or oat, or of altogether, and some acorns among; of which scourge the poorest do soonest taste, since they are least able to provide themselves better. I will not say that this extremity is oft so well to be seen in time of plenty as of dearth; but if I should, I could easily bring my trial.'

Bread was the staple of the diet and people of different statuses ate bread of different qualities. *Manchet* was a very fine white bread made from wheat flour with a little bran and wheat germ added, creamy-yellow in colour and the bread of the nobility. *Raveled* bread, *ravel* or yeoman's bread, was made from coarser whole-wheat flour with the bran left in. It was a darker colour and less expensive than manchet. 'Carter's Bread' was dark brown or black bread, the bread that the poorest people ate. It was made from *maslin,* a mixture of rye and wheat; or from *drage*, a mixture of barley and wheat; or from rye alone. 'Horse-corn' was bread made from peas, beans, lentils and oats, eaten by the poor when the wheat harvest failed. The bread would have been kept in an 'ark', a wooden box, to protect it from mice and damp.

For the wealthier, joints of meat were often cooked in thick pastry cases to keep them moist and the pastry was then discarded. Meat and good fish were luxuries reserved for the rich, who could choose among 'brown meats' such as beef, veal, pork, lamb, mutton, venison, as well as rabbit, fowl, salmon, trout, eel and shellfish. If not placed in a pie, most meats were cooked by 'seething' (boiling). Salting and pickling of meat and fish was common practice, since there was no refrigeration. Baking was carried out in iron boxes laid on fire embers, or for wealthier families, in a brick oven set into the side of the fireplace.

Sugar and currants were used in prodigious quantities when available to the rich later in the period. Sugar had always come from Morocco and the Barbary Coast, but quantities came flooding into Europe from the Spanish and Portuguese colonies in the West Indies, much being captured by privateers. From the 1540s London was converting and purifying coarse sugar into white crystalline cones weighing up to 14 pounds. These were then grated for sale or sold in hunks for grating in the great kitchens. The annual national consumption of sugar rose to a pound a head in Elizabeth's time, the vast amount being eaten by the aristocracy. Paul Hentzner noted the English addiction and its effect upon the teeth of the topless queen and her courtiers, in *A Description of Elizabeth I & her Court at Greenwich, from Journey into England* (1598):

First went gentlemen, barons, earls, knights of the garter, all richly dressed, and bare-headed; next came the Chancellor, bearing the seals in a red silk purse, between two, one of which carried the royal sceptre, the other the sword of state, in a red scabbard, studded with golden fleur-de-lis, the points upwards. Next came the Queen, in the sixty-fifth year of her age, as we are told, very majestic. Her face oblong, fair but wrinkled, her eyes small, yet black and pleasant, her nose a little hooked, her lips narrow and her teeth black (a defect the English seem subject to, from their too great use of sugar). She had in the ears two pearls with very rich drops. She wore false hair and that red. Upon her head, she had a small crown, reputed to be made of some of the gold of the celebrated Luneburg table. Her bosom was uncovered, as all English ladies have it till they marry, and she had on a necklace of exceeding fine jewels.

The Yule Boar, a boar's head garnished with bay and rosemary, often served as the centrepiece of Christmas feasts. The rich also ate bittern, duck, goose, owl, pheasant, blackbird, swan, peacock, pigeon, robin, lark, sparrow, heron, crane, woodcock, gull, grouse, partridge and blackbird. People would also eat badger, hedgehog, otter and tortoise. Whole peacock was served dressed in its own iridescent blue feathers (which were plucked, then replaced after the bird had been cooked), with its beak gilded in gold leaf. Swan was often presented to the table with a gold crown upon its head, and English law still stipulates that all mute swans are owned by the Crown and may not be eaten without permission from the queen. The Tudors enjoyed spicy sauces and pies. Pies could be open, as in the later Homity Pie, which contains potatoes and leek, covered with cheese. However, most were closed, in the manner of Cardiff's Clark's Pies, where an aluminium tray is not required to protect the contents falling from a 'soggy bottom'. Knives and forks are not needed, as the pastry is thick enough to pick up and eat the whole meat and gravy pie in the upright position, without crumbling. I have seen the musician-comedian Frank Hennessey deliver the routine which includes the lines: 'I can't remember not having a Clark's Pie. As soon as Cardiffians saw the Millennium Stadium they fell in love with it. They didn't realise why. It's like a giant Clark's pie with four cocktail sticks in it.'

The menu for a nobleman's dinner of around 1550 included roast beef, powder (salted) beef, veal, leg of mutton with 'gallandine sauce', turkey, boiled capon, hen boiled with leeks, partridge, pheasant, larks, quails, snipe, woodcock, salmon, sole, turbot, whiting, lobster, crayfish, shrimps, eel, pike, young rabbit, leverets (young hares), (bone) marrow on toast, artichokes, turnips, green peas, cucumbers, olives, quince pie, tart of almonds, fruit tarts and cheese. A merchant's dinner might include sausage, cabbage, porridge, pike with a 'high Dutch sauce', stewed carp, roasted blackbirds, larks, woodcock and partridge. Indeed, birds were constantly hunted by all classes, but only the rich were allowed to eat the larger birds. We have archaeological evidence of the Tudors eating: Great Auk (extinct 1840s), Little Auk, Blackbird, Bustard (extinct and reintroduced), Chicken, Coot, Cormorant, Crane, Curlew, Dotterel, Duck (all types), Finch (all types), Gannet, Godwit, Goose, Grouse, Guillemot, Gull (all types), Heron, Knot, Lapwing, Lark, Moorhen, Oystercatcher, Partridge, Peacock, Pheasant, Plover, Puffin, Quail, Razorbill, Rock Dove, Ruff, Sandpiper, Snipe, Sparrow, Spoonbill, Stork, Swan, Tern, Missel Thrush, Song Thrush, Turkey, Turtle Dove, Water Rail, Woodcock and Wood Pigeon.

Yeoman farmers' wives grew a variety of vegetables, herbs and flowers. Pottages were made thicker and richer with the addition of peas, milk, egg yolks, breadcrumbs and parsley. Herbs were important for flavouring, and the rich would have had a separate herb garden to grow mint, rosemary, thyme, sage, parsley and the like. Cloves, cinnamon, mace and nutmeg came from the Spice Islands and were very expensive. Pepper came from India and cinnamon from Ceylon. The quest for spices drove the early explorers to cross the Atlantic, and later the Pacific, in search of a direct sea route to the Spice Islands. Spices were used to make spiced wines, to flavour foods such as fish, jam and soup and, especially, meat dishes. The increasing popularity of spices saw European countries scramble for possessions in India and Asia.

In the sixteenth century food was used to 'illustrate splendour and largesse'. As Elizabeth's servants were seen to be a manifestation of her personal glory, her care of them symbolically showed how generous she could be, not just to them, but to all of her subjects. Her servants were allowed privileges known as *bouge of court*. They were thus allocated specific amounts of 'bread, wine, beer, fuel and light' each day, and also the enormous leftovers from state meals. In *The Tudor Court*, David Loades tells us that there was 'considerable manoeuvring and competition among the courtiers to obtain their rations' from the Privy Kitchen, because the food was better and they shared in the queen's prestige if they ate the food that had been prepared for her. As if to encourage this, 'the kitchen never closed, and the wine and beer cellars, far from being properly regulated, were also open all night to all comers.'

In 1563 William Cecil introduced 'Cecil's Fast', which imposed punishments for eating meat during Lent and on certain other days of the week. This was imposed to ensure the population ate enough fish, so that an adequate number of seamen could earn their living. It would therefore be possible to maintain sufficient ships and crews who could defend England in time of war. (The English navy was small, most ships were privately owned and the most substantial made a living privateering). In the 1580s Cecil also attempted to restrict the consumption within the royal household, ordering that 'the cofferer, clerks comptroller, and clerks of the Greencloth be allowed only "six dishes" instead of seven at dinner, and that on two days a week no supper be served in the household.' This was generally disregarded by the queen's servants.

Rather than a three meal per day routine, most people had a two meal one, as many people did not eat breakfast. The household ordinances of the nobility and gentry regularly specify who was allowed to eat breakfast, and who was not. In the *Black Book* of Edward IV, careful attention was paid to the ranks in his household who were allowed to eat breakfast. The main meal, dinner, was held at about 10.30 or 11 in the morning, and supper about five hours later. However, while household servants were regularly denied breakfasts in the fifteenth century, Thomas More wrote in 1528 'men should go to Mass as well after supper as before breakfast'. Thomas Elyot recommended eating breakfast four hours before dinner in *The Castell of Health* (1539). In 1542, Andrew Boorde in his *Dietary of Health* (1542) wrote that 'a labourer may eat three times a day but that two meals are adequate for a rest man'.

Noblemen's breakfasts of the sixteenth century became increasingly elaborate. In 1501, the Duke of Buckingham built himself a dedicated breakfast room at Queenhithe, to eat in the company of about thirty important guests and members of his household. On the 'fish days' of Wednesday, Friday and Saturday, when eating meat was forbidden, his breakfast consisted of pike, plaice, roach, butter and eggs. Ten years later the 5th Earl of Northumberland

and his countess sat down each 'fish-day' morning to: 'two manchets, two pints of beer, three pints of wine, two pieces of salt fish, six smoked herrings, four white herring or a dish of sprats.' On 'meat days' they replaced the fish with a neck of mutton or boiled beef. The servants in the earl's household were also given breakfast. The countess's lady companions were given a loaf of household bread, beer and boiled mutton or beef, but the grooms in the stables received only a small amount of household bread and beer. In 1558 the executors of Henry Willoughby's estate were given a breakfast of bread, ale and a sweet dish made of eggs, butter, sugar and currants. Thomas Cogan remarked in *The Haven of Health* (1584) that 'bread and butter' was a countryman's breakfast, and butter became increasingly imporant. Various herbs were added, such as sage 'to sharpen the wits.'

Elizabethan food grew dramatically in range and breadth, with an almost global trade. New fruit, food and spices reached London and the great houses competed to prepare and serve the most lavish meals. In the sixteenth century new foods were introduced from the Americas. Columbus landed in the 'Indies' on his first voyage, and Haiti on his second, where he discovered the chilli pepper. New foods came to Europe including maize, potatoes, chocolate, peanuts, vanilla, tomatoes, pineapples, lima beans, sweet (capsicum) and chilli peppers, tapioca and the turkey. The turkey arrived in Europe in 1523 or 1524 and in England shortly after that.

3

Tudor Drink

Britain, consisting of the two kingdoms of England and Scotland, is the largest island in the world, encompassed by the ocean, the German and French seas. The largest and southern part of it is England, so named from the *Angli*, who quitting the little territory yet called Angel in the kingdom of Denmark, took possession here … There are but few rivers; though the soil is productive, it bears no wine; but that want is supplied from abroad by the best kinds, as of Orleans, Gascon, Rhenish, and Spanish. The general drink is beer, which is prepared from barley, and is excellently well tasted, but strong, and what soon fuddles.

Paul Hentzner, 1598

Meat and fish were heavily salted for preservation, and made people thirsty. Water was extremely unsafe to drink, especially in cities where supplies became contaminated with sewage, from people cleaning clothes or from animal carcasses in the water supply. In the cities, water-carriers delivered water from the countryside to the rich. Courtiers were allowed a certain amount of wine each day, but generally servants were allowed to drink ale or beer. Before Henry VIII closed the monasteries, they provided a place where people could stay for a night and have a meal. After their closure, inns took over this role and inns, alehouses and taverns became far more common. A 1577 survey revealed 19,000 such establishments in England and Wales, to serve a population of about 4 million, one for every 200 people.

Fresh water, even in casks, would not keep for long and from early times wine or beer was substituted. The usual ration at sea was a gallon per day per man. The explorer Sir Martin Frobisher (1535–94) of North West Passage fame, is quoted as saying 'We'll sail as long as the beer lasts'. One of the major problems on board ship was that beer 'went off' very quickly, and poor water could bring typhus, dysentery and death. Beer was taken at breakfast, often with gruel, and at supper, with hunks of bread. Brewing was considered part of the housewife's function of cooking for the household, although women almost uniformly had full-time jobs as well. Women had to make it palatable, or there would be nothing to drink. Larger houses, monasteries and castles had their own brew-houses with dedicated brewers, and beer (and/or cider) formed part of the wages for many servants and workers.

Alcohol 'purified' water, and home-brewed ale or beer was the usual drink at most meals, including breakfast. Even children drank beer, which was weaker than that drunk by adults and was known as 'small beer'. This was sometimes made of fermented herbs or weak cider, but because of its lower alcohol content, there was more chance of contamination. Wine had to be imported from the Continent and was an expensive luxury. Wine was sometimes diluted with water, even though there was a risk of pollution, and was often served warm and spiced. Other drinks in sixteenth century England included sherry, known as 'sack', and brandy. Whiskey was being distilled in Scotland, Wales and Ireland and was a popular 'medicinal' drink. The earliest form of the word in English was *uskebeaghe* (1581), and it was made all over the British Isles by monks. After the Dissolution, it was made in homes.

People would occasionally drink milk, but because it was unpasteurised and there was no way of keeping it cool, it did not stay fresh for long. It was far more valuable being made into nourishing butter and cheese and preserved, sold or eaten. The main drinks were ale, cider, perry, mead and wine. Ale was a fermented drink made from grain and water, the main drink of ordinary people in the early sixteenth century but beer, using hops, gradually became more common. Beer and ale acted as a food, giving essential carbohydrates and nutrients for people who often worked from dawn to dusk. Cider was made from apples and drunk by poorer people; perry was a fermented drink made from pears; and mead was an alcoholic mixture of honey and spices.

The thirteenth refrain from the *Barley Mow* drinking song is: 'Oh, the company, brewer, cooper (or bookie), slavey, drayer, daughter, landlady, landlord, barrel, half-barrel, gallon, half-gallon, quart pot, pint pot, half a pint, gill pot, half a gill, quarter gill, nipperkin, and a round (or brown) bowl – Here's good luck (good luck!), good luck to the barley mow.' The twelve terms from 'barrel' to 'round bowl' were used to measure the volume of alcoholic beverages. A round bowl indicates either a simple, wooden bowl, or a person's hands cupped together into the shape of a bowl. The nipperkin is one-half of a quarter-gill, one-eighth of a gill, or one thirty-second of an English pint, from which we had the old request for a 'nip' of spirits.

ALE AND BEER

In his *Compendyous Regiment* of 1542 Andrew Boorde notes that beer is growing in popularity. Boorde thus warns the English that they will get fat-bellied and appear like Dutchmen, unless they stick with good English ale. He considers that ale is the natural drink of an Englishman, while the far inferior beer is the natural drink of a Dutchman (some spellings modernised): 'Ale is made of malt and water; and those who do put any other thing to ale than is rehearsed, except yeast, barm, or goddes good, doth sophisticate their ale. Ale for an English man is a natural drink. Ale must have these properties, it must be fresh and clear, it must not be ropy, nor smoky, nor it must have no werte nor tayle. Ale should not be drunk under 5 days old. New Ale is unwholesome for all men. And sour ale, and dead ale, and ale which doth stand a little, is good for no man. Barley malt maketh better Ale than Oat malt or any other corn doth: it doth engender gross humours: but it maketh a man strong. Beer is made of malt, of hops and water. It is a natural drink for a Dutch man. And now of late days it is much used in England to the detriment of many English men; specially it killeth them the which be troubled with the Colic and the stone, and the strained colon; for the drink is a cold drink. Yet it doth make a man fat, and doth inflate the belly, as it doth appear by the Dutch mens faces and bellies.'

We now tend to interchange the terms 'ale' and 'beer', but until the seventeenth century ale only referred to unhopped, fermented malt liquor. Hopped malt liquor from the Low Countries first appeared in England in the fifteenth century, and in Tudor times the new fashionable drink became more popular. It took more time to spread to rural districts, so 'ale' began to be the term for 'rustic' country drinks, although it might now use hops, while 'beer' was the term used in towns and cities. Country beer tended to be lighter, while London beer was darker, again giving a distinction between ale and beer, although both might use hops. Hops counteracted sweetness, acted as a preservative and helped to 'fine' the brew, i.e. make it less cloudy. Hops were not commercially grown in England until the 1520s, and soon the fashion for English-brewed beer spread. Though many still regarded unhopped ale as the more 'natural' English drink, by the end of the Tudor period far more beer than ale was being drunk. By nineteenth century the term ale came to be associated with stronger beers, while beer referred to weaker household or table beers.

Hops were never forbidden in England, as some writers have asserted, but from around 1440 to 1540 attempts were made to maintain the distinction between unhopped English ale, and beer, the hopped malted cereal drink.

Thus some authorities prevented ale brewers, who remained an entirely separate group of men and women from the beer brewers until at least the reign of James I, from putting hops into their ale. Beer brewers, however, were allowed unrestricted access to hopping. In 1483 the London ale brewers, again trying to maintain the difference between unhopped ale and hopped beer, persuaded the city authorities to rule that in order for ale to be brewed in 'the good and holesome manner of bruying of ale of old tyme used', no one should 'put in any ale or licour [water] whereof ale shal be made or in the wirkyng and bruying of any maner of ale any hoppes, herbes or other like thing but only licour, malt and yeste'.

Henry VIII's ale brewer at Eltham Palace, near London, was instructed in a document of January 1530, that was attempting to reform sundry 'misuses' in the royal household, not to use hops or brimstone, which would have been used for fumigating casks, when brewing. More regulations laid down by the Treasurer of the Household at another of Henry's palaces, Hampton Court, in 1539 included a rule that the ale brewers 'put neither Hoppes nor Brimstone in their ale in the pipes [120-gallon casks], soe that it may be found good, wholesome and perfect stuff and worth the King's money.'

As well as an ale brewer, Henry VIII had a beer brewer, whose work gave him special privileges. John Pope, Henry VIII's personal beer brewer in 1542, received permission to have as many as twelve 'persons born out of the King's Dominions', probably meaning beer-brewing experts from the Low Countries, to work in his household 'for the said feat of beer-brewing'. This was despite Tudor law that no Englishman should employ more than four foreigners at a time. The Tudor army required hopped beer when it was campaigning. In July 1544, during an English invasion of Picardy, the commander of Henry VIII's forces complained that his army was so short of supplies they had drunk no beer 'these last ten days, which is strange for English men to do with so little grudging.'

A weekly brew was made upon the fire, and had to be drunk fairly quickly, as when fermented, beer was not bottled, as glass was an expensive commodity. When rich men moved home, they took their windows with them at this time. In richer homes, beer may have been barrelled, but in poorer homes beer was simply taken as desired from the pot or cauldron it had been brewed in. The poor did not have the same access to hops as the upper classes, and ale was still the poor man's beer. In general, half a pound of hops was added to a bushel of malt in brewing. Sir Hugh Plat in 1594 noted that Flemish hops were far stronger than English hops and care had to be taken in choosing the correct hopping not to make the beer too bitter. Drinking over-hopped beer gave him and his family 'great looseness'.

Herbs and spices have always been of great importance in the preparation of alcoholic beverages. They were added to wines, beers and other drinks as flavourings, preservatives, colouring agents and for their remedial properties in medicinal beverages. Before the introduction of hops, many English ales were given extra relish by the addition of aromatic herbs or a mixture of spices. While not as efficient as hops, many also served to counteract sweetness, to fine (clear) and help preserve the brew. The most common hop substitute was Ale-hoof, *Nepeta glechoma,* also known as Tun-Hoof, Ground-Ivy, Cat's-Foot, Gill-go-by-the-Ground, Gill-Creep-by-Ground, Hay-Maids, Coin Grass, Creeping Jenny, Creeping Charlie, Run-Away-Robin, Field Balm and Hedgehove. Culpeper recommended it for many ailments, and its dried leaves were used for centuries before and after the introduction of hops, as an infusion to make 'gill-ale.' Bitter 'long peppers' were also used in gill-ale and other ales.

Not only the above ale-hoof, but clary (wild sage), mugwort, tansy, maudlin and costmary were all found to act as preservatives. Iris roots hung in ale were said to prevent it turning sour. Sir Hugh Plat was dismissive of hops, which had only 'weak and feeble virtues' compared to wormwood, and also recommended centaury and artichokes in brewing. 'Gale beer' was brewed from bog myrtle and heather ale from *Erica vulgaris* blossoms. Unhopped strong ale named *ebulon* was flavoured with elderberries and ginger. There are many superb Belgian spiced beers today, and in Tudor times dried herbs and spices such as sage, rosemary, betony, hyssop, pennyroyal, balm, broom, tansy, eyebright, dandelion, cherries, blackberries, cowslips and even 'good hay' were used in flavouring and brewing. William Harrison in 1512 describes his wife brewing with 'half an ounce of arras and half a quarter of an ounce of bayberries finely powdered... some, instead of arras and bays, add so much long pepper only.' While barley formed the basis of the malt, in some areas 'white beer' was brewed using wheat, again a popular Belgian drink today. The ancient honey drink *metheglin* relied for its peculiar flavour on the leaves of borage, bugloss and other aromatic plants. During the medieval and early modern period, brewers added herbs to their malt liquors in order to improve their keeping properties. Before citrus fruits became generally available, country people warded off scurvy with regular draughts of scurvy-grass ale, a bitter brew prepared from *Cochlearia officinalis*, a member of the cabbage family which is rich in vitamin C.

The 1610 Ordnance Roll of Cowbridge, Glamorgan, is based upon older documents, and lays out the 'rules' for keeping order in the walled town. It describes different types of ales, ordaining that 'all Brewers shall brewe good and wholesome Ale, third drincke and small drincke'. Hops were mashed to make strong beer and used again to make weak beer (small drincke), and reused a final time to make beer fit for children to sup (third drincke). Alcohol was sold by the gallon (8 pints), pottle (4 pints) or quart (2 pints). Dice, cards and bowls were forbidden in the town, and women found guilty of being 'scolds' were put in the 'Cuckinge stoole' for one hour for a first offence, two hours for a second offence, and ducked under water tied to the 'Cuckinge stoole' for a third misdemeanour. There was a ten shilling fine if any inhabitant kept bawds, suspected harlots, vagabonds, loiterers or 'naughtipackes' in their houses, naughtipackes being promiscuous men or women.

Thoroton, in his account *Nottinghamshire*, gives an account of a shepherd who kept ale to sell in the Church of Thorpe. He was the sole inhabitant of a village depopulated by enclosure. At the time there were Bid-Ales, Bride-Ales, Give-Ales, Cuckoo-Ales, Help-Ales, Tithe-Ales, Leet-Ales, Lamb-Ales, Midsummer-Ales, Scot-Ales and Weddyn-Ales. Bride-Ale, also called Bride-bush, Bride-wain and Bride-stake, was the custom of the bride selling ale on the wedding day, for which she received any sum or present which her friends chose to give her. In the *Christen State of Matrimony* (1545) we read: 'When they come home from the church, then beginneth excesse of eatyng and drynking, and as much is waisted in one daye as were sufficient for the two newe-married folkes halfe si yeare to lyve upon.' Modern wedding breakfasts and presents are descendants of this old custom.

To 'con' or 'cun' is to have knowledge, and a cunning woman meant a wise woman. A 'conner' was 'one who tries, tests, or examines,' and an ale-conner was 'an officer appointed by a court leet or other local authority to test for the assize the ale brewed (and sometimes the bread baked) in his or her jurisdiction.' Officers such as ale-conners, beadles, brokers, sheriffs and so on had to swear an oath before taking up their positions. The oaths of various officials of the City of London were recorded in the first book of English common law, *Liber Albus: the White Book of the City of London*, published in 1419 by John Carpenter. From it we read:

'Oath of the Ale-Conners.

You shall swear, that you shall know of no brewer or brewster, cook, or pie-baker, in your Ward, who sells the gallon of best ale for more than one penny halfpenny, or the gallon of second for more than one penny, or otherwise than by measure sealed and full of clear ale; or who brews less than he used to do before this cry, by reason hereof, or withdraws himself from following his trade the rather by reason of this cry; or if any persons shall do contrary to any one of these points, you shall certify the Alderman of your Ward [thereof] and of their names. And that you, so soon as you shall be required to taste any ale of a brewer or brewster, shall be ready to do the same; and in case that it be less good than it used to be before this cry, you, by assent of your Alderman, shall set a reasonable price thereon, according to your discretion; and if any one shall afterwards sell the same above the said price, unto your said Alderman you shall certify the same. And that for gift, promise, knowledge, hate, or other cause whatsoever, no brewer, brewster, huckster, cook, or pie-baker, who acts against any one of the points aforesaid, you shall conceal, spare, or tortuously aggrieve; nor when you are required to taste ale, shall absent yourself without reasonable cause and true; but all things which unto your office pertain to do, you shall well and lawfully do. – So God you help, and the Saints.'

From around 1480, the *Harleian MS 541* has this wonderful drinking song from the 'Ipswich Minstrel':

> Bryng us in good ale, and bryng us in good ale;
> For owr blyssyd lady sak, bryng us in good ale.
> Bryng us in no browne bred, fore that is made of brane,
> Nor bryng us in no whyt bred, for therin is no game;
> But bryng us in good ale.
> Bryng us in no befe, for there is many bonys;
> But bryng us in good ale, for that goth downe at onys,
> And bryng us in good ale.
> Bryng us in no bacon, for that is passing fate;
> But bryng us in good ale, and gyfe us i-nought of that,
> And bryng us in good ale.
> Bryng us in no mutton, for that is often lene,
> Nor bryng us in no trypes, for thei be syldom clene;
> But bryng us in good ale.
> Bryng us in no eggys, for ther ar many schelles;
> But bryng us in good ale, and gyfe us no[th]yng ellys,
> And bryng us in good ale.
> Bryng us in no butter, for therin ar many herys
> Nor bryng us in no pygges flesch, for that will make us borys;
> But bryng us in good ale.
> Bryng us in no podynges, for therin is al Godes-good;
> Nor bryng us in no venesen, for that is not for owr blood;
> But bryng us in good ale.
> Bryng us in no capons flesch, for that is ofte der;
> Nor bryng us in no dokes flesche, for thei slober in the mer;
> But bryng us in good ale.

CIDER

From 1066 Normans took over the monasteries and churches, bringing a strong tradition of apple growing and cider making. They established vast cider apple orchards, and the Middle Ages found monks pressing and selling large quantities of apple ciders and spirits. The Normans introduced many apple types to Britain, the first recorded being the Pearmain and the Costard. The Old English Pearmain was first recorded in 1204 and was of great use in cider-making. The manor of Runham (Norfolk) had to pay the Exchequer each year 200 Pearmains, as well as four hogsheads of cider made from Pearmains. The capacity of a hogshead varied, but would be about 54 gallons, or 432 pints. The Costard was first recorded in 1296 when 100 apples were sold for a shilling. In 1325, 29 Costard apple trees were recorded as having been sold for three shillings. The name Costard is preserved in the word 'costermonger', originally a seller of Costard apples.

The Black Death and the Wars of the Roses had led to a decline in population and in fruit cultivation, but upon Henry VIII's instructions, Richard Harris, fruiterer to the king, began to import apple trees from France in 1533. Harris planted a model orchard at Teynham which was then used to distribute trees to other growers, and there was an expansion of cider orchards. Cider could be transported for sale as, unlike beer, it could be kept for some time. The price was between 2½–4*d* a gallon, while wages were between 1*d* and 4*d* a day. There are many more references to beer than cider, partly because beer was regulated by the state and the manor, but also as it was much more important than cider. Beer was cheaper to make than cider so was priced at ¾d to 1½*d* a gallon depending on quality and area. Cider apple trees are easier to grow than barley, but the laborious crushing of the apples, without investment in cider mills and presses, took more work. To make cider, apples must be ground to a fine pulp, or *pomace*, using a crusher. This initiates cellular breakdown and releases the juices inside. Wild yeasts then convert apple sugar into alcohol.

Jim Franklin, an orcharder in Hereford's Teme Valley, explained the importance of cider to farm workers in particular:

'Before 1900, cider was so important, so important through the Teme Valley, in Devon, in Somerset, it was a complete way of life. It was paid as wages, it was drunk because the water was so foul and it was used for medicinal purposes. It was taken on ships to stop scurvy, I mean it was a complete product in its own right. Previously to, I suppose, to the 1200s there's reasonable records that they called it wine, it wasn't called cider and that's probably where the origin came, cider went one way and wine went another way but I cannot see really what's the difference, between an apple being made into wine or an apple being made into cider, it's just that it picked up this name and I don't know exactly what the origins of this name is but I think it's supposed to mean "strong drink" but maybe it was because it was so plentiful that it was quite a dangerous product. And it was, unless it was used properly, a lot of people were drunk for most of their life, which is probably the best way to go through life anyway.'

This author's ninety-four-year-old father remembers being given cider as a fourteen-year-old boy working on a Welsh farm before the Second World War. In the Vale of Glamorgan, many bridges over streams have a small shelf underneath them, just below the water level. The men used to place their 4, or 8-pint earthenware jars of farmhouse cider there to keep them cool while working in the fields in the summer months.

Cider apple seeds were taken by the Pilgrim Fathers to America. George Washington and John Adams were extremely fond of the drink, with Adams drinking a tankard of strong cider every morning before breakfast to soothe his stomach and quell flatulence. Most of the cider apples grown were different to those of today, being small, high in tannin and very varied, some types restricted to just one or two orchards. Like the renowned *pomewater* recommended in many Tudor recipes, many varieties of apple have died out, but if we simply look at the names of some of the remaining apple varieties (of which only some are used for cider) we can appreciate both their variety and the need to keep these wonderful British trees in existence:

Brown Snout, *Glan Sevin o Langadog*, Chisel Jersey, Fillbarrel, Harry Master's, Carlisle Codlin, Beauty of Kent, Caroline Baxter's Pearmain, Bedfordshire Foundling, Catshead, Blenheim Pippin, Dumelow's Seedling, Brownlee's Russet, Dredge's Fame, Greenup's Pippin, Hambledon *Deux Ans*, Emperor Alexander, Hanwell Souring, Flower of Kent, Herefordshire Costard, Foxwhelp, Hoary Morning, Glory of the West, Holland Pippin, Gloucestershire Costard, Golden Noble, Grand Duke Constantine, Grange's Pearmain, Kentish Fill-Basket, Lane's Prince Albert, Minchull Crab, Minier's Dumpling, Red Hawthornden, Nonesuch, Norfolk Beefing; Northern Greening; Round Winter Nonesuch, Norfolk Stone Pippin, Royal Pearmain, Omar Pasha, Royal Russet, *Twyn y Sheriff*, Royal Somerset, Porters Perfection, Rymer, Small's Admirable, Toker's Incomparable, Tower of Glammis, Striped Beefing, Sugarloaf Pippin, *Cadwaladr*, Monmouth Beauty, Winter Colman, Summer Pearmain, Winter Greening, Summer Stibbert, Sweeny Nonpareil, Winter Quoining, Winter Majetin, Warner's King, Watson's Dumpling, Aromatic Russet, Cockle's Pippin, Ashmead's Kernel, Coe's Golden Drop, Cornish Aromatic, Cornish

Gilliflower, Beachamwell, Cox's Orange Pippin, Crofton Scarlet, D'Arcy Spice, Devonshire Quarrenden, Early Harvest, Harvey's Wiltshire Defiance, Early Nonpareil, Holbert's Victoria, Hughes Golden Pippin, Hunt's Deux Ans, *Gwell na Mil* (Welsh, translated as 'Better than a Thousand'), Forman's Crew, Hunt's Duke of Gloucester, Irish Peach, Golden Harvey, Golden Knob, Joaneting, Golden Nonpareil, Golden Pippin, Keddleston Pippin, Golden Reinette, Keeping Russet, Golden Russet, Golden Winter Pearmain, Lamb Abbey Pearmain, Old King of the Pippins, Large Yellow Bough, Lord Burghley, Packhorse, Lucombe's Pine Apple, Padley's Pippin, Margaret Pearson's Plate, Maclean's Favourite, Pine Golden Pippin, Pineapple Russet, Melon, Morris's Court of Wick, Pitmaston Pine Apple, Nanny, Pomeroy of Hereford, New Rock Pippin, *Nonpareil*, Northern Spy, Sack and Sugar, *Cox Cymraeg* (Welsh Cox), Shakespere, Stoke Edith Pippin, Ronald's Gooseberry Pippin, Rushock Pearmain, Yellow Ingestrie, Wormsley Pippin, Bran Rose, Munn's Red, Cider Lady's Finger, Cherry Norman, Old Bromley, Pym Square, *Cwmmy*, Red Splash, Red-streak, Forest Styre, Skyrme's Kernel, South Quoining, Garter, Strawberry Norman, Gennet Moyle, Hagloe Crab, White Norman, Handsome Norman, White Must, White Styre, Hangdown, Channel Beauty, *Llwyd Haner Goch*, Baker's Delicious, Red Cluster, Pound Apple, Sweet Elford [Alfred], Soldier, Tom Putt, Northwood Black Hereford, Foxwhelp, *Nant Gwrtheyrn*, Pigeon's Beak, Diamond, Pigskin, Bloody (or Blood) Butcher, *Pig Aderyn, Marged Nicolas*, Gennet Moyle, Hangdown, Greasy, Champagne, Anglesey Pig's Snout (*Trwyn Mochyn*), Goose's Arse and Slack ma [my] Girdle (now extinct).

The Welsh name for Bardsey, *Ynys Enlli*, means 'Isle of the Currents', and the difficult two-mile crossing, even by motorboat, has been known to take two hours. It is often unreachable except by helicopter. Its former name, *Ynys Afallach* (Isle of Apples), has traditionally been associated with Merlin and Avalon. A few years ago, a single stunted apple tree was found on the island and has since been propagated for sale. It is said that this 'Bardsey Island Apple' dates from Arthurian times. Merlin was said to have hidden his treasure on the island, and Arthur was rowed there to be healed after his last battle with his cousin Mordred. *Nant Gwrtheyrn* refers to Vortigern, the fabled king of the Britons. The *Pren Glas* was found in the grounds of the ruined St Dogmael's Abbey. The rare *Llwyd Haner Goch* means Grey Half Red, and dates from at least the sixteenth century, at Dinefwr (Dynevor) Castle. If you buy and plant a Bardsey Island apple tree, just like a Foxwhelp, a Kentish Fill-Basket or a Brown Snout, you are perpetuating romance and history in your garden, rather than laying paving slabs and causing run-offs and local flooding.

Cider is making a comeback with new breweries setting up, and it is a refreshing drink. According to Mark Twain, 'Cider and doughnuts make old people's tales and old jokes sound fresh and crisp and enchanting'. In 1542, Andrew Boorde wrote that 'Cider does little harm in harvest-time,' understanding that workers in the fields needed such nourishment while working fourteen-hour days. Cider, however, was popular only in certain localities. Wales, its borders, the West Country and Kent were favoured areas. Barely filtered strong cider is known as 'scrumpy', derived from the slang 'scrumping', stealing windfalls from an orchard. Scrumpy originally was cider made from windfalls (scrumps). For most people it means a rough, cloudy and unsophisticated cider and is most often applied to young cider, only a few months old and yet to undergo maturation. Old hands sometimes called scrumpy 'squeal pig cider' because of the sound new drinkers made when sampling it unaware. However, for some cider makers, scrumpy can be the finest cider, slowly fermented from selected apples and matured for longer. A lager and cider mix is known as 'snakebite', an extremely quick way to become inebriated, and mixed with rum, is known as 'stonewall.' Today's additive-free Breton cider is extremely refreshing, brewed by many farmers. In Brittany, *lambig* is a splendid and little-known *eau de vie* made from distilling cider.

MEAD

Under the Tudor dynasty, mead was an extremely popular drink. However, from the seventeenth century sugar was imported from the West Indies, replacing honey as a sweetener, and mead declined in the face of cheaper competition from ale, gin and rum. From Greek through Celtic times, mead was drunk across Europe. Mead is not a beer, as beer is an alcoholic beverage made from grains. European beers were made mainly from barley or wheat grains, but mead is made solely from water, honey and yeast. It is also not a wine, as the sugars involved in fermentation are not derived from fruit. For mead brewing, the initial mixture of water, honey and yeast is termed a *must* and the yeast converts the sugars in honey into alcohol, at which point the 'must' becomes mead. It is possible to create different flavours by adding ingredients such as fruit or spices into the must or by putting them into the mead when fermentation has stopped. Mead is the simple alcoholic honey drink made without the addition of any spices or fruit. *Metheglin* is mead with spices, with sack mead and sack metheglin being sweeter versions of both. In Tudor times, *melomel* was honey 'wine' made with fruit. The two main types of melomel are *pyment* (honey alcohol made with grapes) and *cyser* (honey alcohol made with apple juice).

The Greeks called mead a *'food of the gods'*, and Norsemen celebrated weddings with mead for a whole lunar month, hence the word *'honeymoon'*. However, Welsh monasteries found that the drink was too strong and often diluted mead with fruit juices. *The Laws of Hywel Dda* (*c*. 920–40) gave permission for his court stewards to have a daily ration of mead and laid down rules for its production. Ty Brethyn Meadery, at Maesmor Hall near Corwen, makes traditional meads, including a pink one using redcurrants for use at weddings. Mead is sometimes made from barley and honey and is still popular in Brittany, where it is known as *'chouchen'*, and in the West Country. Mead was so strong and popular that the church tried to persuade people to turn to ale, and by the middle of the nineteenth century, mead had become very much a minority drink in Wales. The following quotation was found in *'Yr Haul'*, the magazine of the Church in Wales, in July 1932; 'Getting drunk on mead meant a dreadful drunkenness, damaging to the body, people getting so drunk that they could not sober up for many days. In addition to this, its effect on the body's equilibrium was very different from the effect of getting drunk on beer. A man who gets drunk drinking beer leans forward, and such a drunkard moves forward, but mead would make one lean backwards, and a drunkard drunk on mead would be impelled 'backwards' despite all efforts to move forwards.' It is now usually used as the drink for toasts or at recreations of medieval and Tudor banquets in stately homes and castles.

METHEGLYN

Metheglyn is mead spiced with cloves, ginger, rosemary, hyssop and thyme. Elizabeth I had her finest *'metheglyn'* sent annually to her court from Anglesey. The Welsh parson Sir Hugh Evans in Shakespeare's *The Merrie Wives of Windsor* (1602) accuses Sir John Falstaff of 'being given to fornications and to taverns and sack and wine and metheglins, and to drinkings and swearings and starings, pribbles and prabbles.' Metheglyn was first mentioned by Andrew Boorde in the chapter on Wales in his *Fyrst Boke of the Introduction of Knowledge* of 1542: 'metheglin, fined, is better than mead.' In the book, Boorde also makes the earliest known reference to the tasty savoury snack of cooked cheese being eaten in the British Isles (see chapter on snacks): 'I do loue cawse boby, good rosted chese; / And swyshe swash e metheglyn I take for my fees.' *Swish-swash* was made of honeycombs and water, another type of mead.

WINES

Strong, sweet wine was the most popular drink with the royal court, which was stored by the barrel in palaces and lodges. Only rich people drank wine, imported from France, Austria, the Rhinelands, Greece, Portugal, Madeira, Spain and Cyprus, although there were some attempts at vineyards in south-east England. *Malmsey* was the name of the mulled and spiced Madeira wine, made from the grapes which the Portuguese brought there from Cyprus in 1420. Although Malmsey should have come from the island of Madeira, such was the popularity of the fortified sweet wine that it was also made with water, honey, clary (sage) juice, beer grounds and brandy. Sweet wines were in high demand and foreign visitors remarked on the English habit of adding sugar to drinks. Many Tudor wines were made with infusions of wormwood, myrtle, hyssop and rosemary, mixed with sweetened wine and flavoured with honey. Wines composed of spices, Asiatic aromatics and honey were generally called white wines. Wines were also made from the juices of certain fruits, with no grapes. Tudors had cherry, currant, raspberry and pomegranate wines. *Moré* was a wine made from the mulberry. Alcoholic and non-alcoholic drinks were also made from filberts, milk of almonds, the syrups of apricots and strawberries and cherry and raspberry waters.

HIPPOCRAS

This strong and very popular rich man's drink was taken at the end of a meal as a *digestif*. It was made with a mixture of spices in red or white wine, sweetened with sugar or honey. Many forms of this name occur in early recipes, the most common being *ypocras, vpocrate, ipocras, ipocrist, hipocras, ippocras, hvpocras, hvppocras, hypocrace, hvpocraze* and *ippocrass*. The word is derived from the Middle English *Ipocras*, the Greek physician Hippocrates. Its Latin name was *Vinum Hippocraticum* – wine of Hippocrates. The spices were filtered through a bag known to apothecaries as a *manicum hippocraticum* – the sleeve of Hippocrates, which gave the drink its name. A '*hippocras gyle*' was the spice mixture which was infused in the wine to make this ancient drink, and usually included galingale, cardamom, cinnamon, grains of paradise, cubebs and long pepper.

One of the rarest spices used in the production of hippocras was *carpobalsamum*, the aromatic flower buds of the Balsam of Judea Tree. Musk seeds, another Egyptian spice, were also sometimes used to scent hippocras, though the most popular perfuming ingredients for the beverage were the animal products of musk and ambergris. Scented hippocras was served with the bridecakes at rich Tudor weddings, along with a variety of sweetmeats or 'banquetting stuffes'. As well as having alleged digestive effects, the 'hot' spices in hippocras were thought to 'provoke venery'. It was sometimes served with other 'provocative' sweetmeats, such as aphrodisiac *eryngo* roots, and quince marmalade struck with 'Spanish comfits', which themselves contained musk.

The syrupy drink was fortified by adding brandy, usually in the proportion of a quarter of a pint to one gallon of wine. The wines most commonly used were claret for red hippocras and white Spanish and Portuguese wines for white. Taken at the end a meal with wafers and comfits, it was usually brought to table cold. Throughout Europe it was an important item in the court table ritual known as the *void* or *issue de table*. Later, when spices were more readily available, it became a popular drink at wedding and christening feasts. During the evolution of the banquet course during the Tudor and Jacobean eras, hippocras was gradually displaced by stronger distilled and infused cordial waters, the ancestors of modern liqueurs.

WASSAIL

Wassail has several associated meanings. It can be the ale or mulled wine that is drunk from a decorated or special wassail cup; the toasts or salutations of the season; the songs being sung; festivities with much drinking; and also the drinking carousers. There was a custom of taking the wassail cup or bowl, crying 'Wassail!', drinking from it, and passing it to the answering cry of 'Drinkhail!', recorded in a mid-fourteenth-century text by Robert Mannyng and Peter de Langtoft. In 1480 Caxton traced the history of wassail to an encounter between the beautiful Ronewen, daughter of the Saxon mercenary Hengist and Vortigern, King of the Britons: 'And whan nyght come that the kyng Vortiger shold gone in to his chambre for to take ther his nyghtes reste Ronewen that was Engistes doughter come with a coupe of gold in hir honde and kneled beforne the kyng and said to hym wassaille and the kyng wist not what it was to mene ne what he sholde ansuere for as moch as hym selfe ne none of his Britons yit coude none Englissh speken ne vnderstond it but speken tho the same langage that Britons yit done. Nothelees a latymer tolde the kyng the full vnderstondyng ther of wassaille and that othir sholde an suere drynke haille. And that was the fyrst tyme that wassaille and drynkhaille come vp in this land and from that tyme vn to this tyme it is will vsed in this lande.' The legend by which Vortigern was seduced into allowing the Saxons into Britain is repeated in the *Cronycles of the londe of Englod*, dated 1493.

In the fifteenth century John Speed recorded Edward II's English troops, before battle with the Scots, 'in his Campe, Wassaile, and Drinkehaile were thundered extraordinarily.'

Around 1511, Edward Hall wrote that Henry VIII's Christmas festivities at Richmond ended thus: 'and then was the wassaill or banket brought in, and so brake vp Christmas.' By this time the custom of wassail had become part of the Christmas, Twelfth Night or other festive holiday celebrations. Ronald Hutton provides this text of wassailing song from *c.* 1550: 'Wassail, wassail, out of the milk pail, Wassail, wassail, as white as my nail, / Wassail, wassail, in snow, frost and hail, / Wassail, wassail, that much doth avail, / Wassail, wassail, that never will fail.'

MEASURES

The academy of armory, *c.* 1640 by Randle Holme of Chester, gives us

'Several sorts of Vessells made after the Form and Fashion of Barrells. A Dryfett. A Tunn, is eight Barrells. An Hogshead, is two Barrells. A Pipe, is a Barrel and half. An half Pipe, is three Firkins. A Barrel, is four Firkins, or thirty six Gallons. An half Barrel, is two Firkins. A Firkin. A Kilderkin. An half Firkin. A Rundlet of thirty six quarts, all other Vessels less are called Rundlets of twelve, ten, six, four quarts &c. till you come to a Rundlet for Oysters pickled, containing about a quart, or a pint and a half.' Soon after, Holme makes slight differences to the list: 'The Measure of these kind of Vessels. A Tun contains 8 Barrels. A Hogshead, is two barrels. A Terce, is a Barrel and an half. A Barrel is 36 Gallons, but of Ale it is 32 Gallons. A Kilderkin or Half Barrel, is 2 Firkins. A Firkin is the fourth part of a Barrel, containing nine Gallons. A Rundlet, is any Vessel under a Firkin, and of any measure from a Pint to 9 Gallons, which are called Rundlets of such or such a measure or quantity.' Note the distinction between beer and ale barrels. Liquid measures are also given in the section dealing with distilling equipment, winepresses and surgical instruments: '2 Half Gills makes a Gill, or Quadran. 2 Gills makes an Half Pint. 2 Half Pints makes a Pint. 2 Pints makes a Quart. 2 Quarts makes a Pottle. 2 Pottles makes a Gallon. By these measures, Wine, Water, Ale, and Beer, are measured; yet with this difference, that the Barrel of Beer is 36 gallons, all other Liquors, but 32 gallons'.

4

Tudor Kitchens and Hampton Court

Bread was the vital part of the Tudor diet and it was eaten with most meals, but took a great deal of time to make. Only the upper classes had kitchens with an oven for baking bread which was heated with burning bundles of twigs called faggots. Castles and mansions had a separate bakehouse, where pastries and bread were cooked in a dome-shaped oven, heated by wood. The fire was raked out onto the floor and then pushed into a space under the oven before the food was put inside. Long wooden paddles were used to place and remove loaves of bread, much as one sees in a traditional pizzeria.

In richer homes, 'turnspits' were kitchen assistants who roasted pork, beef, mutton and poultry on iron spits over open fires, constantly bathing drier meat with water, dripping or lard to prevent it drying out. The valuable dripping or lard was caught in trays under the spit. Handled cauldrons hung from hooks on racks over the fire, and the racks could be raised or lowered to vary the cooking temperature. Soups and sauces were cooked in smaller pans and pots that stood on trivets above the fire.

Kitchens had work tables, long boards on trestles where servants prepared food. A table was called a *messe*, and it was the scullion's job to 'clear up the messe', when all the work had been done, preparatory to preparing new meals. Near the kitchen would be the buttery, which held barrels of wine and ale, oils and vinegars, and was where other liquids could be kept. Generally, people in the better houses ate at smaller messes, with four to a table, and the word survives in today's military eating in the mess.

THE KITCHENS AT HAMPTON COURT PALACE

Peter Brears' *All the King's Cooks* is the definitive work upon the kitchens at Hampton Court, so it is not intended to replicate that excellent work here.

Henry VIII had great kitchens at all his palaces and he extended those at Hampton Court to feed from 600 to 1,200 members of court, twice a day, and often throughout the day. They are often still used to prepare Tudor feasts. The royal kitchens were a central part of palace life and were larger than those of any modern hotel. The kitchens employed many master cooks, each with a team of yeomen and sergeants working with them. The annual provision of meat at Hampton Court for one year in Elizabeth I's reign was 1,240 oxen, 8,200 sheep, 1,870 pigs, 2,330 deer, 760 calves and 53 wild boar (pork or boar meat was called *brawn* at this time). This does not include countless birds such as teal, cygnet, gull and shoveler duck, as well as quail, pheasant and chicken. Ale was drunk fairly quickly, not stored, and 600,000 gallons of ale were drunk each year at Hampton Court alone, enough to fill an Olympic-size swimming pool. Also imbibed annually at court were around 75,000 gallons of wine.

Henry VIII extended the kitchens at Hampton Court from 1529–32 to comprise fifty-five rooms, covering 3,000 square feet, permanently staffed by 200 servants. In August 1546, Henry entertained the French ambassador and 200 companions, plus 1,300 of the English court for six days, which must have placed a terrific strain on the kitchen workers. Located on the cooler, north side of the palace, the kitchens were accessed through their own gatehouse, which was occupied by the *cofferer*, who acted as the kitchen accountant. His assistants, the *clerks of the greencloth*, checked all the goods and staff going into the kitchens and made sure that nothing was smuggled out. The *office of spicery* was responsible for the massive quantities of fruit produced in the palace gardens, including apples and pears from Hampton's two orchards. The spicery was filled with spices imported from the Orient and Europe, as well as English mustard and herbs grown in the herb garden. Paul Hentzner in 1598 noted another use of rosemary: 'Afterwards we were led into the [Hampton Court] gardens, which are moſt pleaſant; here we ſaw roſemary ſo planted and nailed to the walls as to cover them entirely, which is a method exceeding common in England.' In the *confectionery*, delicacies were prepared for the more important members of the Court. In the *pastry house* both sweet and savoury pies and pasties were prepared in four great ovens. Meat stock and boiled meat were produced in the *boiling house* in a great boiling-copper which had a capacity of an enormous 75 gallons.

There were three larders in the Tudor kitchens: the flesh larder for meat; the wet larder for fish; and the dry larder for pulses and nuts. Meat was supplied from various sources including the palace's own pheasant yard, rabbit warrens and hutches and venison from its deer park. Fish (eaten on Fridays and during Lent) came from the palace's Pond Garden. The palace also had three cellars. The wine cellar, with an attached drinking house for wine tasting, held 300 casks of wine for courtiers. Wine and ale for the sovereign was kept in the separate *privy cellar*, for fear of poisoning. Ale and later beer was stored in the *great cellar*. This had two locks on the door, with the keys being held by two different officials for extra security. The *great kitchen* had six fireplaces with spit-racks, only one of which remains. Liveried serving men collected finished dishes from the serving hatches at the far end of the great kitchen and took them to the Great Hall. Henry spent £62,000, a labour cost of £130 million at today's prices, building the Great Hall and a Royal Tennis court.

Tudor court cookery was affected by European standards. The king's dignity would be damaged if his table could not provide similar to the French or Spanish courts, e.g. if olives were available in Italy, then Henry would have served them in his court also. Roasted meat was consumed at almost every meal on non-fish days, as it was an expression of wealth for the rich. The poor ate meat rarely, and then it was usually preserved, whereas freshly slaughtered meat was available all year round to the rich. Most people would have boiled their meat, if they could afford it, to get rid of the salt, but the upper classes could afford to roast it before a fire, a technique that wastes most of the fuel, and they would employ a 'spit boy', who sat all day turning the spit and ensuring the meat did not dry out.

The Field of the Cloth of Gold, near Calais, was the site of a meeting between Henry VIII and François I of France in 1520. To show off his wealth and sophistication, Henry built two fountains which spouted hundreds of gallons of free wine for his courtiers and their French guests to enjoy. One French participant observed that the fountains 'continually spouted white wine and claret, the best that could be found, with large silver cups for any one to drink – which was a remarkable thing!' A contemporary painting of the fountains even depicts some people vomiting after having too much to drink. A replica of one fountain was built, after a major archaeological dig in 2008 discovered the remains of a sixteenth century conduit at Hampton Court. The 13-feet-tall replica, made of timber, lead, bronze and gold leaf, stands on the site of the excavated fountain in Hampton Court's largest inner courtyard, Base Court, where Henry's guests were welcomed and received by court officials. It is painted to look like white and red marble, features a naked gold figure of the Greek god of wine, Bacchus, and bears the motto *faicte bonne chere quy vouldra* – French for 'let he who wishes make good cheer.' Gravity was formerly used to force the water from cisterns through pipes and out through the fountain's holes. It was common in Tudor times during festivals and celebrations for wine to be run through public fountains in a show of the monarch's largesse to the population, most of whom would normally have drunk beer. One such occasion was the coronation of Anne Boleyn in 1533.

Henry VIII's wine cellar is one of the few remaining parts of Whitehall Palace, the main London residence of monarchs for over 150 years. Whitehall was once the biggest palace in Europe, bigger than the Vatican or Versailles, covering over 93,000 square metres between the Thames and Green Park. It became a royal palace when Henry VIII confiscated York Place from Cardinal Wolsey. As well as being Lord Chancellor of England, Wolsey was also Archbishop of York, and since the thirteenth century the archbishops' London seat had been York Place. In 1514 Thomas Wolsey had been made Archbishop of York and began work to further extend York Place, which soon became a favourite visiting place for Henry VIII, especially as the old royal palace at Westminster had been destroyed by fire in 1512. When Wolsey failed to have Henry's marriage to Catherine of Aragon annulled, his property became forfeit to the Crown and Henry VIII took Hampton Court Palace and York Place. Henry then spent enormous sums developing and expanding both residences.

York Place was to become known as Whitehall after the white stone used for the great hall. Shakespeare, in *King Henry the Eighth*, recorded: 'You must no more call it York Place: that is past; / For since the Cardinal fell that title's lost. / 'Tis now the King's, and called Whitehall.' Henry married Anne Boleyn at Whitehall in 1533, Jane Seymour there in 1536 and died there in 1547. After terrible fires in 1691 and 1698 all that remains are the Banqueting House, Queen Mary's Steps and Henry's wine cellar. In 1949 the Ministry of Defence wanted to destroy the cellar for new building, but Queen Elizabeth requested that it be saved. It could not be dismantled as Tudor brick is too soft, so builders dug around and underneath it and encased the whole cellar in steel and concrete. It was moved nine feet to the west and nineteen feet lower, but is not generally open to the public. Thus unfortunately buried under the Ministry of Defence in Whitehall, is an extraordinary historical survivor.

The Venetian ambassador described York Place, as 'a very fine palace, where one traverses eight rooms before reaching the audience chamber.' Henry VIII acquired a large plot of land opposite his new acquisition of York Place. Here he built a series of pleasure buildings including tennis courts, a tiltyard for tournaments and a cockpit. The main buildings of the palace, including the great hall, chapel and royal apartments, stretched from the site of the present Banqueting House to the Thames.

The street was spanned by two splendid gateways, the King Street Gate and Holbein Gate, which enabled members of the court to pass from St James's Park to the palace without crossing the public road. On Henry VIII's death the palace covered 23 acres and was the largest royal palace in Europe.

Whitehall Palace had a number of large communal spaces for entertainment that included the great hall and the chapel, but some temporary structures were constructed for special occasions. The largest of these was built by Queen Elizabeth I who erected a large banqueting house to hold entertainments connected with her marriage negotiations with the Duke of Alençon in 1581. This building occupied the site of the present Banqueting House. The Banqueting House of 1581 was meant to be temporary but it lasted for 25 years. In 1606 James I of England and VI of Scotland (1602–25) decided to replace it with a permanent building. Built of brick and stone and completed in 1609, the new banqueting house had a large hall above a ground floor basement. James I's new banqueting house was specifically built to provide an appropriate setting for a new and elaborate type of court entertainment, the masque. Unfortunately it burnt down in 1619 but James immediately decided to rebuild it.

No household detail was too small to be included in the regulations of major households – they had to be run like businesses. The fate of every single item of household waste: candle stubs; poultry feathers; bones; broken casks; fireplace ash etc., was specifically determined. Many were perquisites that formed part of the payment of household staff, being eminently useable, reusable or saleable in times when recycling was a way of life. Food waste was particularly detested and thought of as sinful. During these times wealthy households were also expected to assist the poor in the community, and this responsibility was taken very seriously. The two obligations of helping the poor and avoiding the sin of waste were served by the distribution of food leftovers to the poor waiting at the gate.

Henry VIII's *Ordinances for the Household Made at Eltham* in 1526, was very explicit in respect of the fate of 'broken meate', i.e. leftover food. The rules of Henry's household were quite clear: all food scraps were to be collected, and all were to be distributed as alms to the poor, on pain of the King's displeasure:

No Vessell To Be Cast Abroade Out Of The Chambers.
And semblably all such as have their lodgeings within the court shall give straight charge to the mynisters and keepers of their chambers, that they do not cast, have, or lay any manner of dishes, platters, saucers, or broken meate, either in the said galleryes, or at their chamber doores, or in the court, or other place; but immediately after they shall have occupied them, to carry them into the squillery [scullery], leaving the broken meate and relliques being in the fame, in a vessell, which by the officers of the almonry shall be sett abroad in a place to be deputed for that purpose; and likewise to put the relliques of their ale into another vessell, semblably to be ordeyned for the same, which vessells the said officers of the almonry shall sett out in a place convenient,

giveing their attendance upon the same, from time to time, upon paine of imprisonment, with further aggravation of punishment as their negligence shall require, soe that broken meate and drinke be in no wise lost, cast away, or eaten with dogges, nor lye abroad in the galleryes and courtes, but may daily be saved for the reliefe of poore folks, and to be administered unto them by the almoners as apperteyneth: and in cafe any of those which have allowance of lodgeing within the court doe make default in the ordering of their servants and keepers of their chambers in manner and forme aforesaid, they shall, for the first time, be by the head officers admonished to reforme the same, and at the second default lack their liverie for that time, and for their third forfeite loose their allowance, lodgeing, and bouch of court [meals]

Relicts and Fragments of Meate and Drinke.

And because heretofore the relicts and fragments of such meate and drinke, as dayly hath been spent in the King and Queen's chamber and household, have not been duely distributed unto poore folkes, by way of almes, as was convenient; it is therefore the King's pleasure, that from henceforth speciall regard be had, that all the said reliques and fragments be saved and gathered by the officers of the almonry, and from day to day to be given to poore people at the utter court gate, by oversight of the under almnor; without diminishing, embesselling, or purloyning any parte thereof; and that neither in the chamber, nor other place where allowance of meate is had, the meate be given away by any sitting or wayting there; but the relliques to be imployed to the almes as is aforesaid.

The Booke of the Household of Queene Elizabeth in 1601 went into fine detail of who took what:

THE SCALDING HOUSE.

YEOMEN. ... and they have for their fees, all the fethers of such provision and fowle as come into the scalding house; and the heades, feet, heartes, and guizardes of geese, and of all other things that the heades and feet are to be cut off before they be roasted.

COQUIN. IMPRIMIS, the cheife clerke of the kitchen hath for his fee, all the girdles of fresh sturgeon spent within the house.

ITEM, the master Cookes have to fee all the salmon's tailes, the heades of breats, hellibuts, porpose, chines, finnes, and tailes, pigges heades, the toiling of the leade, the lambes, and kiddes heades, skinnes, and appurtenances, from Candlemas to Lammas, except such as shall be to serve the King and Queen's grace; they have also the skinnes and tallow of all the oxen presented to the King and Queene, the Serjant of the Acatry being partaker with them.

ITEM, the yeomen of the kitchen and larder have to fee of the mutton and veales three joynts of the cragge, the two hinder legges and the rumpe, and of the oxe the fore legges stricken in the first joynte, and one peece of the neck stricken in the first joynte.

ITEM, the groomes of the kitchen and larder have to fee of the mutton, two joyntes of the cragge, andin lent brent oyle.

THE BOYLING HOUSE.

Item, the boylers have to fee, the dripping of the roste, the strippings cut of from the briskets, the surloine peece of the beefe, and the grease coming of the draweing of the beefe out of the leade, being in the kittles or pannes.

LARDER.

IMPRIMIS.The Sargent hath for his fee of the oxe two jointes of the rump chine, two jointes of the cragge, and two cloddes of the bore of the heade, and the four feet, the belly peeces, and the hinder quarters to the arse bone; excepte so many heades as shal be necessary for the expenses of the King and Queen, all empty barrels of herrings and eeles, salt salmon and sturgeon, and all the panniers of sea fish.

PULLET.

The serjant hath to fee, the grey conie skinnes from Hallomas till Shrovetide. The Clerke hath to fee, all the blacke and dunne conie skinnes and the barrels. The Groomes have to fee, all the grey conie skinnes from Midsomer till Hollantide.

Note in the last extract, different coloured rabbit skins are allocated to specific persons.

Here we have noted the Clerk of the Kitchen, Master Cookes, Serjant of the Acatry, Yeomen of the Kitchen and Larder, Groomes of the Kitchen, Boylers, Sargent of the Larder, Sargent of the Pullet and the Clerk and Groomes of the Pullet, among Elizabeth's household staff. Because of Elizabeth I's great progresses around her kingdom, which purposefully saved her a fortune in outgoings and entertainments, all the great houses of the day had to have massive kitchens and excellent cooks. Burghley, Wollaton, Cowdray, Longleat, Lacock and Hardwick were all able to provide enormous feasts for the queen and her entourage. Generally, the household steward acted as a modern-day chief executive in the running of the domestic staff of these huge mansions and their estates. He would then delegate control of the buying of provisions, the kitchen and its staff to a clerk in the kitchen. In the case of Elizabeth, the Lord Chamberlain directed her clerk (Clarke) to the kitchen, who had eleven officers such as Serjeants (spelling is variable in Elizabethan times), Chief Clerks and Master Cooks, to supervise around 150 staff.

The Serjeant of the Accatry (provisioning and purchasing) brought in beef, veal, mutton, pork, lard, fish, vegetable and fruit as required from the queen's estates. He would also purchase spices, salt and fish and overseas foods that could not be sourced from royal lands. These were sent to the Serjeant of the Larder for checking and storage, under whose direction the Yeoman of the Boyling House would boil the meats in huge copper boilers. The Serjeant of the Poultry, or Pullet, was responsible for game birds, poultry and lambs (despite mutton being in the domain of the Accatry). His Yeoman of the Scalding House scalded, plucked and drew poultry and game birds in preparation for the cooks. The Yeoman Garnetor worked under the Serjeant of the Bakehouse to prepare supplies of corn and flour. Yeomen Pervayers took these supplies into the bakehouses, and other yeomen and grooms baked breads for the queen's table and for the household and attendant guests and soldiers.

Separate ovens were used by the Serjeant of the Pastry to prepare baked meats, pastries and pies. He was ordered to make sure that they were all 'well seasoned with that proportion of spice which is allowed them, and well filled, and made according to the rate which is appointed to them … and see that no waste be made of sauces.' There was a Chief Clarke to the Spicery, who was in charge of more detailed aspects of bakery. He had yeomen to powder spices with pestles and mortars, and yeomen to make pastries and waffles using decorated iron wafer-tongs to sometimes impress stamps upon sweetmeats and biscuits. This clerk also controlled the confectionary, and supplied wardens (pears), apples, figs, raisins and other fruits. The Serjeant of the Scullery was in charge of all silver and pewter dishes, knives, spoons and candlesticks, as well as all the kitchen equipment, issuing 'chistes, guarde or irons, tubes, trays, baskets, flaskets [long, shallow baskets], scoopes, boraches [spits], peeles and such like.' The Master Cooke controlled cookery and the Serjeant of the Pantrey supervised the Yeomen for the Mouthe. These were grooms and pages who took trenchers, cutlery, bread and salt to the queen's table, before returning with the main courses. The Serjeant of the Seller was in charge of all wines, and his Yeomen of the Pitcher-House supplied drinking vessels. Yeomen for the Mouthe also served wines from the cellars and other drinks from the Buttery at table.

The job of recording the comings and goings from the household and the management of the accounts fell to the steward, who kept a detailed day-to-day tally in the Household Book. Some of the surviving household books are a marvellous source of information on daily life on a manorial estate, and the Duke of Buckingham's household book records the guests and provisions for the Christmas of 1507 at Thornbury Castle:

Thornbury, The Feast of the Nativity, Saturday 25th December 1507. Dined 95 gentry, 107 yeoman, 97 garcons. Supped 84 gentry, 114 yeoman, 92 garcons.

Archates [purchases, from the French *acheter*, to buy]: 4 swans price 12*s*, 4 geese 2*s*, 5 suckling pigs 20*d*, 14 capons 8*s*, 18 chickens 18*d*, 21 rabbits 3/6*d*, 1 peacock 2*s*, 3 mallards 8*d*, 5 widgeons 10*d*, 12 teals 12*d*, 3 woodcocks 8*d*, 22 syntes [snipe] 12*d*, 12 large birds 3*d*, 400 hens eggs 3/4*d*, 2 dishes of butter 20*d*, 10 flagons of milk 10*d*, 1 flagon of rum 6*d*, 2 flagons of frumety 4*d*, in herbs 1*d*. *Kitchen spent of the Lord's store*: 1 carcase and seven rounds of beef 20*s*; 9 carcases of mutton price 16*s*; 4 pigs 8*s*; 1½ calves 4*s*.

Cellar spent: 11 bottles and 3 quarts of Gascony wine price 13*s*; 1½ pitchers of Rhenish wine price 15*d*; ½ pitcher Malvoisey price 6*d*; Butter: Spent in aile [ale] 171 flagons, 1 quart, price 13*s* 7½*d*.

5

Tudor Etiquette at Table, the Waist of Henry VIII, Progresses, Banquets, Sumptuary Laws and Glutton Mass

After its importance as food, the most useful role bread played at table was as a plate, or 'trencher'. A trencher could be made of many different materials, earthenware, wood, or metal, but well into the sixteenth century it was often made of bread. The word is derived from the French *trenchier* or *trancher*, to cut, and the plate was made freshly for each meal by cutting off a slice from the loaf. It was often stale, so as to hold the contents better. It soaked up gravy, and could be eaten by the diner or taken away with all the other remains and given to the poor. A clean trencher was prepared once or twice during an elaborate meal as the table was swept clean between each course, the servants removing 'all broke cromys, bonys and trenchours before the secunde cours and servise be served.' The quality of bread improved under the Tudors, but it may be that 'any man who ate his own trencher must have been particularly hungry, as the bread used was rather coarse and stale, to make it solid enough for the purpose'. The flour was unbolted and the loaf itself several days old: 'trencher bred iii dayes [old] is convenyent and agreeable.' *The Goodman of Paris* adds that a trencher should be quite thick, 'half a foot wide and four inches high'. It was said to be firm enough to be used sometimes as a candle holder.

An ordinary diner made his own trencher after he sat down at the table, by cutting off a slice from the nearest loaf, but the most important people expected to be served. One manual suggests three trenchers for the master of the household, two for his son and one for the least distinguished at the table. Portions of food were taken from a shared dish and put on trenchers. In noble houses, the trenchers were not eaten at table but collected after use into baskets, which were then distributed as alms to the poor, by which time the rich meat juices and gravy had soaked into the bread and softened it so that it was edible. A major change in dining habits in the sixteenth century was the decline of serving food upon these square trenchers of firm wholemeal bread.

They were replaced by similar sized thick wooden boards. In the centre was a wooden hollow, perhaps six inches across, to contain meat and gravy, while a smaller hollow in a corner was for the diner's own serving of salt. The slab bread was replaced in dishes with 'sops' added. These were small pieces of bread placed underneath the meat, to absorb sauce. The poor, however, generally made do with deep wooden bowls, or cups, to contain their food. Illustrative of the increased use of wooden trenchers is the vast numbers rescued from Henry VIII's ship *Mary Rose*, which sank in 1545, indicating that even common soldiers used them.

Pottery also gained in popularity, becoming more affordable. Diners began to use individual beakers, whereas earlier they would signal if they wanted a drink during a meal, which they took from a communal flagon before handing it back to the server. Drinking cups and bowls were traditionally turned from ash, but the century saw them being replaced by earthenware in wealthier homes. The rich ate off pewter, silver, or earthenware, and in 1567 two tin-glazed earthenware factories were set up in London and Norwich, making white plates capable of being painted. However, the wealthy's pewter and silver was possibly reserved for special occasions, as they generally used wooden trenchers and bowls for everyday meals. Nobles would have pewter for daily use and silver for special occasions. The extremely wealthy had glass goblets. The general population drank out of wooden, earthenware or leather cups, as pewter cups were a luxury. Pewter is an alloy of tin, copper and a small amount of lead. It has a relatively low melting point and can easily be used in moulds. Once polished it can resemble silver, and at only 6*d* or 7*d* a pound in weight (a working man's daily wage) it allowed people who were not so wealthy to build up an impressive display of what resembled silver plate.

However, since pewter is a soft metal which scratches and damages easily, those who used it routinely would commonly still use a wooden platter in order to cut up meat before eating. The later Tudors took great pride in their mealtimes as it allowed them to show off their wealth and importance, not only in the fancy dishes or 'kickshaws' which used an abundance of exotic spices and food colourings, but in the wealth of plate: gold, silver or parcel gilt which was silver plated with gold. All these treasures, from bowls and dishes to candlesticks and toothpicks, were stored in court cupboards when not in use.

Although a meal in a large household might consist of two or three courses, some of which might involve several different dishes, not every guest or diner had everything offered to them. The food was graded according to the status of the diner. For example, the top table and the two sides nearest to that might be offered roast venison, but those lower down, junior members of the household, might be offered 'umble pie' made from the internal organs of the same deer. The 'humbles', or intestines and organs, would be boiled in a stew with dried fruit, apples, suet, spices, sugar and salt and then baked in pastry. This has given us the term 'eating humble pie' i.e. knowing one's inferior position or place. The servants and those placed well away from the top table would not expect to be offered the fancy dishes and elaborate spiced sauces made for the lord and his guests. Some dishes, such as chicken, tended to be reserved for visiting clergy, as it was thought to be less likely to inflame their passions than eating red meat. This idea was based on the belief that the body was composed of four humours. Up until the reign of Mary there were dietary restrictions placed on clergy by the church. Fasting rules also applied to the laity, but the wealthy who had money at their disposal found ways to circumvent the restrictions created by Lent, Advent and Friday fasting.

Under Henry VII lords still dined at a table on a raised platform or dais at the top of the hall, while servants rushed backwards and forwards at the other end of the hall along a screened passage to kitchens, which were usually some way away to minimise the risk of fire. For the lords and gentry, dinner in Tudor times was served at eleven in the morning and supper between five and six in the evening and on special occasions were extended into banquets.

In and around London alone, Henry VIII kept court at the Tower of London, Hampton Court, Whitehall, the Palace of Westminster, Baynard's Castle (near St Paul's Cathedral), Greenwich, Richmond and Eltham. There were palaces at Richmond and Eltham. All the activities at court were planned to show Henry's talents and interests, so the court became the fashionable centre for art, music, dance, poetry and tournaments. Courtiers had their own rooms in Henry's palaces. They brought their own servants with them who often had to make do with sleeping in the corridors. Sometimes nobles' sons served at court. Knowing how to cut your bread and what to do with your napkin was a social signal and every young noble learned to serve at table and how to carve. In *The Squyr of Lowe Degree* printed around 1520 by Wynkyn de Worde, we read of a squire serving dinner to Henry VIII:

> He toke a white yeard in his hande,
> Before the kynge than gane he stande,
> And sone he sat hym on his knee,
> And serued [served] the kynge ryght royally
> With deynty meates that were dere,
> With Partryche, Pecocke, and Plouere [plover],

With byrdes in bread ybake,
The Tele [teal], the Ducke, and the Drake,
The Cocke, the Corlewe, and the Crane,
With Fesauntes fayre, theyr ware no wane,
Both Storkes and Snytes [snipes] ther were also,
And venyson freshe of Bucke and Do [doe],
And other deyntés [dainties] many one,
For to set afore the kynge anone.

In the *Household Books of the third and fourth Earls of Derby*, as published by The Chetham Society in 1853, we read that Henry Stanley inherited the title in 1572 on the death of his father, Edward, 3rd Earl of Stanley. His household included 140 servants, plus a constant stream of visitors and guests, and there was also the obligation to feed the large number of 'indigent dependants' who flocked to the hall to receive their dole of leftovers. The Chetham Society record says:

'The extent of the Earl's domain supplied him with most of these necessaries of life. His flocks and herds were the produce of his own lands, his park furnished his family with venison, and his warrens and fishponds readily supplied game and fish for the table. The malt was made in his own kilns, and the hops apparently grown on his own lands, whilst the ale, in no stinted quantity, was brewed by experienced hands. The ordinary weekly consumption of the household was about one ox, a dozen calves, a score of sheep, fifteen hogsheads of ale, and plenty of bread, fish, and poultry. [Ale consumption for 140 was thus around seven pints per servant per day] The low lands around Lathom furnished turves [peat], and the lordly forests around Knowsley logs of wood for fires, whilst the capacious vaults of stone, called ovens, capable of containing more than an ox at one time, and seldom disused, were kept heated with this homely fuel of the country. Fossil coal abounded in the neighbourhood, but was apparently unknown.'

Candles of wax, but principally of tallow, proving that rushlights were not ordinarily used, were made by the household Chandler, whilst Carpenters and Rough casters were constantly employed in attending to the repairs and decorations of the massive half-timbered halls. Panelling of oak was little used at this time, and Arras men were engaged throughout the year in making tapestry and embroidering hangings for the superior rooms in the several houses of the Earl. Confectionaries, sweetmeats, and fruits are not mentioned by name, and the produce of the gardens might not have been large, as only one gardener is named in the Roll of Servants. Landscape scenery and picturesque views, now largely popular, were little regarded at the time, even by a person of Lord Bacon's refined taste. Wine is also omitted in the accounts of Earl Henry, although in 1569 Gilbert, Earl of Shrewsbury, stated that two tons in a month did not suffice for the consumption of his household, and it is an important item in the expenditure of Edward, Earl of Derby, a little earlier. In 1563 the Steward paid 6 1. [pounds] a ton for wine, whilst so great was the increase in the price of luxuries during the reign of Elizabeth, that in 1606 half a ton of wine for the use of the Earl of Cumberland's household amounted to 8 1. 5s. No delicacies are specified, but these might be included under the general and somewhat comprehensive word Acates, and, like the ordinary fare, would be most abundantly supplied at a Christening, at the great festivals of the Church, and at large entertainments.'

An order was made that dogs were not allowed in the dining hall for they would steal from the alms tubs and annoy the guests with their barking and fighting. Elsewhere there was a regulation that only a few people were allowed to be present when the Earl's dinner was being dressed, to reduce the chance of poison being added.

From *Orders for Household Servants* by John Haryngton (Harrington) we obtain a real insight into the internal government of a country gentleman's house in 1566. All these fines were deducted by the steward at the quarterly payment of the men's wages:

A servant who is absent from prayers to be fined. For uttering an oath, 1*d*; and the same sum for leaving a door open.

A fine of 2*d*, from Lady Day to Michaelmas, for all who are in bed after six, or out after ten.

The same fine, from Michaelmas to Lady Day, for all who are in bed after seven, or out after nine.

A fine of 1*d* for any bed unmade, fire unlit, or candle-box uncleaned after eight.

A fine of 4*d* for any man detected teaching the children obscene words.

A fine of 1*d* for any man waiting without a trencher, or who is absent at a meal.

For any one breaking any of the butler's glass, 12*d*.

A fine of 2*d* for any one who has not laid the table for dinner by half-past ten, or the supper by six.

A fine of 4*d* for any one absent a day without leave.

For any man striking another, a fine of 1*d*.

For any follower visiting the cook, 1*d*.

A fine of 1*d* for any man appearing in a foul shirt, broken hose, untied shoes, or torn doublet.

A fine of 1*d* for any stranger's room left for four hours after he be dressed.

A fine of 1*d* if the hall be not cleansed by eight in winter and seven in summer.

The porter to be fined 1*d* if the court-gate be not shut during meals.

A fine of 3*d* if the stairs be not cleaned every Friday after dinner.

ETIQUETTE AT TABLE

The upper levels of society developed complex and formal rules about how diners should behave together at meal times, starting with the necessity of handwashing before sitting down. Both men and women could be noticed for their courtly and genteel manner of eating or criticised for their poor behaviour. Good table manners could sometimes lead to promotion, and thus it was important to learn the right way to behave. Most table manners were practical, concentrating on cleanliness and consideration for others who would be sharing the food. At table it was considered bad form to place chewed bones back on the shared central plate, to spit, to pick one's teeth, to put too much food in one's mouth, to scratch out head lice, to nose pick, to scratch one's ears, or to blow one's nose on the tablecloth. To allow 'guns blasting from your hinder parts', was also frowned upon. 'Muck minders', the innovation of handkerchiefs, seemed to first appear in Elizabethan times.

In gentry and upper-class households, hands would be washed before a meal, often in water sweetened with roses or rosemary. Before eating there would be the saying of grace. If a man had servants, they would pass from guest to guest with each dish, and the guests would help themselves to as much as they liked from each plate. There was a predetermined order of serving courses within each meal, laid out in several books of etiquette. Manners were thought so important that they were both written down by hand and learned, and later were put into printed instruction books in rhyming format which made them easier to learn. Below is a brief extract from the *Schoole of Vertue and Booke of Goode Nourture for Chyldren* of 1577, with spelling modernised:

> For rudeness it is thy pottage to sup,
> Or speak to any, his head in his cup.
> The knife see be sharp to cut fair thy meat;
> Thy mouth not too full when thou dost eat;
> Not smacking thy lips, As commonly do hogs,
> Nor gnawing the bones, As if were dogs;
> Such rudeness abhor, Such beastliness fly,
> At the table behave thyself mannerly...

Pick not thy teeth at the table sitting,
Nor use at thy meat, Over much spitting;
This rudeness of youth is to be abhorred;
Thy self mannerly, Behave at the board.

The host was not expected to supply utensils for guests, who would bring their own knives and spoons in ornamental cases. They used a spoon for serving, a knife for cutting the food and their fingers for eating solids. All men carried knives, the poor in their belts, while they often carried a spoon in their hats. There were no pockets at this time. The shared bowl or trencher would be placed between the diners and they would spear small pieces of meat using the knives that everyone, men and women, usually carried about them. Forks were an Italian novelty that seem to have made a first appearance during the reign of Henry VIII, but did not come into vogue until Stuart times. Elizabethan colonists in America had no forks and there being no forks, the fingers were generally used for picking out the tastiest morsels from a central dish – but one did not return to the dish anything one had touched. If no servants were available, women and children of the house would serve the dishes, sitting down to eat after all the men and guests had taken what they wanted. Young nobles would serve higher nobles to gain an understanding of court etiquette. Men ate with their hats on, only removing them out of deference to a particularly high-ranking member of the dinner party. The upper classes had a clean, white napkin on the left shoulder or wrist, upon which soiled fingers or knives could be wiped.

The servants who attended table were hatless, as they could not doff their hats to their superiors while carrying dishes. Conversation at the table was considered polite and was expected. Books were written upon how to hold polite conversation upon various topics. Wynkyn de Worde's *The Boke of Keruying* (The Book of Carving, 1508) lists the rules and customs which should be followed by those preparing and by those serving the dishes. It includes everything from handwashing ceremonies to the exact placement of the trenchers by the carver, who could only touch the food with his left hand, by a thumb and two fingers. One instruction is: 'Place the salt on the right side of your Lord's seat, and the trenchers to the left of the salt. Then take the knives and arrange the loaves of bread side by side, with the spoons and napkins neatly folded by the bread. Cover your bread and trenchers, spoons and knives, and set a salt cellar with two trencher loaves at each end of the table … then serve your Lord faultlessly.'

A hornblower (or several at the king's court) would announce that it was time to wash hands and begin the meal and the steward oversaw the serving.

The butler and his servants served ale and wine to the guests, cupbearers presented the lord's and lady's cups on bended knee, while *pantlers* delivered bread and butter to the table. Carvers cut the meat or held the meat for the lord to carve it with a long knife. Bones were never wasted; they were placed in a 'voiding dish' for use later or for giving to servants or the poor to make stock. It was usual for two or four people to share a portion of food, known as a *messe*. The term also came to be applied to the table, or board, they shared. Long boards were placed upon trestles and could be easily cleared away. During and after the meal, there may have been musicians, mummers and jugglers performing during and after the meal.

A Tudor writer, describing the huge range of food offered at a feast given by the Earl of Northumberland, tells us that the reason for so much was to allow everyone to eat what they enjoyed, as well as ensuring enough food remained for the servants who had waited at table and ate later. Noble households could routinely expect to provide a hundred or more meals at dinner time. Gentlemen 'did not over eat, but were strictly moderate' in their diet and habits, although variety and novelty were highly prized. Spices were highly valued not to disguise tainted food, but to give variety to a bland diet.

Paul Hentzner, a German visitor to England in 1598, described dinner for Queen Elizabeth at Greenwich Palace during his stay:

'But while she was still at prayers, we saw her table set out with the following solemnity: A gentleman entered the room bearing a rod, and along with him another who had a table-cloth, which, after they had both kneeled three times with the utmost veneration, he spread upon the table, and after kneeling again, they both retired. Then came two others, one with the rod again, the other with a salt-seller, a plate and bread; when they had kneeled, as the others had done, and placed what was brought upon the table, they too retired with the same ceremonies performed by the first. At last came an unmarried lady (we were told she was a countess) and along with her a married one, bearing a tasting-knife; the former was dressed in white silk, who, when she had prostrated herself three times in the most graceful manner, approached the table, and rubbed the plates with bread and salt, with as much awe, as if the queen had been present.'

When they had waited there a little while, the yeomen of the guards entered, bareheaded, clothed in scarlet, with a golden rose upon their backs, bringing in at each turn a course of twenty-four dishes, served in plate, most of it gilt; these dishes were received by a gentleman in the same order they were brought, and placed upon the table, while the lady-taster gave to each of the guard a mouthful to eat, of the particular dish he had brought for fear of any poison. During the time that this guard, which consists of the tallest and stoutest men that can be found in all England, being carefully selected for this service, were bringing dinner, twelve trumpets and two kettle-drums made the hall ring for half an hour together. At the end of all this ceremonial a number of unmarried ladies appeared, who, with particular solemnity, lifted the meat off the table, and conveyed it into the queen's inner and more private chamber, where, after she had chosen for herself, the rest goes to the ladies of the court. The queen dines and sups alone with very few attendants; and it is very seldom that any body, foreigner or native, is admitted at that time, and then only at the intercession of somebody in power.'

THE WAIST OF HENRY VIII

Henry VIII usually dined in the quiet of his Privy Chamber and ate after the master cook had first checked his food and drink for poison. While there was at least one occasion when Henry threw sugarplums at his guests, meals were generally gentile affairs. The king had a special fingerbowl with spiced water, heated in a chafing dish, and a designated napkin to protect his fine manchet roll. When he had eaten enough, he stood and washed his hands while an usher brushed crumbs from his clothes.

An ambassador at the Tudor court reported: 'His Majesty is the most handsomest potentate I have ever set eyes on. Above the usual height with an extremely fine calf to his leg and a round face so very beautiful it would become a pretty woman.' Henry may have suffered a bout of smallpox at the age of twenty-three, and aged thirty he appears to have contracted malaria, which is thought to have returned throughout his life. His health was worsened by two factors: open sores on his legs and sporting injuries. Varicose ulcers began on his left leg when he was thirty-six, and later affected his right, and may have been caused by the restrictive garters he wore to show off his calves. They never healed and they increasingly restricted his mobility. He also suffered various injuries because of his love of sports. He excelled, like his father, at archery, and also wrestled and played tennis. Whilst playing the latter game he seriously injured his foot. However, in 1524 his first serious accident occurred in jousting when he failed to lower the visor on his helmet and was hit by his opponent's lance just above the right eye. Following this accident, he almost constantly suffered from migraines.

In 1536, he was nearly killed while jousting at Greenwich, when a fall left him 'speechless' for two hours. The forty-four-year-old Henry, in full armour, was thrown from his horse, itself armoured, which then fell on top of him.

Anne Boleyn was told that he would die and the shock of the news, she said, caused her to miscarry the male child she was expecting. Immediately after this, Henry told Anne they would clearly never have male children together and he had her executed six months later. Some historians, such as Lucy Worsley, believe that the accident 'provides the explanation for his personality change from sporty, promising, generous young prince, to cruel, paranoid and vicious tyrant... From that date the turnover of the wives really speeds up, and people begin to talk about him in quite a new and negative way.' Henry may have suffered a brain injury, Dr Worsley explains: 'Damage to the frontal lobe of the brain can perfectly well result in personality change.'

The incident, which ended his jousting career, aggravated his serious leg problems which plagued him for the rest of his life. The end of his jousting, combined with his leg ulcers restricting his movement, saw Henry begin to rapidly gain weight. He may have eaten up to thirteen dishes a day, the majority comprising meat such as lamb, chicken, beef, game, rabbit and a variety of birds like peacock and swan, and he may have drunk ten pints of ale a day as well as wine, as water was unsafe. He has been described as a 'comfort-eating paranoid recluse – a 28 stone man-mountain.' Between his 20s and his 50s, the 6-foot 1-inch monarch's waist grew from 32 inches to 52 inches, and his chest expanded from 39 inches to 53 inches. By the time of his death, his doctors recorded that he had badly ulcerated legs, was unable to walk, his eyesight was fading and he was plagued by paranoia and melancholy.

PROGRESSES AND BANQUETS

Feasts were used to commemorate the 'procession' or progress of the monarch in the summer months, when the king or queen would travel through a circuit of other nobles' lands. This was carried out both to avoid the plague season of London, and to alleviate the royal finances, drained through the winter to provide for the needs of the royal family and court. This would include a few days or even a week of feasting in each noble's home, who depending on his or her display of fashion, generosity and entertainment, could achieve elevated status in court for months or even years. On one occasion in 1519, the 3rd Duke of Buckingham entertained Henry VIII at Penshurst Place at a cost of over a million pounds in today's money. Two years later, such largesse had been forgotten, Buckingham was executed on a charge of treason and Henry acquired his lands.

Queen Elizabeth I made many 'progresses' around the country during her long reign. Progresses were massive undertakings. Virtually the whole court and the key administrators of the country, hundreds of people, left the royal residences in London and moved for weeks or months around provincial locations. It was an honour to accommodate the Queen and her retinue and naturally she was not charged for rent and meals by the aristocratic subjects and towns who provided this service. The costs were staggering, of course, and it is said that some were bankrupted in the process.

The Tudor banquet was very different from our modern perception and stems from the medieval 'ceremony of the *voide*'. After dinner, the guests would stand and drink sweet wine and spices while the table was cleared, or 'voided'. Not until the seventeenth century would *voide* be replaced with the *dessert*. During the sixteenth century, guests would no longer stand in the great chamber while the table was cleared and the room prepared for entertainment, instead retiring to the parlour or banqueting room. As the idea of banqueting developed, it could take place at any time during the day and had much more in common with the later practice of taking tea. Banqueting rooms varied greatly from house to house, but were generally on an intimate scale, either in a garden room or inside the mansion, such as in the small banqueting turrets in Longleat House.

To avoid the noise and disturbance of clearing away the main meal, it became fashionable for those seated at the top table to withdraw at the end of a meal to another room where special luxuries, *banquettes*, could be enjoyed. During Elizabeth's reign ever more fanciful banqueting houses, both temporary and permanent, were being built, often on the rooftops of new houses which are now known as 'prodigy houses'. Nowadays we think of a banquet as a full meal, but when banquets became fashionable during the reign of Elizabeth I, the word applied only to a final concluding course of fruit, cakes, biscuits and sticky preserves all of which featured sugar in various degrees. The centrepiece of these sugar banquets would be a fabulous and decorative subtlety, often of marchpane, which was made from sugar, rosewater and almonds which, like sugar, had to be pounded or ground to a powder before use.

Around the same time that banquets became fashionable, forks, first mentioned as sucket forks, double-ended with spoons in an inventory for Henry VIII, began to be more widely available. They were ideal for spearing sticky, sugary delights, but it took time for them to become widely accepted and used. As they did, the need for pointed knives for picking up food waned, and their shape slowly evolved into the rounded end commonly used today. However, well into the seventeenth century and even later, travellers routinely still carried their eating equipment with them. Another essential item that evolved alongside the banquet was a small, flat, wooden platter or banqueting plate. These were often made of beech or sycamore which could be cleaned, but left no taint on the delicately flavoured food. They were often served with a decorated side uppermost and turned over for actual use, which allowed the sticky plain side to be scrubbed clean afterwards.

In 1529, John, 3rd Earl of Atholl, built a huge hunting and feasting 'palace' in the woodlands to entertain the seventeen-year-old James V of Scotland, Margaret the Queen Mother (Henry VIII's sister), the papal nuncio and 'a numerous train of followers'. His magnificent entertainment took the shape of a hunt, at which the king was 'as well served and eased, with all things necessary to his Estate, as if he had been in his own palace in Edinburgh'. Atholl had a special woodland palace built of green timber, the floor strewn with rushes and flowers and the walls hung with tapestry and arrases of silk, with incredibly valuable glass in the windows. The banquet held within this massive folly, twenty miles from any dwelling, included ale, beer, wine, both white and claret, and aqua vitae. For food, there was every kind of meat from beef, mutton and venison, to swan and peacock and fish including salmon, pike and eels, with gingerbread and sweetmeats.

A thousand men were employed to herd deer to the hunting grounds and the king's party killed 'thirty score hart and hynd, with other small beasts, as roe, wolf, fox and wild cats'. The king remained there for three days and three nights. The whole entertainment was supposed to have cost Atholl £1000 a day, and the papal nuncio summed up his reaction. He thought it a 'great marvel that such a thing could be in Scotland, considering it was named the arse of the world in other countries.' As soon as the king left, Atholl told his followers to set fire to the palace and huts which had been constructed for the occasion, 'that the king and the ambassador might see them on fire. Then the ambassador said to the king, "I marvel sir, that you should thole your fair palace to be burnt, that your grace has been so well lodged int" – then the king answered the ambassador and said, "it is the use of our highlandmen, though they never be so well lodged, to burn their lodgings when they depart."'

SUMPTUARY LAWS

In 1517 the Sumptuary Laws on feasting were passed, setting out the number of courses different ranks were permitted to eat during one meal. Cardinals were allowed nine, dukes and bishops seven, and so on, while those without a title but with an annual income of between £40 and £100 could ask for no more than three. The motivation for the promulgation of sumptuary laws was varied. A particularly devout leader may have felt that excessive and conspicuous consumption would bring the wrath of God upon the nation.

Archbishop Cranmer and his bishops in 1541 made some very specific orders as to the exact number of courses and dishes that the various ranks of the clergy might eat, it being seen that men of religion had moved too far from the concepts of simplicity and abstemiousness, to the point of becoming gluttonous. However, in Cranmer's own words, 'this order was kept for two or three months, till, by the disusing of certain wilful persons, it came again to the old excesses.' Sometimes the motivation for such laws was more to do with maintaining one's position. To some rulers, it was wrong that a lesser mortal might emulate or surpass one in finery or at the dining table. Most often, sumptuary laws applied to clothing and they were frequently quite detailed as to colours, fabrics, trims, styles and so on, but sometimes, as in the example of Archbishop Cranmer, they applied to food.

GLUTTON MASS

In 1833, Isaac Disraeli wrote *Curiosities of Literature*, and in the chapter on *Ancient and Modern Saturnalia*, he noted a 'glutton mass': 'We had in Leicester, in 1415, what was called a glutton mass; during the five days of the festival of the Virgin Mary. The people rose early to mass, during which they practised eating and drinking with the most zealous velocity, and, as in France, drew from the corners of the altar the rich puddings placed there.' Ralph Barnes Grindrod published *Bacchus, an essay on intemperance*, in 1839, and we read:

'The manners of the clergy in the fourteenth and fifteenth century, were extremely gross and discreditable to the cause of religion. The luxury and intemperance of the high dignitaries of the church, afforded a pernicious example to its inferior officers, whose conduct is thus described by a modern historian... The secular clergy, were no enemies to the pleasures of the table, and some of them contrived to convert gluttony and drunkenness into religious ceremonies, by the celebration of "glutton-masses", as they very properly called them. These glutton-masses were celebrated five times a year, in honour of the Virgin Mary, in this manner: Early in the morning, the people of the parish assembled in the church, loaded with ample stores of meats and drinks of all kinds. As soon as mass ended, the feast began, in which the clergy and laity engaged with equal ardour. The church was turned into a tavern, and became a scene of excessive riot and intemperance. The priests and people of different parishes entered into formal contests, which of them should have the greatest glutton-mass, i.e. which of them should devour the greatest quantities of meat and drink in honour of the Virgin Mary.'

Part 2

Tudor Recipes

6

First Courses

I have placed what we would today call 'starters' into this section, but for the Tudor upper classes first courses were far more substantial. A typical feast menu on a meat day might have had a first course of wild boar or pork served with a pepper or mustard sauce. It could be accompanied with venison and frumenty, or bacon and pease pottage. The rest of the first course would consist of various roast or boiled meats and perhaps meat pies and pasties. In the royal household a second course would be more roast meats including game birds, pottages of meat and poultry and fish in sauce. The last course was pastries, fritters, sweetmeats and jellies. On great occasions a *sotiltee* or subtlety was the climax of each course, often modelled with *marchpane*. *Sotiltee* refers to the elaborate sculptures that often adorned the tables at grand feasts. These displays, usually made of sugar, paste, jelly or wax, depicted magnificent objects: armed ships, buildings with vanes and towers, eagles. They were also known as 'warners,' as they were served at the beginning of a banquet to 'warn' (or notify) the guests of the approaching dinner.

Some Account of London (1790) gives a description of a spectacular 'warner' at the enthronement feast of William Warham as Archbishop of Canterbury in 1504.

'The first course was preceded by "a warner, conveyed upon a rounde boorde of viii panes, with viii towres embatteled and made with flowres, standynge on every towre a bedil in his habite, with his staffe: and in the fame boorde, first the king syttinge in his parliament, with his lordes about hym in their robes and Saint Wylliam, lyke an arcbishop, sytting on the ryght hand of the kyng: then the chaunceler of Oxforde, with other doctors about hym, presented the said lord Wylliam, kneelyng, in a doctor's habite, unto the kyng, with his commend of vertue and cunnynge, &c. &c. And on the third boorde of the fame warner, the Holy Ghoste appeared with bryght beames proceedyng from hym of the gyftes of grace towarde the fayde lorde of the feaste." This is a specimen, of the antient sotelties. This was a Lenten feast of the most luxurious kind. Many of the sotelties were suited to the occasion, and of the legendary nature others historical; but all, without doubt, contrived "with great cunnynge.'"

Such subtleties are given in *The Boke of Nurture* for a meat day:

A dynere of flesche.
The First Course.
Furst set forthe mustard /& brawne / of boore, be wild swyne,
Suche potage / as þe cooke hathe made / of yerbis / spice /& wyne,
Beeff, moton / Stewed feysaund / Swan with the Chawdwyn,
Capoun, pigge / vensoun bake, leche lombard / fruture viaunt fyne;
A Sotelte And þan a Sotelte: Maydon mary þat holy virgyne, And Gabrielle gretynge hur / with an Ave. [A device, or subtlety, of Mary the holy virgin, and another of Gabriel greeting Mary]
The Second Course.
Two potages, blanger mangere, & Also Iely:
For a standard / vensoun rost / kyd, favne, or cony,
Bustard, stork / crane / pecok in hakille ryally,
heiron-sew or / betowre, with-serue with bred, yf þat drynk be by;
Partriche, wodcok / plovere / egret / Rabettes sowkere;
Gret briddes / larkes / gentille breme de mere,
Dowcets, amber Leche, dowcettes, payne puff, with leche / Ioly Ambere,
Fretoure powche / a sotelte folowynge in fere,
þe course for to fullfylle,
An angelle goodly kan appere,
and syngynge with a mery chere,
Vn-to .iij. sheperdes vppon an hille. [A subtlety of an Angel appearing and singing to three Shepherds on a hill.]
The Third Course.
Creme of almondes, & mameny, þe iij. course in coost,
Curlew / brew / snytes / quayles / sparows / mertenettes rost,
Perche in gely / Crevise dewe dou / pety perueiswith þe moost,
Quynces bake / leche dugard / Fruture sage / y speke of cost,
and soteltees fulle soleyn:
þat lady þat conseuyd by the holygost

hym þat distroyed þe fendes boost,

presentid plesauntly by þe kynges of coleyn. [Subtlety of the Mother of Christ presented by the Kings of Cologne.]

Dessert.

Afftur þis, delicatis mo.

White apples, caraways, wafers and Ypocras.

Blaunderelle, or pepyns, with carawey in confite,

Waffurs to ete / ypocras to drynk with delite.

now þis fest is fynysched / voyd þe table quyte

Go we to þe fysche fest while we haue respite,

& þan with goddes grace þe fest wille be do.

This is the bill of fare for the 1486 nuptial feast, again with subtleties, of Henry VII and Elizabeth of York, as given in *Some Account of London* by Thomas Pennant, 1790.

NUPTIAL TABLE Henry VII

First Course.

A Warner byfor the Course

Sheldes of Brawne in Armor

Frumetye with Venison

Bruet riche

Hart powdered graunt Chars

Fesaunt intram de Royall

Swan with Chawdron

Capons of high Goe

Lampervey in Galantine

Crane with Cretney

Pik in Latymer Sawce

Heronusew with his Sique

Carpe in Foile

Kid reversed

Perche in Jeloye depte

Conys of high Grece

Moten Roiall richely garnysed

Valance baked

Custarde Royall

Tarte Poleyn

Leyse Damask

Frutt Synoper

Frutt Formage

A Soteltie, with writing of Balads.

Second Course.

A Warner byfor the Course

Joly Ypocras

Mamane with Lozengs of Golds

Pekok in Hakell

Bittowre

Fesawnte

Browes

Egrets in Beorwetye

Cokks

Patrieche

Sturgyn freshe Fenell

Plovers

Rabett Sowker

Seyle in Fenyn entirely served richely

Red Shankks

Snytes

Quayles

Larkes ingraylede

Creves de Endence

Venesone in Paste Royall

Quince Baked

Marche Payne Royall

A colde bake Mete flourishede

Lethe Ciprus

Lethe Rube

Fruter Augeo

Fruter Mouniteyne

Castells of Jely in Temple wise made

A Soteltie.

John Russell's *The Boke of Nurture* of 1460–70 gives a model menu for a *Feast for a Franklin*, a freeholder not of noble birth. For this middle-class man, he suggests as a first course brawn (pork) with mustard, boiled chicken, stewed beef or mutton, bacon with pease pottage, roast goose or pork and a capon pie or a *crustard*, a type of quiche. The franklin's second course would begin with *mortrewes* (a thickened meat or fish broth), or a savoury breadcrumbed pudding. As a third course he would have a series of roasts: veal or lamb; kid or rabbit; chicken or pigeon, with a meat pie or pasty. A third course would be fritters and slices of sweet and savoury puddings. He would then have stewed or baked spiced apples and pears, bread and cheese. The fifth and final course would be spiced cakes and wafers, with spiced ale and mead.

A fest for a franklen.
A Franklen may make a feste Improberabille,
brawne with mustard is concordable, [first course]
bakon serued with peson,
beef or moton stewed seruysable,
Boyled Chykon or capon agreable,
convenyent for þe seson;
Rosted goose & pygge fulle profitable,
Capon / Bakemete, or Custade Costable,
when eggis & crayme be geson.
Þerfore stuffe of household is behoveable,
Mortrowes or Iusselle ar delectable
for þe second course by reson. [second course]
Than veel, lambe, kyd, or cony,
Chykon or pigeon rosted tendurly,
bakemetes or dowcettes with alle.
þen followynge, frytowrs & a leche lovely; [third course]
Suche seruyse in sesoun is fulle semely
To serue with bothe chambur & halle.
Then appuls & peris with spices delicately
Aftur þe terme of þe yere fulle deynteithly,
with bred and chese to calle.
Spised cakes and wafurs worthily
withe bragot &methe, þus men may meryly
plese welle bothe gret & smalle.'

Nearly all of the above dishes will be described in the following pages. Please note that any following modern redactions of Tudor recipes are purely indicative. It was very rare for cooks to disclose their cooking times or quantities of ingredients. To make matters even worse, some measurements were in Tudor measures of cups and spoons. Any meal here can be a main course, if wished. The ingredients are given as guidance for experimentation with the recipes. In most cases, spellings of the original recipes have been modernised, but a few examples have been left in. However, the recipes begin with Britain's oldest recipe, a staple of 6000 BCE, which the Tudor poor ate, is still made today and is a popular soup in better restaurants.

NETTLES TWO WAYS

Stone Age people would mix nettles and other leaves such as dandelion and sorrel, adding salt, water and later barley flour to make a nourishing nettle pudding or pottage. Nettles taste like spinach, cabbage or broccoli and are rich in iron, potassium and vitamins. Best of all, they are free, and soaking, drying, cooking, refrigerating or wilting all neutralise their sting. Pick while young in March and April, wearing rubber gloves to pick only the top 4–6 leaves. Using gloves, discard stems and stalks.

Ingredients 1: nettles; butter.

Method 1: Wash nettle leaves, place in a pan of boiling water for 3–4 minutes or until leaves have wilted. Drain through a colander, keeping the liquid for stock. Press out the excess water and chop to eat, like spinach. Add butter for a side dish, or make into a soup, or add to risotto, pasta, pizza topping, scrambled eggs etc.

Ingredients 2: 150 g nettle tops; 1 l chicken or vegetable stock; clove of chopped garlic; 2 chopped celery sticks; 1 chopped onion; 1 finely sliced leek; knob of butter.

Method 2: Melt butter into a pan, add onion, leeks, celery and garlic, cover and allow to sweat for 10 minutes. Add stock and simmer for 10 minutes. Add nettles and simmer for 5 minutes or until tender. Season with salt and pepper and then purée. Serve with chopped chives and yoghurt.

SALMON SALLET FOR FISH DAYS – SALMON AND ONION SALAD WITH VIOLETS – PANSY SALMON

Thomas Dawson's *The Good Huswifes Jewell*, 1585, 1594, 1596

Colours and presentation were extremely important at the rich man's table, especially when demonstrating one's wealth and power, to guests. Many types of edible flower were used, both for taste and visual appeal, and flowers were also set at table to enhance the presentation. Large and elaborate sculptures and settings of 'flowers,' were even made of cut vegetables and herbs if attractive flowers were not in season. This has a resonance today. With a well-presented dish, in attractive settings, we often think that the meal is a small portion and we eat it more slowly. We then realise that we are full and consequently tend to eat less in quantity than when a mound of food is heaped on our plates. One can easily make this a main meal, and substitute or add other edible flowers such as nasturtiums, pot marigolds, roses, borage, flowers of basil (sparingly), pinks, chive flowers, etc. Violet flowers have a lettuce-like flavour, making decorative addition to a green salad or to garnish a pâté or dessert. They can also be crystallised and used on cakes, biscuits or creamy desserts. Varieties to use are *Viola cornuta* (horned pansy), *Viola hybrida* or *Viola x williamsiana* (pansy), *Viola tricolour* (wild pansy, heartsease), or *Viola odorata* (sweet violet).

'Salmon cut long waies with slices of onyons upon it layd and upon that to cast Violets, Oyle and Vineger'.

Ingredients: (for four servings) Salmon fillet cut into 4 strips; large onion, very thinly sliced (use a red onion as it is milder); 2 tbsp white wine vinegar; 1 tbsp lemon juice; ¼ cup extra virgin olive oil; 1 tsp sugar; ¾ cup viola flowers; salt and pepper to taste.

Method: Place the vinegar and lemon juice in a bowl. Slowly whisk in the olive oil. Season to taste and then add the sliced onion to the vinaigrette. Wait a few minutes, and remove the onion to save for later. Lightly coat salmon with some of the vinaigrette and place under a preheated medium grill, on foil. Cook for 3 to 4 minutes each side, or until firm. Place a mound of the onion in the centre of each dish, with the salmon strip on top. Drizzle the rest of the vinaigrette over the salmon, and scatter violets across the top. Serve with crusty brown bread and butter. Simple and delicious.

FINE RISE PORREDGE – RICE PORRIDGE WITH ALMONDS

John Partridge's *The Treasurie of Commodious Conceits & Hidden Secrets*, 1573

'To make fine Rise Porredge. Take half a pound of Jordan Almonds, and half a pound of Rice and a gallon of running water, and a handful of Oak bark, and let the bark be boiled in the running water, and the Almonds beaten with the hulls and all on, and so strained to make the Rice Porridge withal.' (spellings modernised)

EVERIN IN BRUET – EGG, CHEESE AND SAFFRON BROTH

The Master-Cook of Richard II, *The Forme of Cury, c.* 1390

The Forme of Cury means the form of cooking, from the French *cuire*, to cook. This was a common Tudor dish, but the only recipe this author can find dates from the previous century. *Eyerin* or *everin* is a relict name for eggs.

'For to make eyerin in bruet: Nym water and welle it and break eyerin and co them in and grind pepper and saffron and temper up with sweet milk and boil it and hack cheese small and cast therein and mix it forth.'

Ingredients: 2½ cups milk; ⅛ tsp saffron; ⅛ tsp ground pepper; ½ tsp salt; 2 beaten eggs; ½ cup grated cheese.

Method: Heat milk, saffron, pepper and salt to boiling point. Stir in cheese and cook, stirring, for 1 minute. Blend eggs into the soup, stirring constantly. Serve as soon as the eggs are set.

IUSSELL – BREAD AND EGG SOUP

The Babees Book, or A 'Lytyl Reporte' of How Young People Should Behave, MS. Harl. 5086, c. 1475

Iusselle (*or jusshel, jushel, dyshelle, dishel* etc.) is described in the *Middle English Dictionary* as 'a thick soup of eggs and grated bread.' *Dishel* is elsewhere called 'a compound of eggs, grated bread, saffron and sage, boiled together.' The following reference appears to be the first time the word 'recipe' appears.

'Recipe brede gratyd, and eggis; and swyng þam to-gydere, and do þerto sawge, and saferon, and salt; þan take gode brothe, and cast it þer-to, and bole it enforesayd, and do þer-to as to charlete.'

BREAKFAST SOUP – BUBBLY BEER CHEESE BREAKFAST SOUP

Traditional medieval/Tudor/Stuart

The average English family member drank six pints of beer (or cider) a day, including children, needing the carbohydrates for hard work and the colder winters. Only in some rural areas was it safe to drink water. Breakfast could often be hot beer soup, enriched with butter. A couple of whisked eggs were added to it and it was usually poured over bread. In Germany, *biersuppe* was spiced beer thickened with a roux of flour and butter, enriched with egg yolks and cream. This probably evolved into what we know as *posset*, made from spiced milk and ale. Another traditional dish was *Berliner biersuppe*, consisting of beer, thickened with a browned roux, flavoured with cinnamon, ginger, salt, nutmeg, rum, white wine, egg yolk and sugar. In Alsace, *soupe de la bière* is a traditional savoury purée, still made from local beer, chicken broth, onions, bread and a pinch of nutmeg. In Wales, cheese was traditionally added and is the following beer and cheese soup. As a start to the day on a cold winter morning, this is even better than a fried breakfast.

The Duchess Élisabeth Charlotte d'Orléans (1676–1744) wrote in her letters: 'Tea makes me think of hay and dung, coffee of soot and lupin-seed, and chocolate is too sweet for me – it gives me a stomach ache. How much I would prefer a good beer soup, that wouldn't give me a stomach ache.' Many, many housewives brewed beer, and there seem to be no particular surviving recipes for this medieval dish, but the following is a modern version.

Ingredients: 2 pints of chicken broth; small chopped onion; 2 pints skimmed milk; 4 tbsp soy sauce (although not available in Tudor times); ¾ pound grated Cheddar or Caerphilly cheese; 1 cup beer; 1 tsp pepper; 1 tsp paprika; 2½ pounds chopped sweet potatoes. Use normal potatoes if sweet are not available, although they were not used in Tudor times.

Method: Bring the chicken broth to the boil, add the potatoes and onion and simmer for 30 minutes. Remove from the heat and allow the broth to cool a little, before stirring in the milk. (If you add milk to very hot broth, it will curdle). In small batches, remove the mixture and purée in a food processor, returning the mixture to another cooking pot. Stir in the soy sauce and pepper, and on a low heat bring back to the simmer, stirring occasionally. Now gradually stir in the grated cheese. When the cheese is melted, stir in the beer and ladle into bowls, adding a pinch of paprika on top if desired. You can easily add bread or toast to the soup to make a main meal.

AN EXCELLENT BOILED SALLAT ON SIPPETS – SALAD OF BOILED SPINACH WITH CURRANTS SERVED ON TOAST

Gervase Markham's *Countrey Contentments, or, The English Hus-wife*, 1615

'Sippets' are small pieces of toast or bread, often soaked in gravy or juices to act as a garnish. In the recipe, you can use toasted slices of bread quartered into triangles.

'To make an excellent compound boiled Sallat: take of Spinage well washed two or three handfuls, and put it into fair water and boil it till it be exceeding soft and tender as pap; then put it into a Colander and drain the water from it, which done, with the backside of your Chopping-knife chop it and bruise it as small as may be: then put it into a Pipkin with a good lump of sweet butter and boil it over again; then take a good handful of Currants clean washed and put to it, and stir them well together, then put to as much Vinegar as will make it reasonably tart, and then with sugar season it according to the taste of the Master of the house, and so serve it upon sippets.'

Ingredients: 300 g spinach; 40 g butter; 140 g currants; 3 tbsp wine vinegar; 4 tbsp sugar; 450 g loaf of bread, sliced thickly and toasted.

Method: Boil some water in a pan and add the spinach, boiling for 3 minutes. Drain and immediately rinse under cold water. Wring the spinach to drain and chop finely before heating the butter in a frying pan. Add the spinach to the butter and after about a minute, add the currants. Fry for another two minutes, then add the vinegar and sugar. Toss the ingredients together and spoon over the sippets, serving immediately.

MORTROSE OF FYSHE – MORTRESS OF FISH

Gentyll Manly Cokere, MS Pepys 1047, c. 1490, also in *The Forme of Cury*, 1390

Mortrews was a common dish of finely ground food boiled in broth, etc., named for the mortar in which it was prepared. A *Mortrew, Mortrose, Mortis* or *Mortress* was generally a dish of mixed meats, but the following was a dish for fish days. By 'houndfish', the writer probably meant dogfish.

'To make mortrews of fish. Take houndfish, haddock or cod. Boil it and pick it clean from the bones. Take away the skin and grind the liver there with blanched almonds. And temper thy milk with the broth of the fresh fish and make a gode milk of it. Do there to crumbs of white bread and sugar. Set it to the fire. When it boils look it be standing. Mess [portion out]. Serve it forth. Strew on white powder.'

Ingredients: 450 g cod or haddock, but you can use any white fish; 75 g ground almonds; 175 g fresh white breadcrumbs; 15 ml sugar; 15 ml icing sugar; 5 ml ground ginger.

Method: Place the fish in a shallow pan and just cover with water. Simmer for about 10 minutes until tender. Take out the fish, remove the skin and bones and break it up into flakes. To simplify the recipe, buy pre-prepared cod, and also fish stock. Blend the almonds with 425 ml of the fish stock from the pan, and blend in the fish flakes, breadcrumbs and sugar. Pour the mixture into a pan and cook for a few minutes, stirring continuously until it thickens. Pour it into serving dishes and leave to cool. Mix the icing sugar and ginger and sprinkle over before serving.

MORTIS – TUDOR CHICKEN PATÉ
Thomas Dawson's *The Good Huswifes Jewell*, 1585, 1594, 1596

In Latin, *mortis* means 'of death', as in *rigor mortis*. However, the name probably derives from the use of a pestle and mortar to crush the almonds and grind the chicken meat.

'To make a mortis: Take almonds and blanch them, and beat them in a mortar, and boil a Chicken, and take all the flesh of him, and beat it, and strain them together, with milk and water and so put them into the pot, and put in Sugar and stir them still, and when it hath boiled a good while, take it of, and set it a cooling in a pail of water, and strain it again with Rose water into a dish.'

Ingredients: 4 chicken breasts or thighs; 60 g blanched almonds; 120 ml milk; large pinch of salt; 1 tbsp brown sugar; 1 tbsp rose water.

Method: Place the chicken in a saucepan, cover with water, add salt and bring to the boil. Reduce to a simmer, cooking for about 45 minutes until tender. As the chicken is cooking, blanch the almonds, grind them and then add milk to form a smooth paste. Remove the chicken and if using the thighs take all the meat from the bones. Chop the chicken meat and add to the almond paste in a food processor, grinding until it forms a paste. Place the mixture in a saucepan, add the sugar and heat gently for about 15 minutes, stirring continuously to prevent the mixture from sticking to the saucepan's base. Then immediately cool the saucepan in a bowl of cold water, and beat in the rose water. Spoon the resulting paté into individual ramekins and chill for 15 minutes in the fridge before serving.

ELIZABETHAN PICKLED MUSHROOMS
The Whole Body of Cookery Dissected, 1675

There are about 3,600 species of fungi in the United Kingdom alone, of which 50–100 are dangerous. Culpeper refers to some different types for medical use, and the following shows the variety of wonderful names for some of these fungi. Edible Fungi: Beefsteak Fungus; Brittlegills – Powdery, Greencracked, Common Yellow, Yellow Swamp; Fairy Ring Champignon; Mushrooms – Field, Oyster, Macro, St George's, Horse, Wood, Blushing Wood, Hedgehog; Puffballs – Common, Stump, Meadow, Giant; Charcoal Burner; Chanterelle; Porcelain Fungus; Saffron Milkcap; Oak Milkcap; The Blusher; The Deceiver; Parasol; Shaggy Parasol; Waxcaps – Crimson, Scarlet, Meadow; Tawny Grisette; Trumpet Chanterelle; Wood Blewit; Field Blewit; Shaggy Inkcap; Oak Milkcap; Horn of Plenty, The Prince; Boletes – Bay, Orange Birch, Orange Oak, Scarletina; Velvet Shank; The Miller; Morels; Summer Truffle; Jelly Ear; Chicken of the Woods; Cauliflower Fungus and Slippery Jack.

This author used to 'go mushrooming' with his father and grandfather on weekends but gathering edible mushrooms today is seen as increasingly dangerous. Undoubtedly in Tudor times there would have been fatalities. Among the poisonous fungi are: Devil's Bolete; Sickener; Beechwood Sickener; Panthercap (can kill); Destroying Angel; Livid Pinkgill; Splendid Webcap (deadly poisonous, smelling of pepper); Deadly Webcap (deadly poisonous, but similar to edible chanterelles); Fool's and other Webcaps; Funeral Bell (can kill); Deadly Fibrecap; Fool's Funnel (seriously poisonous, can be deadly); Fenugreek Milkcap; The Dapperlings including the Star, Deadly and Fatal Dapperling; Fly Agaric; The Sickeners; Silky Pinkgill; Poisonpies; Common Inkcap; Inky Mushroom; Bitter Bolete; False Morel (can kill); Sulphur Tuft; Inky Mushroom; and Brown Roll Rim. This last can kill if eaten uncooked, but is sometimes edible if cooked. The Yellow Stainer is the most likely to cause stomach upsets, as it is similar in appearance to some of the edible agaric mushrooms.

Liberty Caps are also now known as Magic Mushrooms for their hallucinogenic properties, but are classed as poisonous and are the only fungi which are illegal to pick, being considered a class-A drug. The Common Inkcap is edible, but strangely poisonous if taken with alcohol. Deathcap is aptly named, as if untreated there is a 50–90 per cent mortality rate. Even with expert hospital care, there is only a 20 per cent survival rate. It is responsible for 90 per cent of all fungus deaths and is not uncommon, found in mixed woods and looking similar to agaric mushrooms. However, the 'Trumpet of Death', also called the Black Trumpet, Black Chanterelle and Horn of Plenty, the evil-looking *Cratellerus Fallax* is edible. Strangely, its French name is also '*Trompette de la Morte*'. (– from *Breverton's Complete Herbal*).

'Take a bushel of mushrooms, blanch them over the crown, barm them beneath; if they are new, they look red as a Cherry; if old, black; this being done, throw them into a pan of boiling water, then take them forth and let them drain; when they are cold, put them up into your Pot or Glass, put thereto Cloves, Mace, Ginger, Nutmegs, whole Pepper; Then take white wine, a little Vinegar, with a little quantity of salt, so pour the Liquor into your Mushrooms, and stop them close for your use all the year.'

Ingredients: 230 g chestnut or closed cup mushrooms, about 3 cm in diameter; two cloves; one large sliver of mace; one thin slice of fresh root ginger; ½ nutmeg sliced into fragments; 180 ml white wine; 480 ml water; 1 tbsp vinegar; 1 tsp salt; 1 tsp peppercorns.

Method: Wash the mushrooms with a damp cloth. If you wash under running water, they will absorb the liquid and will not pickle properly. Slice off the stems within 1 cm of the cap. Add 480 ml water to a saucepan. Add half the salt and the mushrooms and then bring to the boil. Once the mushrooms have started to boil, drain immediately and place them in a large screw-top jar. Add the spices and the remainder of the salt, and then pour the wine and the vinegar over the top. If there is insufficient liquid, top-up with more white wine vinegar. Cover the jar with cling film or plastic to protect the cap from corrosion. Invert the jar several times over the next day to make sure that the spices are evenly distributed in the pickling liquid. Store in a cool place for around three to four days before using.

CAWL BLAWD CEIRCH – LEEK, CARROT AND OATMEAL SOUP
Traditional Welsh

Fried oatmeal, leeks, onion and carrots in a milk and white stock base, this makes an excellent soup starter for a St David's Day feast.

Ingredients: 1 large onion, peeled and chopped; 2 leeks, washed and chopped; 2 carrots, scraped and chopped; 2 tbsp butter; 50 g medium oatmeal; 600 ml white stock or vegetable stock; 450 ml milk; salt and freshly-ground black pepper, to taste; ½ tsp fresh thyme, chopped; 6 tbsp fresh parsley, chopped.

Method: Combine the onion, leeks and carrots in a pan with the butter. Heat until the butter has melted, then toss the vegetables to coat evenly. Add the oatmeal and continue frying gently, stirring constantly, for 3 minutes. Then stir in the stock and bring the mixture to a simmer. Cover the pan and cook slowly for 45 minutes before adjusting the seasoning to taste. Now add the thyme and parsley. When ready to serve, take off the heat and stir in the milk. Return to the heat, bring back to a simmer and serve immediately.

VENYSON IN BROTH – STEWED VENISON RIBS
Two Fifteenth Century Cookbooks – Harleian MS. 279, c. 1440

This can be a main meal, but was also served as a first course. To make a main dish, serve with *Frumenty,* as in the following recipe. Venison is an underrated and very healthy meat.

'Venison in Broth. Take ribs of venison, and wash them clean in fair water, and strain the same water through a strainer into a pot, and add there-to Venison, also Parsley, Sage, powder pepper, Cloves, Mace, Vinegar, and a little red wine add there-to; and then let it boil until it is done, and serve forth.'

Ingredients: 900 g venison roasting joint, or venison ribs; 2½ ml chopped sage; 2½ ml chopped parsley; 30 ml red wine vinegar; 150 ml red wine; pinch each of cloves, mace and salt and black pepper to taste.

Method: Place the joint or ribs in a stockpot and cover with water. Bring to the boil, add the spices, vinegar and red wine and return to the boil. Reduce the heat to a simmer and cook for 60 minutes. Adjust the seasoning and continue cooking until the venison is tender. Serve hot.

FRUMENTY – TUDOR PORRIDGE
Liber Cure Cocorum, Sloane MS. 1486, 1430

Frumenty was a Christmas staple for much of the nation. Its precise nature varied depending upon time and place, but most recipes consisted of cracked wheat boiled into a thick porridge using almond milk, cream, milk or eggs. In wealthier households, this would be spiced with saffron, cinnamon or mace. The poor ate it on its own, the rich as an accompaniment to venison, mutton or as in *The Forme of Cury*, porpoise. Once grain had been harvested it was only ground to flour as needed, as it was subject to attack by weevils, so whole grain was more readily available than it is now. Any grains could be used, cracked lightly in a pestle and mortar. *Seethe* is an old word for simmer, so the recipe instructs the reader to bring the grain to the boil and simmer gently. Letting it stand allows the grain to swell and soften. Egg yolks are used to thicken the mixture further. You can add raisins, currants, honey, sugar, ginger and cinnamon to taste. The dish was also known as *firmity*, and *frumenty* stayed in the cook's repertoire until well into the nineteenth century. It was strong alcohol-spiced *firmity* that led Henchard into selling his wife in Thomas Hardy's *Mayor of Casterbridge*. There are more recipes for *frumenty* in the chapter on side dishes.

'Seethe the cracked grains for about 15 minutes and allow them to stand for as long again. Add some milk, saffron and 2 yolks of eggs. Stir softly till it be thick.'

Warning: If a discontented husband, do not add alcohol to the dish.

SUBTLE BROTH FROM ENGLAND

Le Ménagier De Paris, 1393

Long pepper was the pepper generally available until Elizabethan times. It is a native of Java, Malabar and Bengal. Long Pepper (*Piper longum*) is closely related to the more familiar *Piper nigrum*, from which we now obtain the familiar black, white and green peppercorns. Long pepper was highly prized in ancient times for both its medicinal and culinary uses, but was eclipsed by black pepper when this became cheaper and more easily available. Its virtual death knell in European cuisine was assured by the opening up of the New World and the increasing familiarity of chilli pepper, and it is now little used outside its natural homelands. Black pepper, *piper nigrum*, was cultivated at Malacca, Java and Sumatra. From these islands pepper is exported to every part of the world where a regular commerce has been established. The common white pepper is the fruit of the same plant but is prepared differently. A great deal of the heat of the pepper is taken off by this process, so that the white kind is more suitable for many purposes than the black.

'Subtle Broth from England. Take cooked peeled sweet chestnuts, and as many or more hard-boiled egg yolks and pork liver: grind all together, mix with warm water, then put through a sieve; then grind ginger, cinnamon, clove, grain, long pepper, galingale and saffron to give it colour and set to boil together.'

MAKEROUNS – MACARONI CHEESE

The Master-Cook of Richard II, *The Forme of Cury, c.* 1390

This writer grew up after the war, not tasting any type of pasta until the 1960s. In Tudor times, fresh pasta was layered with cheese and butter in a baking dish, before being oven baked and served.

'Makerouns. Take and make a thynne foyle of dowh, and kerue it on pieces, and cast hym on boiling water and seeþ it wele. Take chese and grate it, and butter imelte, cast bynethen and abouven as losyns; and serue forth.'

'Macaroni. Take a piece of thin pastry dough and cut it in pieces, place in boiling water and cook. Take grated cheese, melted butter, and arrange in layers like lasagne; serve.'

MACARONI WITH PERMASENT [PARMESAN] CHEESE

Certaine Philosophical Preparations of Foode and Beverage for Sea-men, 1607 (and 1595)

This dish seems astonishing, but simply shows how adventurous Tudor cooking could be. Plat's cook's recipes date from Tudor times, and it is wonderful to think of Elizabethan privateers eating pasta. Hugh Plat (1552–1608) was an independently wealthy courtier, inventor and writer. He wrote on many topics, particularly within the fields of domestic economy, agriculture, science and medicine. This is a very early English reference to macaroni being used by the Elizabethan explorers, by which he meant pasta in general. Plat extolled the virtues of macaroni in *Sundrie new and Artificiall remedies against Famine*, published in 1595. In summary, he notes that the advantages of pasta as a food for seamen were that it kept well, even in hot conditions and it was relatively light in weight. On expeditions on land, one man could carry enough to feed two hundred men for a day. Pasta cooked quickly – a bonus to the cook in the tiny cramped galley – and the saving in fuel translated to more saved space. It was also a welcome alternative to the salt meat staple of the seaman's diet. It served 'both in steede of bread and meate, wherby it performeth a double service.' Unused macaroni could be used to supply a second voyage, it lent itself to variation and enrichment and the ingredients for making macaroni were available all year. Plat also knew of couscous, which has only become a regular item in supermarkets in the last fifteen years.

'And first for Food. A cheap, fresh and lasting victual, called by the name of Macaroni amongst the Italians, and not unlike (save only in form) to the Cus-cus (couscous) in Barbary may be upon reasonable warning provided in any quantity to serve either for change and variety of meat, or in the want of fresh victual. With this, the Author furnished Sir Francis Drake and Sir John Hawkins, in their last voyage.'

It was over a century before pasta recipes began to appear in cookery books, e.g.

'To Dress Macaroni with Permasent [Parmesan] Cheese'.

The Experienced English Housekeeper, Elizabeth Raffald (1769)

'Boil four Ounces of Macaroni 'till it be quite tender, and lay it on a Sieve to drain, then put it in a Tossing Pan, with about a Gill of good Cream, a Lump of Butter rolled in flour, boil it five Minutes, pour it on a Plate, lay all over it Permasent Cheese toasted; send it to the Table on a Water Plate, for it soon goes cold.'

SALLAT OF CARRETS – ELIZABETHAN CARROT SALAD

William Vaughan, *Approved Directions for Health, both Natural and Artificial: derived from the best physitians as well moderne as auncient*, 1612

This is a herbed salad of cooked baby carrots. Orange carrots were fairly rare at this time, with the vegetables, smaller than today's, being purple, white, red and yellow, so multicoloured carrots could make a dish appear more attractive. Carrots were often cut into shapes for effect in adorning dishes, being cut into 'knots, escutcheons, birds, beasts' etc. Interestingly, Vaughan declared in his book that 'tobacco well dried, and taken in a clean Pipe fasting, in a moist morninge, during the Spring or Autumne, cureth the megrim [migraine], the toothache, obstructions proceeding of cold and helpeth the fits of the mother.' However, he also warned that it could be abused. In 1612 John Cotta also wrote about tobacco's use as a panacea: 'Is not this high-blased remedy now manifestly discovered, through intemperance and custome, to be a monster of many diseases?' Dr James Hart in 1633 also claimed that its use reaped little benefit, but it was to be another four centuries before real doubts were raised again about the efficacy of tobacco.

'Carrets boyled and eaten with vinegar, Oyle, and Pepper serve for a special good salad to stirre up appetite, and to purifie blood'.

Ingredients: 450 g baby carrots; 700 ml water; ½ tsp salt; ¼ tsp chervil; ¼ tsp white pepper; leaves of a large bunch of flat-leaf parsley; 120 ml white wine vinegar; extra virgin olive oil.

Method: Clean the carrots by scrubbing with a brush and cut off their green tops. Put the water in a saucepan and add salt. Bring to the boil and add roughly-chopped chervil and the carrots. Cover the pot and reduce to a simmer. Cook for around ten minutes, or until the carrots are tender. In a large bowl mix the vinegar, oil and pepper. Once the carrots are cooked, drain and toss them in the dressing to coat them thoroughly. Cover the bowl and leave to marinade for at least an hour. Wash the parsley leaves and place on a large plate. Arrange the carrots around the leaves, pour a little of the dressing on top and serve.

A SIMPLE PLAIN SALLET – MIXED SALAD WITH BOILED VEGETABLES

Gervase Markham's *The English Huswife: Containing the inward and outward Vertues which ought to be in a Compleat Woman – A Work generally approved, and now the Ninth time much Augmented, Purged, and made most profitable and necessary for all men, and the general good …*, 1615, 1683 (Markham's works were updated throughout the seventeenth century, but based in Tudor times)

We rarely have cooked salads today, but the Tudors believed that cooking ingredients improved things for health, by making food more artificial. Artificial was good, because the hand of man, directed by God, was there. Animals ate raw foods and thus cooking distanced man from the animals and made him closer to God.

'First then to speak of Sallets, there be some simple, some compounded, some only to furnish out the Table, and some both for use and adornation: your simple Sallets are Chibols pilled [peeled green onion], washt clean, and half of the green tops cut clean away, and so served on a fruit dish, or Chives, Scallions, Rhaddish roots, boyled Carrets, Skirrets and Turnips, with such like served up simply: Also, all young Lettuce, Cabbage-Lettuce, Purslane, and divers other herbs which may be served simply without any thing but a little Vinegar, Sallet Oyl and Sugar; Onions boyled; and stript from their rind, and served up with Vinegar, Oyl and Pepper, is a good simple Sallet; so is Camphire, Bean-cods [green beans], Sparagus, and Cucumbers, served in likewise with Oyl, Venegar and Pepper, with a world of others, too tedious to nominate.'

Method: It seems that the chibols, scallions, chives and radishes are served in side dishes. 'Cabbage-lettuce' is a headed lettuce, as opposed to loose-leaved, and along with purslane is served with a mixture of herbed vinegar, salad oil and sugar. Boiled onions are served with vinegar, oil and pepper. Cooked samphire, cucumber, steamed asparagus and boiled green beans can also be served, and carrots, turnips and skirrets must be boiled before adding them.

MY LADY OF PORTLANDAS MINCE PYES – LADY PORTLAND'S MINCE PIES

The Closet of the Eminently Learned Sir Kenelme Digbie Kt Opened, 1669

The recipe is an evolution of the medieval Christmas pie, which used beef and venison offal, often with apples. It was always a spiced meat-based dish, but Digbie's version has more fruit than meat in it and so seems to be a precursor of the fruit and suet-based mince pie that we now know at Christmas. The beef version makes a great winter treat, but minced venison is a healthier option if available. As ever, the secret is to measure out all your spices and ingredients before commencing to cook. 'Neats' are oxen, and parboiled ox-tongue was Digbie's preference for this dish. 'Orangiadoe' is a bitter orange. These were also known as 'shred pies'.

'Take four pounds of Beef, Veal or Neats-Tongues, and eight pounds of suet; and mince both the meat and Suet very small, before you put them together. Then mingle them well together and mince it very small, and put to it six pounds of Currants washed and picked very clean. Then take the Peel of two Lemons, and half a score of Pippins, and mince them very small. Then take above and Ounce of Nutmeg, and a quarter of an ounce of Mace, some Cloves and Cinnamon, and put them together, and sweeten them with Rose-water and Sugar. And when you are ready to put them into your Paste, take Citron and Orangiadoe, and slice them very thin, and lay them upon the meat. If you please, put dates upon the top of them. And put amongst the meat an Ounce of Caraway seeds. Be sure you have very fine Paste.'

Ingredients: 600 g minced beef; 400 g minced beef suet; 900 g seedless currants; 2 cooking apples; grated rind of one lemon; 1 tsp freshly-grated nutmeg; ¼ tsp ground mace; pinch of ground cloves; ¼ tsp ground cinnamon; 80 g dates, quartered lengthways; 1 lemon, sliced into rings; 1 small, tart orange sliced into rings.

Method: The dish calls for 'fine paste', i.e. shortcrust pastry, in which you can use saffron if you wish. Make or buy enough pastry to line both the base of a 10-inch-diameter pie dish and to provide a lid for the pie. Heat some olive oil in a frying pan and fry the mince for a few minutes until lightly browned. Place in a large bowl and allow to cool. When cooled, add the suet, currants, grated apples, grated lemon and spices. Mix together well and put the mixture in the pastry-lined pie dish. Cover with the dates, and then with the lemon and orange slices, and add the pastry topping. Bind the bottom and top pieces of pastry together by pressing down with a fork. Prick the surface of the pastry lid a few times to allow steam to escape. Place in an oven preheated to 160°C and bake for about 40 minutes or until the pastry is a light golden brown in colour. Serve warm.

A GOOD POTTAGE – BOILED LAMB (OR BEEF) AND OATMEAL POTTAGE

Gervase Markham's *Countrey Contentments, or, The English Hus-wife*, 1615

Ingredients: 900 kg lamb or rolled brisket of beef; 8 spring onions; 60 ml medium oatmeal; 5 ml salt; 60 ml of herbs chosen from chicory, marigold petals, violet leaves; strawberry leaves, parsley, spinach, endive.

Method: Chop the onions finely. Also chop the herbs finely and mix with the onions. Place the mixture in a deep saucepan half-full of water. Bring to the boil, stirring constantly, and then add the meat, making sure that the liquid covers it. Reduce the heat to a simmer and skim off any scum, trying not to remove the herbs. (In Elizabethan times vegetables and herbs were often both designated as herbs). Cover and cook gently for 90 minutes, stirring now and again, and then stir in the oatmeal. Cook for another 30 minutes, stirring now and then. Serve the boiled meat as a separate dish and stir in the salt to the liquid to accompany as pottage.

MUTTON POTTAGE WITH WHOLE HERBS – LAMB (OR VEAL) AND VEGETABLE STEW

Gervase Markham's *Countrey Contentments, or, The English Hus-wife*, 1615

This is similar to the above dish, but flavoured with vegetables and greens. Mutton was a far more popular dish than today, primarily because lambs were much smaller. Fully grown sheep were about a third of the size of today's breeds. Also, especially with sheep, their fleece was valuable and they could have one to two lambs a year. They were worth more alive than dead to many people and eating mutton for the poorer classes was restricted to when a sheep died rather than was killed.

'Take mutton, veal or kid, break the bones but do not cut up the flesh, wash, put in a pot with water. When ready to boil and well-skimmed, add a handful or two of small oatmeal. Take whole lettuce, the best inner leaves, whole spinach, whole endive, whole chicory, whole leaves of colaflorry or the inward parts of white cabbage, with two or three onions. Put all into the pot until done. Season with salt and as much verjuice as will only turn the taste of the pottage; serve up covering meat with whole herbs and adorning the dish with sippets.'

Ingredients: 900 g joint of mutton, beef or lamb; 50 g medium oatmeal; 3 sliced onions; 100 g each of the whole leaves of lettuce, spinach, chicory, endive, white cabbage; 10 cauliflower florets; 5–10 ml salt; 60 ml verjuice or wine vinegar; 12 sippets.

Method: Add the meat to a stockpot with enough water to just cover it. Bring the water to the boil and skim off any excess fat. Mix the oatmeal with 275 ml of cold water and stir into the stockpot. Add all the vegetables and bring back to the boil. Lower the heat to a simmer and keep on cooking for about 90 minutes until the meat is tender. Check the dish regularly and skim off any surface fat. When cooked, pour the liquid into a bowl, take the meat out and break into strips. Add this to the liquid. Toast thick slices of white bread and quarter into triangles. Place these on top of the pottage and serve. Alternatively, lift the meat out onto a serving dish, and lift the vegetables out with a skimmer and place on top of the meat, decorating the edges with the sippets (toast pieces). Keep this warm for a main course, while first eating the remaining pottage as soup.

CHAWETTYS – BEEF, VEAL, HAM OR PORK PIES TWO WAYS

Two Fifteenth Century Cookbooks – Harleian MS. 279 & Harl. MS. 4016, c. 1440

These can also easily be served as a main dish – see *Chauet of Beef* in Mains.

'Take buttes of veal, and mince them small, or pork, and put on a pot, take wine, and caste thereto powder of ginger, pepper, and saffron, and salt, and a little verjuice, and do them in a coffins; then take yolks of eggs and cut dates and roysorys of currants, cloves, maces, and then cover thine coffin and let it bake till it be enough.'

Ingredients for Method 1: 1 lb chopped stewing beef; 5 tbsp currants; 5 figs; ⅛ tsp ginger; ⅛ tsp pepper; ¹⁄₁₆ tsp cloves; ⅛ tsp mace; 5 tsp plum wine; pastry.

Method 1: Fry minced meat until lightly browned, and stew it. When cooked, add to other ingredients, and bake in pies.

Ingredients for Method 2: 18 oz chopped pork or veal; ¾ tsp salt; ⅜ cup currants; ¾ cup red wine; 1 tsp wine vinegar; ¼ tsp cloves; 5 threads saffron; 9 egg yolks; ½ tsp mace; ¾ tsp ginger; ⅜ cup dates; double 9-inch pie crust; ¾ tsp pepper.

Method 2: Cut the meat into ½ inch cubes. Simmer it in a cup and a half of water for about 20 minutes. Make the pie crust, and fill with the meat, chopped dates and currants. Mix spices, wine, vinegar and egg yolks and pour over. Put on a top pastry crust. Bake in a 180°C oven for 50 minutes, then 200°C for 20 minutes, or until the crust looks cooked.

CAWL LLYSIAU'R GAEAF – WINTER VEGETABLE STEW
Traditional Welsh

A simple vegetarian soup, making use of seasonal ingredients. Sweet potatoes would have been used in Tudor times, but today's potatoes work fine. Cream was often a by-product and its calorific value was important in winter.

Ingredients: 4 potatoes, quartered; 2 onions, finely chopped; 1 leek, finely sliced; 2 tsp olive oil; 1 swede, cubed; 4 carrots, chopped; 2 parsnips, chopped; 2 bay leaves; 1.2 l water; salt and black pepper, to taste.

Method: Fry the onion and leeks in olive oil for about 5 minutes, or until softened. Add the carrots, swede and parsnip, allowing them to thoroughly heat through. Add the potatoes and fry for a further 10 minutes, stirring constantly. Add the bay leaves and water. Season with salt and pepper and bring to the boil, then reduce to a simmer. Cover the pot and simmer for 2 hours. Take off the heat and allow the soup to cool a little. Discard the bay leaves. Remove half the vegetables and set aside. Place the remaining stock and vegetables in a food processor and render to a smooth purée. Return this to the pan and stir in the removed vegetables. Reheat the mixture, and when hot transfer to warmed soup bowls and serve. Serve immediately, with cream if desired, and hunks of crusty bread.

GRUEL OF FORCE – PORK GRUEL
Two Fifteenth Century Cookbooks – Harleian MS. 279 & Harl. MS. 4016, c. 1440

Ingredients: 150 g pinhead oatmeal – cut oats not rolled into flakes, as oatmeal is usually sold; 150 g lean cooked pork; 900 ml beef stock; 2 tsp salt.

Method: Sprinkle the oatmeal onto the stock in a pan, stirring while bringing to the boil. Simmer for about 30 minutes until cooked. Grind the pork into a smooth paste and stir it into the gruel with the salt. Cook for another five minutes before serving.

SALMAGUNDI GRAND SALLET – SOLOMON GUNDY'S GRAND SALAD

The Good Hous-Wives Treasurie, 1588

A mix of boiled chicken, eggs, fish, greens, beans, wild flowers, fruit, nuts, potatoes and herbs. English pirates and privateers would throw anything they could get into a huge cauldron, with green turtle being especially popular. While this is thought of as a seventeenth and eighteenth century dish, it existed long before. Hannah Glasse described a *salmagundi* in 1747 consisting of romaine lettuce, covered with sliced roast chicken, diced lemon, parsley, cooked egg yolks, anchovies and vinaigrette, garnished with grapes or beans and nasturtium leaves. If you were served this now, you would think it a fresh and modern idea. The name derives from the French *salmigondis*, a disparate assembly of things, ideas or people that forms an incoherent whole. This dish was somehow transmuted into the nursery rhyme: 'Solomon Grundy, / Born on a Monday, / Christened on Tuesday, / Married on Wednesday, / Took ill on Thursday, / Grew worse on Friday, / Died on Saturday, / Buried on Sunday. / That was the end, / Of Solomon Grundy.' Basically, you can throw whatever you wish into this dish. It is difficult to give a Tudor version, as every meal could have been different according to the availability of ingredients. A simplified modern version to serve two is as follows:

Ingredients: 2 cups of diced, cooked chicken; ¾ cup cooked ham, diced; 3 hard-boiled eggs, diced; 1 head romaine lettuce; shredded; 2 stalks celery, diced; 2 medium tomatoes, diced (although tomatoes would not have been available, they help 'make' the dish); vinaigrette; 2 tablespoons anchovies, minced (optional).

Method: Place the lettuce on two plates and arrange the remaining ingredients in strips or small mounds on the lettuce. Serve with your favourite vinaigrette

SAVOURY POTTAGE – SIR KENELM DIGBY'S BEEF AND BARLEY STEW

The Closet of the Eminently Learned Sir Kenelme Digbie Kt Opened, 1669

A traditional thick barley stew with beef, chicken, herbs and spinach. Violet leaves were used commonly in stews as they exude a thickening agent. You can also use pheasant or guinea fowl in this recipe.

'Make it of beef, mutton and veal; at last adding a Capon, or Pigeons. Put in at first a quartered Onion or two, some Oat-meal, or French barley, some bottom of a Venison-pasty-crust, twenty whole grains of Pepper; four or five Cloves at last, and a little bundle of sweet-herbs, store of Marigold-flowers. You may put in Parsley or other herbs.'

Ingredients: 200 g cubed beef or cubed mutton; 4 chicken drumsticks; 2

medium onions, roughly chopped; 200 g pearl barley; 500 ml beef stock (you can use a stock cube); ½ tsp freshly-ground pepper; ¼ tsp ground cinnamon; 150 g fresh spinach washed and shredded; large bunch of parsley, finely chopped; bunch of chives, finely chopped; 20 g violet leaves, chopped (if available – if not, use a thickening agent); 50 g breadcrumbs.

Method: Fry the beef cubes to brown on each side, then set aside. In the same pan (do not wash it), brown the chicken pieces and then set these aside. Again using the same pan, add the onions and fry until soft. Add the onions to the bottom of a large stock pot and pour in about 500 ml of beef stock. Add the spices and stir, and then add the beef, chicken and pearl barley. Cook on a low heat either on top of, or in, the oven for at least 80 minutes, then take out the chicken pieces and add the breadcrumbs. Remove the meat from the chicken bones, shred and return to the pot. Add the 'sweet herbs', which will depend on the season. Remember that the term 'herb' referred to any green vegetable. Continue to cook for a further five minutes then serve.

TARTE OF BEANS – COTTAGE CHEESE AND BEAN PIE
The Proper Newe Booke of Cookerye, c. 1557

'A Tarte of Beans. Take beanes and boyle them tender in fayre water, then take theym oute and breake them in a morter and strayne them with the yolckes of foure egges, curde made of mylke, then ceason it up with suger and halfe a dysche of butter and a lytle synamon and bake it.' … 'To make short paest for tarte. Take fyne floure and a curscy of fayre water and a dysche of swete butter and a lyttel saffron, and the yolkes of two egges and make it thynne and as tender as ye maye.'

Ingredients for the filling: 250 g dried broad beans; 4 egg yolks; 120 g cottage cheese (curds); 4 tbsp sugar; 90 g butter; 4 tsp ground cinnamon.

Ingredients for the pastry: 225 g plain flour; 90 g softened butter; 2 egg yolks; 6 saffron threads ground into 1 tbsp warm water in a pestle and mortar; 1 cup flour; 5–6 tbsp very soft butter; 2 egg yolks.

Method for filling: Put beans in 2½ cups of water, bring to boil and turn off heat. Allow to rest, covered, for 90 minutes. Add another cup of water and boil for about 50 minutes, until soft. Drain the beans and blend in food processor, then cool the bean paste. When cool, mix in the egg yolks (if you do this when warm, the yolks will cook). Now add the cottage cheese, without draining it. Add sugar, butter (soft or in small bits) and cinnamon. Mash together into a thick liquid.

Method for pie crust: To make the crust, mix the saffron water into flour. Add egg yolks and mix well. Add 4 tbsp butter and mix well. Add enough of remaining butter to make a smooth paste. Roll smooth and place in a 9-inch pie plate, crimping the edge. Pour filling into raw crust and bake at 180°C for about 50 minutes.

DEVISED MEAT AFTER THE ROMANE MANNER – RIGATONI WITH CHEESE SAUCE

Epulario, or The Italian Banquet, 1598 translation of 1516 edition

Many continental cookbooks were translated into English, or were available in the widely understood Latin or French. This meal serves 6–8, and reminds us that the Tudors knew more about foreign cuisine than did this author as a young man.

'Take white flour, and make paste of it somewhat thicker than a pancake, and roule it about a staffe, then take out the staffe, then cut the past in peeces of the length of thy little finger, whereby they will be hollow like a pudding and round or close, them seeth them in fat broth or in water as time serveth, but the broth or water must boile when you put them in. And if you seethem them in water put a little sweet Butter and salt it, and when they are sod, dish them with Cheese, Butter, and spices.'

SAVOURY TOASTED CHEESE

The Closet of the Eminently Learned Sir Kenelme Digbie Kt Opened, 1669

Toasted bread smothered in a cheese and butter sauce. There is also a similar dish, *Caws Pobi*, in the chapter on snacks.

'Cut pieces of quick, fat, rich, well tasted cheese, (as the best of Brye, Cheshire, or sharp thick Cream-Cheese) into a dish of thick beaten melted Butter, that hath served for Sparages or the like, or pease, or other boiled Sallet, or ragout of meat, or gravy of Mutton: and, if you will, Chop some of the Asparages among it, or slices of Gambon of Bacon, or fresh-collops, or Onions, or Sibboulets, or Anchovies, and set all this to melt upon a Chafing-dish of Coals, and stir all well together, to Incorporate them; and when all is of an equal consistence, strew some gross White-Pepper on it, and eat it with tosts or crusts of White-bread. You may scorch it at the top with a hot Fire-Shovel.'

Ingredients: 230 g butter; 230 g cream cheese; 60 g brie or any other strong soft cheese; ¼ tsp white pepper. Vegetables or bacon as desired.

Method: Melt the butter in a pan. Cut the cheese into small pieces and place in the butter. Use a whisk for simplicity to blend the two together. When the sauce takes on a creamy consistency, it is ready. Pour over bacon, or cooked vegetables such as asparagus, onions or broccoli, or over toast.

BLAWMANGER – WHITE CHICKEN BROTH
Utilis Coquinario part III of *Curye on Inglysch*, Fourteenth century
'For blankmanger, that made he with the beste' – *The Prologue to the Canterbury Tales*, Geoffrey Chaucer (1343–1400). Chaucer's cook was an expert at making *blankmanger*, 'white food', which was extremely popular from medieval through to Stuart times. *Blankmanger* was a bland, white pottage based on almond milk. Except for a few fish-day versions, it usually contained ground poultry, thickened with rice flour. The usual English 'flesh-day' version was ground capon or chicken with rice and almond milk. In some recipes the poultry is in chunks, rather than ground up. Today's *blancmange* is a type of rice-pudding dessert, obviously bearing little resemblance to the medieval forerunner.

'Blawmanger. Tak the two del of rys, the thridde pert of almoundes; wash clene the rys in leuk water and turne and seth hem til thay breke and lat it kele, and tak the melk and do it to the rys and boyle hem togedere. and do therto whit gres and braun of hennes grounde smale, and stere it wel, and salte it and dresch it in disches. and frye almaundes in fresch gres til they be browne, and set hem in the dissches, and strawe theron sugre and serue it forth.'

Ingredients: 1 cup rice; 3 cups almond milk; 1 cup ground cooked chicken; dash salt; ¼ cup fried or slivered almonds; sugar to garnish.

Method: Bring to a boil the rice, milk and salt. Reduce heat, stir in the chicken and cover. Cook gently, stirring occasionally, until the liquid is absorbed and rice is fluffy. Garnish with almonds and a sprinkling of sugar.

CAWL – WELSH STEW
Traditional Welsh recipe
A classic soup of leeks, onions, carrots, parsnips and neck of lamb in stock, in this instance thickened with rice. It was a cheap and nourishing winter meal served as a starter and often with potato. If you put chopped potatoes in first, they can serve as a useful thickener. *Cawl* is often served in Welsh pubs in the interval when watching Wales play rugby, and in the old days everyone's 'mam' could cook a good *cawl*. You can add swede, turnip or anything to hand.

Ingredients: 4 medium leeks, chopped; 2 onions, chopped; 3 carrots, peeled and cubed; 2 parsnips, peeled and cubed; 675 g neck of lamb, trimmed of fat; 80 g rice (or thickener); bunch of parsley, finely chopped; salt; freshly-ground black pepper.

Method: Add all the ingredients to a large pan, cover with plenty of water, bring to a boil then season and skim any fat from the surface. Cover and simmer gently for 2 hours. Remove the meat bones, take the meat off and add back to the cawl. Adjust the seasoning and serve sprinkled with parsley. Serve with hunks of buttered wholemeal bread as a main course.

CAWL CENNIN – LEEK SOUP

Derived from the above and a favourite dish across Wales. If you use vegetable stock, it can be vegetarian.

Ingredients: 575 g finely-chopped leeks; 1 small onion, roughly chopped; 115 g roughly-chopped leeks; 60 g butter; 2 stalks of celery, finely cubed; 2.4 l mutton or lamb stock; 30 g finely-chopped parsley; 150 ml double cream; salt and pepper to taste.

Method: Finely chop the largest portion of leeks and chop the remainder more coarsely. Melt butter in a saucepan and when liquid turn down the heat. Add the finely-chopped leek, onion and celery. Toss the vegetables in the butter then cover with a lid and leave to cook until the leeks have softened. Once they are truly soft, before they turn brown, add the stock and raise the heat to bring the stock to the boil. Lower to a simmer and allow to cook for an hour. Leave the *cawl* to cool a little, then pour into a liquidizer and purée. Transfer back to a saucepan and add the remaining leeks and the parsley. Bring back to the boil then turn the heat down. Allow to simmer for twenty minutes, then remove from the heat, allow the *cawl* to cool a little and stir in the cream. Ladle into bowls, sprinkle some parsley on top and serve immediately.

RAPES IN POTAGE – BALDRICK'S TURNIP BROTH

The Master-Cook of Richard II, *The Forme of Cury*, *c*. 1390

This dish is titled in honour of Blackadder's servant Baldrick. Pre-cooking the turnips reduces the natural strength of the turnip flavour and makes about four cups of soup.

'Rapes in Potage. V. Take rapus [turnips] and make hem [them] clene and waissh hem clene. quare [quarter] hem. parboile hem. take hem up. cast hem in a gode broth and seeþ [simmer] hem. mynce Oynouns and cast þerto Safroun and salt and messe it forth with powdour douce. the wise make of Pasturnakes [parsnips] and skyrwates [skirrets].'

Ingredients: 4–5 turnips, cut into half-inch cubes; ½ medium onion, chopped; 2 cups chicken or vegetable broth; ¼ tsp salt; ½ tsp powder douce; pinch of saffron.

Method: Place turnips into a pot with enough water to cover them. Bring to a boil, and allow to simmer for about 10 minutes, until they start to soften. Drain and add remaining ingredients. Return to boil, reduce heat, and continue to cook until cooked. Serve hot.

7

Main Courses

For many years it was believed that the Tudor upper classes ate few vegetables, but unless they were imported, such items would not appear upon household accounts, as they were grown by servants. *Palladius on Husbondrie* was translated around 1420 in Colchester Castle and lists vegetables and fruit which are hardly or never known in recipes of the period. However, their names appear in English form, so they must have been known in the country. Included are cucumber, figs, asparagus, garlic, orange trees, dates, grapes, olives, peaches, pomegranates, pistachios (*pistaces*, grown in Turkey and Greece), gourds and coriander. Equally, it was thought that there was a preponderance of potages, or stews in the diet, because these dishes featured prominently in cookery books and surviving recipes. However, if meat was simply roasted or boiled, there would not have been any need to pass on recipes. Thus we read of 'gilded capon' dishes, but not of roast chicken or boiled beef. There was a rigid order for the serving of dishes during feasts, with diners taking a piece from each dish. Remainders were reused in cooking or given to servants and the poor. The Brandenburg lawyer Paul Hentzner, writing *Of the Manners of the English* in 1598, in his *Itinerarium Germaniae, Galliae, Angliae, Italiae, cum Indice Locorum, Rerum atque Verborum* (published 1612) was one of the few to tell us of the eating of roast meat and sugar in these times:

> The English are serious, like the Germans; lovers of show, liking to be followed wherever they go by whole troops of servants, who wear their masters' arms in silver, fastened to their left arms, a ridicule they deservedly lay under. They excel in dancing and music, for they are active and lively, though of a thicker make than the French; they cut their hair close on the middle of the head, letting it grow on either fide they are good sailors, and better pirates, cunning,

treacherous, and thievish; above three hundred are said to be hanged annually at London; beheading with them is less infamous than hanging; they give the wall as the place of honour; hawking is the general sport of the gentry; they are more polite in eating than the French, devouring less bread, but more meat, which they roast in perfection; they put a great deal of sugar in their drink; their beds are covered with tapestry, even those of farmers; they are often molested with the scurvy, said to have first crept into England with the Norman conquest; their houses are commonly of two storeys, except in London, where they are of three and four, though but seldom of four; they are built of wood, those of the richer sort with bricks; their roofs are low, and, where the owner has money, covered with lead.

They are powerful in the field, successful against their enemies, impatient of any thing like slavery; vastly fond of great noises that fill the ear, such as the firing of cannon, drums, and the ringing of bells, so that it is common for a number of them, that have got a glass in their heads, to go up into some belfry, and ring the bells for hours together for the sake of exercise. If they see a foreigner very well made, or particularly handsome, they will say, 'tis a pity he is not an Englishman.

ORDER OF MEATES FOR FLESH DAYES
Thomas Dawson's *A Booke of Cokerie*, 1620

'Heere followeth the order of Meates, how they must bee served at the Table. Services for Flesh dayes at Dinner.

The first Course.
Pottage or stewed broath, boyled meate or stewed meats, Chickins and Bacon, powdered Beefe, Pyes, Pigge Roasted, Beefe roasted Veale, Custard.

The second course.
Roasted Lambe, rosted Capons, roasted Conyes [rabbits], Chickens, Peahens, Baked Venison, Salt.

The first course at Supper.
A sallet, Pigges Petitoes [trotters], Powdered Beefe sliced, a Shoulder of Mutton, or a breast Veale, Lambe, Custard.

The second course.
Capons roasted, Conyes roasted, Chickins roasted, Pigions roasted, Larkes rosted, a Pye of Pigions or Chickins, Baked Venison, Tart.'

ORDER OF SERVICE FOR FISH DAYES
Thomas Dawson's *A Booke of Cokerie*, 1620

Not only were the fish served in specific order, but most had particular sauces allocated to them.

The first course.

'Butter, a Sallet with hard Egges, red Herring greene broiled, white Herring, Ling, Haberdine [dried, salted cod], sauce Mustard, salt Salmon minced, sauce Mustard and Verjuyce and a little Suger, powdered Conger, Shad, Mackrell, sauce Vinegar, Whiting, sauce with the Liver and Mustard, Playce, sauce Sorrrell, Wine and Salt, Mustard, or Verjuce, Thornebacke [thornback ray], sauce Liver and Mustard, Pepper and Salt strewed upon, after it is brused, fresh Cod, sauce Greene sauce, Dace, Mullet, Eeles upon soppes, Roche upon soppes, Perch, Pike in pike sauce, Trowte upon soppes, Tench in Gelly, or Gorefish [needlefish?], Custard.

The second course.

Flounders or flookes, pike sauce, fresh Salmon, fresh Conger, Brette, Turbut, Breame upon soppes, Carpe upon soppes, Soles or any other fish fryed, roasted Eele sauce the dripping, rosted Lamperns*, rosted Porpos [porpoise], fresh Sturgion, sauce Galentine, Crevis [crayfish], Crab, Shrimps, sauce Vinegar. Baked Lamprey, Tart, figges, Apples, Almonds blaunched, Cheese, Raysins, Peares.' [*This is a lamprey, but as lampreys are mentioned later, it is possibly a river lamprey rather than a saltwater lamprey, or vice versa].

HODGEPODGE – MUTTON AND VEGGIE STEW

A Booke of Cookrye Very Necessary for all such as delight therin, 1591

A hodgepodge, or hotchpotch, has come to mean a random selection of things. People of less opulent means, in an attempt to emulate the wealthy, also wished to season their foods, but were far more likely to use local herbs than imported spices. Balinese long peppers were the first peppers imported into Europe and were used in many Tudor dishes.

'Hodge-Podge (Cold Meat Cookery) – To make a Hodgepodge. Boyle a neck of Mutton or a fat rump of Beef, and when it is well boyled, take the best of the broth and put it into a pipkin and put a good many onyons to it, two handfull of marigold flowers, and a handfull of percely fine picked and groce shredde and not too small, and so boyle them in the broth and thicke it with strained bread, putting therin groce beaten pepper, and a spoonfull of Vinagre, and let it boyle somwhat thick and so lay it upon your meat.'

Ingredients: To bring the redaction bang up-to-date, I use an 1865 version of the recipe from *Mrs. Beeton's Dictionary of Every-day Cookery*: 'About 1 lb of underdone cold mutton, 2 lettuces, 1 pint of green peas, 5 or 6 green onions, 2 oz of butter, pepper and salt to taste, 4 teacupfuls of water.

Method: Mince the mutton and cut up the lettuces and onions in slices. Put these in a stewpan, with all the ingredients except the peas and let these simmer very gently for 1 hour, keeping them well stirred. Boil the peas separately, mix these with the mutton, and serve very hot. Time – ¾ hour. Sufficient for 3 or 4 persons. Seasonable from the end of May to August.

HERB-STUFFED TROUT (OR MACKEREL)

Gervase Markham's *Countrey Contentments, or, The English Hus-wife*, 1615

Fish days were part of the medieval church calendar, so there are many fish recipes recorded. Fishing rights were not available to the poor, although fish could be purchased at markets. Wealthier families ate freshwater fish from their own ponds or rivers. Sugar and mace would make this a very expensive dish, so a middle-class household would be unlikely to use these in a meal, and they are omitted from the following recipe. Serve with *frumenty* [see above and side dishes] and seasonal vegetables.

'Take a large trout, fair trimmed, and wash it and put in a deep pewter dish, then take half a pint of white wine, with a lump of butter and a little mace, parsley, savoury and thyme and put them into the trout's belly (minced fine) and so let it stew a quarter of an hour, then mince the yolk of a hard egg and strew it on the trout and laying herbs about it, and scraping on sugar, serve it up.'

Ingredients: 1 trout or mackerel per person; 25 g butter; 1 sprig each of parsley and thyme; 300 ml white wine or fish stock; 2 hard boiled eggs for decoration.

Method: Place parsley and thyme herb butter inside the fish and tie it closed. Pour the stock or wine into a pan, large enough to simmer the fish. Simmer for about 15 minutes or until the fish is done. Use two fish slices, or spatula, to carefully lift the fish whole from the pan. Cut off the string and decorate with sliced or crumbled eggs.

CAPON BAKED WITH EGG YOLKS – FOWL PIE

John Partridge's *The Treasurie of Commodious Conceits & Hidden Secrets*, 1573

Capon meat is more moist, tender and flavoured than that of a cockerel or a hen, a capon being a large, castrated cockerel, which was often force fed. Modern versions of medieval cookery, in the absence of capons, often substitute goose, but a large chicken or small turkey could be used. The bird was placed into a fireproof container. In the recipe, eight boiled egg yolks, each pricked with five cloves, were added, along with ginger and salt and then baked for three hours over an open fire. A serving sauce was made from two egg yolks beaten into a cupful of verjuice, with a good quantity of sugar. As the cooking time was three hours, the 'coffyn', or pastry pie case, would be charred and inedible, being used simply to contain the ingredients. A coffyn was basically a container which could contain anything being cooked, and pastry coffyns, the forerunners of our pies, usually held savoury rather than sweet fillings. The pastry from which coffyns were constructed was fairly inedible in pre-Tudor times, simply made from a flour and water paste. It was kneaded into stiff dough, being sometimes several inches thick to make it strong enough to hold its contents. It was seldom actually consumed by the nobility, but passed 'below the salt' to those of lesser rank, or handed out to the poor. Although the pastry was tough and blackened, it would have absorbed some of the gravy and juices from the contents. However, coffyns or pastries became better and pies, particularly meat pies, began to make up a large part of the diet. An Elizabethan saying was 'If it's good, 'tis better in a Coffyn.'

Coffyns were often square, not round, in particular the Twelfth Night coffyn or pie. This festive dish was always rectangular to represent the manger in which Christ slept. Even when consumption shifted from the Twelfth Night pie to the 'Christmas Pie' during Tudor and Elizabethan times, it still retained its rectangular shape. Not until the Protectorate of Oliver Cromwell did the Christmas pie become round. The Puritans forbade dancing and many celebrations of festivities, such as May Day and Christmas. A rectangular Christmas pie on the table was an offence, so cooks began making their pies round and they have stayed so ever since. In the early periods, single crust pies, i.e pies with no top crust, were called 'traps', but by Elizabethan times they had become known as tarts.

'When the Capon is made redi, trusse him in the ye Coffyn: then take viii yolks of egges sodden hard, and pricke into every of them v Cloves, and put the yolks into the Coffyn with the Capon: then take a quantitie of gynger and salt, and cast it on the Capon, and let it bake iii Houres. Then take ii raw yolkes of egges beaten into a Gobblet of Verjuice, with a good quantitie of sugre sodden togither, put it into ye Coffyn and to serve it.'

Ingredients: Goose, chicken or turkey; 10 egg yolks; 40 cloves; ginger; salt; cup of verjuice; sugar; pie crust pastry (optional).

Method: If you are making a pie, as in the recipe, you will need to first cook and then chop up the bird. Place the fowl into a large casserole. Eight boiled egg yolks, each pricked with five cloves, are added, along with ginger and salt and the whole baked for three hours, covered. A serving sauce is made from two egg yolks beaten into a cupful of verjuice, with a good quantity of sugar.

A PECOKE – PEACOCK WITH GINGER SAUCE
Gentyll Manly Cokere, MS Pepys 1047, c. 1490

The peacock was used in medieval feasts for its symbolic reputation and beauty, but its meat was considered tough and stringy. Peacocks are still available today from peacock farms, but turkeys, large ducks or geese are easier to cook and provide better meat. Turkeys began replacing peacock as a 'rich man's bird' in Elizabethan times. Leave out the grapefruit and replace with semi-sweetened lemons if you want a true Tudor meal, as grapefruit only dates from a Barbadian hybrid of the eighteenth century.

'A peacock. Cut him in (the) neck and scald him. Cut off the feet and head. Cast him on a spit. Bake him well. The sauce is ginger.'

Ingredients: 1 whole peacock, or preferably a turkey, large duck or goose; olive oil for basting; 1 tsp cornflour; 1 tbsp olive oil; 1 tsp grated fresh ginger; 1 tsp clear honey; juice of 2 oranges; 1 orange peeled and cut into segments; 1 grapefruit, peeled and cut into segments.

Method: Place your bird in a large roasting pan. Put in an oven preheated to 220°C. Roast for 20 minutes for each pound and ensure that internal temperature reaches 90°C. When the bird is cooked, remove and allow to rest. To make the ginger sauce, add the orange juice, ginger and honey to the roasting pan and gently bring to the boil. Mix the cornflour with 1 tbsp cold water and stir into the sauce. Keep stirring on a gentle heat until thickened and syrupy, like a sweet and sour sauce, then season to taste. Return the bird to the pan, add the orange and grapefruit segments and heat through gently. Cut the bird into serving portions and pour the ginger sauce over. Scatter 1 tbsp freshly-cut chives or chopped parsley over the dish.

BOILED MEATS ORDINARY – LAMB AND GREENS STEW

Gervase Markham's *Countrey Contentments, or, The English Hus-wife*, 1615

'You shall take a racke of mutton cut into peeces, or a leg of mutton cut in peeces: for this meat and these joints, are the best, Although any other joint, or any fresh beefe will likewise make good pottage: and having washt your meat well, put it into a cleane pot with faire water, and set it on the fire: then take violet leaves, endive, succory [chicory], strawberie leaves, spinage, langdebeefe [bristly oxtongue, a type of daisy], marygold flowers, Scallions, and a little persly, and chop them very small together, then take halfe so much oatmeale well beaten as there is herbes, and mix it with the herbes, and chop all very wel together: then when the pot is ready to boile, skumme it very wel and then put in your herbes: And so let it boil with a quicke fire, stirring the meat oft in the pot, till the meat be boild enough, and that the hearbes and water mixt together without any separation, which will be after the consumption of more then a third part: then season them with salt, and serve them up with the meat either with sippets or without.'

Ingredients: 1 kg boned lamb (or mutton); 1.2 l water; 600 g oatmeal; ½ tbsp salt; 550 g mixed greens (spring onions, chicory, endives, parsley, spinach, mustard greens, watercress etc.)

Method: Cut the lamb into bite-sized cubes and add to a stockpot along with the water and salt. Bring to the boil and add the oatmeal and the finely-chopped greens. Simmer for about an hour and serve. If you wish, you can make a smooth paste out of the vegetables and oats by grinding them together in a pestle and mortar before adding to the boiling water.

GOOD AND PERFECTLY OPTIMAL ROAST PORK IN SWEET AND SOUR SAUCE

Anonymous, Venetian *Libro di cucina/ Libro per cuoco*, 14th–15th century

'If you want to make a roast in sweet/sour sauce. Take a loin of pork and roast it. Take cooked and raw eggs and grind them together, add good white wine and vinegar and put it to boil in a pan. Take slices of the roast and put it to boil in the sauce and add chopped dates and pine nuts and well washed Saracen grapes [a specific dried raisin variety] and spices, and when it is cooked lift it from the fire and it will be good.'

TO BAKE A GAMMON OF BACON

A.W., *A Book of Cookrey*, 1584

A gammon is the cut of bacon from the back end near the leg. The original recipe called for boiling a second time, to reduce the amount of salt as the meat had probably been salted for storage.

'To bake a gammon of Bacon. Take your Bacon and boyle it, and stuffe it with Parcely and Sage, and yolks of hard Egges, and when it is boyled, stuffe it and let it boyle againe, season it with Pepper, cloves and mace, whole cloves stick fast in, so then lay it in your paste with salt butter.'

Ingredients: 2 lb unsliced bacon; ½ cup chopped fresh parsley; ¼ cup chopped fresh sage; 6 egg yolks, hard boiled; ½ tsp pepper; ¼ tsp cloves; ⅛ tsp mace.

Method: Remove any skin from the bacon and place the bacon in a stockpot with enough water to cover it. Put on a lid, bring to the boil and cook for 30 minutes. Place the parsley, sage, egg yolks and spices in a bowl and mix well. Remove bacon from the pot, cut open and stuff with mixture. Wrap in pastry and bake for about an hour at 180°C until done.

ALLOES OF BEEF – BEEF OLIVES

Gentyll Manly Cokere MS Pepys 1047, c. 1500

Beef rolls, stuffed with onions and herbs and roasted on skewers. Alloes, or aloes, were meant to resemble larks or small birds and are sometimes translated as 'veal birds'.

'To make Alloes of beef: Take lean beef and cut him in thin pieces and lay it on a board. Then take suet of mutton or of beef and herbs and onions hacked small together. Then strew thy slices of beef with powder of pepper and a little salt and strew on your suet and the herbs. And roll them up there in, put them on a spit [or skewer] and roast them and serve them up hot.'

Ingredients: 6 large, thin frying steaks; 75 g suet; 1 tsp chopped sage; 1 tsp chopped thyme; 1 large chopped onion; salt and pepper.

Method: Lightly beat the steaks and sprinkle with salt and pepper. Mix the onion, suet and herbs and spread over the steaks. Roll up the steaks with the mixture on the inside and tie securely with string. Thread each roll to a skewer supported across a baking tin and cook at 170°C for about 40 minutes. Cut off the string and serve.

CAPON LARDED WITH LEMONS, ON THE FRENCH FASHION

John Murrel's *A New Booke of Cookerie*, 1615

'To boyle a Capon Larded with Lemons, on the French fashion. Scald your Capon, and take a little dusty Oatmeale to make it boile white. Then take two or three ladlefuls of Mutton broth, a Fagot of sweet Hearbes [bouquet garni], two or three Dates, cut in long pieces, a few parboyld Currins [currants], a little whole Pepper, a piece of whole Mace, and one Nutmeg. Thicken it with Almonds. Season it with Uergis [Verjuice], Sugar, and a little sweet Butter. Then take vp your Capon, and larde it very thicke with a preserued Lemmon. Then lay your Capon in a deepe Meat-dish for boyld meates, and poure the broth vpon it. Garnish your Dish with Suckets [sweetmeats] and preserued Barberries.'

FANTASTIC CRAYFISH OR LOBSTER TART

Anonymous, Venetian *Libro di cucina/ Libro per cuoco*, 14th–15th century

'Take boiled crayfish and pull the flesh from the tails, and take a quantity of good herbs, and chop all well together and put with them almond milk, fine spices and currants. And of this batter make a thin tart between two crusts, and above the filling should be potent with sweet spices and currants, and the crust should be good and yellow.'

STEW OF FLESH – BEEF AND CHICKEN STEW

Gentyll manly Cokere MS Pepys 1047, c. 1500

This is an unappetising description of a rich man's meal. Of course with modern sensibilities we now refer to meat rather than flesh; pork rather than pig; beef rather than cow; veal rather than calf; and mutton rather than sheep. Curiously, of all our popular red meats, only lamb is referred to as lamb. See the side dish *cressee* for information upon *saunders*, a red food colouring.

'To make a stew of flesh. If your pot is 4 gallons, put in a quart of wine. Take good beef of the fore loin or of the hind loin and mince it, and add good capons to all of this. Add pepper, good cinnamon powder, ginger, currants, cloves, mace, saffron, and sandalwood. Add onions, parsley, sage, rosemary, thyme, hyssop, savory, clarified honey, and a large amount of bruised almonds; bring to a boil. But your fire needs to be of coals, and not a large fire but a small fire good for boiling. Boil thoroughly while it stews. Be sure that the pot is well covered and that no heat escapes in any way. And in this way you can stew all sorts of meat.'

Ingredients: Red wine; stewing beef, chopped; chicken in pieces; pepper; cinnamon; ginger; currants; cloves; mace; saffron; sandalwood; onions; parsley; sage; rosemary; thyme; hyssop; savory; clarified honey; almonds, slightly crushed or bruised. One can experiment with the quantities, depending upon the amount of meat used, but an updated version is given in the next recipe.

Method: Pour the wine into a stockpot and add the chopped beef and chicken pieces. Add the spices, currants and the colouring agents (saffron for yellow and sandalwood for red). Add the chopped onions and fresh herbs, honey, and almonds. If not using clarified honey, you will need to remove any honey scum that will surface during cooking. Bring to a boil and then reduce the heat to a gentle simmer until the stew is thoroughly cooked, keeping the pot covered with a tight-fitting lid.

SERGEANT OF THE KING'S MEAT STEW

Gentyll manly Cokere MS Pepys 1047, c. 1500

The above recipe has been modified by the cooks who specialise in Tudor feasts in Hampton Court, and is as follows:

Ingredients: 1.35 kg lean beef steak; 1.15 litres of red wine; 1 lb sliced English onions; 2 tbsp honey; 100 g raisins; 50 g bruised ground almonds; pinch of saffron; herbs 2½ ml each of chopped rosemary, sage, thyme and hyssop; spices 1½ ml each of ground cloves, ginger, mace and pepper; 225 g white bread, cut into one inch cubes.

Method: Place all ingredients in a large pan except the bread. Simmer for 2.5–3 hours, stirring only occasionally. Arrange the bread on the bottom of deep individual dishes and pour the stew on top.

MOCK STURGEON

Curye on Inglysch, 14th century

Under British law whales and sturgeon are royal fish, the property of the monarch. This particular royal prerogative dates from the time of Edward

II, and in 2004 a Llanelli fisherman was investigated for landing a 10-foot sturgeon in Swansea Bay and selling it in Plymouth for £650. Sturgeon are very rare in European waters and cooks avoided controversy by making their own 'sturgeon' as follows.

'To Make Sturgyn. Take veal shanks and calf's feet and simmer them in honey. When you have simmered them until the meat falls apart, take out the bones. If there are large pieces of flesh, chop them smaller and put it (the flesh removed from the broth) in a clean piece of canvas and press it well. Then take it and slice into thin slices. Take onions, vinegar and parsley and lay thereon. Serve.'

PYE OF ALOWES – LAMB PIE
Proper Newe Booke of Cookerye, c. 1557

Strips of cooked lamb or mutton are stuffed with egg yolks and herbs in a thick, red wine sauce. The word 'aloe' is the Old French for lark. Originally they were rolls of meat with various stuffings that were prepared by roasting on a spit. As they cooked they became similar in appearance to small birds without heads, feet and wings, hence the name.

'To make a pye of alowes. Take a legge of mutton and cutte it in thyn flyces, and for ftuffing of the fame take perfely, tyme and fauerye, and chop them fmal, then temper among them thre or, iiii. yolckes of harde egges chops fmal, and fmall reyfons, dates cutte with mace, and a lyttle falte, then laye all thefe in the ftekes, and then role them together. This done make youre pye, and laye all thefe therein, then ceafon theym wyth a lyttle fuger and fynamon, fafron and falte, then ca.st vpon theym the yolckes of three or foure harde egges, and cut dates, wyth fmall rayfynges, to clofe youre pye, and bake hym. Then for a fyrope for it, take roofted breade, and a lyttle claret wyne, and ftrayne them thyn togeather, and put thereto a lytle fuger, fynamon, and gynger, and putte it into youre pye, and then ferue it forthe.'

Ingredients: Leftover roast leg of lamb or leg of mutton; 4 tbsp parsley, finely chopped; 2 tsp fresh thyme, minced; 2 tsp savory, minced; 4 hard-boiled egg yolks, chopped; 2 tbsp raisins; 6 dates, pitted and finely chopped; ¼ tsp ground mace; salt, to taste; 300 ml clarrey – claret wine mulled with spices and honey, see the drinks chapter; enough pie crust dough for a 9-inch diameter double-crust pie; 4 tbsp toasted bread, crumbed in a food processor; 2 tbsp brown sugar; ground cinnamon and ground ginger, to taste.

Method: Slice the lamb into long, thin slices. Mix together the thyme, savory, parsley, egg yolks, raisins, dates, mace and salt in a bowl until you have a paste-like mixture. Spread about 1 tsp of this mixture over each strip of lamb. Take just over half your pastry and roll out until large enough to cover the base and sides of your pie dish. Take the covered lamb slices and roll them up tightly lengthways so that the stuffing is enclosed in the meat. Arrange these in the pastry shell, filling the pie completely. Now take the remaining pastry and roll out large enough to form a lid. Use this to cover the pie then crimp the edges securely together. Trim off any excess. Take a sharp knife and cut a cross in the centre of the pie about 2 inches wide. Using the point of the knife, carefully peel back the cut points of pastry to leave a hole and a decorative pattern around it, as you will add the gravy through here. Place the pie on a baking dish and transfer to an oven preheated to 180°C. Bake for about 35 minutes or until the pastry is golden brown and cooked through. While baking, prepare the sauce. Pour the clarrey into a pan and bring to a simmer. Whisk in the breadcrumbs and continue simmering until the sauce has thickened, which will take around 20 minutes. Press this mixture through a fine-meshed sieve, then stir in the sugar until dissolved and season to taste with cinnamon and ginger. Place back on the heat to keep warm. As soon as you remove the pie from the oven pour the clarrey syrup into it. Serve any remaining syrup to accompany the pie.

TARTE OWTE OF LENT – TUDOR CREAM CHEESE PIE
Gentyll Manly Cokere, MS Pepys 1047, c. 1490

The name derives from the fact that it contains all the things the Tudors were not allowed to eat during Lent – cheese, cream and eggs – cooked in a light pastry case.

'Take neshe [soft] chese and pare hit and grynd hit yn A morter and breke egges and do ther to and then put yn buttur and creme and mell all well to gethur put not to moche butter ther yn if the chese be fatte make A coffyn of dowe and close hit a bove with dowe and collor hit a bove with the yolkes of eggs and bake hit well and serue hit furth.'

Ingredients: 100 g Cheshire or Caerphilly cheese; 150 ml cream; medium sized egg; 30 g butter; salt and pepper; any high butter pastry, such as shortcrust; egg yolks for glazing.

Method: Chop the cheese and then pound in a mortar. Add cream, egg and butter and mix together to make a thick cream about the consistency of cottage cheese. Add more cream if too dry, more cheese if too wet.Season with salt and pepper to taste. Make a pastry tart case, about 10 inches in diameter, and a thin pastry lid. (Use a tart tin if easier). Fill with the cheese, cream, egg and butter mixture. Put on the pastry lid, seal and glaze with egg yolks. Bake at 220°C for 40 minutes or until golden. Allow to cool a little and serve.

BAKED CONIES, RABETS, OR HARES

A Booke of Cookrye Very Necessary for all such as delight therin, 1591

Coney, or cunny, was the name for a rabbit kept in a warren and comes from the Latin *cuniculus*. It seems also that a coney was an adult rabbit and a rabbit was a juvenile. They are no longer popular food, possibly because of outbreaks of myxomatosis. Rabbit looks and tastes like dark chicken meat and nowadays often seems to contain lead pellets.

'How to bake Conies, Rabets, or Hares, with fruit or without fruit. Season them with Pepper and Salte, Cloves and mace, and so laye them into your paste with Corance or Prunes, great Raisins and if you will: butter and a little vergious.'

CONYNGYS IN GRAVEYE – MINCED RABBIT BROTH

Two Fifteenth Century Cookbooks – Harleian MS. 279 & Harl. MS. 4016, c. 1440

The recipe specifies adult rabbit (coney), and is made by larding and roasting joints of rabbit, and then chopping the meat into smaller pieces (perhaps like mince) before cooking it again in a rich meaty broth thickened with ground almonds and rice flour, and spiced with saffron, ginger, galangal, cinnamon, sugar, cloves and mace.

'Conyngys in graueye. Take Conyngys, and make hem clene, and hakke hem in gobettys, and sethe hem, oþer larde hem and Rost hem; and þanne hakke hem, and take Almaundys, and grynde hem, and temper hem vppe with gode Freysshe brothe of Flesshe, and coloure it wyth Safroun, and do þer-to a porcyon of flowre of Rys, and do þer-to þen pouder Gyngere, Galyngale, Canel, Sugre, Clowys, Maces, and boyle it onys and seþe it; þen take þe Conyngys, and putte þer-on, and dresse it and serue it forth.'

BAKED SMALL MEATS

A Booke of Cookrye Very Necessary for all such as delight therin, 1591

Such recipes were simply memory aids for experienced cooks, hence the very minimalist nature.

'To bake small meats. Take Egges and seethe them hard, then take the yolkes out of them and braye them in the morter, and temper them with Creme, and then straine them, and put to them Pepper, Saffron, Cloves, Mace, small raisins, Almonds blanched and small shred and grated bread.'

MAWMENY – CHICKEN STEW

The Babees Book, or A 'Lytyl Reporte' of How Young People Should Behave, MS. Harl. 5086, c. 1475

'Recipe brawne of Capons or of hennys, and dry þam wele, and towse þam smalle; þan take thyk mylk of almondes, and put þe saide brawn þer-to, and styr it wele ouer þe fyre, and seson it with suger, and powder of Canelle, with mase, quibibs, and anneys in confete, and serve it forthe.'

Ingredients: 1 lb chicken; 2 cups almond milk; 2 egg yolks; 2 tbsp. rice flour; 1 tbsp sugar; ¼ tsp galingale; ¼ tsp salt; ⅛ tsp cinnamon; ⅛ tsp cloves; ⅛ tsp mace; pinch of saffron.

Method: Finely chop the chicken and place in a large pot. Whisk together almond milk, egg yolks and rice flour, and add to the chicken. Add spices and bring to a low boil. Simmer until thick and serve hot over bread or rice.

COMARYE – ROAST PORK MARINATED IN RED WINE

The Master-Cook of Richard II, *The Forme of Cury*, c. 1390

Pork is marinated in red wine and sauces, then roasted, and served with a sauce of the pan juices mixed with broth and boiled.

'Take coriander, finely-ground caraway, powdered pepper and garlic ground in red wine. Mix all these together and season with salt. Take uncooked loins of pork and remove the skin and prick all over with a knife and lay it in the sauce [marinade], then roast the meat and keep the juices in the roasting tray. Boil the pan juices in a small pan with clean broth and serve it to accompany the roast.'

Ingredients: 1 loin of pork (about 1 kg); 1 tsp coriander seeds; 1 tsp caraway seeds; ½ tsp freshly-ground black pepper; 6 garlic cloves; 80 ml red wine; 300 ml 'good broth' (see preserves); 100 ml red wine; salt, to taste.

Method: Grind the coriander, caraway and black pepper to a powder in a mortar or food processor and place the 'good powder' in a bowl. Pound the garlic cloves to a paste in a mortar and then blend in the 80 ml of red wine to make a smooth paste. Mix the paste with the spice paste and season with salt. Trim and prepare the pork loin, and rub into it the spice paste. Place in a dish, cover with a cloth and set aside to marinate for an hour or two. Put the meat in a roasting tin. Pour the 100 ml red wine around the base and then beat in any leftover marinade. Transfer to an oven preheated to 220°C and roast for 30 minutes, then reduce the oven temperature to 160°C and continue roasting for 50 minutes per kg, basting occasionally with the pan juices. When cooked, check that the meat juices run clear when it is pierced in its thickest part with a skewer. Transfer the pork to a chopping block, cover with foil and set aside to rest for 15 minutes. While it is resting, strain the juices into a clean pan and add the 'good broth'. Bring to a boil and cook until thickened. Serve the meat sliced and accompanied by the sauce.

SHAMBLES MEAT FOR A LARK

Gervase Markham's *Countrey Contentments, or, The English Hus-wife*, 1615

'Shambles meat' was meat bought from 'the shambles', the butchers' markets, and the meat sold there was generally the larger beasts – cattle, sheep and pigs. The word derives from the Latin *scamellum*, meaning a small *scamnum* or bench. By the tenth century, in Old English, it was a general word for a table or counter used for such activities as selling goods or counting money. Four hundred years later the word had become applied specifically to a stall where meat was sold. To make this dish you need a large spit over an open fire, with someone turning it by hand. This is one of the strangest meals, cooking a tiny lark between huge pieces of meat.

'If you will Roast a Chine of Beef, a loyn of Mutton, a Capon, and a Lark, all at one instant, and at one fire, and have all ready together and none burnt, you shall first take your Chine of Beef, and parboyl it more than half through: Then first take your Capon, being large and fat, and spit it next the hand of the turner, with the legs from the fire, then spit the Chine of Beef, then the Lark, and lastly the Loyn of Mutton, and place the Lark so as it may be covered over with the Beef and the fat part of the Loyn of Mutton, without any part disclosed, and then baste your Capon and your loyn of Mutton, with cold water and salt, the Chine of beef with boyling Lard, then when you see the beef is almost enough, which you shall hasten by scotching and opening of it, then with a clean cloth you shall wipe the mutton and Capon all over, and then baste them with sweet butter till all be enough rosted, then with your knife lay the Lark open, which by this time will be stewed between the beef and mutton, and basting it also with dredge altogether, draw them and serve them up.'

SOWCED PIGGE – MUSTARDED SHOULDER OF PORK

Thomas Dawson's *The Good Huswifes Jewell*, 1585, 1594, 1596

Dawson served up 'a quarter of the pigge' in a dish. Rolled shoulder of pork, marinated in a mustard-spiced wine and herb mixture before serving makes an excellent cold Christmas joint. If you do not wish to prepare the meat, ask your butcher to prepare a boned pork loin, by removing all but a very thin layer of fat from its upper surface. Roll the meat tightly and place in the middle of muslin, about 80 cm square. Roll this around the meat, tie firmly with butcher's string and knot the free ends of the muslin.

'To Sowce a Pigge. take white Wine and a little sweet broth, and half a score nutmegs cut into quarters, then take Rosemarie, Baies, Time, and sweet margerum, and let them boyle altogether, skum them very cleane, and when they be boyled, put them in an earthen pan and the syrop also, and when yee serve them, a quarter of a pig in a dish, and the Bays and nutmegs on top.'

Ingredients: 900 g rolled pork shoulder; 1 bottle white wine; 1 piece of chopped root ginger; 3 tbsp salt; half a crushed nutmeg; 2 tsp peppercorns; 3 bay leaves. You can amend the dish over time by adding rosemary, marjoram or mustard powder to suit your taste. You can also use strong ale instead of wine and spices, or substitute half of the wine with chicken broth.

Method: You can use Markham's method, as above, but this is simpler. Pour 575 ml of water in a stockpot, add the wine, spices and bay leaves and bring to the boil. Put in the meat and skim it once it returns to the boil. Simmer gently for around 2 hours until the meat is tender. Dissolve the salt in 1.7 l of water. When the meat is cooked, place it into this cold brine. Leave in a cool place until it is due to be served, within the next 2–3 days. Use the stock as in the next recipe.

BRAWN POTTAGE

Thomas Dawson's *The Good Huswifes Jewell*, 1585, 1594, 1596

You can easily make a pottage from the leftover stock from the above dish, as Dawson recommended, by stirring in 2 tbsp medium oatmeal and 1 tsp dried thyme or sage, previously mixed in a little cold water. Add two roughly chopped onions, bring to the boil and simmer for 40–45 minutes. Add salt and pepper to taste before serving.

TO SOUSE A YOUNG PIGGE – PORK SHOULDER AND TROTTERS IN JELLY

Sir Hugh Plat's *Delightes for Ladies*, 1602

Pork cooked in a spiced blend of water and wine, cooked down until the stock jellifies and where the meat is kept in the jelly. This author had a memorable meal in Reggio Emilia where he was taken to a special and expensive 'peasant food' restaurant, as it was the favourite eating house of the rich principal of an educational academy. A massive metal trolley was wheeled in, steaming and smelling quite unpleasant. When uncovered, the meal only consisted of steamed pig brain, assorted unexplained offal and trotters. Everything was coloured a pale cream. There were no sauces or accompaniments except for a few sprigs of wilted lettuce. The trotters were the only edible item for this squeamish writer, eaten for politeness' sake. Bay is an easy and decorative small shrub for your gardens.

'To foufe a young Pigge.Take a young Pigge being fcalded, boile it in a faire water and white wine, put thereto fome Baye leaues, fome whole Ginger, and fome Nutmegs quartered, a fewe whole cloues, boyle it thoroughly, and leaue it in the fame broth it an earthen pot.'

Ingredients: 3 pigs' trotters; 1 pork shoulder with bone; 1.5 l water; 500 ml dry white wine; 3 bay leaves; 2 quartered nutmegs; 6 cloves.

Method: Tie the nutmegs and cloves in a muslin bag. Add to a large pot along with the pork pieces and bay leaves. Pour over the water and white wine and bring to the boil. Reduce to a simmer, cover and cook gently for 3 hours, or until the meat is completely tender. Take off the lid, bring to a boil and reduce the liquid until it barely covers the meat. Take the pot from the heat, remove the meat and set aside. When cold enough to be handled, strip all the pork from the bones and arrange in an earthenware casserole dish. Skim all the fat from the stock, and then strain it over the meat. Set aside to cool, and when it jellifies, store in the refrigerator until needed.

TARTE OF SPINAGE – ELIZABETHAN SPINACH PIE
The Proper Newe Booke of Cookerye, c. 1557

'Take Spynage and perboyle it tender, then take it up and wrynge oute the water cleane, and chop it very small, and set it uppon the fyre wyth swete butter in a frying panne and season it, and set it in a platter to coole then fyll your and so bake it.

To make short paest for tarte, take fyne floure and a curscy of fayre water and a dysche of swete butter and a lyttel saffron, and the yolkes of two egges and make it thynne and as tender as ye maye.'

Ingredients for the Pie Filling: 550 g spinach; 115 g butter; 1 tbsp sugar; 1 tsp cinnamon; ¼ tsp each of mace and salt.

Ingredients for the Pastry: 225 g flour; 90 g softened butter; 2 egg yolks; 6 saffron threads ground into 1 tbsp warm water with a pestle and mortar; sugar; cinnamon; butter.

Method: Bring a pan of unsalted water to the boil, add the spinach and cook for 3 minutes. Drain and immediately rinse the spinach under cold water. Wring the spinach dry. Heat the butter in a frying pan, add the spices and fry the spinach in this for 2–3 minutes. Remove from the heat and allow to cool. To make the pie crust pastry, sift the flour into a bowl, add the saffron threads and their steeping water along with the egg yolks and mix together well. Then add three-quarters of the softened butter and mix in well. If all the flour does not come together into a dough, add a little more butter. Once the dough comes into a ball cut it into two pieces, one slightly larger than the other. Roll the larger piece of dough out and use this to line a 9-inch pie dish. Cut off the excess pastry around the edge. Fill the middle of the pie with the spinach mixture. Roll out the smaller piece of pastry and place on top of the pie. Use the back of a fork to crimp the upper and lower pieces of pastry together. Pierce the top pastry a few times to allow steam to escape. Cook in an oven preheated to 180°C for about 40 minutes, or until the upper crust has just turned golden. Brush the top surface of the pie with a mixture of sugar, molten butter and cinnamon.

ROAST CAPON – SPICE ROAST CHICKEN

Gervase Markham's *Countrey Contentments, or, The English Hus-wife*, 1615

A capon was a castrated cockerel which grew larger than a normal chicken. Free-range and corn-fed, these birds had a special flavour, gamier than normal chickens. The recipe would originally have been made with a slowly roasted whole bird, but this recipe uses chicken thighs. Being muscular, they are the tastiest parts of a chicken.

Ingredients: 6 chicken thighs, with skin; 60 g unsalted butter; 40 g extra virgin olive oil; 1 tsp powdered cinnamon; 1 tsp ground cloves; 1 tsp powdered mace.

Method: Place the butter, olive oil and spices in a small pan and heat to melt the butter. Preheat oven to 180°C. Baste the chicken thighs with the butter mixture, place in a baking dish and roast for about 35 minutes until the thighs are a rich golden brown. Every 5 minutes or so take the thighs from the oven and baste with more of the butter mixture. Serve immediately.

SEISIG MORGANNWG – GLAMORGAN SAUSAGES

Traditional Welsh

This savoury vegetarian sausage, incorporating breadcrumbs, cheese and leek, made use of what was existing in poorer Welsh homes when meat was not affordable. It can be a starter, a main course or a snack. Cheddar was first noted in the 1580s as a recognisable cheese. A couple of splashes of Worcester sauce make it more savoury. Farmhouse Caerphilly cheese production died out during the Second World War, as all milk had to be diverted to the Cheddar factories to help the war effort. After the war, these factories started making their version of Caerphilly to help their cash flow, as crumbly Caerphilly matures more quickly than Cheddar.

Ingredients: 150 g breadcrumbs; 75 g Caerphilly or Cheddar cheese; small leek; 30 g butter; generous pinch of mustard powder; 20 g chopped parsley; 2 tbsp flour; ¼ tsp black pepper; 1 egg.

Method: Finely chop the leek and fry in butter until softened. When the leek has cooled, add it to the breadcrumbs and grated cheese. Mix in the chopped parsley, salt and pepper before adding the egg yolk as a binding agent. Mix together then shape the mixture into sausages. Roll in flour and fry gently upon each side until the sausages are golden brown and crisp.

TO STEW A RUMP OF BEEF – BEEF IN RED WINE WITH A CHEESE AND CABBAGE SAUCE

The Closet of the Eminently Learned Sir Kenelme Digbie Kt Opened, 1669

'To Stew a Rump of Beef: Take a rump of Beef, break all the bones; season it with Pepper and Salt to your liking; Take three or four Nutmegs, and a quantity of Mace, beat them grossly; Then take a bunch of very good sweet herbs, and one good Onion cut in quarters, or Garlike, as you like it. Put in half a pint of White-wine Vinegar, and one pint of good Claret, one handful of Sugar; and a piece or two of beef suet or Butter; shred some cabbage under and over, and scrape in a pound of good old cheese. Put all these into an earthen pot, and let it stand in an oven with brown bread four or five hours; but let the pot be covered close with paste.'

Ingredients: 1.2–1.5 kg piece of boned beef rump; 1 tsp lesser calamint, or a mix of mint and oregano; 1 tsp ground nutmeg; 1 tsp ground mace; 50 g each of parsley, winter savory, marjoram, chicory – add basil if one is missing; 4 or 5 sage leaves; 1 large onion, chopped; 450 g shredded cabbage; 3 cloves of garlic; 300 ml white wine vinegar; 600 ml red wine, such as claret; 100 g butter or beef suet; 100 g sugar; 150 g Cheddar cheese; 350 g flour; water.

Method: Trim the beef and brown on all sides in a frying pan. Layer half the cabbage on the bottom of a heavy casserole dish. Add the onion and garlic on top. Place the beef on top and add the liquid ingredients, along with the butter or suet, cheese, herbs and spices and cover with the remaining cabbage. Place the flour into a bowl and add just enough water to form dense, but pliable, dough. Use this to line the rim of the casserole dish and place the casserole lid firmly on top of the dough, pressing gently into place. This allows the casserole to simmer gently in the oven for over 5 hours without drying out. Preheat oven to 130°C and place the beef in the oven, leaving for about 5.5 hours. After about 5 hours, increase the temperature to 160°C for the last 30 minutes. Remove from oven, remove the pastry rim, take out the beef and shred it. Place the sauce and the cabbage in a dish, cover with the shredded beef and serve immediately. This is a great meal to come home to, if you are out for the afternoon or morning, as it is simply left alone for 5 hours.

BOYLED FLOUNDER OR PICKEREL OF THE FRENCH FASHION – FLATFISH OR PIKE IN WHITE WINE SAUCE

Sir Hugh Plat's *Delightes for Ladies*, 1602

Pickerel was a small pike, weighing up to 3 pounds, costing around 2½*d* a pound in medieval markets. The flavoursome pike is not popular at present, except in Eastern European cuisine and with Poles living in Britain, probably because of the incredible amount of fiddly bones. It is interesting that there is no distinction between cooking the freshwater pike and saltwater flounder. Flounder is a lean, flaky fish with a firm texture and a mild, sweet taste. While often best served sautéed, there are a variety of ways to incorporate this tasty fish into lunch or dinner. Flounder is a name often given to sole, halibut, turbot, plaice, fluke or dab. All are flatfish, members of the order *Pleuronectiforme*s, and adults carry both eyes on the darker top side of the head. Flounder and plaice were among the cheapest saltwater fish sold in Staffordshire markets in 1461, at around ½*d* each, with only herring being cheaper at ¼ d. The most expensive were saltfish (salted white fish) at 8*d* and stockfish (dried cod) at 3*d*.

'To boyle a flounder or Pickerel, of the French faſhion. Take a pinte of white wine, the tops of young time and Roſemary, a little whole mace, a little whole pepper ſeaſoned with Veriuice, ſalt, and a peece of ſweete butter, and ſo ſerue it: this broth will ſerue to boyle Fiſh twiſe or thriſe in.'

Ingredients: 2 flounders or 1 pike, gutted and scaled (your fishmonger will do this); 500 ml white wine; 2 tsp thyme sprigs; 4 fresh rosemary tips; 2 blades of mace; 1 tsp black peppercorns; 60 ml verjuice (or white wine vinegar); salt to taste; 2 tbsp unsalted butter.

Method: Combine all ingredients in a fish kettle or large casserole dish. Place the fish inside and bring to a simmer on the hob. Cover with a tight-fitting lid and poach the fish gently for 20–40 minutes, depending on size, or until the flesh flakes easily with a fork. Divide the fish into portions and serve with a little of the sauce. Strain the sauce before serving.

SAMON ROSTYD IN SAUCE – GRILLED SALMON IN WINE SAUCE
Gentyll Manly Cokere, MS Pepys 1047, c. 1490

Try to buy non-farmed salmon, e.g. Pacific salmon. Atlantic salmon is becoming scarce and farmed salmon is often unpleasant. The copious grey slime in the meat of the fish is because it has not properly developed muscle meat in the Atlantic Ocean and unhealthy farmed salmon almost uniformly have lice and other problems which transfer to non-farmed salmon as they pass the fish farms to breed.

'Samon rostyd in sause. Cut thy salmon in round pieces and roast it on a grid iron.Take wine and powder of cinnamon and draw them through a strainer. Add thereto onions minced small. Boil it well. Take vinegar or verjuice and powder of ginger and salt. Add thereto. Lay the salmon in dishes and pour the syrup thereon and serve forth'.

Ingredients: 6 salmon steaks; 1 large onion; 1 tsp ground cinnamon; 5 ml ground ginger; 575 ml red wine; 1 tbsp wine vinegar; 5 ml salt.

Method: Finely chop the onion, place in a saucepan with the wine and cinnamon, cover and cook for 15 minutes. Place the salmon on a grill and cook for 4–7 minutes each side, dependent upon thickness. When the salmon and onions are cooked, place the salmon on a hot dish. Stir the vinegar, ginger and salt into the onions and pour over the salmon just before serving.

PYKE IN SAUCE – FISH IN SAUCE
A Proper Newe Booke of Cokerye, 1545

In Staffordshire in 1461, Pike was the most expensive freshwater fish sold in markets, probably because of its size, with 12*d* being the median price paid and 8*d* for a pickerel (young pike). It was followed by tench 6*d*, bream 5*d*, chub 4½*d*, perch 2*d* and eel 1½*d*. Along with roach, all could be kept in ponds. All fish had different sauces recommended for them. Salmon, trout, dace, grayling, carp, ruff, barbell, burbot, gudgeon and even minnow were eaten.

'A Pyke sauce for a Pyke, Breme, Perche, Roche, Carpe, Eles, Floykes [flukes] and al maner of brouke [brook] fyshe. Take a posye of Rosemary and time and bynde them together, and put in also a quantitye of perselye not bounde, and put into the caudron of water, salte and yeste, and the herbes, and lette them boyle a pretye whyle, then putte in the fysshe and a good quantitye of butter, and let them boyle a good season, and you shall have good Pyke sauce. For all those fysshes above written yf they muste bee broyled, take sauce for them, butter, peepper and veneger and boyle it upon a chafyngdyshe and then laye the broyled fyshe uppon the dysche; but for Eeles and freshe Salmon nothing but Pepper and vyneger over boyled. And also yf you wyll frye them, you muste take a good quantitie of persely, after the fyshe is fryed, put in the persely into the fryinge panne, and let it frye in the butter and take it up and put it on the fryed fyshe, and frye place, whyttinge and suche other fyshe, excepte Eles, freshe Salmon, Conger, which be never fryed but baken, boyled, roosted or sodden.'

STEWED HERYNGS – HERRINGS IN MUSTARD ALE SAUCE
Gentyll Manly Cokere, MS Pepys 1047, c. 1490

When buying food, a hundred did not always equal 10 x 10. This did not matter to the ordinary household cook, but it was very important to anyone buying or selling commodities, or buyers for the great households. In 1440, in the fishing port of Yarmouth, a regulation was established that: 'Hearings [herrings] are sold freshe by the meise, which is five hundred, eche hundred contayning vj xx.' Thus a 'hundred' of herrings was actually one hundred and twenty herrings. This was technically a 'long hundred', but the 'long' was often understood. The problem was that the actual number represented by a 'long hundred' depended upon both the item and the era. Fish were commonly traded in long hundreds and this usually indicated six score, or 120, as in the fifteenth century reference above. It could mean more however. A reference in the *Household Ordinances of Edward II* (1284–1327) noted that 'Of somme manner of fish the hundred containeth six score, and of some other sort, nine score [180].' A seventeenth century reference says 'Ling, Cod, or Haberdine [salt or sun-dried cod], have 124 to the Hundred.' Also at this time, it could be as much as nine score (180) depending upon the item and market. Other items commonly counted in long hundreds were eggs (120); sheep in some areas (106); and dried salt fish (160). Even more confusingly, 225 onions or garlic bulbs counted as 100, made up of 15 'ropes' of 15 heads each.

'For to stew heryng. Se thy heryng be well watered and take owte the bone and take the myltys [spleen] and lay them yn A fayre dysch of water and wesche both the heryng and the mylt to gether then take a litell percely so muche tyme a Fewe unyons and mell all to gether as small as ye can make hit and then bruse all your herbes and the mylts together And take poder of pepur a litell suger and rasyns of Curance and a litell myed [crumbled] of White brede and put all thes together and stew thy heryng with all. When they be stuffed lay them on A dyshe and take ale a gode porcon and put ther to musterd and cast vpon them grete Rasyns and cover them with a dyshe and set them on þe fyre and so serue them furth.'

Ingredients: 600 ml mild ale; 25 g soft white breadcrumbs; 25 ml chopped parsley and thyme; pinch of ground black pepper; 50 g raisins; 2 tsp mustard powder; 5 ml chopped onion; 25 ml sugar. The above filling will be enough for one large herring, so multiply the quantities accordingly.

Method: Ask your fishmonger to open the herring down the belly and to remove the gut, gills, spine and bones. Cook the same day. The recipe calls for you to grind the milts and roe with the bread, currants, onion, pepper, sugar and herbs to form a smooth paste, but the milts and roe have been omitted from the present dish. Use the paste to stuff the herring, holding it in place by skewering the fish belly together. Place in a shallow pan with ale, mustard and raisins and simmer gently for 10 minutes before draining and serving.

A DISH OF PARTICULAR COLOURS – MULTICOLOURED CHICKENS

Sabina Welser's *And Thus You Have a Lordly Dish: Fancy and Showpiece Cookery in an Augsberg Patrician Kitchen*, 1553

White, brown, yellow, green and black roasted chickens. If you fancy serving a green or black chicken, ensure it is to a guest you never want to see again…

'Item, a dish that in each part has a particular colour is made thus. Roast hens on a spit and do not put them too close together. And when they are roasted make six colours. Make them white thus: take the whites of eggs, put a little flour in it. Make a thick paste. Item, make brown thus: take cherry electuary and mix it with eggs and flour to a brown paste. The yellow make thus: take the yolks of eggs, a little good flour, saffron, and three or four eggs. From that make a paste. Make green thus: take parsley. Put it through a cloth with eggs. Put a little flour with it and make a paste. Black: take flour and eggs; make a paste of them. Add crushed cloves which have soaked overnight in beaten eggs. Put enough in and it will be good black. When you have made these five colours, then baste each hen with its colour, and be careful that you don't heat them too much. And when the colouring has dried, then take the hens from the fire and lay them next to other roasts on a platter.'

TO DRESSE A CRABE – DRESSED CRAB
The Proper Newe Booke of Cookerye, c. 1557
Crabmeat mixed with cinnamon, sugar and wine, served in the empty crab shell with the crab claws.

'To dresse a crabe Fyrste take awaye all the legges, and the heades, and then take all the fyſh out of the ſhelle, and make the ſhell as cleane as ye canne, and putte the meate into a dyſſhe, and butter it vppon a chafyng dyſſhe of coles, and putte therto ſynamon and ſuger and a lytle vyneger, and when ye haue chafed it and ſeaſoned it, then putte the meate in the ſhelle agayne, and bruſe the heades, and ſet them vpon the dyſſhe ſyde and ſerue it.'

Ingredients: 4 cooked crabs, steamed or boiled; ½ tsp ground cinnamon; 2 tbsp brown sugar; 2 tbsp white wine vinegar; 50 g butter.

Method: Remove the legs from the freshly-cooked crabs. Open the shells and keep the top shells. Carefully take out the meat and set aside. Melt the butter in a frying pan then sprinkle over the cinnamon, brown sugar and white wine vinegar. When the sugar has dissolved, add the crab meat and stir well on a low heat until heated through. Divide the seasoned and warmed crab meat between the reserved top shells of the crabs. Arrange on a dish, bruise the claws so that they may be opened more easily and arrange these on the dish with the crab meat. Serve immediately.

TO DYGHT A CRABE – CRAB MEAT DRESSED IN SHELL (Two Ways)
Gentyll Manly Cokere, MS Pepys 1047, c. 1490
'To prepare a crab. Take out all in the crab and lay it in a little vinegar. Take and put a little red wine thereto and strain all through a strainer. Take powder of ginger, cinnamon, and sugar and mix all together. And put him in the shell. And set it on the fire til he boils and when it is boiled take it off and cast powder of cinnamon and sugar upon and serve it forth.'

Ingredients 1: Crab meat, cooked and shredded – save the shell if using fresh

crab; red wine vinegar or cider vinegar; red wine; ginger; cinnamon; sugar; whole crab shell or ramekin; pinch of sugar and cinnamon.

Method 1: Blend crab, vinegar, wine, ginger, cinnamon and sugar thoroughly with a fork or food processor to the consistency of a paté or a stuffing. Use more or less wine as needed. Fill the crab shell or ramekin with the crab meat; brown in an oven or under a broiler. Sprinkle a little cinnamon and sugar on top. Serve hot.

Ingredients 2: 1 dressed, cooked crab in shell; 2 tbsp red wine vinegar; 1 tbsp sweet red wine; pinch of ground ginger; pinch of ground cinnamon; ½ sugar.

Method 2: Soak the cooked crab meat in the vinegar and wine for 20 minutes, then chop finely and rub it through a sieve. Stir in a little more wine and vinegar if necessary to make a smooth paste. Stir in the spices and sugar, return the mix to the shell and place over a gentle heat. Stir until it boils and serve immediately with a pinch of ground cinnamon and sugar, in its shell or a ramekin.

CHAUET OF BEEF – STEAK AND CHICKEN PIE

An Ordinance of Pottage, Beinecke MS 163, 1460
Each pie serves 6 to 8 people – also see *Chawettys* in Starters.

'Take Befe cut smal, do thereto poudyr of gynger, clovis and othir good poudrs, grapes vergys, and salt, Toyled togedyr Do chickenys chopped in coffyns and yolkes brockyd and cromyd small; Bake hem and hem forth.'

Ingredients for two pies: 1½ lbs chicken, boned and chopped into bite-size pieces; 2 lbs beef mince; 1 tsp ginger; 2 tsp powder fort; ½ tsp cloves; 5 tbsp wine vinegar (or verjuice); 12 cooked egg yolks, crumbled; 2 pinches of saffron; 1 tsp salt. You can make your own 'coffyns' or buy 2 packs of frozen fold-out pie crusts.

Method: Fry the beef till almost done and drain the fat. Pat it dry with a kitchen towel, if desired. Boil the chicken until cooked and chop up. Mix all ingredients together, divide and place in two pies, baking in a hot oven until the pastry is cooked.

CHAWETTYS (CHEWETTS) – VEAL OR PORK PIES

Two Fifteenth Century Cookbooks – Harleian MS. 279 & Harl. MS. 4016, c. 1440

'Chawettys. Take joints of Veal and mince them small, or Pork, and put on a pot; take Wine, and caste thereto powder of Ginger, Pepper, and Saffron, and Salt, and a little verjuice, and do them in a coffin (pie) with 3 yolks of Egg, and cut Dates and Raisons or Currants, Cloves, Mace, and then place in the coffin and let it bake until it be enough.'

TO MAKE PYES – LAMB PYE WITH FRUITE – MUTTON OR BEEF FRUIT PIES

Proper Newe Booke of Cookerye, c. 1577

Yet another melding of sweet and savoury in an excellent combination. For *paest royall* see the recipe in the chapter on Sweets.

'To make Pyes. Pyes of mutton or beif must be fyne mynced and seasoned with pepper and salte and a lytel saffron to colour it / suet or marrow a good quantitie / a lytell vynegre / pruynes / great reasons / and dates / take the fattest of the broath of powdred beefe. And if you will have paest royall / take butter and yolkes of egges and so to temper the floure to make the paest.'

Ingredients: 675 g beef and/or lamb roasting joint, cooked and minced into very small pieces; ½ tsp ground black pepper; ½ tsp salt; 120 g beef suet, diced; 60ml red wine vinegar or cider vinegar; 100 g pitted and sliced prunes; 60 g raisins; 60 g chopped dates; 500 ml beef broth; *paest royall* or shortcrust pastry.

Method: Combine the meat, spices, suet, vinegar and fruit in a large bowl, adding just enough beef broth to thoroughly wet the mixture, which should be fairly runny. Line a 9-inch pie dish with the *paest royall* and fill with the meat mixture. Add a pastry lid, pierce the lid and place the pie in an oven preheated to 190°C. Bake for about 45 minutes to an hour, until the filling is bubbling and the pastry is a golden brown.

TO BOYLE A LEG OF MUTTON WITH LEMMONS – LEMONED LAMB

A.W., *The Booke of Goode Cookry Very Necessary for all Such as Delight Therein*, 1584, 1591

'To boyle a Leg of Mutton with Lemmons. When your mutton is half boyled, take it up, cut it in small peeces, put it into a Pipkin and cover it close, and put therto the best of the broth, as much as shall cover your Mutton, your Lemmons being sliced very Thin and quartered and corance: put in pepper groce beaten, and so let them boile together, and when they be well boiled, seson it with a little vergious, Sugar, Pepper groce beaten, and a little sanders, so lay it in fine dishes upon sops, it wil make iv messe for the table.'

Ingredients: 900 g leg of lamb or mutton; 115 ml lamb stock; 575 ml white wine; 150 ml wine vinegar; 1 thinly sliced lemon; thinly shredded zest of half an orange peel; 15 ml sugar; 1.5 ml cinnamon; 1.5 ml ginger; 225 g cubed white bread; 25 g fresh white breadcrumbs; 1.5 ml salt.

Method: Preheat the oven to 180°C. Place the meat in a roasting tin to bake for 15 minutes. Remove it from the oven and place a metal plate on top, pressing it down as hard as possible. Slash the meat with a knife, press again and pour the meat juices into a small saucepan. Put the meat back in the oven for 10 minutes, take it out and press again. Gather more juice to make about 3 tbsps in total in the small saucepan and set aside. Now use a large stockpot, and in it mix the lamb stock with the wine and vinegar, bringing to the boil. Place the partly-roasted lamb into the stockpot, reduce to a simmer and cook for another 45 minutes or until tender. Add the salt, lemon slices, orange zest, sugar, cinnamon, ginger and breadcrumbs to the simmering lamb. Ladle out 425 ml of the stock that the lamb is simmering in and add to the small saucepan containing the meat juices. Cook for 5 minutes to make a savoury sauce. Line the base of a deep dish with the cubed bread and place the meat on top. Pour the sauce over and arrange the lemon slices over the meat.

TO BOILE A LEG OF MUTTON WITH HEARBES – HERBED LAMB
A.W., *The Booke of Goode Cookry Very Necessary for all Such as Delight Therein*, 1584, 1591
Follow the recipe for Lemoned Lamb above, omitting the lemon, orange zest and currants, but use herbs instead to make a herbed sauce for pouring over the lamb.

'To boile Mutton with Endive, Borage, or Lettice, or any kinde of hearbes that may serve therunto. When your Mutton is well boyled, take the best of the broth, and put it in a Pipkin, and put therto an handfull of Endive, borage, or what herbs you list, and cast therto a few corance, and let them boyle well, and put therto a peece of upper crust of white bread, season it with pepper groce beaten, and a little Vergious, and a little sugar, and so poure it upon your meat.'

SEETHED FRESH SALMON – ELIZABETHAN HERB POACHED SALMON
The Good Huswifes Handmaide for the Kitchin, 1594, 1597, 1588
'To seeth Fresh Salmon. Take a little water, and as much Beere and salt, and put therto Parsley, Time and Rosemarie, and let all these boyle togeathere. Then put in your Salmon, and make your broth Sharpe with some Vinigar.'
Ingredients: 4 salmon steaks; 240 ml water; 240 ml beer or ale; 60 ml white wine vinegar; 3 tbsp chopped parsely; 1 tsp thyme; 1 tsp rosemary leaves; ¼ tsp salt.
Method: Combine all ingredients, except the fish, in a pan and bring to the boil. Reduce the heat to a simmer. Place the fish in a shallow baking dish and add enough of the poaching liquid to cover two-thirds of the salmon steaks. Cover the dish and place in an oven preheated to 200°C and bake for about 20 minutes, or until the fish becomes tender and flakes easily with a fork.

TO BAKE A STOCKFISH – ELIZABETHAN VINEGARED COD PIE
A.W., *The Booke of Goode Cookry Very Necessary for all Such as Delight Therein*, 1584, 1591

Until the twentieth century, cod were so plentiful that they grew to an enormous size and were the cheapest fish available, being easily harvested off Newfoundland and in the North Sea. Overfishing by industrial trawlers in the twentieth century caused the Atlantic cod population to collapse, with immature cod taken before they could breed. Cod can live for over thirteen years and reach five feet long and over 100 pounds, but now most caught are less than a fifth of that weight. In recent years, 'fish and chips' has become proportionately far more expensive, with smaller cod portions as a result of overfishing. Stockfish is unsalted white fish, usually cod, dried by cold air and wind on wooden racks on the foreshore and has a storage life of several years. The method is cheap and effective in cold climates such as Norway and Newfoundland and is easily transported to market. Before it can be eaten, salt cod must be rehydrated and desalinated by soaking in cold water for one to three days, changing the water two to three times a day.

'To bake a Stockfish. Season your Stockfish with pepper and salt and lay it into the paste, and put good store of butter to it, and shred onions small, and percely, and cast it upon the stockfish, and put a little vergious [verjuice] unto it, and bake it.'

Ingredients: Use either 450 g skinned cod fillets, or salted fish which has been soaked in water for 24 hours; 1 small chopped onion; 15 ml cider vinegar or wine vinegar; 15 ml chopped parsley; 25 g butter; a little milk; salt and pepper to taste. For the pastry you will need 350 g plain flour; 125 g lard; 60–90 ml cold water.

Method: Mix the onion, parsley, salt and pepper. Rub the lard into the flour, mix in just enough water to make a stiff shortcrust pastry and knead lightly. Roll the pastry out to form a large rectangle. Spread a layer of onion mixture across half of the rectangle and arrange some of the fish on top of it. Add the remaining onion and fish in alternate layers, dotting with butter. Moisten the edges of the pastry with a little milk. Fold the empty half of the pastry over the fish and onion mixture, sealing and rolling the edges all around. Pierce a hole in the top to pour in the wine vinegar. Glaze the pie with milk and bake at 220°C for 45 minutes.

TEWKESBURY MUSTARD BALLS – PORK IN TEWKESBURY MUSTARD
Fifteenth century to present.

This author's favourite mustard is a blend of mustard flour and grated horseradish root. By the seventeenth century it had become a staple condiment of kitchens. Shakespeare mentions it in *Henry IV Part 2*, where Falstaff describes his friend Ned Poins: 'his wit's as thick as Tewkesbury Mustard.' Legend has it that Tewkesbury Mustard Balls covered in gold leaf were presented to Henry VIII, when he visited Tewkesbury in Gloucestershire in 1535. The women of Tewkesbury gathered the ingredients from the fields and the Severn riverbanks about the town. A cannonball in an iron mortar was used to crush the mustard grain to a fine flour, then it was sieved to produce a fineness and purity. Horseradish was a common weed around Tewkesbury and was used to make the mustard hotter, but it caused great suffering during the preparation of the root as, before being soaked in cider or cider vinegar, the fumes are a painful irritant to the eyes. Originally the mustard was prepared by grinding the mustard seeds into mustard flour, combining this with finely-grated horseradish (and sometimes herbs and spices), then forming the mixture into balls which were then dried to aid preservation. The mustard balls would then be transported and sold in this form.

To use the balls, they would be broken apart then mixed with a liquid such as water, vinegar, wine, ale, beer, cider or fruit juice to soften them, and then mixed to a thick, creamy consistency. Often a sweetener such as honey would be added. The resulting mixture would then be used as a condiment or as a cure for ailments. The Tewkesbury mustard that was so popular from the sixteenth to nineteenth centuries was only sold in ball form, never in jars or other containers. Although the precise recipe has been lost, the ingredients were simply local grown mustard seed, mixed with an infusion of horseradish, formed into balls and then allowed to dry on a board. The customer would then cut off as much as was required and steep it in his chosen liquor until it was workable. The resultant mustard was 'thick and pungent'. By 1662 Tewkesbury mustard was considered by Thomas Fuller, in *The History of the Worthies of England*, to be the best in England. Manufacture of Tewkesbury mustard died out only at the beginning of the nineteenth century, perhaps coincidentally with a Mr Coleman of Norwich inventing his new process for producing mustard flour. The tradition is now restored as a cottage industry in the borough. Mustard balls are produced to order and on special occasions such as the re-enactment of the Battle of Tewkesbury in July of each year. Handmade mustard using local ingredients can still be purchased in Tewkesbury. There is some evidence that Tewkesbury Mustard Balls came to be used as slang for incendiary 'fire-balls'.

Ingredients: 1–2 pork tenderloins weighing about 500–600 g; salt and freshly ground black pepper; vegetable oil for frying; knob of chilled butter; 4 shallots, peeled, halved and finely chopped; 2 tsp Tewkesbury mustard; 250 g crème fraiche; 1 tbsp chopped parsley.

Method: Cut the pork into 8 slices and flatten them slightly with the palm of your hand. Heat a tablespoon or so of vegetable oil in a heavy or non-stick frying pan and fry the pork pieces on a high heat for a couple of minutes on each side. Remove from the pan and keep warm. Add the butter to the pan and cook the shallots for 20–30 seconds, add the mustard and stir in the crème fraiche and simmer until the sauce thickens, then add the parsley and season to taste. Arrange the pork pieces on warmed serving plates and spoon the sauce on top.

BOYLED MALLARD AND CABAGE
The Good Huswifes Handmaide for the Kitchin, 1594

'To boyle a Mallard with Cabage. Take the Cabage and pick them cleane, and wash them, and parboile them in faire water: then put them in a colender, and let the water runne from them, then put them in a faire pot, and as much beefe broth as will couer them, and the Marie of three Mary bones whole. Then take a Mallard, and with your knife giue him a launce along vppon each side of the breast. Then take him of, and put him into your Cabage, and his dripping with him, for he must be roasted halfe ynough, and his dripping saued, and so let them stew the space of one hower. Then put in some pepper and a litle salt, and serue in your Mallard vpon sops, and the Cabage about him, and of the vppermost of the broth.'

CAPON STUE – CHICKEN STEW
A.W., *A Book of Cookrye*, 1584, 1591

'To stue a Capon. Take the best of the Broth of the pot, and put it in a pipkin, and put to it Corance and great raisins, Dates quartered and onions fine minced, strayned bread and time, and let them boile well togither: when they be well boyled, put in your prunes, season it with cloves, mace, pepper and very little Salte, a spoonfull or two of Vergious, and let it not be too thick. And your Capon being boyled in a pot by it selfe in fair water and salt to keepe it faire, and thus you may boyle a Chicken, vele, beef or mutton after this sort.'

Ingredients: 1 lb chicken; 8 cups chicken or vegetable broth; ⅓ cup raisins; ⅓ cup chopped dates; ½ cup sliced onion; 4 slices bread; ¼ tsp thyme; ⅓ cup prunes, chopped; ⅛ tsp cloves; ⅛ tsp mace; ¼ tsp pepper; ¼ tsp verjuice or lemon juice; salt to taste.

Method: Place chicken in a pot of boiling water and cook until done, taking about 20 minutes. Remove the chicken, allow to cool and cut into bite-sized pieces. Throw away the cooking water. Put broth, raisins, dates and onion into a stockpot and bring to a boil. Tear up the bread into large pieces and place in a small bowl. Add some of the broth and allow to soak for a few minutes, stirring occasionally to break the bread up. Strain into the pot, discarding the solids. Add remaining ingredients and chicken. Bring to a boil and allow to simmer for about 15 minutes.

CAPONS STEWED – HERBED CHICKEN IN SPICED WINE SAUCE
Gentyll manly Cokere MS Pepys 1047, c. 1500
Capon stuffed with herbs, stewed in wine and served in a wine and fruit syrup with beef ribs. Chicken in the following recipe has been substituted for capon and beef ribs have been omitted.
Ingredients: 2.7 kg chicken; 75 cl white wine; 37 cl red wine; 50 g chopped dates; 25 g currants; 1.5 ml ground ginger; 1.5 ml ground cinnamon; 1.5 ml salt; 30 ml sugar; large quantity of fresh parsley, sage, rosemary and thyme; 225 g white bread cut into 1-inch cubes.
Method: Stuff the chicken with half the herbs and place on a grid or grill in a large stockpot to prevent it sticking to the bottom of the pan. Cover with water and stir in the rest of the herbs. Bring to the boil, skim, cover and simmer for 2 hours. Ten minutes before serving, mix and heat the wine, dates, currants, ginger, cinnamon and salt to make a sauce. Arrange the bread in a deep dish, place the drained chicken on top and pour the sauce over it just before serving.

FRICASE OF A GOOD HADDOCK OR WHITING – FISH FRICASSÉE
A.W., The Booke of Goode Cookry Very Necessary for all Such as Delight Therein, 1584, 1591
'To make a Fricase of a good Haddock or Whiting. First seeth the fish and scum it, and pick out the bones, take Onions and chop them small then fry them in Butter or Oyle till they be enough, and put in your Fish, and frye them till it be drye, that doon: serve it forth with pouder of Ginger on it.'

CAPONS IN DORRE – CHICKEN IN GOLDEN ALMOND MILK
Gentyll manly Cokere MS Pepys 1047, c. 1500
A dish of toasted bread in a sweet, golden almond milk.
'Blanched almonds grind them, temper them up with fair water unto a good milk. And draw it through a strainer into a pot. Add thereto saffron for if thou wilt, thou may colour it a little therewith, and add thereto sugar and salt and set it on the fire. Stir it well and when it is at the boiling add thereto a little good wine. Take it from the fire and stir it well, and then take white bread and cut it manner of brewes thin. Toast them a little on a roast iron that they be somewhat brown and then dip them a little in wine and toast them better and add a little milk in dishes and couch 3 or 4 toasts in a dish and pour more milk upon and serve forth. Probotum est.'

Ingredients: One medium-sized chicken; 100 g ground almonds; 275 ml white wine; 30 ml sugar; butter or oil for roasting; 2.5 ml salt; pinch of saffron; 225 g white bread cut in 2.5 cm cubes, toasted golden brown.

Method: Roast the chicken with a little butter or oil at 200°C, allowing 20 minutes per 450 g, plus a further 20 minutes. Soak the almonds in water for 30 minutes, drain, then grind with 575 ml of water, adding and pouring it off little by little and straining through a cloth to make almond milk. Put the almond milk in a small saucepan, adding the saffron to colour it golden, along with sugar and salt. Bring to the boil, stir in half the wine and set on one side. Arrange the toasted bread in a deep dish, and pour the rest of the wine over it. Leave for five minutes. Pour the almond milk sauce over, and place the roast chicken on top before serving.

MEAT PYES
A Proper Newe Booke of Cokerye, 1545

'To make Pyes. Pyes of mutton or beif must be fyne mynced and ceasoned wyth pepper and salte, and a lyttle saffron to coloure it, suet or marrow a good quantite, a lyttle vyneger, prumes, greate raysins, and dates, take the fattest of the broathe of powdred beyfe, and yf you wyll haue paest royall, take butter and yolkes of egges, and to tempre the flowre to make the paste.'

Ingredients: 1 to 2 lbs minced mutton or beef; ¼ cup chopped prunes; ¼ cup chopped dates; ¼ cup raisins; 2 tbsp vinegar; ½ tsp pepper; ½ tsp salt; pinch of ground saffron (optional); short pastry.

Method: Mix the filling ingredients and set aside. Cut the butter into the flour thoroughly. Mix in egg yolk and enough water to let the dough hold together. Separate into eight portions and roll out. Place one-eighth of the filling into each, fold over and seal with water. Bake for about 30 minutes at 180°C until crust is golden.

STEWED TRYPES – **TRIPE AND ONION TOAST**
The Proper Newe Booke of Cookerye, c. 1557

Sliced tripe boiled with claret and onions, served on a bed of toast.

'To ftewe Trypes. Take a pynte of claret wyne, and fet it vpon the frre, and cutte youre trypes in fmall peces, and thereto putte in a good quantitye of fynamon and gynger, and alfo a flyced onyon or twayne, and fo let them boyle half an houre, and then ferue them von foppes.'

Ingredients: 500 ml clarrey – mulled claret wine, see drinks chapter; 300 g prepared, washed tripe, sliced into small pieces; ¼ tsp ground ginger; ¼ tsp ground cinnamon; 1 medium onion, peeled and sliced into thin rings; 4 thin slices of toasted white bread.

Method: Combine the tripe, ginger, cinnamon and onion in a pan with a tight-fitting lid. Pour over the wine then bring to a simmer. Cover with a lid and simmer gently for about 40 minutes, or until the tripe is very tender. Take the sliced bread, cut each piece into four triangles and arrange on the serving dish. Spoon over the tripe and onion mixture and serve.

TO FRYE TRYPES – FRIED TRIPE
A Proper Newe Booke of Cokerye, c. 1545
'To Frye Trypes. Take your Trypes and cutte them in small peces and put them into a panne and put therto an onyon or two and a dysche of swete butter, and let them frye tyll they be browne, and then take them oute and set them upon a chaffindysh and put thereto a lyttle verges [verjuice] and gynger and serue it.'

CAPON WITH SIRROP
Thomas Dawson's *A Booke of Cokerie*, 1620
'To boyle a Capon with sirrop. Boyle your Capon in sweet broath, and put in grosse Pepper and whole Mace into the Capons belly and make your sirrop with Spinage, white wine, and Currants, Suger, Cinnamon and Ginger, and sweete Butter and so let them boyle, and when your Capon is ready to serve, put the sirrop on the Capon, and boyle your Spinage before you make your sirrop.'

TO FRY WHITINGS [OR HADDOCK] – FRIED WHITEFISH IN APPLE OR ONION SAUCE
A.W., *The Booke of Goode Cookry Very Necessary for all Such as Delight Therein*, 1584, 1591
'To fry Whitings. First flay them and wash them clean and scale them, that doon, lap them in floure and fry them in Butter and oyle. Then to serve them, mince apples or onions and fry them, then put them into a vessel with white wine, vergious, salt, pepper, cloves and mace, and boile them togither on the Coles, and serve it upon the Whitings.'
Ingredients: Either skin and fillet the fish or buy it pre-prepared: 700 g whiting, haddock or other white fish; 100 g butter or 100 ml olive oil; 225 g finely-chopped onions or apples; 1.5 ml mace; pinch of ground cloves; 275 ml white wine; 15 ml wine vinegar; 1.5 ml pepper; 5 ml salt; a little flour.
Method: Fry the onions or apples gently in a saucepan, in a little of the oil or butter, until cooked but not browned. Stir in the wine, vinegar, salt, pepper, cinnamon and mace and cook for a few minutes more. Keep hot, ready for use. Dust the fish with flour and gently fry in the remaining oil or butter for 5–10 minutes. Serve with the onion or apple sauce.

TO BAKE AN OLYVE-PYE – BEEF OLIVE OPEN PIE

Gervase Markham's *Countrey Contentments, or, The English Hus-wife*, 1615
Beef olives (stuffed rolled beef) baked in a pie.

'To make an excellent Olyve Pye: take sweet hearbs as Violet leaves, Strawberry leaves, Spinage, Succory, Endive, Tyme and Sorrel, and chop them as small as may be, and if there be a Scallion or two amongst them, it will give the better taste. Then take the yolks of Hard Eggs, with Currants, Cinnamon, Cloves, and Mace, and chop them among the hearbs also; Then having cut out long Olives (thin slices) of a leg of Veal, roule up more than three parts of the hearbs so mixed within the Olives, together with a good deal of sweet butter. Then having raised your crust of the finest and best paste, strow [strew = scatter] in the bottom the remainder of the hearbs, with a few great Raisins, having the stones pickt out. Then put in the Olives, and cover them with great Raisins, and a few Prunes: then over all lay good store of butter, and so bake them. Then being sufficiently bak't, take Claret Wine, Sugar, Cinamon, and two or three spoonfuls of Wine Vinegar, and boyl them together, and then drawing the Pye, at a vent in the top of the lid, put in the same, and then set it into the Oven again a little space, and so serve it forth.'

Ingredients for the filling: 5 or 6 slices of beef topside minute steaks; 200 g spinach; 150 g sorrel; 50 g chicory (this used to be called succory); 15 g strawberry leaves (if available); 15 g violet leaves (if available, they were used for thickening); 30 g endives; 3 spring onions, finely chopped; 1 tsp fresh thyme, finely chopped; 60 ml red wine; generous pinch of salt; 2 hard-boiled eggs, finely chopped; 1 hard-boiled egg yolk, finely chopped; 30 g currants; 30 g raisins; 30 g stoned prunes, finely chopped; 60 g softened butter; pinch each of cinnamon, mace and cloves.

Ingredients for the pastry: 225 g flour; 90 g softened butter; 2 egg yolks; 6 saffron threads ground into 1 tbsp warm water in a pestle and mortar.

Method for pastry: Sift the flour into a bowl, add the saffron threads and their steeping water along with the egg yolks and mix together well. Add three-quarters of the softened butter and mix in well. If all the flour does not come together into a dough, add a little more butter. Once the dough comes into a ball cut it into two pieces, one slightly larger than the other. Roll the larger piece of dough out and use this to line a 9-inch flan dish or other deep-sided dish. Cut off the excess pastry around the edge and place baking beads or dried beans in the pie base. Blind bake in an oven preheated to 200°C for 10 minutes. Reduce the heat to 180°C and continue baking for a further 5 minutes. Take the pastry from the oven and set aside to cool.

Method for filling: While baking, roughly chop the greens. Place a pan on the heat and add the wine, chopped greens, thyme and spring onions into the pan. Add a generous pinch of salt, cover and cook on medium heat for about four minutes, or until the greens have begun wilting. Drain immediately, reserving the cooking liquid. Prepare the meat by beating it out until thin and flat. Set aside and start making the filling. Place the chopped eggs, along with the currants, spices and two tablespoons of the reserved cooking liquid in a bowl and mix together. Divide this mixture amongst the steaks and top with a knob of butter, before rolling the meat (olives) up neatly and securing with a cocktail stick. Place the wilted greens in a bowl, add the raisins and prunes and mix together well. Line the bottom of the pastry with this mixture and arrange the rolled beef olives on top. Dot with the remaining butter and place in an oven at 190°C for about 35 minutes, or until the beef has cooked. Remove the cocktail sticks from the meat and serve.

FLORENTINES – MEAT FLORENTINE

A.W., *The Booke of Goode Cookry Very Necessary for all Such as Delight Therein*, 1584, 1591

Florentines now are biscuits, but in Tudor times were savouries.

'To make Florentines. Take Vele and some of the Kidney of the Loyne, or colde Veale roasted, colde capon or Phesant, which of them you wil, and mince it very small with sweet suet, put unto it two or three yolks of Egs, being hard sod, Corance and dates small shred, season it with a little sinamon and ginger, a very little cloves and mace, with a little Salte and sugar, a little Time being finely shred. Make your paste fine with butter and yolkes of Egs and Sugar, role it very thin and so lay it in a platter with butter underneath: and so cut your cover and lay it upon it.'

FLORENTINE – VEAL KIDNEY PIE

A.W., *The Booke of Goode Cookry Very Necessary for all Such as Delight Therein*, 1584, 1591

'To make a Florentine. Take the Kidney of Veale and boyle it a little, choppe it very fine. Then take Cloves, Mace and Pepper, and season it withall, then take an ounce of Biskets and as much of Carowayes, and put into your stuffe, make your paste of fine floure, butter Egges and Sugar and drive your paste very thin, and lay a sheet of paste in a dish and under it lay a little butter, and spread it abroad with your thumb, then lay your meat aloft on it in the dishe, then make the other sheet and cut it and lay it upon your meat. Then close it and cut it round about like a Starre, and set it in the Oven and let it abide a quarter of an houre, then take it out and wet it over with Butter, then cast sugar wet with rosewater upon it, then set it into the Oven again a little while, then take it out and serve it in.'

FLORENTINES WITH EELS FOR FISH DAYES – EEL FLORENTINE

A.W., *The Booke of Goode Cookry Very Necessary for all Such as Delight Therein*, 1584, 1591

'To make Florentines with Eeles for Fish dayes. Take great Eeles, fleye them and perboyle them a little, then take the fishe from the bones, and mince it small with some Wardens amongst it to make it to mince small, and season it with cloves and mace, pepper, Corance and Dates, and when you lay it into your paste, take a little fine Sugar and lay it upon before you cover it, and when it is halfe baked or altogither, laye a peece of sweet Butter upon cover, and a little rosewater and sugar. After the same manner, minced pyes of Eeles.'

A FLORENTINE OF FLESH – VEAL KIDNEY FLORENTINE

A.W., *The Booke of Goode Cookry Very Necessary for all Such as Delight Therein*, 1584, 1591

'A Florentine of Flesh. Take the Kidneies of Veale and chop them very small with Corance, dates, sinamon and Ginger, Sugar, salt, and the yolks of three Egs, and mingle altogither, and make a fine paste with yolks of egges, and butter, and let there be Butter in your dishe bottome, then drive them to small Cakes, and put one in the dish bottom, and lay your meat in, then lay your other upon your meat, and close them togither, and cut the cover and it, when it is baked then strew Sugar and serve it out.'

A FLORENTINE OF FISH – MOCK FISH FLORENTINE

A.W., *The Booke of Goode Cookry Very Necessary for all Such as Delight Therein*, 1584, 1591

'A Florentine of Fish. Take apples, grated bread, Corance, and chop your apples verye fine, and mingle your stuffe with yolkes of Egs, and drive out your paste as you do the other, put butter in your dish bottom and so serve it out.'

BAKED CHEKINS IN LYKE PAEST – FRUIT AND CHICKEN PIE

The Proper Newe Booke of Cookerye, c. 1557

A raised chicken pie layered with fruit.

'To bake chekins in lyke paeſt. Take youre chekins and ceaſon them with a lytle Ginger and ſalte, and ſo putte them into youre cofin, and ſo put in them barberies, grapes, or gooſe beryes, and halfe a dyſhe of butter, ſo clooſe them vp, and ſette them in the ouen, and when they are baken, take the yolkes of fyxe egges, and a dyſhfull of vergis and drawe them through a ſtreyner and ſette it vpon a chafingdyſhe, then drawe youre baken chekins and put thereto this fore ſayde egges and vergys, and thus ſerue them hoate.'

CHEKYNS FARSED – ROAST HERB-STUFFED CHICKEN

Gentyll Manly Cokere, MS Pepys 1047, c. 1490

Chickens roasted with an herb stuffing between the skin and meat.

'Chickens stuffed. Break the skin at the neck behind and blow him that the skin may arise from the flesh. Draw them, wash them clean and chop off the heads. Take the lean of fat pork boiled and hacked small with raw yolks of eggs and hard yolks minced small and raisins of Courance and other powders and herbs parboiled and hewed small. And put in saffron and salt. Do together all these and stuff thy chickens there with between the flesh and the skin and plunge them in hot broth and then make them smooth with thy hands that the stuff lay even under the skin. The parboil them a little, then roast them. And serve them forth.'

Ingredients: 1 large chicken; small tin of chopped pork; 3 hard-boiled egg yolks; 1 large egg, beaten; 25 g currants; 5 ml each of parsley, sage and thyme.

Method: Place the herbs in a drainer, scald and leave to cool. Mix the cooked egg yolks, the raw egg, pork, currants and herbs to form a smooth forcemeat. Make a space between the skin and body of the chicken by inserting the fingers from both ends. Pack the forcemeat as evenly as possible between the skin and flesh, then truss the chicken with string for roasting. Preheat the oven to 200°C. Plunge the chicken into a large pan of boiling water for 15 minutes and then remove. Place on a grid in a roasting tin and roast in the oven for 20 minutes per 450 g, plus a further 20 minutes. If you wish, after the chicken has been in the oven for 30 minutes, remove it, dredge with flour and baste with butter and put it back, to give a better colour.

ALLOWES OF EELS – ROAST STUFFED EELS

A.W., *The Booke of Goode Cookry Very Necessary for all Such as Delight Therein*, 1584, 1591

Possibly a starter or snack, to 'splat' an eel must mean to split it. I am unsure of the meaning of 'culpines'.

'To make Allowes of Eeles. Take and splat an Eele by the back, and keepe the belly whole, and so take out the bone, then take onions, percely, Time, and Rosemary chopped together, and put therto pepper and salt, and a little Saffron, and so lay it upon the Eeles, and then wrap it up in Culpines, and put them upon a spit and so roast them.'

BOYLED PIGEONS WITH RICE – PIGEONS (CHICKEN) IN RICE PUDDING

Sir Hugh Plat's *Delightes for Ladies*, 1602

This seems to us a strange combination, yet again, but it works well. 'Sweet herbs' referred to those herbs that could be eaten raw or could be added directly to stews and pottages. All other herbs were 'pot-herbs' and required blanching before consumption. Those most usually employed for purposes of cooking, such as the flavouring of soups, sauces, forcemeats, etc., were thyme, sage, mint, marjoram, savory and basil. They were sometimes tied into a bunch, much like a bouquet garni, but this latter method was more likely to be used for pot-herbs, to remove from the dish prior to serving. Sweet herbs were typically soft-leaved herbs used in enhancing the flavour of a dish, while 'savoury herbs' or 'pot-herbs' with strong, penetrating flavours were used to flavour stews cooked in pots. Sweet herbs tend to be annual in nature, are not woody and have aromatic oils that give a pleasant fragrance when crushed. They break down into the stock and do not need to be removed. They can often be eaten raw and can be added to salads to improve the flavour.

'To boyle Pigeons with rice. Boyle them in mutton broth, putting fweete hearbes in their bellies, then take a little Rice and boyle it in Creame, with a little whole mace, feason it with fugar, lay it thick on their breafts, wringing alfo the iuice of a Lemmon vpon them, and fo ferue them.'

Ingredients: 4 pigeons, or 6 chicken breasts; 400 ml mutton broth; sweet herbs in any combination of thyme, sage, mint, marjoram, savory and basil, for stuffing; 100 g rice; 500 ml single cream; 4 tbsp sugar; 2 blades of mace; 1 lemon.

Method: Use the herbs to stuff the pigeons then place in a pan with the mutton broth. Bring to the boil, reduce to a gentle simmer, cover and continue cooking for about 40 minutes, or until the pigeons are tender. In the meanwhile, wash the rice and place in a saucepan with the cream and mace. Bring to a simmer and cook, stirring constantly for about 30 minutes, or until the rice is tender and the mixture is thick. Remove the mace and stir in the sugar. When the pigeons are done, transfer to serving dishes. Spoon over the rice mixture then squeeze over the juice from the lemon and serve.

BOYLED CAPON IN WHITE BROTH – SWEET AND SOUR ALMOND CHICKEN

Sir Hugh Plat's *Delightes for Ladies*, 1602

This is a traditional Elizabethan recipe for boiled chicken (or rabbit) served in a sweet and sour mutton broth and white wine base, with mixed greens and herbs.

'To boyle a Capon in white broth. Boyle your Capon by it felfe in faire water, then take a ladlefull or two of mutton broth and a little white wine, a little whole mace, a bundle of fweete hearbs, a little marrowe, thicken it with Almonds, feafon it with fugar, and a little veriuyce, boyle a fewe currants by themſelues, and a Date quartered, leaſt you diſcolor your broth, and put it on the breaſt of your Capon, Chicken or Rabbet: if you haue no Almonds, thicken it with Creame, or with yolkes of egges, garniſh your diſhes on the ſides with a Lemmon ſliced and ſugar.'

Ingredients: 1 capon or large chicken; half a large onion; 400 ml mutton broth; 100 ml white wine; 100 g ground almonds; 1 blade of mace; 1 bunch of sweet herbs, securely tied; 50 g beef marrow, finely chopped; 1 tbsp sugar; 2 tbsp verjuice or white wine vinegar; 4 tbsp currants; 1 quartered date.

Method: Wash and dry the chicken. Place into a large pot, cover with water and the halved onion and bring to the boil. Reduce to a simmer, cover and cook for about 2 hours, or until the chicken is cooked through and tender. In the meanwhile, prepare the sauce. Combine the mutton broth and white wine in a small pan. Bring to a boil and then remove from the heat and pour over the ground almonds. Mix together well, pour the mixture into a food processor and purée. Pour the resultant almond milk into a clean pan and add the mace, sweet herbs and beef marrow. Bring to a simmer and cook for 10 minutes until thickened and flavoured by the herbs. Remove from the heat and set aside to infuse. Around 10 minutes before the chicken is due to be ready, strain the flavoured almond milk and pour into a pan. Stir in the sugar and verjuice and bring to a simmer. Combine the currants and quartered date in a small pan. Barely cover with water, bring to a simmer and cook for a few minutes, until the fruit are tender and plumped up. Drain and set aside. When the chicken is ready, remove from the pan, pat dry and arrange on a serving dish. Pour over the almond milk mixture, garnish with the fruit and serve.

BAKED FISH

A.W., *The Booke of Goode Cookry Very Necessary for all Such as Delight Therein*, 1584, 1591

'To bake Carp, Bream, Mullet, Pike, Trout, Roche or any other kinde of Fish. Season them with Cloves and Mace, and pepper, and bake them with smal raisins, sweete butter and Vergious, great raisins, and some prunes.'

BAKED EELES – EEL PIE

John Murrel's *A New Booke of Cookerie*, 1615

'To bake Eeles. Cut your Eeles about the length of your finger: season them with Pepper, Salt, and Ginger, and so put them into a Coffin, with a good piece of sweet Butter. Put into your Pye great Razins of the Sunne, and an Onyon minst small, and so close it and bake it.'

Ingredients: 2 lbs eel, cut into slivers; ½ cup onion, finely chopped; ½ cup raisins; 1 tsp pepper; 1 tsp ginger; ½ tsp salt; 1½ tbsp butter; pie crust.

Method: Mix all ingredients, except the butter, and put into pie crust. Smooth butter over the mixture and cover the pie. Bake at 180°C for 45–50 minutes, or until eel is cooked.

BLANK DESSORRE – CHICKEN IN WHITE ALMOND SAUCE

Two Fifteenth Century Cookbooks – Harleian MS. 279 & Harl. MS. 4016, c. 1440

'Take blanched almonds, grind them and temper them with white wine, or on a flesh day with broth and cast therein the flour of rice or amydoun [wheat flour starch] and thicken it therewith. Take the ground flesh of capons. Take sugar and salt and place in the broth and garnish with white aniseed comfits. Take a vessel, put in saffron, mix with the blank dessorre and serve it forth.'

Ingredients: 300 g cooked chicken, minced; 400 ml almond milk; 3 tbsp rice flour; sugar and salt to taste.

Method: Add the almond milk to a pan, stir in the rice flour and add the chicken. Bring to the boil then reduce to a simmer and cook for 20 minutes, or until the mixture thickens appreciably. Add salt and sugar to taste, then serve it immediately in side bowls or over meat or fish.

TO BOYLE A CHINE OF VEALE – VEAL OR CHICKEN IN SWEET AND SOUR HERB SAUCE

Sir Hugh Plat's *Delightes for Ladies*, 1602

Chine is the backbone and surrounding meat of an animal. Chicken is preferred to veal, but any other white meat can be used.

'To boyle a chine of veale, or a chicken in fharpe broth with hearbes. Take a little mutton broth, white wine and veriuice, and a little whole mace, then take Lettuce, Spinage, and Parfley, and bruife it, and put it into your broth, feasoning it with veriuice, pepper and a little fugar, and fo ferue it.

Ingredients: 1 chicken; 500 ml mutton broth; 150 ml white wine; 60 ml verjuice or white wine vinegar; 2 blades of mace; 2 'Little Gem' lettuce, shredded; 100 g spinach, washed and shredded; 1 bunch of shredded parsley; verjuice, to taste; freshly-ground black pepper to taste; sugar to taste.

Method: Clean and gut the chicken or buy pre-prepared. Cover and boil in water until tender. Cut or joint the meat into serving pieces and set aside. Combine the mutton broth, white wine, verjuice and mace in a pan and bring to a simmer. Combine the lettuce, spinach and parsley in a mortar and bruise lightly then mix into the stock. Bring to a simmer, add the meat and cook until all the ingredients have heated through. Season with black pepper to taste, Adjust the sweet and sour balance with the verjuice or white wine vinegar and sugar. Serve hot, ladled into bowls and upon bread.

THE SYDES OF A DERE OF HYE GRECE ROSTYDE – ROASTED VENISON

Gentyll Manlie Cokerie MS Pepys 1047, c. 1490

'The venison first shall be the lord o' th' feast' – *Cymbeline*, William Shakespeare. This recipe describes the actions of turning the spit and using the fat to baste the meat. Describing deer in his *A Description of Elizabethan England* in 1577, William Harrison wrote: 'Of these also the stag is accounted for the most noble game, the fallow deer is the next, then the roe, whereof we have indifferent store.' Venison was very much a noble's dish, as Andrew Boorde described in his *A Compendyous Regiment or a Dyetary of Healthe* (1546): 'I haue gone rounde about Chrystendome, and ouerthwarte Chrystendome, and a thousande or two and moore myles out of Chrystendome, Yet there is not so moche pleasure for Harte and Hynde, Bucke and Doe, and for Roo-Bucke and Doe, as is in Englande lande: and although the flesshe be dispraysed in physicke, – I praye God to sende me parte of flesshe toeate, physicke notwithstanding – all physicions sayth that Venson … doth ingendre colorycke humours; and of trueth it doth so: Wherefore let them take the skynne, and let me haue the flesshe. I am sure it is a Lordes dysshe, and I am sure it is good for an Englysheman, for it doth anymate hym to be as he is: whiche is stronge and hardy. But I do aduertyse euery man, for all my wordes, not to kyll and so to eate of it, excepte it be lawfully, for it is a meate for great men. And great men do not set so moche by the meate, as they doth by the pastyme of kyllynge of it.'

'Wash the sides of a deer. Remove the fillets and put them on a spit and roast them. Put them on the spit outer-wards and a loaf of bread crosswise. Take red wine, powder of pepper and salt, and baste them with this until done. Have a charger underneath to keep the drippings. Baste again with the drippings then serve it forth.'

ROAST VENISON, FIRST PARBOILED

A.W., *The Booke of Goode Cookry Very Necessary for all Such as Delight Therein*, 1584, 1591

'First perboile it, and then make it tender cast it into cold water, then Lard it and roste it, and for sauce take broth, Vinagre, Pepper, Cloves and mace, with a little salt and boile these togither and serve it upon your Venison.'

STEWED COLOPES OF VENISON – VENISON STEW

A Noble Boke of Cookry – Holkham MSS, c. 1468–75

According to recipes indexed in the *Concordance of English Recipes*, between the thirteenth and fifteenth centuries venison was served in *brewet*, stewed, served in broth, in sauce, in pastry or in pies and with frumenty. It was baked, roasted, preserved, salted and served as steaks or collops. At least six recipes were for noumbles or humbles of venison and another three recipes were for venison with *pevorade* sauce. Collops, or *colopes*, usually referred to slices of bacon.

'To mak stewed colopes tak collopes of venyson rostid and put them in a pot and do therto hole cloves, pouder of pepper, canelle and other spice and boille it up with a gret part of swet brothe and sesson it up with pouder gyngir and the venyson and serve it.'

VENISON COFFINS – DEER PASTIES

A.W., *The Booke of Goode Cookry Very Necessary for all Such as Delight Therein*, 1584, 1591

'Cut the Venison in faire peeces, in quantitie as you will have your pasties, and perboyle it, that doon stick the grain side ful of Cloves, and Lard the lean side with good lard, and season it with pepper, salt, and all manner of spices; then put the grained side of the venison downwards into the coffin of brown paste, and so close it and bake it, and when it is open turn the grain side upward.'

VINEGARED RED DEARE PYE

Thomas Dawson's *The Good Huswifes Jewell*, 1585, 1594, 1596

'To bake Red deare. Take a hand full of time, and a hand full of rosemarie, a hand full of winter savorie, a hand full of bay leaves and a hand full of fennel, and when your liquor seethes that you perboyle your venison in, put in your hearbes also and perboyle your venison untill it be halfe enough. Then take it out and lay it upon a faire boorde that the water may runne out from it, then take a knife and pricke it full of holes, and while it is warme have a faire traye with vineger therein, and so put your venison therein from morning vntill night, and ever nowe and then turne it up side downe, and then at night have your coffin ready, and this done season it with synamome, ginger, and nutmegges, pepper and salte, and when you have seasoned it, put it into your coffin, and put a good quantitie of sweete butter into it. And then put it into the Oven at night, when you goe to bedde, and in the morning drawe it forth, and put in a saucer full of vineger into your pye at a hole above in the toppe of it, so that the vineger may runne into everie place of it, and then stop the whole againe and turne the bottome upward and so serve it in.'

RED DEERE, FALLOW-DEERE, SWANNE OR RAMME MUTTON COFFINS – VENISON/SWAN, MUTTON PIES

Gervase Markham's *Countrey Contentments, or, The English Hus-wife*, 1615

'When you bake red Deere, you shall first parboile it and take out the bones, then you shall if it be leane larde it, if fat save the charge, then put it into a presse to squeese out the blood; then for a night lay it in a meare sauce made of Vinegar, small drinke and salt, and then taking it forth, season it well with Pepper finely beaten, and salt well mixt together, and see that you lay good store there of, both upon and in every open and hollow place of the Venison. But by no meanes cut any slashes to put in the pepper, for it will of it selfe sinke fast enough into the flesh, and be more pleasant in the eating. Then having raised the coffin, lay in the bottome a thicke course of butter, then lay the flesh thereon and couer it all over with butter, and so bake it as much as if you did bake great browne bread. Then when you draw it, melt more butter with three or fowre spoonefull of Vinegar, and twice so much Claret wine, and at a vent hole on the toppe of the lidde powre in the same till it can receive no more, and so let it stand and coole. And in this sort you may bake Fallow-deere, or Swanne, or whatsoever else you please to keepe colde, the meare sauce only being left out which is only proper to red Deere. And if to your meare sauce you adde a little Turnesole, and therein steepe beefe, or Ramme mutton. You may also in the same manner take the first for Red-deere Venison, and the latter for Fallow, and a very good iudgement shall not be able to say otherwise, then that it is of it selfe perfect Venison, both in taste, colour, and the manner of cutting.'

BOYLED PIGS PETITOES – **PIGS' TROTTERS**

Thomas Dawson's A Booke of Cokerie, *1620*

Petit toes, small toes, was the original term for pigs' feet, or trotters.

'To boyle a Pigs Petitoes. Take and boyle them in a pint of Vergice and Mastard; take 4 Dates minced with a few small Raisins, then take a little Time and chop it small and season it with a little Sinamon and Ginger, and a quantity of Vergice.'

BLEWE MANGER – **WHITE CHICKEN PATÉ**

The Proper Newe Booke of Cookerye, c. 1557

The use of *blanc* (white) and *manger* (to eat), meant white food, often using almond milk. The original recipe specifies a 'pottle' each of milk and cream, but a pottle was half a gallon of liquid and would call for eight pints of liquid. The recipe also calls for the 'brawne' of a chicken, i.e. dark meat, but as the dish should be very pale, chicken breast is best. This can also be served as a first course and a different recipe is given in that chapter. Rye flour is used as a thickener, so you could substitute rice flour, plain flour or cornflour.

'To make Blewe manger. Take a capon and cut out the brawne of hym a lyue and perboyle the brawne tyll the fleſſhe come from the bone, and then drye hym as drye as you canne, in a fayre clothe, then take a payre of cardes, and carde hym as fmall as is poffyble, and then take a pottell of mylke and a pottel of creame, and halfe a pounde of Rye flower, and your carded brawne of the capon, and putte all into a pan, and ftere it al together and fet it vpon the fyre, and whait begynneth to boyle put thereto halfe a pounde of beaten Suger and a faufer full of Rofe water, and fo let it boyle tyll it be very thicke, then put it into a charger tyll it be colde, and then ye maye flyce it as ye doe lieche and fo ferue it in.'

Ingredients: 4 chicken breasts; 500 ml single cream; 500 ml whole milk; 50 g caster sugar; 4 tbsp rose water; 50 g rye flour.

Method: Bring a pan of lightly salted water to the boil. Add the chicken and simmer for about 40 minutes, or until tender. Take out the chicken, remove the skin and chop the meat as finely as possible. This is easier with a food processor. Mix the milk and cream in a jug and work some of this into the rye flour to make a smooth paste. Pour the remaining milk and cream mixture into a pan, then whisk in the rye flour paste and the chopped chicken meat until smooth. Bring to a simmer and then stir in the sugar until dissolved. Continue cooking gently whilst stirring constantly, until the mixture is thick like custard. Now stir in the rose water and continue cooking for a few minutes. Remove from the heat. Line a small loaf tin or a dish with a sheet of cling film and pour in the blancmange mixture. Set aside to cool until hardened then turn out and cut into slices for serving.

YMBRE DAY TARTE – EMBER DAY SWEET QUICHE

The Master-Cook of Richard II, *The Forme of Cury, c.* 1390

This can form a starter, snack or part of a main meal. Ember days are four separate sets of three days within the same week, Wednesday, Friday and Saturday, roughly equidistant in the circuit of the year, that were formerly set aside for special fasting and prayer. The days were considered especially suitable for the ordination of clergy. Eating meat was forbidden and an Ember Day Tart was a filling dish served on these fasting days. The recipe uses galingale but you can use ginger as a substitute, if it is not easily available.

'Tart in embre day: take and parboile onynons; presse out the water and hewe hem smale; take brede and bray it in a mortar, and temper it up with ayren [eggs]; do perto butter, safron, spice and salt and corans and a ltel sugar with powdor douce, and bake it in a trap, and serve it forth.'

Ingredients: 2 large onions; 1 tbsp melted butter; 4 eggs; 2 tbsp breadcrumbs; a pinch each of saffron, galingale and mace; ⅛ tsp sugar; ½ tsp salt; 2 tbsp currants; 250 g of shortcrust pastry.

Method: Chop the onions and parboil for about 5 minutes. Strain, add the butter and then set aside to cool. Mix the remaining ingredients in a bowl and add the onions. Make either an 8-inch pastry case or 12 individual-sized cases. If making the latter, roll out the pastry, cut into small circles using the top of a cup and place on a baking tray. Spoon the mixture into the pastry cases. Bake at 180°C for 30–40 minutes for the large pie or 15–20 minutes for the individual tarts. The filling should be set and the pastry lightly browned.

YMBRE DAY TARTE – EMBER DAY SAVOURY QUICHE

Curye on Inglysch, fourteenth century

'Grene chese' is any well-aged cheese. Other versions have bread instead of cheese, so you could use a mix of both.

'Tart in ymbre day. Take and perboile oynouns and erbis and presse out þe water and hewe hem smale. Take grene chese and bray it in a morter, and temper it vp with ayren. Do þerto butter, saffroun and salt, and raisons corauns, and a litel sugur with powdour douce, and bake it in a trap, and serue it forth.'

Ingredients: 3–4 small onions, chopped; 2 bunches of chopped parsley; 1 cup shredded Cheddar cheese (or ½ cup unseasoned bread crumbs); 8 beaten eggs; 1 tbsp melted butter; ⅛ tsp saffron; ½ tsp salt; ¼ cup currants; ¼ tsp. sugar; ⅛ tsp each cloves and mace; 1 9-inch pie shell; spices – you can use ½ tsp of any 'sweet' herbs such as sage, basil, thyme, etc. (optional).

Method: Parboil or sauté the onions and parsley, drain well. Mix with all other ingredients and place in pie shell. Bake at 180°C for 35–40 minutes or until pastry is golden brown and the filling is set.

PYGGE Y-FARSYD – STUFFED PIGLET, GOAT OR SHEEP

A Noble Boke off Cookry ffor a Prynce Houssolde, Holkham MSS 674, 1480. Also in *Two Fifteenth-Century Cookery-Books, Liber Cure Cocorum.*

There are many medieval recipes for stuffed pig, goat or sheep. In the absence of a goat or pig, I have substituted an 8-pound pork loin, closed and tied with string.

'Pygge y-farsyd. Take raw Eyroun, and draw hem thorw a straynoure; than grate fayre brede; take Safroun and Salt, and pouder of Pepir, and Swet of a schepe, and melle alle to-gederys in a fayre bolle; then broche thin Pygge; then farce hym, and sewe the hole, and lat hym roste; and than serue forth.'

Ingredients: 8 lb joint of pork loin, tied; 4 eggs; 8 slices bread, ground; ½ cup raisins; ½ tsp ginger; ½ tsp salt; ½ tsp pepper; pinch of saffron.

Method: Pass the uncooked eggs through a strainer and mix in the ground bread and raisins. In a small bowl, mix the spices well, then add to the eggs and bread, again mixing well. Stuff your 'piglet' and bake at 180°C, until done. If you have a meat thermometer, the internal temperature should be 70°C.

VAUTES – SWEET AND SOUR FRUIT AND KIDNEY OMELETTE

The Proper Newe Booke of Cookerye, c. 1557

'Take the kydney of veale and perboyle it tyll it be tender, then take and choppe it fmall wyth the yolkes of three or foure egges, then ceafon it wyth dates fmall cutte, fmall Reyfons, Gynger, fuger, fyamon, faffron, and a lyttle falte, and for the paeft to laye it in, take a dofen of egges, bothe the whyte and the yolkes, and beate theym well altogether, then take butter, and put it into a frying panne, and frye them as thynne as a pancake, then laye your ftuffe therein, and fo frye them together in a panne, and cafte fuger and gynger vpon it, and fo ferue it forthe.'

Ingredients: 1 veal kidney or mutton kidney; 3 egg yolks; 3 finely-chopped dates; 3 tbsp seedless raisins; ¼ tsp ground ginger; 1 tbsp brown sugar; ¼ tsp ground cinnamon; pinch of crumbled saffron; salt to taste; 6 beaten eggs; 30 g butter for frying; sugar and ginger for seasoning. Cayenne pepper, thyme or parsley (optional).

Method: Clean the kidney, removing any membranes. Add the kidney to a pot of boiling water and simmer for about 30 minutes, or until tender. Remove the kidney, allow to cool and then core and chop the meat finely. Mix well in a bowl with the 3 egg yolks, dates, raisins, ginger, cinnamon and saffron. You could add a little cayenne pepper for taste, although it is not a Tudor addition. Cover and set aside in the refrigerator for about 20 minutes, for the dates and raisins to expand. Beat the 6 eggs in a bowl. Add thyme or parsley if you like a herb omelette. Melt the butter in a large frying pan, add the eggs and fry a very thin omelette. A few minutes before the omelette is completely set, place the meat and fruit filling over one half. Fold the omelette over and fry for about 2 minutes more or until the base is browned. Place under a hot grill and cook until the top is golden. Serve garnished with a little sugar and ginger.

STOCKE FRYTURES – FRUIT AND KIDNEY PASTY OR FRITTERS

The Proper Newe Booke of Cookerye, c. 1557

This is similar to a Cornish pasty, with a blend of cooked kidney and fruit that can be baked or fried.

Ingredients: Filling as for *Vautes*, the above recipe; 1 batch of pie crust pastry.

Method: While the mixture is cooling, prepare the pastry by dividing in half and rolling into two circles, about the size of a saucer each. Arrange the filling over one half of both pastry circles, then fold over the other half to produce a crescent shape. Pinch the edges of the pasties closed and place on a baking tray in an oven preheated to 180°C. Bake for about 25 minutes, or until golden brown. Alternatively, heat olive oil to a depth of about 1 cm in a deep frying pan. When hot add the stocke frytures and fry for about 8 minutes per side, or until golden brown.

THE CORNISH (OR DEVON) PASTY
Traditional Tudor – The Cornish Pasty Association

While the above dish is similar to a Devon or Cornish pasty, it is worthwhile considering its history. Pastry dishes became very popular at this time, with many recipes for both sweet and savoury fillings baked in pie crusts or 'coffyns'. It is commonly held that the Cornish pasty was made for Cornish tin and copper miners as their midday meal. Tin, and its associated mineral arsenic, are poisonous and it is thought that the crust was held along its edge, while the sweet and savoury filling was eaten. Pasties were also common in the great Welsh copper mines. Some of the first references to a 'pasty' appear during the reign of Henry III (1207–72) but the OED suggests that 'pasty' was identified around 1300.

Great Yarmouth was bound in Henry III's time to send to the sheriffs of Norwich one hundred herrings every year, baked in twenty-four pasties, to be conveyed to the King. The pasty became commonplace in the sixteenth and seventeenth centuries and only really attained its Cornish identity during the last 200 years. By the eighteenth century it was firmly established as a Cornish food eaten by poorer working families who could only afford cheap ingredients such as potatoes, swede or turnip and onion. Miners and farm workers took this portable and easy to eat convenience food with them to work because it was so well suited to the purpose. Its size and shape made it easy to carry, its pastry case insulated the contents and was durable enough to survive, while its wholesome ingredients provided enough sustenance to see the workers through their long and arduous working days. They were also taken down the Welsh coal pits.

There is an early reference to pasties in a letter from a baker to Jane Seymour which includes: 'hope this pasty reaches in better condition than the last one …' Also in Shakespeare's *All's Well That Ends Well*, Parolles says: 'I will confess to what I know without constraint: if ye pinch me like a pasty, I can say no more'. Shakespeare also writes, in *The Merry Wives of Windsor* (1600), 'Come, we have a hot pasty to dinner.' The shout 'Oggie, Oggie, Oggie' is said to originate from Cornish miners calling for their pasties (also known as *oggies* or *tiddy oggies*). The crimped dirty crust was then left for the 'knockers', ghosts, which were said to exist down the mines. It was said that the devil would never dare to cross the River Tamar into Cornwall for fear of ending up as a filling in a Cornish pasty.

The English word pasty derives from the Old French word 'paste', meaning a pie filled with venison, salmon or other meat, vegetables or cheese and baked without a dish. The earliest version of *Le Viandier* has been dated to around 1300 and contains several pasty recipes, and in 1393, *Le Menagier de Paris* contains recipes for *pasté* with venison, veal, beef or mutton. No less than 5,500 venison pasties were served at the installation feast of George Neville, Archbishop of York and chancellor of England, in 1465.

In 2006, a researcher in Devon discovered a recipe for a pasty tucked inside an audit book and dated 1510, which replaced the previous oldest recipe, dated 1746, held by the Cornwall Records Office. The Devon dish at the time was cooked with venison, at the Mount Edgecumbe estate of one of Henry VII's greatest supporters, Richard Edgecumbe. The recipe details the ingredients of flour, pepper and venison that was used in the pasties and calculates the cost of the items and labour involved in making them. The Devon ledger also included the price of a pasty in Plymouth in 1509. Some sources state that the difference between a Devon and a Cornish pasty is that a Devon pasty has a top-crimp and is oval in shape, whereas the Cornish pasty is semicircular and side-crimped along the curve. Pasties with a top crimp have been made in Cornwall for generations, but the Cornish bakers who favour this method can no longer legally call their pasties 'Cornish.'

Catherine Brown, co-author of *The Taste of Britain*, points out that the pasty was only one of many regional variations on a theme: 'Hand-held pies were developed as a solution for people who didn't have ready access to tables or knives and forks, they were a working-class version of the festive and symbolic pies that graced the tables of the upper classes. It was actually the first takeaway food.' In the same tradition were 'Scotch pies', made with lamb and topped with gravy, beans or vegetables, carried by working men everywhere, or the small pork pies of the English shires, made for farm labourers to eat in the fields. In Cornwall, there were 'two course' pasties, made with fruit at one end, and meat and vegetables at the other. A similar suet crust dumpling made in Bedfordshire was known as a 'Bedfordshire Clanger.' The 'clanger' would usually have diced potatoes and vegetables at one end and jam or sweetened apple at the other. A crimp mark would signify which end of the pasty to begin eating first. The sugar content in the sweet part would provide an instant energy boost, whilst the carbohydrates in the pastry and potatoes would provide a slower release of energy.

Today's pasties usually contain a filling of beef steak, onion, potato and swede with salt and white pepper, but historically workingmens' pasties had a variety of different fillings. In Cornwall, 'turmut, 'tates and mate', turnip, potatoes and meat was a common filling. The 'licky pasty' contained mostly leeks and the herb pasty contained watercress, parsley and shallots. Pasties were also often made with sweet fillings such as jam, apple, blackberry, plums or cherries. The Cornish Pasty Association tells us that this is the recipe for a traditional Cornish pasty, enough to make four good sized pasties. Of course, potatoes would have been added after Tudor times, with turnips or other vegetables being used as filler, owing to the lesser likelihood of having a meat filling, except for the upper classes.

Ingredients for the pastry: It is important to use a stronger flour than normal, as you need the extra strength in the gluten to produce strong pliable pastry. 500 g strong bread flour; 120 g white shortening; 25 g cake margarine; 5 g salt; 175 g cold water.

Ingredients for the filling: 450 g good quality beef, e.g. skirt; 450 g Maris Piper or Wilja potatoes; 250 g swede; 200 g onion; salt and pepper to taste (2/1 ratio); clotted cream or butter (optional).

Method: Mix the fat lightly into the flour until it resembles breadcrumbs. Add water and beat in a food mixer until the pastry clears and becomes elastic. This will take longer than normal pastry, but it gives the pastry the strength that it needs to hold the filling and retain a good shape. Leave to rest for 3 hours in a refrigerator. This is a very important stage as it is almost impossible to roll and shape pastry when fresh. For the filling, chop the ingredients finely then add them to the rolled out circles of pastry. Layer the vegetables and meat, adding plenty of seasoning. Put your knob of cream or butter on top. Then bring the pastry around and crimp with a fork.

Cooking time and temperature: Gas No.6, approx 50–60 minutes; electric 210°C, approx 50–60 minutes; fan-assisted 165°C, approx 40 mins.

MORE AND MORE PASTIES
Le Ménagier de Paris, 1393

'Come, we have a hot Venison pasty to dinner' – *The Merry Wives of Windsor*
Under Richard II in 1379, certain regulations were laid down to specify what might be included in a pasty and what must not be included. The regulations also spelled out the punishment for offending pasty-makers. His *Ordinances of the Pastelers, or Piebakers, as to pasties* reads: 'Because the Pastelers of the City of London have heretofore baked in pasties rabbits, geese, and garbage, not befitting, and sometimes stinking, in deceit of the people; and also, have baked beef in pasties, and sold the same for venison, in deceit of the people; it is therefore, by assent of the four Master Pastelers, and at their prayer, it is ordered and assented to.- In the first place, – that no one of the said trade

shall bake rabbits in pasties for sale, on pain of paying, the first time, if found guilty thereof, 6s 8d, to the use of the Chamber, and of going bodily to prison, at the will of the Mayor; the second time, 13s 4d, to the use of the Chamber, and of going etc. Also, – that no one of the said trade shall buy of any cook of Bredestret, or, at the hostels of the great lords, of the cooks of such lords, and garbage from capons, hens, or geese, to bake in a pasty, and sell, under the same penalty. Also, – that no one of the said trade shall bake either whole geese in a pasty, halves of geese, or quarters of geese, for sale, on the pain aforesaid.' Can one imagine cooking a whole goose in a pasty?

'Fresh VENISON PASTY. You must parboil the venison, and skim it, then lard it and make pastry: this is the way to make pasties of all fresh venison; and it should be cut in big, long pieces like rolling-pins, and this is called "pasty of larded boiled meat."

BEEF PASTIES. Have good young beef and remove all the fat, and the less good parts are cut in pieces to be used for stock, and then it is carried to the pastry-cook to be chopped up: and the grease with beef marrow. The meat of a leg of beef is sliced up and put in pastry; and when the pastry is cooked, it is appropriate to throw a wild duck sauce into it.

MUTTON PASTIES. Chopped very small with scallions.

VEAL PASTIES. Take the round part of the thigh, and put with it almost as much beef fat; and with this you make six good pasties in platters.'

ROASTED HARE

A.W., *The Booke of Goode Cookry Very Necessary for all Such as Delight Therein*, 1584, 1591

'Wash him in faire water, then perboile him, and lay him in colde water againe, then Larde him and roast him on a Broche, then to make sauce for him, take red vinagre, Salt, Pepper, ginger, Cloves, Mace, and put them togither, then mince apples and onions, and fry them in a Panne, then put your sauce to them with a little sugar, and let them boyle well togither, then baste it upon your Hare, and so serve it.'

STEWED STEKES OF MUTTON – LAMB AND ALE CASSEROLE

The Proper Newe Booke of Cookerye, c. 1557

Ingredients: 1 kg mutton (or lamb) leg steaks, cut into strips; 500 ml bottle of good quality ale, porter or stout; 2 large onions, sliced into rings; 50 g unsalted butter; salt and freshly-ground black pepper, to taste.

Method: Combine the meat and onions in a casserole dish. Pour the beer over and bring to a simmer. Skim any scum from the surface and then add the butter. Reduce to a simmer and cover the casserole with a tight-fitting lid.

Cook gently for about 40 minutes, until the meat is very tender. Season to taste and serve.

CAPOUN IN SALOME – ROAST CHICKEN WITH A MARBLED SAUCE
Potage Dyvers, 1430–40

This recipe has sandalwood (saunders) in it. Sandalwood is now considered incense and has a very strong flavour, so use the very barest pinch.

'Take a capon and scald it, and roast it. Then take thick almond milk, mix it with white wine or red. Take a little sandalwood and a little saffron, and make it marble coloured, and cover with this at your kitchen dresser. Sprinkle with milk so that it is most comely, and serve forth.'

Ingredients: 1 roasted chicken; 1 cup melted fat, from the chicken; 1 cup almond milk; 1 tsp saffron; a very small pinch of sandalwood; ½ cup red or white wine.

Method: Melt the fat from the chicken, including the jellified part, and add the almond milk and the saffron. Stir the sandalwood in and taste, before you think of adding more. Simmer the sauce until slightly reduced and pour over the roast chicken.

VAUNT – EGG, PRUNE, DATE AND CURRANT PIE
The Good Huswifes Handmaide for the Kitchin, 1594, 1597 (and 1588)

The first reference to a *vaunt* occurs in 1508 in Wynkyn de Worde's *Boke of Kervynge* (Book of Carving). The recipe includes beef marrow and in Tudor times fatty bone marrow was commonly included in such fruit dishes to add richness.

'To make a Vaunt. Take marrow of Beefe, as much as you can hold in both your hands, cut it as big as great dice. Then take ten Dates, cut them as big as smal dice: then take thirtie Prunes and cut the fruite from the stones, then take halfe a handfull of Corrans, washe them and picke them, then put your marrow in a cleane platter, and your Dates, Prunes, and Corrans: then take ten yolks of Egs, and put into your stuffe afore rehearsed. Then take a quartern of Sugar, and more, and beat it smal and put to your marow. Then take two spoonfuls of Synamon, and a spoonful of Sugar, and put them to your stuffe, and mingle them all together, then take eight yolkes of Egs, and four spoonfuls of Rosewater, straine them, and put a litle Sugar to it. Then take a fair frying pan, and put a litle peece of butter in it, as much as a Walnut, and set it vpon a good fire, and when it looketh almost blacke, put it out of your pan, and as fast as you can, put halfe of the yolkes of Egs, into the midst of your pan, and let it run all the bredth of your pan, and frie it faire and yellow, and when it is fryed put it in a faire dish, and put your stuffe therein, and spread it al the bottome of the dish, and then make another vaunt euen as you made the other, and set it vpon a faire borde and cut it in faire slices, of the breadth of your litle finger, as long as your Vaunt is; then lay it vpon your stuffe after the fashion of a lattice window, and then cut off the ends of them, as much as lyeth without the inward compasse of the dish. Then set the dish within the Oven or in a baking pan, and let it bake with leisure, and when it is baken ynough the marrow will come faire out of the vaunt, vnto the brim of the dish. Then draw it out, and cast theron a litle sugar, and so you may serue it in.'

POMPYS – DECORATED MEATBALLS
Potage Dyvers, 1430–40

'Take beef, pork or veal, one of them, and raw. Chop it up at the dresser, then grind it in a mortar as small as you can. Then add raw yolks of eggs, wine, and a little white sugar. Also add powdered pepper, mace, cloves, cubeb [a pungent Indonesian spice], canella [an inferior form of cinnamon], cinnamon, and salt, and a little saffron. Then make it into small pellets, round enough. Make sure you have a good pot of fresh broth of beef or capon, and ladle it on and let it boil till they are done enough. Then take good milk of almonds, with cold fresh broth of beef, veal, mutton or capon, and mix it with rice flour and with the spices. And at the dresser, put the pellets in a dish, and then pour on the sauce, and serve. Or else make a good syrup and lay the pellets on top at the dresser, and that is good service.'

Ingredients: Lean pork meat (or beef or veal); 1 l beef stock; 125 g ground almonds; 1 tbsp rice flour; 1 tbsp currants; ¼ tsbp ground mace; 3 ground cloves; salt and freshly ground black pepper; 1 tbsp olive oil; to garnish – white sugar, ground mace and small colourful flowers.

Method: Place the pork in a small saucepan and pour in the beef stock. Bring to the boil and allow to gently simmer until just cooked through. Remove the meat and set the stock aside to cool. Meanwhile make some almond milk by pouring 270 ml of the warm stock over the ground almonds. Allow to stand for 10 minutes or so, and then pass through a fine strainer, pressing all of the liquid out. Discard the almond solids. Add the rice flour to the almond milk, stir well to dissolve and set aside. The consistency should be a little thinner than pouring cream. Cut the pork into slices and mix with the currants, ground mace, cloves, salt and pepper. Form the mixture into tablespoon-sized balls and refrigerate for 10 minutes. Heat the oil in a frying pan over medium heat and lightly brown the meatballs. Arrange the meatballs on a plate, coat each one with some of the almond milk and sprinkle over the sugar, ground mace and fresh flowers.

PUMPES – MEATBALLS IN WHITE SAUCE

Two Fifteenth Century Cookbooks – Harleian MS. 279 & Harl. MS. 4016, c. 1440

This is a different version of the above recipe.

'Take an sethe a gode gobet of Porke, and not to lene as tendyr as thou may; than take hem uppe and choppe hem as small as thou may; than take clowes and maces and choppe forth with-alle and also choppe forth with Roysonys of coraunce; than take hem and rolle him a round as thou may, lyke to smale pelettys, a .ij. inches a-bowte, than ley hem on a dysshe be hem selue; than make a gode Almaunde mylke, and a lye it with floure of Rys, and lat it boyle wyle, but loke that it be clene rennyng; and at the dressoure, ley .v. pompys in a dysshe and pore thin potage ther-on. An if thou wolt, sette on euery pompe a flos campy flour, and a-boue straw on Sugre y-now, and Maces: and serue hem forth. And sum men make the pellettys of vele or Beeff, but porke ys beste and fairest.'

Ingredients and Method for meatballs: ½ lb beef mince; ⅛ cup raisins; pinch of mace and cloves. Form into meatballs and fry until cooked.

Ingredients and Method for sauce: ½ cup almonds; 1 cup milk; 2 or 3 tbsp flour; oregano; bay leaf; salt; pepper; mace. Make a white sauce with the almond milk and flour. Add spices to taste and pour over meatballs.

FILLETS OF BEEFE OR CLODS INSTEAD OF RED DEARE – COUNTERFEIT VENISON

Thomas Dawson's *The Good Huswifes Jewell*, 1585, 1594, 1596

For those times when venison was not available or one had guests to impress, there are a number of recipes for counterfeiting venison out of beef.

'To make fillets of beefe or clods instead of red Deare. First take your Beefe, and Larde it very thicke, and then season it with pepper, and Salt, Sinamon and ginger, Cloves and Mace good store, with a greate deale more quantitie of pepepr and Salte, then you would a peece of Venison, and put it in covered Paste, and when it is baked, take vineger and suger, Sinamon and Ginger, and put in, and shake the Pastie, and stope it close, and let it stande almost a fortnyght before you cut it up.'

LAMPREY PIE – POLITICIANS' PIE

Hannah Woolley's *The Queen-like Closet, or Rich Cabinet, Scored with all manner of Rare Receipts fo Preserving, Candying and Cookery*, 1672

This is an Elizabethan recipe from the book by Hannah Woolley (1622–75). The medieval tradition of the City of Gloucester sending a lamprey pie to the Royal household died out during the Industrial Revolution, but was resurrected in time for the Queen's coronation in 1953. In 1135 Henry I died of food poisoning after eating 'a surfeit of lampreys', while Samuel Pepys' diaries speak of the their popularity among 'medieval epicures'. It is rare for the lamprey, which can grow over a yard long, to attach itself to non-fish species, but attacks on humans are not unknown. There are three lamprey species (brook, river and sea) in the River Severn. Dwindling numbers have now seen it classified as an endangered species and protected by law, so for the queen's 60th Jubilee, Gloucester had to source lampreys from Canada's Great Lakes, where they are a pest. The main ingredient in Gloucester's delicacy is not the prettiest of creatures. It is jawless, with no scales or gill covers, with a round sucker-like mouth and its skeleton is made of cartilage. It is a backbone-less, secretive, primitive, blood-sucking, worm-like parasite and for these reasons I have renamed it Politicians' Pie.

'Take your Lamprey and gut him, and take away the black string in the back, wash him very well, and dry him, and season him with Nutmeg, Pepper and Salt, then lay him into your Pie in pieces with Butter in the bottom, and some Shelots and Bay Leaves and more Butter, so close it and bake it, and fill it up with melted Butter, and keep it cold, and serve it in with some Mustard and Sugar.'

LAMPRAYES IN BROWET – **LAMPREYS IN BROTH**
Liber Cure Cocorum, c. 1430
'Take lamprayes and scalde hom by kynde,
Sythyn, rost hom on gredyl, and grynde
Peper and safrone; welle hit with alle,
Do þo lampreyes and serve hit in sale.'
Take lampreys and scald them by kind,
Then, roast them on griddle, and grind
Pepper and saffron; boil it withal,
Add the lampreys and serve it in hall.'

STEW AFTER THE GUISE OF BEYONDE THE SEA – **HERBED LAMB STEW**
A Proper Newe Booke of Cokerye, 1545
'To make a stew after the guise of beyonde the Sea. Take a pottell of fayre water / and as muche wyne and a brest of mutton chopt in peces / than set it on the fyre and scome it clene / than put thereto a disshe ful of sliced onions and a quantite of synamon / gynger / Cloues and Mace / with salte and stew them all togither / and than serue them with soppes.'
Ingredients: 3 cups water; 3 cups red wine; 2–2½ lb lamb, bone in; large onion; ½ tsp each of cinnamon, ginger, cloves, mace; 1 tsp salt.

Method: Bring wine and water to boil, add the lamb, bring to the boil and reduce to simmer. Remove scum and add onions and spices. Simmer for around 1½ hours.

HOW TO MAKE A FRIED MEAT OF TURNEPS – BALDRICK'S ERSATZ MEAT

Epulario, Or, The Italian Banquet, English translation of 1598

'Roast the Turneps in the embers or else boil them whole, then cut or slice them in pieces as thick as half the shaft of a knife, which done, take cheese and cut it in the same form and quantity, but somewhat thinner. Then take Sugar, Pepper, and other spices mingled together, and put them in a pan under the pieces of cheese, as if you would make a crust under the cheese, and on top of them likewise. And over it you shall lay the pieces of Turnips, covering them over with the spices aforesaid, and plenty of good Butter, and so you shall do with the said cheese and Turnips till the pan be full, letting them cook the space of a quarter of an hour, or more, like a Tart, and this would be one of your last Dishes.'

Ingredients: 1 medium size turnip; 16–18 oz cheese such as mozzarella; up to 2 tbsp butter; mixture of 2 tsp sugar; ⅛ tsp ginger; 1 tsp cinnamon; ½ tsp ground cloves; 1 tsp salt; ½ pepper to taste.

Method: Peel turnip and blanch in salted water for 5 minutes to lessen strong taste. Throw water away. Cover with salted water and cook for 1–1½ hours, if whole, until tender, less time is required if you quarter the turnip. Remove turnip and allow to cool. Slice into rectangular pieces about 2 x ½ x ½ inches. Slice the cheese into similar shapes, only thinner. Sprinkle some of the spice mixture on the bottom of a 9-inch layer cake pan or pie plate. Place on it a layer of cheese, then spice the turnips and dot with butter. Repeat with spice, cheese, turnips and butter to fill the pan, making it a little higher in the middle. The top layer should be cheese and spices. Preheat oven to 180°C and bake in oven until cheese is melted and turns an even brown, around 35 minutes. You can also make this with strong Cheddar, but the result is more like cheese macaroni in texture. In this case, cook for only 25 minutes until the Cheddar melts.

HARE IN WORTES – HARE (OR GOOSE) STEW

A Boke of Kokerie, 1440

This was a course served at a feast held for the ordination of the Archbishop of Canterbury in 1443.

'Hare in Wortes. Take cabbages, and strip them faire from the stalks. Take Beets and Borage, avens, Violet, Mallows, parsley, betony, patience, the white of leeks, and the young heads of nettles. Parboil, press out the water, chop them small, and mix. Take good broth of fresh beef, or other good flesh and marrow bones. Put it in a pot and set on the fire. Chop the hare in pieces, and if you wish, wash it in the same broth, and then draw it through a strainer with the blood, and then put all on the fire. And if it is an old hare, let it boil well, before you throw in the herbs; if it is young, throw in all the ingredients together. Let them boil til they are done, and season them with salt. And serve them forth. In the same way you may make wortes of a Goose of a night powdryng [salting], of beef, or any other fresh flesh.'

ROASTED CAPON, PHESANT, PARTRIDGE, QUAILE, CRANE, HERON, CURLEW, BITTER, PLOVER, SNITE AND WOODCOCK

A.W., *The Booke of Goode Cookry Very Necessary for all Such as Delight Therein*, 1584, 1591

A 'bitter' is a bittern, these days very rare, and a 'snite' is a snipe.

'To roast a Capon. You must roste a Capon with his head off, his wings and Legs on whole.

Roste a Phesant. As a Capon, and when you serve him in, stick one of his fethers upon his brest.

Partridge as a Phesant, but no Fether.

Roste a Quaile. With his legs broken and knit one within an other.

Roast a Crane. With his legs turned up behind him, his wings cut of at the ioynt next the bodye, and then winde the neck about the broche, and put the bill into his brest.

Heron, Curlew and Bitter, as a Crane: but the Bittures head must be of.

Roste a Plover. With his head off, and his Legs turned upward upon his back.

Roast a Snite. With his Bill put into his brest, and his Legs turned upward upon his brest.

To roast Woodcocks. First pluck them and draw out the guts, leave the Liver still in them, then stuffe them with lard chopped small, and Jenoper beryes, with his bill put into his brest and his feet as the Snite [snipe], and so roast him on a spit, and set under it a faire large pan with white wine in it, and chopped Percely, Vinagre, salt and ginger, then make tostes of white bread, and toste them upon a grediron, so that they be not brent, then put these tostes in a dish, and lay your woodcocks upon them and put your sauce the same broth upon them, and so serve them forth.'

TO BOYLE A DUCKE WITH TURNEPS – DUCK AND TURNIPS IN SAUCE AND SOPS

Thomas Dawson's *The Good Huswifes Jewell*, 1596

'To boyle a Ducke with Turneps. Take her first, and put her into a potte with stewed broth, then take perselye, and sweete hearbs, and chop them, and perboyle the rootes very well in an other pot, then put unto them sweet butter, Cynamon, Gynger, grosse Pepper and whole Mace, and so season it with salt, and serve it upon soppes.'

Ingredients: Turnips; butter; cinnamon; ginger; pepper; mace; salt; sops (toast pieces).

Method: Place the duck in large stockpot with a meat broth. Cook, and when almost done, add the turnips until they are cooked. Drain. In another pot, place chopped parsley, sweet herbs and the other ingredients and thicken to a sauce. Put the turnips on the toast sops, place the duck on top and pour the sauce over the duck and sops.

BAKED ORENGES – MOCK ORANGE PIES

The Good Huswifes Handmaide for the Kitchin, 1594

This would have been an extremely expensive dish at the time, with oranges and sugar being imported. The dish consists of individual pies made to look like oranges. Each is a hand-raised 'coffin' made with a hot-water crust pastry, spiced and coloured with saffron, filled with candied orange and flavoured with cinnamon and ginger.

'To Bake Orenges. First take twelve Orenges, and pare away the yellow rinde of them, cut in two peeces, and wring out the iuyce [juice] of them, then lay your pilles [peels] in faire water, and when it is boyling hot, put your Orenges therin, let them seeth therin until the water be bitter. Then have another potte of water readie upon the fyre, and when it dooth seeth, put your Orenge pilles therin, and let them seeth again in the same water until they be very tender. Then take your Orenges out of the pot, and put them in a bason of fayre cold water, and with your thombe take out the core of your Orenges and wash them cleane in the same water, and lay them in a faire platter, so that the water may run from them. Then take a quart of Bastard, claret wine, or white wine. If you take a quart of bastard, put thereto a quatern of sugar. If you take claret or white wine, ye must take to everie pint a quaterne of Sugar, and set it to the fire in a faire pot. Then put your Orenges therein, and seeth them till the liquor come to a sirrop.

When it is come to a sirrop, take a fair earthen pot, and put your Orenges and sirrop all together, so that your Orenges may be covered with your sirrop. If you lack sirrop you must take a pint of Claret wine, and a quaterne of Sugar, and make thereof fine sirrop, and put it into your Orenges, and stoppe your pot close, and after this maner you may keep them two moneths. And when you will bake them, take an ounce of Synamon, and half an ounce of ginger, and beat them small. Then take two pounds of sugar, and beat it in like maner. Then put your sugar, Sinamon and Ginger in a faire platter and mingle them together. Then take four handful of fine flower [flour], and lay it upon a faire board, and make a hole in the midst of the flower with your hand. Then take a pinte of fair water, and eight spoonfuls of Oyl, and a little saffron, and make them seeth altogether, and when it seeths, put in it in the hole in the midst of the flowere, and knead your paste therwith. Then make little round coffins of the bignesse of an orange, and when they be made, put a little sugar in the bottom of them. Then take your Orenge pilles and fill them full of sugar and spices afore rehearsed, and put them into your coffins ful of the same sugar and spices. When the spices be in them, close them up, and set them upon papers, and bake them in an oven or baking pan, but your Oven must not be too hot. If your coffins be dry after baking, you may make a little hole with the point of a knife upon the cover of them, and with a spoone put a little of the sirrop to them, at another season you must make your paste with foure handfuls of fine flower, and twelve yolks of egs, and a little saffron, make your paste therewith.'

HATTES IN LENTYN – SALMON OR SEWIN (SEA TROUT) FRIED HATS
Ordinance of Pottage – Beinecke MS 163, c. 1460

These are small fried pastries formed like hats, with a stuffing made of fish and dried fruits. They were a favoured dish for Lent. Sea trout tastes better and will not be factory farmed.

'Make a pastry dough of prepared flour, kneaded with yolks of eggs; and make a stuffing of veal and pork, boiled and ground, with yolks of eggs; marrow diced, and dates minced; currants; sugar, saffron and salt and spices; and mix all together. And make your pastry on round foils of the breadth of a saucer, as thin as may be drawn. Turn it double, that the edges may come to the middle of the foil; then turn it together that the edges on the bigger side meet all about, and the smaller side turn upward without in the manner of a hat. And close well the edges that they hold well. Fill there-on your stuffing. Have a batter of yolks of eggs and wheat flour in the open side that is toward. Look there-in the stuffing be closed, and set it in hot grease upright. When the batter is fried, you may lay it down and fry it all over.'

Ingredients: ¼ lb salmon or sea trout; 1 tbsp chopped dates; 1 tbsp chopped raisins; 1 tbsp chopped pears; saffron; salt; spice powder; dough; 1 cup hotwater to ¼ cup almond powder; pinch of saffron to add to almond milk (optional).
Method: Mix the fish, raisins, figs, pears and spices together. Set aside. Make almond milk out of one cup hot water, pinch of saffron if desired and ¼ cup

ground almonds. Put 1 cup flour in a bowl and add liquid to make stiff dough. Roll into circles and make 'hats', stuffed with the fish mixture. Fry in vegetable oil.

STARREY GAZEY PIE – STARGAZY PIE

16th-century recipe from St. Agnes W.I. in *Cornish Recipes, Ancient & Modern*, The Cornwall Federation of Women's Institutes 1965. First collected and published by Edith Martin, Tregavethan, Truro, 1929, for The Cornwall Friends of W. I.

This is a traditional Cornish dish of baked whole pilchards, along with eggs and potatoes (now in place of turnips or swedes), covered with a pastry crust. Although there are variations with different fish being used, the unique feature of stargazey pie is fish heads (and sometimes tails) protruding through the crust. The heads appear to gaze at the stars. This position allows the oil that is released during cooking to drain into the pie, adding a fuller flavour and ensuring the pie is moist. The dish is said to have originated in the small port of Mousehole (pronounced Muzzel) and is traditionally eaten during the festival of Tom Bawcock's Eve, to celebrate his heroic catch during a stormy winter in the sixteenth century. None of the fishing boats had been able to leave the harbour and as Christmas approached, the villagers, who relied on fish as their primary source of food, were facing starvation.

On 23 December, Tom Bawcock decided to brave the weather and, in difficult seas, managed to catch enough fish to feed the starving village. The entire catch, including seven types of fish, was baked into a pie, which had the fish heads poking through to prove that there were fish inside. There is some evidence that the festival dates back to pre-Christian times. On Tom Bawcock's Eve it is served in The Ship Inn, the only pub in Mousehole, sometimes after a re-enactment of the legend, when the villagers parade a huge stargazey pie with a procession of handmade lanterns, before eating the pie itself. An older feast, held by the fishermen towards the end of December, included a pie cooked with different fish to represent the variety of catches the men hoped to achieve in the coming year. There is a possibility that Tom Bawcock's Eve is an evolution of this festival.

In legend, the pie included pilchards, horse mackerel, sand eels, herring, dogfish, ling and a seventh fish. In a traditional pie, the primary ingredient is now the pilchard (sardine), although mackerel or herring can be used. Any white fish will work for the filling, with pilchards or herring just added for presentation. Along with fish, the other traditional ingredients are thickened milk, eggs and boiled potatoes. Many recipe variations exist, some of which include hard-boiled eggs, bacon, onion, white wine or mustard. Other alternatives to the main fish can be crayfish, rabbit or mutton. The recipes for the stargazey pie are all topped with a pastry lid, generally shortcrust, through which the fish heads protrude. For presentation, one suggestion is that the pilchards are arranged with their tails toward the centre of the pie and their heads poking up through the crust around the edge. The traditional drinking song on Tom Bawcock's Eve is:

'Merry place you may believe, Tiz Mouzel 'pon Tom Bawcock's eve
To be there then who wouldn't wesh, to sup o' sibm soorts o' fish
When morgy brath had cleared the path, Comed lances for a fry
And then us had a bit o' scad an' Starry-gazie pie
As aich we'd clunk, E's health we drunk, in bumpers bremmen high,
And when up came Tom Bawcock's name, We'd prais'd 'un to the sky.'

Ingredients: Dependent on size of pie dish, as many fresh herrings, pilchards or mackerel to fill the dish; sufficient pastry to cover your dish; fresh chopped parsley; up to 6 eggs, or ½ pint of cream; fat bacon rashers; butter; salt and pepper; fine breadcrumbs; 2 tbsp tarragon vinegar.

Method: Scale, clean and bone the fish, retaining heads. Season inside each with salt, pepper and parsley and roll neatly. Butter a dish and sprinkle a thick layer of breadcrumbs on it. Lay in some of the fish, then alternate breadcrumbs and fish until the dish is full. Cover with bacon rashers. Beat eggs with vinegar and pour into pie, or use cream. Cover with shortcrust pastry. Arrange heads on pastry, so as they are looking up. Bake in a hot oven and serve with a sprig of parsley in mouth of each fish.

HERBELADE – HERBED OPEN PORK PIE

Two Fifteenth Century Cookbooks – Harleian MS. 279 & Harl. MS. 4016, c. 1440

'Take Buttes of Porke, and smyte hem in pecys, and sette it ouer the fyre; and sethe hem in fayre Watere; and whan it is y-sothe y-now, ley it on a fayre bord, and pyke owt alle the bonys, and hew it smal, and put it in a fayre bolle; than take ysope, Sawge, Percely a gode quantite, and hew it smal, and putte it in a fayre vesselle; than take a lytel of the brothe, that the porke was sothin in, and draw thorw a straynoure, and caste to the Erbys, and gif it a boyle; thenne take owt the Erbys with a Skymoure fro the brothe, and caste hem to the porke in the bolle; than mynce Datys smal, and caste hem ther-to, and Roysonys of Coraunce, and pynes, and drawe thorw a straynoure yolkes of Eyroun ther-to, and Sugre, and pouder Gyngere, and Salt, and coloure it a lytel with Safroune; and toyle yt with thin hond al thes to-gederys; than make fayre round cofyns, and harde hem a lytel in the ovyn; than take hem owt, and with a dysshe in thin hond, fylle hem fulle of the Stuffe; than sette hem ther-in a-gen; and lat hem bake y-now, and serue forth.'

Ingredients: 3 pork chops; ½ cup chopped dates; ½ tsp salt; 3 cups chopped fresh parsley; ½ cup currants; 1 tbsp sugar; 1 tsp dried leaf sage; ⅓ cup pine nuts; 5 egg yolks; 2 tbsp hyssop; ½ tsp powdered ginger; 9-inch pastry shell.

Method: Boil the chops until cooked. Take out, remove the bones and cut up the meat. Boil herbs in the pork broth. Mix pork, cooked herbs and remaining ingredients in bowl. Make a pie crust and bake for 10 minutes to harden. Place the filling in the pie crust and bake for 30 minutes at 180°C.

MALACHES OF PORK – PORK AND CHEESE QUICHE PIE (TWO WAYS)

Curye on Inglysch, fourteenth century (there are several recipes)

You can make your own 'powdour fort', the strong spice mixture as in the second recipe in the preserves chapter. It is ¼ cup powdered ginger; ¼ cup long pepper, ground; 1½ tsp cloves, ground; ¼ cup ground cinnamon; ¼ cup ground black pepper.

'Hewe pork al to pecys and medle it with ayren and chese igrated. Do therto powdour fort, safroun and pynes with salt. Make a crust in a trap; bake it wel therinne, and serue it forth.'

Ingredients 1: 1 lb cubed lean pork; 4 eggs; 1 cup grated Cheddar or hard strong cheese; ¼ cup pine nuts; ¼ tsp salt; pinch of each, cloves, mace, black pepper; pastry dough for 9-inch pie crust.

Method 1: Preheat oven to 230°C. Line a 9-inch pie pan with the pastry dough and bake it for 5–10 minutes to harden it. Remove it and reduce oven temperature to 180°C. Slowly brown the pork in a frying pan until tender. Beat the eggs and spices together in a bowl. Line the bottom of the pie crust with the browned pork, grated cheese and pine nuts. Pour the egg and spice mixture over them. Place the pie in the oven and bake for 45–50 minutes and cool before serving.

Ingredients 2: 1 lb cubed pork; ¼ cup pine nuts; 3 eggs; 8 threads saffron; ½ tsp salt; ½ lb parmesan cheese; ¾ tsp powder fort – if none available, try 1 part cloves, 1 part mace, 1 part cubebs, 7 parts cinnamon, 7 parts ginger and 7 parts pepper, all ground.

Method 2: Grate cheese and mix with eggs in a bowl. Crush saffron into a teaspoon of warm water and mix into pork, cheese and eggs mixture. Make a 9-inch pie crust and prebake for 5–10 minutes in a preheated oven at 230°C to harden it. Place filling in the crust and bake at 180°C for 45–50 minutes.

PIES OF PAIRIS – PORK AND VEAL PIE

A Noble Boke off Cookry, also *Harleian MS 4016, c.* 1450

This can also be a useful snack for picnics etc.

'To mak pyes of pairis tak and finyt fair buttes of pork and buttes of vele and put it ito gedure in a pot with freshe brothe and put ther to a quantite of wyne and boile it tille it be enoughe then put it in to a treene vesselle and put ther to raw yolks of eggs pouder of guinger sugur salt and mynced dates and raisins of corans and mak a good thyn paiste and mak coffins and put it ther in and bak it welle and serue it.'

Ingredients: 1 lb pork and 1 lb veal, both cut into small pieces; 2 cups beef stock; 1 cup red wine; 3 egg yolks; ⅛ cup currants; ¼ cup minced dates; ½ tsp ginger; ½ tsp salt; 2 tsp sugar; large pie crust.

Method: Boil the pork and veal in stock and wine until they are nearly cooked. Drain meat and mix with the other ingredients. Place into the pie shell and cook at 180°C for 45 minutes, or until the top of the pie begins to brown. You can make a large pie or several smaller ones, which may need a little less time in the oven.

FFESAUNTE ROSTED – ROASTED PHEASANT WITH SAUCE

Two Fifteenth Century Cookbooks – Harleian MS. 279 & Harl. MS. 4016, c. 1440

'Lete a ffesaunte blode in the mouthe as a crane, And lete him blede to dethe; pull him dry, kutte awey his hede and the necke by the body, and the legges by the kne, and putte the kneys in at the vente, and roste him: his sauce is Sugar and mustard.'

Ingredients: Pheasant, pre-prepared, washed and cleaned; ½ lb fatty bacon, or a cheesecloth soaked in melted butter.

Method: Preheat oven to 200°C. Tie pheasant tightly with string so the knees are in at the stomach. Keep the pheasant from drying out by covering with strips of fatty bacon, as with a turkey, or with cheesecloth soaked in melted butter. You can also use both, or cover with foil, occasionally basting with olive oil, later removing the foil to allow to brown. Reduce heat to 180°C when putting the pheasant in the oven and allow 25 minutes per pound. Check if it is done by skewering and seeing if the juices run clear, as you would do with chicken. Allow to rest before carving/serving with the following sauce.

FFESAUNTE ROSTED SAUCE SAUCE – SUGAR AND MUSTARD PHEASANT GLAZE

Two Fifteenth Century Cookbooks – Harleian MS. 279 & Harl. MS. 4016, c. 1440

Ingredients: Brown sugar; strong mustard.

Method: Mix up your favourite strong mustard, such as Tewkesbury. Mix in brown sugar to your required taste. Serve on the side of the plate or thinly glaze the cooked pheasant.

TO BAKE A MALLARD – DUCK IN TUDOR SAUCE PIE

Thomas Dawson's *The Good Huswifes Jewell*, 1585, 1594, 1596

Mallards, being wild ducks, have less fat and are smaller than domestic ones, about 2 lbs compared to 5 lbs for a tame duck.

'To bake a Mallard. Take three or foure Onyons, and stampe them in a morter, then straine them with a saucer full of vergice, then take your mallard and put him into the iuyce of the sayde onyons, and season him with pepper, and salte, cloves and mace, then put your Mallard into the coffin with the saide juyce of the onyons, and a good quantity of Winter-savorye, a little tyme, and perselye chopped small, and sweete Butter, so close it up and bake it.'

Ingredients: 2–3 lbs duck, de-boned and cut into pieces; 3–4 medium onions; ¼ cup verjuice (cup of white wine with a splash of lemon juice); ¼ tsp pepper; ¼ tsp salt; ¼ tsp thyme; ⅛ tsp cloves; ⅛ tsp mace; 2 tbsp butter; 1 tsp chopped parsley; pie crust.

Method: Grind onions in a mortar and pestle or food processor and add verjuice. Strain out the solids, reserving the liquid. In a large bowl, mix the duck, salt, pepper, cloves, mace and the verjuice/onion liquid. Place the mixture into a pie crust and sprinkle with parsley and thyme. Cover with a top crust and bake at 180°C for about an hour, or until done.

TO BAKE CHICKINS, SPARROWS, OR OTHER BIRDS – CHICKEN AND GOOSEBERRY PIE

The Treasurie of Commodious Conceits & Hidden Secrets, 1573

House sparrows are in decline, owing both to the rising cat population and house walls and soffits being in better repair, and thankfully Markham only refers to 'chickins' in his recipe. We see yet again the Tudor taste for sweet and savoury in the same dish, using combinations new to many of us.

'Take and trusse your Chickins, the feete cut off, put them in the Coffin: then for every chickin put in every Pye a handfull of Gooseberies, and a quantity of butter about every Chickin: then take a good quantitie of Suger and Sinimon with sufficient salt, put them into the Pye, let it bake one howre and a halfe, when it is baken take the yolke of an egge and half a Goblet of veriuce with sufficient suger sodden together, put in the pye and serve it.'

CHICKINS WITH GRAPES
John Murrel's *A New Booke of Cookerie*, 1615
'To bake Chickins with Grapes: Trusse and scald your Chickens season them well with Pepper, Salt, and Nutmeg: and put them into your Pye, with a good piece of Butter. Bake it, and cut it vp, and put vpon the breast of your Chickins, Grapes boyld in Uergis, Butter, Nutmegge, and Sugar, with the iuyce of an Orenge.'

BRAWN EN PEVERADE – MEAT WITH PEVORADE SAUCE, THREE WAYS
Two Fifteenth Century Cookbooks – Harleian MS. 279 & Harl. MS. 4016, c. 1440
Brawn was the term for the dark, heavy and slightly fatty meat of poultry or boar, but was also the term for cooked meat made from the head and foreparts of a boar or pig. Richer and fattier than ham, it was regarded as a delicacy for the medieval feast and by Tudor times it had become fare for all twelve days of Christmas. From the thirteenth century onwards it appeared in the last course of the meats, along with the game birds and spicery. It was sometimes incorporated with vinegar, pepper and other spices into a rich pottage called 'brawn en perverde'. It was also sliced and served in a thick, spiced syrup of wine with honey or sugar. By the end of the fourteenth century 'brawn en peverade,' or simple brawn with mustard, had become first course dishes. Details of brawn preparation were first made public in Elizabeth's reign by William Harrison. He described brawn as 'a great piece of service at the table from November untl February be ended, but chiefly in the Christmas time… It is made commonly of the forepart of a tame boar …' *Pevorade* was a popular red wine and mustard sauce of the era, associated with brawn. Being strongly flavoured, served with meat it enhances the flavour but is not overpowering. Most recipes call for the meat to be cooked in the sauce, but the sauce is often preferred on the side of the plate, or poured over, hence the three separate recipes.
'Brawn in Peverade. Take Wine and powdered Cinnamon, and pass it through a strainer, and set it on the fire, and let it boil, and add thereto Cloves, Mace, and powdered Pepper; then take small Onions all whole, and parboil them in hot water, and add thereto. Let them boil together; then take Brawn, and slice it, but not too thin. And if it is soused, let it steep awhile in hot water until it is tender, then add it to the Syrup; then take Sandalwood, and Vinegar, and

add thereto, and let it boil all together until it is done; then take Ginger, and add thereto, and so serve forth; but let it be not too thick nor too thin, but as a pottage should be.'

Ingredients 1: 1 lb stewing beef or pork pieces; chopped large white onion; 1 pint red wine; ½ pint stock; 5 cloves; ⅛ tsp cinnamon; ⅛ tsp mace; ¹⁄₁₆ tsp ginger; ¹⁄₁₆ tsp pepper; 1 tsp vinegar; red food colouring.

Method 1: Lightly fry and cut the meat thin. Parboil white onions and add to boiling wine and stock. Add cloves, cinnamon, mace, ginger and pepper. Add meat and vinegar and a few dashes of red food coloring. Bring to boil and simmer until reduced. As with many dishes, if you leave it a day it will taste better the next.

Ingredients 2: 1 lb beef or pork; ¼ medium onion, sliced; 1 cup red wine; ½ tsp cinnamon; ¼ tsp each of cloves, pepper, ginger; ⅛ tsp mace; ¼ cup red wine vinegar; ¼ cup water; 2 slices bread.

Method 2: Place wine, cinnamon, cloves, mace and pepper in a small saucepan and bring to the boil. Meanwhile, tear the bread into pieces and put into a bowl with the vinegar and water and stir until the bread turns mushy. Strain the liquid into the saucepan and discard the solids. Add onion and ginger and return to the boil. Reduce heat and simmer until the onions are tender. Serve hot over meat.

Ingredients 3: Chicken or pork, thickly sliced. Small onions, parboiled until just tender. Red wine; cinnamon; powdered cloves; mace; pepper; red wine vinegar; ginger; red food colouring or sandalwood.

Method 3: Place wine in a large pot, add cinnamon and bring to the boil. Reduce heat and allow to simmer for several minutes. Remove from heat and allow to slightly cool. Add the cloves, mace, cinnamon and pepper. Bring to the boil, add the parboiled onions and return to the boil. Add the food colouring, vinegar and meat, return to the boil, then reduce heat to a simmer. Allow to cook until the sauce has thickened and reduced into a pottage. Place in a serving dish and sprinkle ginger on top.

BOAR'S HEAD

The Cookbook of Sabina Welserin, 1553

The ceremony of bringing in the boar's head at Christmas dates from 1170 and probably even back to pagan times. Two heralds raised silver trumpets to their lips as the master cook carried in a massive silver platter containing the boar's head, garnished with a wreath of bay, sprigs of rosemary in its ears and a roasted apple in its mouth. The 'lordly dish' was followed by minstrels and other servants carrying in lesser dishes to grace the 'groaning board', as the table was said to 'groan' from the weight of all the food. In England, the procession sang when presenting the Christmas boar's head to the king or queen: 'The Boar's Head in hand bring I, / With garlands gay and rosemary, / I pray you all sing merrily'.

Thomas Tusser, in *Five Hundred Points of Good Husbandry*, suggests dishes that the lady of the house should provide for her guests at Christmas. He mentions mutton, pork, veal souse (pickled pig's feet and ears), brawn, cheese and apples. He also talks of serving turkey, but only as a part of a list of other luxurious items that the housewife should provide. However, in the upper classes, a boar's head was skinned then re-stuffed with meats, spices and fruits and cooked until golden. The head was the centrepiece of the feast held during Christmas with accompanying masques and pageantry. It may be that James I began the tradition of turkey instead of boar for the high table of the great lords and monarchs.

'How to cook a wild boar's head, also how to prepare a sauce for it. A wild boar's head should be boiled well in water and, when it is done, laid on a grate and basted with wine, then it will be thought to have been cooked in wine. Afterward make a black or yellow sauce with it. First, when you would make a black sauce, you should heat up a little fat and brown a small spoonful of wheat flour in the fat and after that put good wine into it and good cherry syrup, so that it becomes black, and sugar, ginger, pepper, cloves and cinnamon, grapes, raisins and finely chopped almonds. And taste it, however it seems good to you, make it so. If you would make a yellow sauce. Then make it in the same way as the black sauce, only take saffron instead of the syrup and put no cloves therein, so you will also have a good sauce.'

RE-DRESSED BOAR'S HEAD

The Cookbook of Sabina Welserin, 1553

'To make a re-dressed boar's head. Take a head, large or small. Boil it in water and wine, and when it is boiled make sure that the bones all stay together next to one another. And remove all the meat from the bones of the head. Strip the skin carefully, the white part from the meat and chop the other meat from the boar's head very small. Put it in a pan. Spice it well with pepper, ginger, and a little cloves, nutmeg, saffron, and let it get very hot over the fire in the broth in which the head was boiled. Next take the boiled head and lay it in a white cloth and lay the skin under it on the cloth. Then spread the chopped meat all around on the head and cover it with the flayed skin. And if you have too little meat from one head, then take it from two and cover the head entirely as if it were whole. Next, pull the snout and the ears out through the cloth. Also, pull the teeth together again with the cloth, so the head is held together while it is still warm, and let it lie overnight. In the morning cut the cloth from around the head. In that way it will stay whole. Then serve it with a cold farce made with apples, almonds, raisins. Thus you have a lordly dish.'

TO BAKE A CAPON WITH YOLKES OF EGGES – CASTRATED COCK AND EGG PIE
The Treasurie of Commodious Conceits & Hidden Secrets, 1573
'To bake a Capon with yolkes of Egges. When the capon is made redi, trusse him in the ye Coffyn: then take viii yolks of egges sodden hard, and pricke into every of them v Cloves, and put the yolks into the Coffyn with the Capon: then take a quantitie of gynger and salt, and cast it on the Capon, and let it bake iii Houres. Then take ii raw yolkes of egges beaten into a Gobblet of Veriuce, with a good quantitie of sugre sodden togither, put it into ye Coffyn and to serve it.'

TO BAKE A FESANT OR CAPON – FALSE AND FIDDLED PHEASANT
The Treasurie of Commodious Conceits & Hidden Secrets, 1573
'To bake a Fesant, or Capon in steede of a Fesant. Dresse your Capon lyke a Phesant trussed, perboyled a little and larded with swete lard: put him into the Coffin, cast theron a little Pepper and Salt: put therto halfe a dish of sweete Butter, let it bake for the space of iii howres, and when it is colde: serve it forth for a Phesant. And thus bake a Phesant.'

BOYL'D BREAM
Thomas Dawson's *A Booke of Cokerie*, 1620
'For Boyl'd Fish. To boyle a Breame. Take white Wine, and put it into a pot, and let it seeth, then take your Breame and cut him in the middest, and put him in, then take an Onyon and chop it small, then take Nutmegs beaten Sinamon and Ginger, whole Mace, and a pound of Butter, and let it boyle altogether, and so season it with salte, serve it upon soppes, and garnish it with fruit.'

1. Tudor mechant's house in Tenby. This is built upon a medieval building. There is both a small hand spit and a swing arm, and there is a bakestone hanging to the left of the utensils. Earthenware containers were uncommon until Stuart times.

2. The Vaughan family's Tretower Court dining hall is unaltered from Tudor times.

3. Trenchers at Cefn Caer medieval hall house, Pennal, laid out for a feast. The bread served to soak up any sauces, which in turn softened the hard bread, and also provided necessary carbohydrates in the absence of potatoes.

4. A typical yeoman's farm larder, with a cheese press in the background. Joints of meat were salted and hung to preserve them. Rabbits were a luxury dish until later times. Rats and mice were an ever-present menace to food stocks, so cats and dogs became a fairly integral part of many homes.

5. Tudor women shopping at one of the many London markets.

6. Early seventeenth-century woodcut of a woman carrying a glass outside an alehouse in London.

7. Woodcut illustrations from 1574 depicting a chicken being butchered (*left*) and a rabbit ripe for catching (*right*).

8. The Tudor 'hogbog' had to be made of stone because a wooden structure would rot or be damaged by the pig. Unlike other farm animals, the pig does not need a field and acres of grassland to survive. The peasant's pig would have been kept in a small enclosure behind his cottage. It was used by farmers and peasants alike to house both pigs and poultry. Pigs occupied the ground space while poultry had a raised hen house, with the design both saving space and avoiding danger to the hens at night.

9. Fishponds like these near the ruins of Valle Crucis Abbey were an important source of protein for the rich and for clerics upon 'fast days'. They were also needed for castle garrisons as a cheap source of food. As long as there was a natural flow of water into the pond, fish required no feeding and were available all year round. There would usually be a series of ponds, as at Valle Crucis, with fish being moved between them as they grew.

10. Ruined dovecots such as this at Marcross Grange, Glamorgan, can be seen around Britain. From Norman times, they were an important source of fresh meat for monasteries and the rich. Especially favoured were 'squabs', young pigeons. Some could hold up to 1,000 birds and had internal revolving ladders to access the nests

Above left: 11. The marriage feast of Sir Henry Unton, English Elizabethan diplomat, *c.* 1596.

Above right: 12. Henry VIII in later life – and with a fuller figure.

Below left: 13. Elizabethan fruit trencher, a small wooden tray for fruit, richly decorated with designs and inscriptions. Trenchers made of wood and pewter gradually replaced bread trenchers in the upper classes. The decoration was for show, as diners reversed their plates to eat off a plain side, which could then be scrubbed clean.

Below right: 14. The earliest known piece of English delftware, a charger plate (a large plate for special occasions) made in 1600 in Aldgate, London. The inscription reads, 'The rose is red, the leaves are greene, God save Elizabeth our queene'. The view is of the Tower of London from the Thames.

15. A Tudor-period woodcut of a cook in a kitchen.

16. Preparing a feast: birds are being spit-roasted by hand, and pages are preparing to bring out the first courses, while the guests dance in the background.

17. A Tudor dinner party.

18. Elizabethan nobles being entertained at table, from a period needlework panel.

19. A spoon rack with different spoons and a ladle, which would have hung on a wall to save space. Spoons were used extensively among the lower classes to eat thickened pottages. In the upper classes, hosts were not required to provide knives for their guests, so guests brought their own.

20. Sixteenth-century jugs, imported earthenware with silver necks applied by English silversmiths.

Below: 21. The cockpit dates from the 1600s, replacing an earlier one at the Hawk and Buckle Inn, Denbigh, and is now in St Fagan's. Men known as 'feeders' trained the birds, who were fitted with sharp spurs, and the 'sport' was not abolished until 1849. An amazing variety of snacks were available from hawkers, 'hawking their trade' and calling out the foods they were selling.

22. A badger depicted in a drawing from a book published in London in 1574. Badger was often eaten in rural areas.

23. Tudor women gutting a fish.

24. Tudor women carrying chickens from the market.

25. A drawing of an otter from a book published in 1574. Stewed otter and porpoise, and grilled beaver tail, were all deemed to be 'fish' dishes suitable for eating during Lent.

26. Wooden storage and mixing bowls plus a pestle and mortar at the Haverfordwest Tudor Trader's House, removed to the St Fagan's National History Museum. The merchant lived in a single storey above his quayside shop, and earthenware or pewter dishes were a luxury.

27. Traditional wooden bowls and spoons, used from time immemorial through to the early twentieth century in rural parts. Each spoon has an identifying mark for its owner, and people used to carry their own spoons and knives with them. Spoons were shaped slightly differently, dependent upon whether one was eating a more liquid pottage or denser food.

28. Tudor liquid measures in pewter jugs: the largest hold ½ pint; the two next-largest are *gills*, ¼ pint; the *jack* is half a gill; then comes the quarter *gill*; a fluid ounce, stamped 20, for one-twentieth; the *nipperkin* or *nip* is one-eighth a *gill*, or a thirty-second of a pint. The *gill* was introduced in the fourteenth century to measure individual servings of spirits or wine. Pronounced with a soft 'g' as jill, the term appears in the nursery rhyme 'Jack and Jill'. In 1625, Charles I scaled down the *jack* or *jackpot* (sometimes known as a double jigger) in order to collect higher sales taxes on drinks. The *jill*, twice the size of the *jack*, was also reduced and 'came tumbling after'.

29. Spices and herbs are best weighed and sorted prior to cooking. Turmeric will give a colour close to saffron much more cheaply, but will not match the taste. Because of their value as status symbols, spices were often publicly displayed. Salt cellars or *nefs*, often in the form of ships, were seen at the tables of the rich, as well as ornate spice containers, their display being an outward and ostentatious show of wealth.

Above: 30. Billingsgate Market, London, drawn in 1598. Billingsgate was both a specialist fish market and a place for buying other foodstuffs brought to London along the Thames.

Below left and right: 31. Tudor bakers at work.

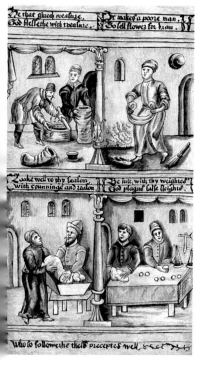

Above left: 32. Elizabeth I's falcon downs a heron. Herons, storks and cranes, then all common birds, were usually spit-roasted like swans.

Above right: 33. Elizabeth I enjoying a picnic following a hunt. Wine and beer is available, along with baskets of roasted fowl for refreshments.

Below left: 34. Elizabeth I is offered a knife to make the first cut in butchering the deer caught by the hunt. Venison was very popular amongst the nobility in Tudor times, and all the Tudor monarchs enjoyed hunting.

Below right: 35. A sixteenth-century salt cellar fit for the Tudor court.

Tying to Poles.

Cutting Roots.

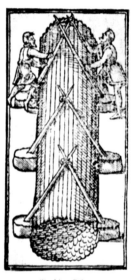

Stacking Poles.

Ramming of Poles.

36. Tudor-era woodcuts of hop cultivation, from a book published in 1574. Specialists from the Continent were brought to Kent to cultivate hops, as beer made from hops began to replace ale, made from grain, and water as the main drink for all classes. Most water was of course unsafe until it had been boiled in the fermentation process.

37. The Tudor Trader's House was originally on the Cleddau quay at Haverfordwest and is now in St Fagan's. The trader lived on the upper floor, and left of his fireplace is a garderobe (toilet) which discharged into a gutter and then the river. The ground-floor vault was used for storing corn, wool, salt, fish, soap, cheese and casks of wine to be exported or sold. It is furnished as in the 1580s, with waffle irons hanging on the wall. The swinging arm followed a cauldron or joint to be placed either over or near the fire to regulate temperature.

38. The central hearth was normal in most homes – chimneys were rare, and smoke escaped through the thatch, open windows or a hole in the roof. Only the very wealthy could afford glass and chimneys. This is a 1508 farmhouse, Hendre'r Ywydd Uchaf, from the Vale of Clwyd, now at St Fagan's, Cardiff. This is where the family lived and cooked in a single-storey 'long house', with animals in the lower section of the home, allowing drainage.

39. A working board for a kitchen. These were often on heavy trestles. There are rudimentary scales, but generally cooks used simple measures such as cups. The barrel would have probably held grains for breadmaking. Bread ovens were only seen in the great houses at this time.

40. The size of the inglenook allowed a bar to carry a cauldron, and firedogs. This chimney was a status symbol at Garreg Fawr Farmhouse, St Fagan's, as was the second story. A toasting fork hangs on the wall, and the later 1620 fireback deflected heat back to the cooking pots and room.

41. Bread trenchers at Cefn Caer medieval hall-house, Pennal.

42. Stargazy pie before baking. The pie is still sold on Tom Bawcock's Eve in the quayside Ship Inn, Mousehole, Cornwall.

43. Homity pie. Many Tudor pies were open, like this, with the pastry 'coffyn' acting as an inedible crust to hold the contents. With this classic vegetable pie, cheese acts as a cover. During the Tudor era, however, flour and pastry became far better in quality.

44. The first record of a turkey being brought to Europe was in 1519, but it was many years before it became our Christmas dinner. For the Tudor rich, the traditional meat on Christmas Day remained swan or goose, as in a medieval Christmas feast. Note that the turkey was then called an 'Indian chicken', and here is named *Gallus Indicus*, Indian cockerel, alongside *Gallus Cornutus*, the 'Cuckold Cockerel'.

Above: 45. Woodcut of an English wild boar from the title page of a book published in London in 1593.

Below left: 46. Title page from Lyte's translation of Dodoen's Herbal, published in London in 1578. Herbals started to become popular in the Tudor period.

Below right: 47. Sixteenth-century drawings of herbs. Note the different spellings – there was no standardised spelling in England at this time.

Right: 48. Early seventeenth-century drawing of Shakespeare's *bon vivant* Sir John Falstaff holding a rare wine glass.

Below left: 49. Potatoes from Gerarde's Herbal, 1597. Potatoes were brought to England in the 1580s but at first few English people ate them, whereas sweet potatoes featured fairly prominently after their discovery. Only in the later sixteenth century did they become a staple food. According to conservative estimates, the introduction of the potato was responsible for a quarter of the growth in Old World population and urbanization between 1700 and 1900.

Below right: 50. A 1509 woodcut drawing of cooks.

51. A Tudor-era woodcut of a shepherd with his sheep. Lambs were rarely eaten as they were too valuable as a source of wool and for breeding more sheep. Sheep were only generally slaughtered at the end of their useful life.

8

Side Dishes

In Tudor times there were not side dishes as we know them today. Instead they were simply a series of many small courses for the nobility, whereas the poor had only one meal. This book has been sectioned to suit modern living, as per a modern restaurant menu, rather than be too unwieldy and each of these chosen 'side' dishes could also be a starter or a main course. We will start with *frumenty* (*frumente, frumentee, furmity, fromity, furmenty* or *fermenty*) which was made across Europe. For several centuries, frumenty was part of the traditional Celtic Christmas meal and came to be served as a festival dish on Twelfth Night. It was said by Florence White to be England's 'oldest national dish' (*Good things in England*, 1932). *Frumenty* was made primarily from boiled, cracked wheat, with its name deriving from the Latin *frumentum* (grain). Frumenty was served with meat as a pottage and traditionally with venison or porpoise.

FRUMENTE – FRUMENTY (1)
Curye on Inglysch, late fourteenth century

The earliest versions were probably made by early farming communities with dried grains. Before potatoes became a staple food, frumenty was generally served as the carbohydrate part of the meal. Roast and boiled meat, fish and game were all served with frumenty through the Middle Ages and into the Tudor and Stuart periods.

Frumenty was still being commonly referred to in Victorian books, although it had fallen out of favour as a dish. The following is a plain frumenty, to serve around six people, made for a worker's meal or breakfast.

'To make frumente. Tak clene whete and braye yt wel in a morter tyl the holes gon of; seethe it til it breste in water. Nym it up and lat it cole. Tak good broth and swete mylk of kyn or of almand and tempere it therwith. Nym yelkes of eyren rawe and saffroun and cast therto; salt it: lat it naught boyle after the etren ben cast therinne. Messe it forth with venesoun or with fat moutoun fresch.'

Ingredients: 275 g bulgar wheat; 150 ml chicken or vegetable stock; 1.1 l water.

Method: Boil the wheat in water for 15 minutes. Remove from the heat and stand for 15 minutes, most of the water should now be absorbed. Add the stock and bring to the boil, serve hot.

HAMPTON COURT FRUMENTY (2)

The Master-Cook of Richard II, *The Forme of Cury*, c. 1390; *Liber Cure Cocorum*, *Sloane MS.*, 1486, 1430 etc.

This thick wheat porridge was traditionally served with venison. It was often made with meat broth or almond milk instead of regular milk, depending on whether it was to be served on a meat or meatless day. There are several methods, but that used by the 'Tudor cooks' at Hampton Court today is as follows:

Ingredients: 150 g whole wheat (or pearl barley for convenience); 2 egg yolks; 100 g ground almonds; large pinch of saffron; 275 ml light stock.

Method: Bruise the wheat in a pestle and mortar. Place it in a pan, scald with hot water and leave in a cool place to soak for 1–2 days. Add more water to the wheat, so that the pan contains three times its volume of water, and leave in a warm oven or on a very gentle heat for at least a day to swell and cook. Leave to cool overnight. Blend the almonds with the stock and strain it to make almond milk. Beat it with the egg yolks and saffron, then beat the mixture into the wheat. Heat the wheat to almost boiling and serve in a deep dish. If you wish to save time, use pearl barley instead of whole wheat. If using barley, simmer in water for 45 minutes, then blend the almonds and so on.

LENT FRUMENTY (3)

Curye on Inglysch, late fourteenth century

There are many versions of frumenty, including a winter dish often served at Christmas with roast meats and vegetables. This makes an excellent side dish, especially alongside strongly flavoured meats. This particular dish was for Lent.

'To make frumente. Tak clene whete and braye yt wel in a morter tyl the holes gon of; seethe it til it breste in water. Nym it up and lat it cole. Tak good broth and swete mylk of kyn or of almand and tempere it therwith. Nym yelkes of eyren rawe and saffroun and cast therto; salt it: lat it naught boyle after the etren ben cast therinne. Messe it forth.'

Ingredients: 140 g cracked bulgar wheat; 1 pint ale or stock; 2 small eggs; 1–2 handfuls of currants; ½ teaspoon of mixed cinnamon, nutmeg and ginger; 3–4 tablespoons of single cream; a jug of water or stock to top up during cooking; a good pinch of saffron (optional).

Method: Soak the wheat in the ale or stock until it begins to swell, taking a few hours. Alternatively, boil for 15 minutes and then leave to stand for 15 minutes. Most of the liquid will be absorbed, but add more liquid if the frumenty begins to dry out when cooking. Add the spices and boil for a few minutes until the wheat is soft. Remove from the heat, add the currants and allow to cool a little so that the eggs will combine rather than cook. Beat the eggs and stir in, along with the cream. Do not allow to boil but cook on a low heat for a few minutes and serve.

A DISHE OF ARTECHOKES

Thomas Dawson's *The Good Huswifes Jewell*, 1585, 1594, 1596

Globe artichokes seem to have been a favourite dish of Henry VIII and this is easy to prepare.

'To make a dishe of Artechokes. Take your Artechokes and pare away all the top even to the meate and boyle them in sweete broth till they be somewhat tender, then take them out, and put them into a dishe, and seethe them with Pepper, synamon and ginger, and then put in your dishe that you meane to bake them in, and put in Marrowe to them good store, and so let them bake, and when they be baked, put in a little Vinegar and butter, and sticke three or foure leaves of the Artechoks in the dishe when you serve them up, and scrape Suger on the dish.'

Ingredients: 10–12 artichoke hearts, cooked; ½ tsp pepper; ½ tsp cinnamon; ½ tsp ginger; 2 tbsp water; 1 tbsp large crystal sugar; 4 tbsp butter; dash of vinegar.

Method: Mix pepper, cinnamon and ginger with water and bring to boil. Immediately remove from heat. Add artichoke hearts and allow to marinate for 15 minutes. Place into a baking dish, adding butter and vinegar. Bake at 180°C for 15 minutes. Sprinkle with sugar and serve.

RYSE OF GENOA – GENOVESE RICE

Gentyll manly Cokere MS Pepys 1047, c. 1500

Rice prepared in beef broth for a non-fasting day, or in almond milk for those frequent times when meat was prohibited.

'Take rice and bring it to boil in water and boil them well. And then take the rice off and place it in a fair vessel and pick them clean and set it on the fire again. And add to the rice fresh beef broth or marrow broth and let it boil well. And add ground saffron and salt, and if it is a fasting day temper it with almond milk and serve it.'

Ingredients: 100 g cooked white rice; 1.7 l beef stock or almond milk; 5 ml salt; large pinch of saffron.

Method: Combine all ingredients and bring to a low simmer. Cook for around 20 minutes until the liquid is absorbed, adding additional stock or almond milk if necessary. Stir occasionally to prevent sticking and burning. Fluff rice with a fork and serve.

DIVERS SALLETS BOYLED – SWEET-COOKED SALAD

John Murrel's *A New Booke of Cookerie*, 1615

This recipe can be used for a diverse range of vegetables, herbs, edible flowers and the like.

'Diuers Sallets boyled. Parboyle Spinage, and chop it fine, with the edges of two hard Trenchers vpon a boord, or the backe of two chopping Kniues: then set them on a Chafingdish of coales with Butter and Uinegar. Season it with Sinamon, Ginger, Sugar, and a few parboyld Currins. Then cut hard Egges into quarters to garnish it withall, and serue it vpon sippets. So may you serue Burrage, Buglosse, Endiffe, Suckory, Coleflowers, Sorrel, Marigold leaues, water Cresses, Leekes boyled, Onions, Sparragus, Rocket, Alexanders. Parboyle them, and season them all alike: whether it be with Oyle and Uinegar, or Butter and Uinegar, Sinamon, Ginger, Sugar, and Butter: Egges are necessary, or at least very good for all boyld Sallets.'

Ingredients: 1 head cauliflower; ¼ tsp cinnamon; ¼ tsp ginger; 1 tsp sugar; 3 tbsp butter; dash vinegar; ⅛ cup currants; 1 hard-boiled egg.

Method: Cut up cauliflower and parboil until just tender, adding currants halfway through. Drain and set aside. Melt butter in a large saucepan, mix in cauliflower florets and add sugar, spices and vinegar. Cut the egg into quarters and use as a garnish. Serve hot.

BRAIN BALLS AND BRAIN CAKES – THE SILENCE OF THE LAMBS

Elizabeth Moxon, *English Housewifry, exemplified in above four hundred and fifty receipts, giving directions in most parts of cookery*, 1764

Brain balls or cakes were a common accompaniment and side dish in Tudor times, but these are later recipes. A restaurant by the name of *Funky Gourmet*, in Athens, serves a sheep's brain. It names the dish 'The silence of the lambs…'

'To make Brain-cakes (1): Take a handful of bread – crumbs, a little shred lemon – peel, pepper, salt, nutmeg, sweet-marjoram, parsley shred fine, and the yolks of three eggs; take the brains and skin them, boil and chop them small, so mix them all together; take a little butter in your pan when you fry them, and drop them in as you do fritters, and if they run in your pan put in a handful more of bread-crumbs.'

Susan MacIver, in *Cookery and Pastry* (1789) gives a similar recipe:

'To Make Brain Cakes. When the head is cloven, take out the brains; take out any strings that may be amongst them, and cast them well with a knife; then put in a little raw egg, a scrape of nutmeg, and a little salt, and mix them with flour to make them stick together; cast them smooth; then drop them like biscuits into a pan of boiling butter, and fry them on both sides a fine brown. Lambs brains are done in the same manner.'

SPEARAGE – ASPARAGUS

John Gerard's *Herball, or Generall Historie of Plantes*, 1597

'Of Spearage or Asparagus. The Vertues. The first sprouts or naked tender shoots hereof oftentimes be sodden in flesh broth and eaten; or boiled in faire water and seasoned with oile, vinegar, salt, and pepper, then are served up as a sallad; they are pleasant to the taste.'

STEAMED ASPARAGUS SPEARS IN ORANGE SAUCE

Elizabethan recipe, originating in Granada, 1599.

Seville oranges are sour, so if using other oranges, add a good dash of lemon juice. '*Para Hazer Escudilla de Esparragos Silvesteres y Domesticos*: Take the most tender part, cause it to boil in hot water until they seem tender, and finish cooking them with good broth of capon or veal: and these want to be served with a little broth. With the wild ones [asparagus] you can put raisins. The cultivated ones can be served with orange juice, sugar, and salt.'

Ingredients: 12 spears of asparagus; juice of 6 Seville oranges; 1 tbsp brown sugar; 1 tbsp butter; pinch of salt.

Method: Cut off the woody base of the asparagus and steam the spears for about 8 minutes, or until tender. Meanwhile, heat the orange juice in a saucepan. Add the sugar and a pinch of salt and whisk in the butter. Allow to thicken for a few minutes. Arrange the asparagus on a plate, pour over the orange sauce and serve immediately.

COMPOST – COLD SPICED VEGETABLES IN WINE AND HONEY SAUCE

The Master-Cook of Richard II, *The Forme of Cury*, *c*. 1390

'Compost. Take rote of parsel. pasternak of rasenns. Scrape hem waisthe hem clene. take rapes and caboches ypared and icorne. take an erthen panne with clene water and set it on the fire. Cast all þise þerinne. whan þey buth boiled cast þerto peeres and parboile hem wel. Take þise thynges up and lat it kele on a fair cloth, do þerto salt whan it is colde in a vessel take vineger and powdour and safroun and do þerto. And lat alle þise thinges lye þerin al nyzt oþer al day. Take wyne greke and hony clarified togider lumbarde mustard and raisouns corance al hool. And grynde powdour of canel powdour douce. And aneys hole and fenell seed. Take alle þise thynges and cast togyder in a pot of erthe. and take þerof whan þou wilt and serue forth.'

Ingredients: 3 parsley roots; 3 parsnips; 3 carrots; 10 radishes; 2 turnips; 1 small cabbage; 2 pears; ½ tsp salt; 1 cup vinegar; ¼ tsp pepper; pinch of saffron, ground; 1 cup sweet wine or Marsala; ½ cup honey; 1 tbsp mustard; ½ cup currants; 1 tsp cinnamon; 1 tsp powder douce; 1 tsp aniseed; 1 tsp fennel seeds.

Method: Peel vegetables and chop into bite-sized pieces. Parboil until just tender, adding sliced pears about halfway through cooking time. Remove from water, drain, place on a tray, sprinkle with salt and allow to cool. Place vegetables in a large bowl and add pepper, saffron and vinegar. Refrigerate for several hours, then put wine and honey into a saucepan, bring to the boil and then simmer for several minutes, removing any scum that forms on the surface. Allow to cool and add currants and remaining spices. Mix well and pour over vegetables. Serve cold.

SPROUTS OF LIFE – ITALIAN SPROUTS

Anonymous, Venetian *Libro di cucina/ Libro per cuoco*, 14th–15th century

'If you want to make sprouts of life, take the rounded cabbage sprouts and boil them for a little while. When they are a parboiled take them off the heat and strain away all the water. And then fry them well in plenty of fat. Take verjuice, parsley, water, spices and salt and mix them well together before putting them on top, and let them boil well together. Then take a little marjoram, temper it with water and put it above and it will be good.'

CRESSEE – GINGER PASTA CHEESE CHESSBOARD SANDWICH

Two Anglo-Normal Culinary Collections Edited from British Library Manuscripts Additional 32085 and Royal 12.C.xii

We think of pasta as a recent Italian addition to British cuisine, but this dish approaches it. The dish is a lattice of yellow and white (or red) noodle strips, to be covered with cheese. Variants were served throughout the Tudor and Stuart ages. Red sandalwood is the heartwood of the *Pterocarpus santalinus*, a tree native of South India, Sri Lanka and the Philippines. Red sandalwood yields a vibrant reddish-scarlet colour, used as a natural dye and in dried potpourri and incense blends. This variety of sandalwood, also known as saunders, red sanders, red saunders and rubywood, is not to be confused with the more aromatic sandalwood (*Santalum album*).

'Here is another dish, which is called cressee. Take best white flour and eggs, and make pasta dough; and in the pasta dough put fine choice ginger and sugar. Take half of the pastry, (which is or should be) coloured with saffron, and half (which is or should be) white, and roll it out on a table to the thickness of your finger; then cut into strips the size of a piece of lath; stretch it out on a table as illustrated; then boil in water; then take a slotted spoon and remove the cressees from the water; then arrange them on, and cover them with, grated cheese, add butter or oil, and serve.'

Ingredients: 1½ cup of unbleached flour; 2 eggs; 2 tbsp sugar; 1 tsp powdered ginger; 1 tsp saffron, good pinch of salt; cheese; 1–2 tbsp water.

Method: Mix the dry ingredients, except the saffron, together, then knead in the eggs until you get a relatively smooth dough. You can use a processor to save time and effort. Divide the dough into two portions. Grind the saffron in a mortar, adding a little warm water to bring out the colour. Mix this into one of the portions and continue kneading until it is yellow and has achieved a smooth consistency. Set aside. Take the other, uncoloured portion, add a little water and knead it until consistently smooth. If you wish, you can add sandalwood or red colouring for this portion. Roll out each piece of dough around ¼ to ½ inch thick and then cut into fairly wide strips. Weave like a lattice-top for a pie. Start in the middle and work your way out symmetrically and tuck the ends in around the edges. Squash the cressee a little to make everything firm. For a ½ inch cressee, cook in boiling salted water for 15 minutes, and for a ¼ inch one cook for 10 minutes. Remove from the water, place on grated cheese on a warmed dish, then some butter or olive oil and some more grated cheese on top. You could also use a pasta machine to cut the two doughs into strips, then place in boiling water and cook until *al dente* as you would with normal pasta. Make a lattice of the strips with alternating colours.

CHAWETTYS – VEAL PIES

Two Fifteenth Century Cookbooks – Harleian MS. 279 & Harl. MS. 4016, c. 1440
You can include half veal and half ham, to make veal and ham pies, or chicken and ham etc.

'Take buttys of vele and mince hem smalle or Pork, and put on a potte, take wine and caste thereto powder of gyngere, pepir, safroun and salt and a little verjuice and do hem in a coffin with yolkeyes of Eyroun and kutte datys and roysonys of coraunce, clowys, mace and then ceuere thin cofyn, and lat it bake tyl it be y-now.'

Ingredients: For 12 small pastry pies: 2 cups flour; 1 egg yolk; ⅓ tsp salt; 4 oz butter; ⅔ cup sour cream.

Method for Pastry: Cut butter into small pieces, mix into the flour and add egg and salt and enough sour cream to make a dough. Chill for an hour or so and make 12 small pies.

Ingredients for pie filling: 1½ lb ground veal; ½ cup wine; ½ tsp salt; ½ tsp pepper; ¾ tsp ginger; 1 tbsp wine vinegar; 3 egg yolks; ¾ cup dates, chopped; ¾ cup raisins; ½ tsp cloves; ½ tsp mace.

Method for Pies: Brown and drain the veal, then add wine, ginger, salt, pepper and allow to simmer for a while. After about 10 minutes, add raisins, dates, mace and cloves and allow to simmer for 5 minutes. Cool before mixing in the egg yolks. Fill tarts and cover with pastry lids, brush with egg yolk and bake at 160°C for about 20 minutes, or until cooked.

SPYNOCHES Y FRYED – CRISPY SPICED SPINACH

The Master-Cook of Richard II, *The Forme of Cury*, *c.* 1390

'Gode powder', a sweet spice blend that usually seasons sweet dishes, is here used in a savoury context, and the recipe is given in the preserves chapter. This is a little like the Chinese or Japanese crispy seaweed.

Ingredients: 300 g washed spinach; olive oil for frying; 3 tsp good powder.

Method: Bring a pan of water to the boil and add washed spinach. Remove after two minutes, drain and roughly chop. Heat oil in a frying pan and add the spinach. Stir and when it starts to crisp, tip into a serving bowl. Sprinkle the 'good powder' over the top and serve.

SAUSEDGES – SMALL SAUSAGES

Thomas Dawson's *The Good Huswifes Jewell*, 1585, 1594, 1596

Perfect for grilling outdoors or as a quick snack, served with Tewkesbury or other mustard. 'Martinmasse beefe' was dried, salted beef, it being common practice to slaughter cattle on the feast-day of St Martin, 11 November, to be preserved for winter. Historically, hiring fairs were held on this day, when farm labourers would seek new posts. Half tsp 'liquid smoke' has been added by some writers to supplement the smoke flavour lost, but they can be grilled over a wood-fired barbecue instead. Being small, they cook through easily.

'To make a sausedge. Take Martinmasse beefe, or if you can not get it, take fresh beefe, or the lean of bacon if you will, and you must mince very small that kinde of flesh that you take, and cut Lard and put into the minced meate, and whole pepper, and the yolkes of seaven Egges, and mingle them altogether, and put the meate into a gut very salt, and hang him in the Chimney where he may dry, and there let him hang a moneth or twoo before you take him downe.'

Ingredients: 1 pound beef; ⅓ pound lard or suet; sausage casing; 1 egg yolk; ½ tbsp salt; 1 tsp pepper.

Method: Grind beef and suet and mix together until uniform. Add the remaining ingredients and enough water to make the meat easy to stuff into your sausage casing. Fry, grill or bake.

PERRY OF PESOUN – A DISH OF PEAS AND ONIONS

The Master-Cook of Richard II, *The Forme of Cury*, *c.* 1390

'A Dish of Peas. Take peas and boil them fast, and cover them, until they burst. Then take them up and cool through a cloth. Take onions and mince them, and boil with the peas, and add oil. Add sugar, salt and saffron, and boil well together, and serve.'

Ingredients: 900 g fresh or frozen peas; 2–3 small, finely-chopped onions; 3 tbsp olive oil; salt; sugar to taste; pinch of saffron.

Method: Place onions and peas in a pan with a little water, bring to the boil and add salt and sugar to taste. Add saffron if available – alternatively the far cheaper turmeric helps colour any dish. Reduce heat slightly and cook until tender. Check seasoning then drain and serve, dressing sparsely with some olive oil.

BUTTERED WORTES – BUTTERED CABBAGE AND LEEKS ON BREAD OR TOAST (2 WAYS)

Gentyll Manly Cokere MS Pepys 1047, *c.* 1500

There are also similar recipes in *Harleian 4016, A Noble Boke of Cookrye* and *Two Fifteenth Century Cookery Books*. Wortes was another name for green vegetables and herbs.

'To make buttyrd Wortys. Take all maner of gode herbys that ye may gette pyke them washe them and hacke them and boyle them vp in fayre water and put ther to butture clarefied A grete quantite And when they be boylde enowgh salt them but let non Ote mele come ther yn And dyse brede in small gobbetts and do hit in dyshys and powre the wortes A pon and serue hit furth.

Ingredients 1: 1 shredded head of cabbage; 2 leeks, cut into roundels; ½ cup parsley, loosely chopped; 100 g clarified butter; 3 slices wheat bread, broken into pieces; salt.

Method 1: Bring a pot of water to the boil, then add cabbage and leeks, cooking until just tender. Add the parsley towards the end, as it does not take as long to cook. Drain and put on top of the bread pieces. Pour butter over the cabbage and salt to taste.

Ingredients 2: A selection of greens such as cabbage, spring onions, spring greens, lettuce, watercress, nettles, cress etc., can be used, with lesser quantities of herbs such as parsley, thyme etc.

Method 2: If you use a lot of different greens, barely cover them with water and boil for 15 minutes or until tender. Drain off the water, stir in the butter and salt and place on a layer of cubed white bread or toast.

SWEET POTATOES IN ROSE AND ORANGE SYRUP
Elinor Fettiplace's Receipt Book, 1605

This work has some of the earliest recipes for sweet potatoes in Britain. Because these were called potatoes in later Tudor and early Stuart recipe books, they are often confused with the newly discovered New World potatoes, which were not being used for cookery at this time. This latter potato was grown widely in Ireland a long time before it became common and popular in the rest of Britain, and John Forster was the first to refer to it as the 'Irish potato', to distinguish it from the sweet potato which was far more widely known. From the beginning, it was considered lowly food, only suitable for pigs, peasants and prisoners. One who did promote the 'Irish potato' in the seventeenth century was John Forster, who published a treatise in 1664 with the snappy title of: *England's Happiness Increased, Or a sure and Easy Remedy Against all Succeeding Dear Years by a Plantation of the Roots called Potatoes: Whereby (with the Addition of Wheat flower) Excellent Good and Wholesome Bread may be Made Every 8 or 9 Months Together, for Half the Charge as Formerly; Also by the Planting of These Roots Ten Thousand Men in England and Wales Who Know Not How to Live, or What to Do to Get a Maintenance for their Families, may on one Acre of Ground make 30 Pounds per Annum. Invented and Published for the Good of the Poorer Sort.* According to Smythe, ambergris was 'a fragrant drug found floating on sea coasts, greyish, light, easily fusible used as a perfume and cordial and in various essences and tinctures'. Ambergris is a waxy substance found floating at sea, or washed up on beaches, secreted by the sperm whale, and still of great value in perfume manufacture. It was often spelt *amber grease/greece*, signifying its colour and function, and was sometimes mixed with salt. It is omitted below.

'Boile your roots in faire water until they bee somewhat tender then pill of the skinne, then make your syrupe, weying to every pound of roots a pound of sugar and a quarter of a pint of faire water, and as much of rose water, and the juice of three or fowre oranges, then boile the syrupe, and boile them till they bee throughlie soaked in the syrupe, before you take it from the fire, put in a little musk and amber greece.'

Ingredients: 3½ lbs sweet potatoes; 1 cup sugar; ½ cup water; ¼ cup orange juice; ¼ cup rosewater; ⅛ cup fresh rose petals; ¼ tsp double strength vanilla.
Method: Bake sweet potatoes till tender, then peel and slice. Mix sugar and water over low heat until liquefied, then add orange juice, rosewater and rose

petals. Stir until heated, then pour over the sliced sweet potatoes. Garnish with fresh rose flowers if available. If using dried rose petals, add with sugar.

POMMES DORRES – FLY BALLS

The Master-Cook of Richard II, *The Forme of Cury*, *c.* 1390

This is a dish of savoury pork meatballs, and *pommes d'or* would mean golden apples. However, *dorre* was a medieval word applied to species of bees or flies, and the addition of raisins and cloves gives the dish the appearance of being covered with flies, hence the semi-humorous translation of 'fly balls' rather than 'fly apples'.

Ingredients: 1 lb ground pork; ½ lb golden raisins, simmered in ½ cup water and 1 tbsp wine; 3 slices dried and crumbed bread; 1 egg; 1 egg white (optional); ¼ tsp cloves; ¼ tsp nutmeg; ⅓ tsp ginger; ½ tsp cinnamon; ⅓ tsp black pepper; 1 tsp salt; 1½ tbsp honey.

Method: Preheat oven to 180°C. Simmer raisins. Once the raisins have absorbed most of the liquid, add them to the remaining ingredients. Knead thoroughly, shaping into balls 1¼-1 ¾ inches in diameter. Bake for 30–40 minutes, depending on size, until done.

SALLET OF ALL KINDE OF HEARBES

Thomas Dawson's *A Booke of Cokerie*, 1620

'To make a Sallet of all kinde of Hearbes. Take your hearbes and pick them very fine into faire water, and picke your flowers by themselves, and wash them cleane, then swing them in a Strayner, and when you put them into a dish, mingle them with Cowcumbers or Lemons payred and sliced, also scrape Suger and put in Vineger and Oyle, then spread the flowers on the top of the Sallet, and with every sorte of the aforesaid thinges, garnish the dish about, then take Egges boyled hard, and lay about the dish and upon the Sallet.'

PAYN RAGON – PINE NUT CANDY

The Master-Cook of Richard II, *The Forme of Cury*, *c.* 1390

This sweetmeat was used as an accompaniment to fried meat or fish. Today this would more likely be served as a snack or treat, but the Tudors saw no problem with mixing sweet and savoury and today's chefs are moving in that same direction. Until recently, the only such British dish was possibly the ubiquitous pineapple ring on a gammon steak. We have also seen the odd addition of pineapples to pizzas.

'Take honey, Cypriot sugar and clarify them together and boil it over a gentle fire, ensuring that it does not burn and when it has boiled a while take out a drop of it with your finger and add to a little water and ensure it hangs together and take it off the heat and add to it a third part [of bread] and ground ginger and stir it together until it begins to thicken and pour it on a wet table. Slice it and serve it forth with fried meat on a flesh day or on fish days.'

Ingredients: 200 g white sugar; 4 tbsp runny honey; 125 ml water; 1½ tbsp pine nuts, coarsely ground; 100 g fine white breadcrumbs; 1 tsp ground ginger.

Method: Combine the sugar, honey and water in a pan, simmer and skim the surface then continue boiling until a thermometer reads 110°C. Immediately turn the mixture into a heated bowl and whisk briskly for about 3 minutes. Then beat in the pine nuts, breadcrumbs and ground ginger until completely incorporated. Turn the resultant mixture onto a greased shallow baking tin and allow to harden. Cut into small slices and serve.

POMESMOILE – APPLE PUDDING
Laud MS 553 Two Fifteenth-Century Cookery-Books

This was a side dish, a little with the consistency of porridge and would also make an excellent breakfast dish.

'Nym rys and bray hem in a morter, tempre hem vp with almande milke, boille hem: nym appelis and kerue hem as small as douste, cast hem yn after ye boillyng, and sugur: colour hit with safron, cast therto goud poudre, and sif hit forth.'

Ingredients: 6 small, unpeeled apples, ground fine; 1½ cups almond milk; ¼ cup cream of rice; ¼ cup sugar; enough saffron (or turmeric) to lightly colour the mixture. If you have no 'goud poudre' available (see preserves for recipe), you can quickly make some with ½ tsp each of ground nutmeg, ground grains of paradise and 1 tsp sugar.

Method: Stir all together in a pan and bring to a slow simmer, stirring occasionally until cooked. Sprinkle good powder over the pudding.

MAKKE – BROAD BEAN PURÉE WITH FRIED ONIONS
The Master-Cook of Richard II, *The Forme of Cury*, c. 1390

'Take drawen benes and feeþ he wel. take he up of the watr and caſt he in a mortr grynde hem al to douſt til þei be white as eny mylk, whawf a litell rede wyne, caſt among in þe gryndyng, to þsat, leþhe it ī diſsh. þanne take Onyonns and mynce hem ſmale and feeþ hem ī oile til þey be al bronn. and floriſsh the diſsh bewith. and sūe it forth.'

Ingredients: 400 g dried, split broad beans; 600 ml beef stock; 250 ml red wine; 6 thinly sliced shallots.

Method: Place the beans in a large bowl and cover with cold water, ensuring there is at least an inch of water above the beans. The following morning, drain the beans, place in a pan and add 600 ml beef stock. Bring to the boil, cover and simmer for about 40 minutes, until the beans have just softened. Add more stock or water if needed. Take off the heat, allow to cool and pour into a food processor. Blend the mixture, then add the red wine and blend again to a smooth paste and return to the saucepan. Gently heat the mixture until it just comes to the boil, then turn off the heat. Meanwhile, add some butter to a frying pan and fry the shallots until they turn brown and slightly crispy. Spoon the bean mixture into a bowl, top with the fried onions and serve immediately.

POMME PORRE – FIG AND PEA POTTAGE
Beinecke MS 163, An Ordinance of Potage
The dish is surprisingly sweet.

'Boyle white pesyn; hool hem. Take hem fro the fyre when they have restyd a whyle, then take the cleryst into anothir pott. Then have mylke of almondes drawyn up with white wyn, figes of amely, sigure and salte, and, yf thou wylte, reysons fryed a lytyll, and do togedyr. Boyle hit; kepe hit, and serve hit forth.'

Ingredients: 1 cup dried whole yellow peas soaked overnight; almond milk made with white wine; ½ cup figs; 1 tsp sugar; lightly-fried raisins (optional); salt to taste.

Method: Place in a cooking pot, uncovered, the soaked peas, the other ingredients and enough almond milk to just cover the mixture. Bring to a simmer, stirring occasionally to prevent sticking. Add a little almond milk at a time to prevent the dish from drying out, until the peas are cooked through. The dish should be like a loose porridge when served.

GOURDES IN POTAGE – PORK AND SQUASH BROTH (TWO WAYS)
The Master-Cook of Richard II, *The Forme of Cury, c.* 1390
The Tudors may have used green Chinese squashes, as New World squashes were possibly only just being introduced into England at the end of Elizabeth's reign. The word squash derives from *askutasquash* (a green thing eaten raw), a word from the Narrangasett language, first documented in 1643 by Roger Williams, the founder of Rhode Island. The squash order *Cucurbitale*, includes pumpkin, gourd, zucchini, courgette and marrow and most can be adapted to this recipe, especially butternut squash. The bottle gourd is of *Lagenaria* genus, part of the same order as the squashes, and includes the calabash, also known as the opo squash, or long melon. Portuguese sailors introduced the *kabocha* squash to Japan in 1541, bringing it with them from Cambodia, and squashes were also being brought into Europe from China. An Asian variety of the winter squash *Cucurbita maxima*, also known as Japanese pumpkin, was possibly the variety used in England. The fact that they are in the recipe

as 'young' indicates that they could have been grown commercially in Europe at this time. There were other edible Asian *cucurbitae* species, such as the Chinese pumpkin or squash *Cucurbita moschata*, known to the Chinese as a 'food melon'.

'Take young gowrdes, pare hem and kerue hem on pecys. Cast hem in gode broth, and do thereto a good pertye of oynouns mynced. Take pork sodden; grynde it and alye it therwith and with 3olkes of ayren. Do therto safroun and salt, and messe it forth with powdour douce.'

Ingredients 1: 1 kg gourd, such as Chinese pumpkin or butternut squash, peeled, seeded and diced; 3 medium onions, finely chopped; 700 ml beef stock; 125 g cubed pork; 2 egg yolks, beaten; salt to taste; 5–6 saffron threads ground into 1 tbsp warm water in a pestle and mortar and allowed to seep; powder douce (see chapter on preserves).

Method 1: Place the pork in a pan and cover with water. Bring to the boil, season with salt and simmer for 40 minutes. When cooked, set the meat aside to cool. Peel and cube the squash and place in a pan with the onions. Pour the broth over this, bring to the boil and reduce to a simmer. Cook for about 15 minutes. Pound the cooked pork in a pestle and mortar or mince the meat finely. When the 15 minutes are up, add the pork and cook for a further 10 minutes, or until the squash is just tender. At the end of the cooking time, stir in the powder douce, the saffron, along with its seeping liquid, and the egg yolks.

Ingredients 2: This is a quicker dish to prepare. Use peeled and chopped courgettes, enough for a side dish; chicken broth or a stock cube; ½ lb or more of pork, chopped and fried; 2 egg yolks; one large chopped onion; salt, saffron, cinnamon, brown sugar, ginger, nutmeg and parsley to taste.

Method 2: Add the chopped courgettes to one cup chicken broth per person, in a stock pot. Add one large chopped onion per 4 persons. Add fried pork and 2 egg yolks. Add salt, saffron, cinnamon, brown sugar, ginger, nutmeg and parsley to taste and simmer until courgette is tender.

BALDRICK'S FRIED TURNIPS
Le Ménagier De Paris, 1393

An excellent accompaniment to a meat dish.

'Turnips are hard and difficult to cook until they have been in the cold and frost; you remove the head, the tail and other whiskers and roots, then they are peeled, then wash in two or three changes of hot water, very hot, then cook in hot meat stock, pork, beef or mutton… when they are cooked, they are sliced and fried in a pan, and powdered spices thrown on.'

Ingredients: 3–4 turnips; 6–8 cups beef broth; butter; powder douce.

Method: Cut the ends off the turnips. Boil the turnips in beef broth until tender. Remove from broth, slice and fry in butter. Sprinkle with powder douce and serve.

TURNIP MEAT – BALDRICK'S CHEESY TURNIPS
Anonymous, Venetian *Libro di cucina/ Libro per cuoco*, 14th–15th century
'Take turnips with small leaves and put them to boil. When they are just about cooked pour away the water and put in enough of grated cheese and let them cook together. When they are cooked and you are ready to serve them put as much of that same cheese over the plate.'

ARMOURED TURNIPS
Anonymous, Venetian *Libro di cucina/ Libro per cuoco*, 14th–15th century
'To make armoured turnips, put the turnips to cook in the fire embers and when they are cooked peel them and cut into thin slices. Take sweet cheese and make thin slices. Between each slice of turnip put one slice of cheese and let them melt well together. If you want you can put them with a hot lid above and they will be done, then powder them with sugar, etc.'

CHYCHES – GARLIC CHICKPEA BROTH
The Master-Cook of Richard II, *The Forme of Cury*, *c.* 1390
This 69-year-old writer had hardly heard of, and never tasted, chickpeas until in his thirties, but they were yet another food, fairly new to late twentieth-century Britain, but common in Tudor times.
'Chyches. Take chickpeas and cover them in ashes all night or all day, or lay them in hot embers. At morrow wash them in clean water, and do them over the fire with clean water. Boil them up and add oil, whole garlic, saffron, powder fort and salt. Boil it and serve it forth.'
Ingredients: 600 g canned chickpeas; cloves from 2 whole garlic heads, peeled but left whole; olive oil; ½ tsp black pepper; ½ tsp ground cloves; pinch of saffron; pinch of salt.
Method: Drain and rinse the chickpeas then place in a single layer on a baking tray and roast in an oven preheated to 200°C for about 45 minutes, turning them over mid-way through so that they cook evenly. They should have a texture and aroma similar to roast nuts when done. Remove from the oven, then place in a pot along with the garlic cloves and just enough water to be 1 cm above the chickpeas. Top with the olive oil, adding just enough to cover the surface of the water. Add the spices then bring to the boil then reduce to a simmer and continue cooking until the garlic softens, which will take about 15 minutes. Drain and serve in the broth.

PYES OF PARYS – PARISIAN MEATBALLS IN SAUCE

A Noble Boke off Cookry ffor a Prynce Houssolde Holkham MSS 674, 1480

This is also featured in *Pleyn Delite* and *Two Fifteenth Century Cookery Books* and makes a perfect buffet or party dish. Cubeb, *Piper cubeba*, was native to Indonesia, particularly Java, and the berries came to Europe via India through Venetian trade with the Arabs. Venetian ships brought most of Henry VII's imports of spices, to be overtaken by the Portuguese as they colonised the 'Eastern World' while Spain was given papal dispensation to take over the Western 'New World'. The Dutch soon followed in Portuguese footsteps and both nations traded with the Tudors extensively. Javanese growers protected their monopoly of the trade by sterilizing the berries by scalding, thus ensuring that the vines were unable to be cultivated elsewhere. Its main use appears to have been in medicine, although its similarity to very expensive pepper made it a handy substitute. Also known as cubeb berries, tailed pepper, tailed cubebs and Java pepper, cubeb is native to the Spice Islands and is still harvested primarily in Indonesia. Beginning in the sixteenth century and for the following 200 years, cubebs were a substitute for pepper throughout Europe, but they never became as popular as white or black peppercorns. The berries, or fruit, are picked before they are ripe and then dried. When harvested the stalk remains attached hence the reference to 'tailed pepper'. Cubebs have a pleasant aroma that is pungent, lightly peppery with hints of allspice. The stalked berries are a little larger than peppercorns, and were thought by the people of Europe to be repulsive to demons.

'To mak pyes of pairis tak and smyt fair buttes of pork and buttes of vele and put it to gedure in a pot with freshe brothe and put ther to a quantite of wyne and boile it tille it be enoughe then put it in to a treene vesselle and put ther to raw yolks of eggs pouder of guinger sugur salt and mynced dates and raissins of corans and mak a good thyn paiste and mak coffyns and put it ther in and bak it welle and serue it.'

Ingredients for the meatballs; 1 pound ground beef; 2 egg yolks; ¼ cup currants; 1 tbsp sugar; ⅛ tsp pepper; ¼ tsp mace; ¼ tsp cloves; ¼ tsp cubebs; ¼ tsp cinnamon; ¼ tsp salt; pinch of saffron; 4 cups beef broth; ¼ cup wine.

Ingredients for the sauce: 2 cups almond milk; 1 tbsp rice flour; 3 tbsp sugar; ⅛ tsp mace; ⅛ tsp cinnamon.

Method 1: Mix ground beef, egg yolks, currants, sugar and spices. Form into small balls, about an inch in diameter. Boil the broth and add the meatballs and wine, simmering for around 15–20 minutes until the meat is cooked. Remove meatballs from the broth and place in serving dish. In a separate pan, mix almond milk, rice flour, sugar and mace. Bring to a boil, reduce heat and simmer over medium heat until thick. Pour just enough sauce over the *pumpes* to thoroughly coat them and serve.

Method 2: To make a pie. Simmer a pound of ground meat in a mixture of red wine and broth (just enough to cover it), until cooked. Add currants and sweet spices such as cinnamon, cloves, etc. Cook until it thickens slightly, then remove from the heat and allow to cool a little, before beating in egg yolks, to help the pie set while baking. Bake as a 1 or 2 crust pie.

ELIZABETHAN SUGARED EGGS THREE WAYS
Le Ménagier De Paris, 1393

'Omelette Fried with Sugar. Take out all the whites and beat the yolks, then put some sugar in a frying-pan and let it melt, and then fry your yolks in it, then put on a plate, with sugar on them.

Lost Eggs. Take four egg-yolks and beat them, add rock and powdered sugar, and let it all be beaten together very well, then poured through a strainer, then fried on the iron skillet and after that cut in lozenges; then let these lozenges be put on a dish with another omelette of poached eggs and finely powdered spices sprinkled on top.

To Make a Beautiful Omelette with Eggs. Take seven eggs and remove the whites from two and put those in a bowl, and break all the others and beat with the two extra yolks, and fry; and it will be yellow. Or, take six or twelve eggs and remove the whites and beat the yolks, and fry in oil, and let it be well spread out over the skillet, and cut in lozenges, and each lozenge should be turned over with the flipper, then put on the plate half an omelette fried in the ordinary way and four lozenges of these yolks, and some of the sugar sort fried in the ordinary way.'

TO MAKE MEAT OF EGGES BEATEN – MOCK PEA SOUP
Epulario, or The Italian Banquet (in English), 1598

The following vegetable soup serves as a side or a starter. If pea water and vegetable broth are unavailable, use a vegetable stock cube boiled in a little water, adding to the egg broth after the egg has been removed. Breadcrumbs are a simple way of using up leftover crusts or bread to thicken sauces instead of making a roux of flour. Never buy packet breadcrumbs, but use stale bread. 'To make meat of Egges beaten, which shall shew like pease. Seethe Egges a little, then take them out of the broth and to make the broth somewhat thicke, take the crummes of a white loaf and straine it through the water, or else take the broth of Pease itself if you can get it, for it is better, and in any of these two broths you shall seeth your egges again, with some spice, safron, parsely and Mint minced very small.'

PESON OF ALMAYNE – GERMAN WHITE PEAS

The Master-Cook of Richard II, *The Forme of Cury*, c. 1390

A Collection of Old English Customs of 1842 tells us of a 'bequest of white peas' which is still being honoured: 'John Huntingtdon of Sawston, Cambridgeshire, England, by will, dated 4th August, 1554, devised lands and tenements to Joice his wife, and his heirs, upon condition that his heirs should yearly forever sow two acres of land, lying together in Linton field, with white peas, one coomb to be yearly bestowed upon each acre, for the relief of the people of Sawston. Two acres, the property of Richard Huddlestone, Esq., the lord of the several manors in the parish, are annually sowed with white peas, as directed by the will, which are gathered green on a day fixed by the occupier of the land, by all the poor indiscriminately, with an complete scene of scramble and confusion ensues, attended with occasional conflicts.' The Town Peas ceremony is still held annually, and peas picked, almost 500 years after the bequest. The Huddlestone family held the Grade 1 listed Tudor manor house, Sawston Hall, and its estate, from 1517 to 1982. As practising Catholics they installed priest holes in the hall.

'German Peas. Take white peas, wash them and boil them a long time. Take them and strain through a cloth. Wash them in cold water until the hulls slip off. Place in a pan and cover tightly so that no steam may escape and boil them thoroughly. And add to this good almond milk and a quantity of rice flour with powdered ginger, saffron and salt.'

Ingredients: 250 g dried white peas; 250 ml almond milk; 4 tbsp rice flour; 1 tsp ground ginger; generous pinch of crumbled saffron; salt, to taste.

Method: Place the peas in a bowl, cover with water and set aside to soak for at least 2 hours. Then drain the peas, place in a pan, cover with water and bring to a boil. Boil for about 2 hours, or until the peas begin to tenderize, then turn into a sieve and drain. Allow to cool, then wash in cold water and allow the hulls to slip off. Place in a pan, just cover with water and bring to the boil. Reduce to a simmer, cover with a tight-fitting lid and cook for about 90 more minutes, or until the peas begin to break down. Mix the rice flour with a little of the almond milk to form a smooth paste. Add the remaining almond milk to the peas along with the saffron and ginger and then work in the rice flour paste. Continue cooking for about 20 minutes until the mixture begins to thicken, then season with salt to taste and serve.

FRIED EGG BALLS

The lady's companion: or, an infallible guide to the fair sex Containing, rules, directions, and observations, for their conduct and behaviour through … of life, as virgins, wives

I make no apologies for including this much later recipe from 1743 as an *amuse-bouche*, as it deserves to be better known! 'Collops' usually refers to slices of bacon, so this could be a traditional breakfast of bacon and eggs with a twist. A later version advises serving with stewed spinach and garnished with orange. 'To fry eggs as round as balls. Having a deep frying-pan, and three pints of clarified butter, heat it as hot as for Fritters, and stir it with a Stick, till it runs round like a Whirl-pool; then break an egg into the middle, and turn it round with your Stick, till it be as hard as a soft poached Egg; the Whirling round of the Butter will make it as round as a Ball, then take it up with a Slice, and put it into a warm Pipkin or Dish set it leaning before the Fire to keep hot: they will keep hot half an Hour and yet be soft; so you may do as many as you please. You may serve them with fry'd or roasted Collops.'

BARA LAWR A'R TOST – LAVERBREAD ON TOAST
Traditional Welsh

This seaweed is harvested on the west coast of the British Isles. It is thoroughly washed several times and is cooked until it becomes soft. It is then minced to convert it into a thick black/green paste-like texture. This made a staple breakfast of laverbread and cockles, *bara lawr a chocos*, to which bacon and eggs were later added. Laver is also a delicacy in Japan, mainly used for *sushi*. Laverbread is nutritious, very low in calories, rich in protein and contains over 50 known minerals and trace elements. The sea-enriched weed provides high quantities of calcium, iron, potassium, magnesium and iodine and vitamins A, B, B2, C and D. Seaweeds such as laverbread enhance the flexibility and mobility of joints, are healing to the mucous membranes and promote healthy skin. Edible seaweeds can be roughly categorised into the finer weeds such as *Laver* and sea lettuce; the short stemmed such as *dulse*, Irish moss or *Carragheen*; and 'horse tail' kelps which grow on or below the tide mark. Laverbread is the most prized for its versatility in cooking and should be far more widely available.

Ingredients: 600 g fresh laver seaweed (use tinned if unavailable); 3 tbsp olive oil; 1–2 tsp fresh lemon juice; salt and pepper to taste; 4 slices bread; butter, to taste.

Method: Wash the seaweed and rinse in clean water several times. Over a low heat, or in a slow cooker, simmer the seaweed for 6 hours until it turns into a dark pulp. However, tinned laverbread has been pre-cooked and is available in delicatessens. Combine the cooked, hot laverbread, olive oil, lemon juice and seasoning and stir through. Toast the bread and butter to taste. Spoon the laverbread onto the hot toast and serve immediately.

PEMBROKESHIRE LAVERBREAD CAKES
Traditional Welsh

Richard Burton called laverbread 'Welsh caviar' and the former recipe gives its full taste and texture, but some might prefer this method of cooking it, as a breakfast dish or accompaniment.

Ingredients: 450 g prepared fresh laverbread (or tinned); 1 teaspoon lemon juice; 200 g rolled oats; 50 g toasted pine nuts (optional); 2–3 tbsp olive oil or bacon fat; salt and pepper to taste.

Method: Combine the laverbread, lemon juice, oats and pine nuts in a mixing bowl, then form into shapes like fishcakes, seasoning well. Warm the oil in a frying pan over a medium heat. Add the laverbread cakes and fry for 5–6 minutes on each side until golden brown. Remove from the pan and serve immediately, preferably with bacon and eggs as a full breakfast.

MANCHET – FINE WHITE BREAD OF THE NOBILITY
The Good Huswifes Handmaide for the Kitchin, 1594, 1597 (and 1588)

In this recipe, as in all other period recipes, the 'fair' water referred to clean spring water, as opposed to rainwater gathered in barrels, which was also used. 'The making of fine Manchet. Take halfe a bushell of fine flower twise boulted [sifted through fine cloth], and a gallon of faire luke warm water, almost a handful of white salt, and almost a pinte of yest, then temper all these together, without any more liquor, as hard as ye can handle it: then let it lie halfe an hower, then take it vp, and make your Manchetts, and let them stande almost an hower in the ouen. Memorandum, that of euery bushell of meale may be made fiue and twentie caste of bread, and euerie loafe to way a pounde beyside the chesill…'

BARA LLECHWAN – BAKESTONE BREAD
Traditional Welsh

Baking a *bara planc*, or risen loaf, on the bakestone was considered an admirable skill and this is a classic soda-type bread that was traditionally cooked in this manner rather than in an oven.

'Roddwch lechwan neu badell ar dân isel cyn ychwanegu'r does. Craswch ar bob ochor nes ei fod wedi ei liwio yn euraidd ac wedi crasu drywodd. Gadewch iddo fferu am ycyhdig o funudau yna torrwch a gweinwch gyda digon o fenyn.'

Ingredients: 360 g plain flour; pinch of salt; 2 tsp baking powder; 1 egg; a little milk.

Method: Sift the flour, salt and baking powder into a bowl. Lightly beat the egg and add to the flour. Mix well then add just enough milk to bring the mixture together into a fairly soft dough. Tip this onto a lightly-floured surface before kneading for about a minute. Place a bakestone or heavy non-stick pan on low heat before adding the dough and spreading it out. Bake upon each side until coloured a golden brown and baked through. Allow to cool for a few minutes before serving with plenty of butter.

QUELQUECHOSE – SOMETHING DIFFERENT FROM PIGS FEET – SHRIMP-SCRAMBLED EGGS

Gervase Markham's *The English House-wife*, 1615

This is more like a fried rice dish than the omelette it appears to be. You can use any leftovers from the fridge in this dish.

'To make a Quelquechose, which is a mixture of many things together; take the Eggs and break them, and do away one half of the Whites, and after they are beaten, put them to a good quantity of sweet Cream, Currants, Cinnamon, Cloves, Mace, Salt, and a little Ginger, Spinage, Endive, and Mary-gold flowers grosly chopt, and beat them all very well together; then take Pigs Petitoes slic'd and grosly chopt, mixt them with the Eggs, and with your hand stir them exceeding well together; then put in sweet Butter in your Frying-pan, and being melted, put in all the rest, and fry it brown without burning, ever and anon turning it, till it be Fryed enough; then dish it upon a flat plate, and so serve it forth. Onely here is to be observed, that your Pettitoes must be very well boyled before you put them into the Fry-case.' Markham added, in *Additions to the House-wife*: 'And in this manner as you make this Quelquechose, so you may make any other, whether it be of flesh, small Birds, sweet Roots, Oysters, Muscles, Cockles, Giblets, Lemmons, Oranges, or any Fruit, Pulse, or other Sallet herb whatsoever; of which to speak severally, were a Labour infinite, because they vary with mens opinion. Onely the composition and work is no other than this before prescribed: and who can do these need no further instruction for the rest. And thus much for Sallets and Fricases.'

Ingredients: You can use boiled pigs feet, small birds, giblets, oysters and the like as above, but here we use: ½ cup cooked shrimp, chopped; 3 whole eggs; 3 egg yolks; 1 cup raw spinach, chopped; 1 cup endive, chopped; ¼ cup currants; 3 tbsp cream; ½ tsp cinnamon; ¼ tsp each of ground cloves, ground mace, ground ginger; pinch of salt; 1 tbsp butter.

Method: Beat eggs, then add cream and all other ingredients, except the butter. Melt the butter in a frying pan, pour in the egg mixture and stir while eggs scramble.

9

Sweets

THE BANQUET

Thomas Dawson, in *The Good Huswifes Jewell* (1596), gave us 'the Names of all thinges necessary for a banquet. Suger, pepper, saffron, anniseedes, cinamon, nutmegs, saunders, coliander (coriander), licoras, all kinds of cumfets, orenges, pomegranet seedes, corneseli, prunes, currans, barberies conserved, pepper white and browne, lemons, rosewater, raisins, rie flower, ginger, cloves and mace, damaske water, dates, cherries conserved, sweete orenges, wafers; for your Marchpane seasoned and unseasoned, Spinndges.' The cost of spices for a banquet could easily exceed the cost of labour. In 1559 the City of London put on a military display at Greenwich for the new queen's benefit, and the expenditures for the banquet that followed were itemized – "'The cooke and his man for thayre labours" were paid a total of five shillings. For a pound of cinnamon, the city paid four shillings; for ¾ pound of pepper, one shilling tenpence; for an ounce of whole mace, one shilling twopence; and for a pound of ginger, two shillings.'

England had gradually developed the practice of a 'banquet', a separate, sweet, course that followed the main meal. In the sixteenth century, a rich man's banquet was remarkably different from today's modern perception and it stems from the medieval 'ceremony of the voide'. While the tables were cleared, or 'voided', dinner guests would drink sweet wine and spices. The *voide* was not replaced with the French *dessert* until the seventeenth century. During the Tudor era, guests would leave the great chamber, while the table was cleared and the room prepared for entertainment. Guests might simply retire to another room with their drinks for the banquet of sweets, but wealthier landowners constructed a separate banqueting house, also called 'prospecting rooms' or a 'pleasure house'.

The word banquet comes from the Italian word *banchetto*, meaning a bench, because the sweet delicacies were often displayed on a long side table, to be admired in advance. Sugar at this time was very, very expensive and was believed to have medicinal qualities, as did most other spices. It was taken as a *digestif*, particularly in the form of sugared, spiced seeds called comfits. It was a status symbol for the wealthy, with 14-pound cones of sugar often given as gifts or bribes. Its use became a fashionable way to impress one's guests and even in very wealthy households the preparation of sugared banquet sweetmeats was the responsibility of the lady of the house and her daughters, as it was too valuable an ingredient to allow the household cook to have access. Much of sixteenth and seventeenth century cookbooks were devoted to recipes for 'banquetting stuffe'. Sugared spices (comfits) and sweetmeats were the earliest delicacies, being classed as 'wet' in a syrup, or dry as in crystallised ginger. Brilliantly coloured and decorated jellies and custards, comfits (sweet-coated spice seeds), suckets (candied fruit peels), wafers, small biscuits, gingerbread, marzipan concoctions, 'composts' and fruit pastes all added to the banquet table. By 1500, cream, cheese and savouries also began to feature.

Gervase Markham (*The English Huswife*, 1615) wrote a brief section on 'The Ordering of Banquets', describing an ideal dessert course: 'I will now proceed to the ordering or setting forth of a banquet; wherein you shall observe that the marchpanes have the first place, the middle place, and the last place; your preserved fruits shall be dished up first, your pastes next, your wet suckets after them, then your dried suckets, then your marmalades and goodinyakes, then your comfits of all kinds; next, your pears, apples, wardens baked, raw or roasted, and your oranges and lemons sliced; and lastly your wafer cakes.' He tells his reader the order in which to organize them before sending them to the dining hall. Sugar paste is to be followed by rose sugar, sugar 'reliefs' (sculptures or 'subtleties'), violet sugar, melted and moulded dragees, large and small round drops of sugar, spun 'candich' (crystalized sugar gobbets); comfits, Manus Christi (boiled sugar gobbets with gold leaf added); and finally red and white 'rusen', poured into moulds, usually with spices. The latter were stiff conserves, served in the shapes of various fruits.

TUDOR SWEET RECIPES

SUGAR PLATE – SUGAR PASTE
The Good Huswifes Handmaide for the Kitchin, 1594, 1597 (and 1588)
Sugar had been known to the Romans and they considered it a medicine. They

preferred honey and wisely saw little culinary value in sugar as it sweetened without adding flavour. However, Crusaders rediscovered sugar for the West, as it was used in the culinary traditions of countries in the East. Sugar came to England with them and a taste for it slowly grew amongst the wealthy. It was a fantastically expensive luxury during the Middle Ages, arriving at ports in rock hard cones of crystallised sugar. This had to be hacked into smaller pieces, before being laboriously ground to a powder in a pestle and mortar. During the sixteenth century more and more elaborate means of working sugar were discovered and it became the basis for both wet and dry 'suckets', variants on crystallised fruit and fruit pulps. It was discovered that adding gum tragacanth in a rose water solution to the sugar created a mouldable sugar paste and this could be used to make more and more fanciful subtleties or edible models, such as one of the St. Paul's church which was presented to Elizabeth I.

Ingredients: 2.5 ml gum tragacanth; 5ml strained lemon juice; 10 ml rose water; 350–450 g icing sugar; half an egg white.

Method: Stir the gum tragacanth into the lemon juice and rose water in a small basin and leave overnight. Alternatively, place the basin in a pan of hot water until the gum tragacanth has dissolved and leave to cool. Stir in the lightly-beaten egg white and you can add a little food colouring at this stage, if desired. Now work in the sifted icing sugar, a little at a time, until you have a paste. Turn this out onto a board with more icing sugar, kneading the mixture until completely smooth. Now roll it into a ball and immediately wrap into a plastic food bag or cling film until needed for use. This is needed as the surface dries out quickly upon exposure to air.

MARCHPANE – MARZIPAN SHAPES

Gervase Markham's *Countrey Contentments, or, The English Hus-wife*, 1615

The Romans made this confection of almonds and egg whites, and it reached its zenith in the sixteenth century as a status piece of the banquet. Marchpane needed three principal ingredients, all of which were imported at great expense – almonds, sugar and rose water. The almonds had to be shelled and then, like the hard crystalline sugar, laboriously pounded in a mortar until they were finely powdered. Special occasions might call for the marchpane to be decorated with gold leaf. For those who could afford them, milk was made by steeping ground almonds in water. This was used to make sauces during the times when dairy produce was forbidden by the church, such as during Lent or Advent. They were also used whole in savoury dishes and sliced as decoration. Markham gives detailed instructions on how a marchpane should be made. The addition of other spices alters the colour significantly.

'To make the best marchpane, take the best Jordan almonds and blanch them in warm water, then put them into a stone mortar, and with a wooden pestle beat them to pap, then take of the finest refined sugar well searced [well sieved], and with it, and damask rose-water, beat it to a good stiff paste, allowing almost to every Jordan almond three spoonful of sugar. Then when it is brought thus to a paste, lay it upon a fair table, and, strewing searced sugar under it, mould it like leaven [raw bread dough]; then with a rolling pin roll it forth, and lay it upon wafers washed with rose water, then pinch it about the sides, and put it into whatever form you please; then strew searced sugar all overit, which done wash it over with rose-water and sugar mixed together, for that will make the ice, then adorn it with comfits [small sugar coated seeds of digestive herbs such as fennel or caraway], gilding, or whatsoever devices you please, and so set it into a hot stove and there bake it crispy and so serve it forth. Some use to mix with the paste cinnamon and ginger finely searced, but I refer that to your particular taste.'

Ingredients: 8 oz ground almonds; 4 oz caster sugar; 3 tsp rose water; small amount of icing sugar.

Method: Work together ingredients with fingers, or a fork, into a stiff paste. Add more rose water if needed, drop by drop. As the almonds become moistened and warm they will release their oil, so do not add too much rose water at the start. Save a small amount of the paste and roll out most of it on greaseproof paper into a circle just under half an inch thick. Pattern the edges by crimping or pressing in a fork handle. Slip the marchpane into a cool oven of not more than 150°C for about 15 minutes. If it shows signs of browning, turn down the heat further. Then leave it for another 10–15 minutes to finish off in the oven, with the heat turned off and the door ajar so that it dries thoroughly without colouring. Whilst it is cooking, roll out the reserved paste quite thinly and cut it into patterns, such as hearts and flowers, and make a thin icing by dripping rose water into icing sugar until it makes a runny paste. Brush the icing paste quickly over the marchpane and attach the decoration shapes. Allow the marchpane icing to dry hard in the remaining warmth of the oven.

MARCHPANE – STIFFENED MARZIPAN SCULPTURES

The Accomplisht Cook Or the Art and Mystery of Cooking – Robert May (1558–*c*. 1654)

Although May's book is later than the Tudor period, it is representative of recipes dating from pre-Tudor times. In the absence of damp, marzipan is virtually indestructible. Marchpane is a stiff form of marzipan that can be moulded into very complex shapes and was often used to generate highly ornate and edible centrepieces for a table setting. Three of the greatest examples of marchpane models were presented to the queen during the New Year celebrations of 1561–2. Wolsey in 1527 had been served with an enormous subtlety of St Paul's Cathedral and a similar one was given to Elizabeth I by her surveyor of the works. At the same time her yeoman of the chamber gave her 'a very faire marshpaine made like a tower with men and artillery in it.' Another copy of a Wolsey speciality was presented to her by her master cook George Webster, a 'faire marchpane being a chessboarde'. At Elizabeth's mother Anne Boleyn's coronation feast in 1533, there were 'subtleties and shippes made of waxe, marvylous, gorgeous to behold.' At Henry VIII's garter dinners, a magnificent 'George on Horseback' was used to introduce the first courses. It is thought that the sugar and marchpane work used the same moulds as used a century before in 1440, 'a soteltee Seint-Jorge on horseback and sleyng the dragon.' This was followed with the third course continuing the legend, with a subtlety of a 'castel that the King and Qwhene comen in for to see how Seint Jorge flogh.'

'To Make a Marchpane. Take two pound of almonds blanched and beaten in a stone mortar, till they begin to come to a fine paste, then take a pound of sifted sugar put it in the mortar with the almonds, and make it into a perfect paste, putting to it now and then in the beating of it a spoonfull of rose-water to keep it from oyling; when you have beaten it to a puff-paste, drive it out as big as a charger, and set an edge about it as you do a quodling tart, and the bottom of wafers under it, thus bake it in an oven or baking-pan; when you see it white, and hard, and dry, take it out, and ice it with rosewater and suger, being made as thick as butter for fritters, so spread it on with a wing feather, and put it into the oven again; when you see it rise high, then take it out and garnish it with come pretty conceits made of the same stuff.'

Ingredients: 350 g ground almonds; 3 tbsp rose water; 175 g icing sugar; 4 wafers of rice paper.

Ingredients for the Glaze: Grated rind of ½ lemon; 1 tbsp rose water; 1 tbsp icing sugar; 1 tbsp rice flour; candied peel for decoration. To make dried peels of citrus fruit, peel with a potato peeler and dry slowly. You can add to the glaze any of allspice, aniseed, cardamom, cinnamon, cloves, coriander, dill seed, nutmeg, star anise, vanilla pods, peel of citrus fruits; roots of angelica, cowslip and shreds of cedarwood, sandalwood and cassia chips.

Method: Grind the almonds in a pestle and mortar until they form a uniform paste. Add a tablespoon of rose water to this and mix in. Add the sugar a little at a time, using the pestle or a wooden spoon to mix into the almond paste. When about half the sugar has been added, mix in the remaining rose water and begin adding the remainder of the sugar, mixing all the while. Do not mix too vigorously as the mixture has a tendency to become oily. When you have created your marchpane, cover a large surface with caster sugar, tip the marchpane onto this and roll out to about 7 mm deep. Cut this into large squares of around 10 cm a side. Line the base of a 20 cm loose-bottomed cake tin with the rice papers, arranging the squares in a fan-like pattern around the inside of the tin so that the entire base is covered. Use any remaining marchpane to cover any holes and then smooth it with the back of a spatula. Remove the marchpane from the tin, and slide onto a greased baking tray. Embed small coloured comfits in the top of the marchpane to create patterns. Mix together the ingredients of your glaze and brush this over the top of the marchpane. Bake in an oven preheated to 170°C for about 30 minutes, or until the marchpane becomes quite firm. Decorate with candied peel and serve. Once you have created a basic marchpane you can try modelling the marchpane into shapes before baking and/or use different marchpanes using different food colourings. Cut patterns in these and place them together to create a colourful shape before baking.

MARCHPANE KNOTTS – MARZIPAN CAKES
Sir Hugh Plat's *Delightes for Ladies*, 1602

You can mould this marchpane into animals or birds as well as rolling into ropes and braiding these before baking. These were the sweetmeats known in Elizabethan times as 'knotts'. Such 'illusion foods' were intended to trick the diner into believing he was receiving something other than what he was actually served. Sir Hugh Plat also described how to fashion life-size marchpane animals covered with 'crums of bread, cinamon and sugar boiled together: and so they will seem as if they were rosted and breaded… By this meanes, a banquet may bee presented in the forme of a supper, being a very rare and strange device.'

'To make a Marchpane. Take two poundes of Almonds being blanched and dryed in a fieue ouer the fire, beate them in a ftone mortar, and when they bee fmall mixe with them two pounde of fugar beeing finely beaten, adding two or three fpoonefuls of Rofewater, and thet will keep your almonds frō oiling: whē your pafte is beaten fine, driue it thin with a rowling pin, and fo lay it on a botome of wafers, then raife vp a little edge on the fide, and fo bake it, then yce it with Rofewater and fugar, then put it into the ouen againe, and when you fee your yce is rifen vp and drie, then take it out of the Ouen and garnifh it with pretie conceipts, as birdes and beafts being caft out of ftanding moldes. Sticke long cōfits vpright in it, caft bisket and carowaies in it, and fo feruce it; guild it before you ferue it: you may alfo print of this Marchpane paſte in your molds for banqueting diſhes. And of this paſte our comfit makers at this day make their letters, knots, Armes, eſcocheons, beaſts, birds, and other fancies.'

Ingredients: 500 g blanched almonds; 500 g caster sugar; 100 g icing sugar; 4–5 tbsp rose water; caraway comfits, to garnish.

Method: Grind the almonds in a blender, then turn into a large stone mortar. Pound the almonds to a smooth paste. If they begin to turn oily, work in 1–2 tbsp of the rose water. Then start to work in the sugar until it makes a smooth paste. Turn this out onto a cold marble slab and roll out to about 1 cm thick. Cut into about 3 cm squares and then carefully raise a lip all the way around. Transfer to lightly-greased baking trays and then place in an oven preheated to 160°C and bake for about 10 minutes. Work the icing sugar and 3 tbsp rose water together until you have a smooth and just spreadable icing. When the marchpanes have been taken out from the oven, cover them with a thin layer of this glaze, then return to the oven and bake for 10 minutes more, or until lightly golden. Remove from the oven and allow to dry, then cut little figures in the shapes.

EXCELLENT MARCHPANE PASTE

Sir Hugh Plat's *Delightes for Ladies*, 1602

In Elizabethan times these were either rolled into moulds so that they would gain the imprint of the mould, or they had stamps imprinted on the upper surface. The recipe begins: 'To make an excellent Marchpane paſte, to print off in molds for banqueting diſhes…'

Ingredients: 250 g blanched almonds; 500 g powdered white sugar; 60 ml rose water; 1 tsp ground cinnamon and/or ground ginger.

Method: Place the almonds in a blender and grind quite firmly. Turn into a mortar and pound until they form a smooth paste. Once you have a smooth paste start working in the spices and sugar. Pound the sugar and almonds together until they become too stiff to handle, then add a little rose water as needed, and continue working in the sugar. Continue until all the sugar has been incorporated and you have a stiff, but still workable paste. Take portions of the mixture and work into balls about 3 cm in diameter. Place these on a marble slab and roll out to about 1 cm thick.

ROSEWATER MARCHPANE

Charles Butler's *The Feminine Monarchie, Or, The Historie of Bees*, 1609

Rose water can be made in summer by steeping rose petals in sugar and boiling water. It is available in most large supermarkets if you do not wish to prepare it, costing around £1.30 for 250 ml. If buying a rose water concentrate, ensure that it is suitable for culinary rather than cosmetic use, as the latter often contains alcohol.

'Marchpane may be made after this manner. Boile and clarifie by it selfe, so much Honie as you thinke meet: when it is cold,take to every pound of Honie the white of an Egge, and beat them together in a Bason, till they bee incorporat together and wax white, and when you haue boiled it againe two or three walmes vpon a fire of coles, continually stirring it, then put to it such quantitie of *blanched Almonds or Nut-kernels stamped, as shall make it of a iust consistence: and after a warme or two more, when it is well mixt, powre it out vpon a Table, and make vp your Marchpane. Afterward you may ice it with Rose-water and Sugar. This is good for the Consumption. *Steepe them a night in cold water, and the peeles will come off.'

WHITE GINGER BREAD – ALMOND GINGERBREAD

A.W., *The Booke of Goode Cookry Very Necessary for all Such as Delight Therein*, 1584, 1591

'To make white Ginger bread. Take Gumma Dragagantis half an once, and steep it in rosewater two daies, then put therto a pound of Sugar beaten and finely serced, and beate them well together, so that it may be wrought like paste, then role it then into two Cakes, then take a fewe Jordain almonds and blaunch them in colde water, then dry them with a faire Cloth, and stampe them in a morter very finelye, adding therto a little rosewater, beat finely also the whitest Sugar you can get and searce it. Then take Ginger, pare it and beat it very small and serce it, then put in sugar to the almonds and beat them togither very well, then take it out and work it at your pleasure, then lay it even upon one of your cakes, and cover it with an other and when you put it in the molde, strewe fine ginger both above and beneath, if you have not great store of Sugar, then take Rice and beat it small and serce it, and put it into the Morter and beat them altogither.'

Ingredients: 225 g marchpane (almond paste); 15 ml ground ginger; 225 g sugar plate. You can use the recipes for marchpane and sugar plate given above.

Method: Knead the ginger into the marchpane and roll it out onto a board dusted with icing sugar to about 7 mm thick. Divide the sugar plate into two. Roll out one piece of the sugar plate into the same size as the marchpane. Dampen one side of the marchpane, then place it damp side down on the sugar plate. Immediately roll out the other piece of sugar plate, dampen the other side of the marchpane and place the sugar plate firmly on this side, to effectively make a layer of marchpane sandwiched between sugar plate. You need to do this quickly, as the sugar plate becomes hardened when exposed to air. Then roll the mixture to about 7 mm thickness. Cut the gingerbread mixture into small diamonds with a pastry jigger. Alternatively, cut into sections, dust with a little cornflour, then press the sections into moulds. Trim off the surplus and leave to dry. You can use the trimmings by simply kneading them and cutting into shapes, so there is no wastage.

TARTYS IN APPLIS – APPLE PIE

The Master-Cook of Richard II, *The Forme of Cury, c.* 1390

This first English cookery manuscript, prepared for the Master Cooks in the King's employ, contains no pastry recipes. It was not considered necessary, as everyone knew how to make dough. Early cookery texts did not give detailed instructions such as a novice could follow, as most were illiterate, and were intended simply as an aide memoire for professionals. Here, the spiced apples were placed in a pastry 'coffin', essentially a container with thick hard walls, which was functional, and would not have been eaten by the well-to-do, but might have been refilled, or broken up and crumbled into stews as a thickener, or given to the poor.

'For To Make Tartys In Applis. Tak gode Applys and gode Spycis and Figys and reysons and Perys and wan they are wel brayed colourd wyth Safroun wel and do yt in a cofyn and do yt forth to bake wel.'

ALMOND BUTTER WITH POMGRANETS – ALMOND BUTTER WITH POMEGRANATE KERNELS

A.W., *The Booke of Goode Cookry Very Necessary for all Such as Delight Therein*, 1584, 1591

The pomegranate tree, *Punica granatum*, came from Iran and Turkey, but was cultivated in Italy and Spain from Roman times. Indeed, the Moors in Spain renamed their province and its capital Granada, from *Gárnata*, the Arabic name for the fruit. The Moors were not expelled from Granada until 1501.

'To make Almond Butter. Blanch two pound of Almonds and bray [break] them small in a Morter, but put no Licour to them of a good while, but bray them as small as you can, and when they be small inough, cast a little water to them into the Morter, then draw them through a Strainer as you can, then put it into a faire put [large pot] with a quarter of a pound of sugar, and set it on the fire, but stir it well for [to prevent] burning, and put in a little Salt, but not too much, and when it boyleth take it from the fire, and put to it a good quantitie of Damaske water or rosewater with an eye [pinch] of saffron, but not too much, then take a faire Cloth of an elle long [a measure from the elbow to the tip of the middle finger, about 18 inches], and lay the butter upon it, and let the cloth be held strait, and draw under the same cloth with a Ladle, that the water may come clean from it, and then draw it above in the midst of the cloth, and knit the corners of the cloth togither, and so hang it up and let it dry, and then dresse it into dishes, and print it as you doo butter, and plant it with kernels of Pomgranets, and so serve it foorth.'

PASTRY OF VARIOUS SORTS

Gervase Markham's *Countrey Contentments, or, The English Hus-wife*, 1615
In Gervase Markham's time, pastry 'coffins' functioned as baking containers – there were no shaped metal dishes until the Industrial Revolution. They would keep the contents edible for a long time, as long as the shell was not breached by cracking or becoming damp. A housewife had to have a repertoire of pastry types and shapes to accommodate different requirements, for example size, contents, longevity and whether it was to be eaten hot or cold. Markham explains what was needed:

'Next to these already rehearsed, our English House-wife must be skilful in Pastry, and know how and in what manner to bake all sorts of meat, and what Paste is fit for every meat, and how to handle and compound such Pastes. As for example, Red Deer,Venison, Wild Boar, Gammons of Bacon, Swans, Elkes, Porpus and suchlike standing dishes, which must be kept long, would be bak't in a moyst, thick, tough, course, and long lasting crust, and therefore of all other, your Rye paste is best for that purpose; your Turkey, Capon, Pheasant, Partridge, Veal, Peacocks, Lamb, and all sorts of Water-Fowl, which are to come to the Table more than once, (yet not many dayes) would be bak't in a good white-crust, somewhat thick: therefore your Wheat is fit for them; your Chickens, Calves-feet, Olives, Potatoes, Quinces, Fallow Deer,and such like which are most commonly eaten hot, would be in the finest, shortest,and thinnest crust, therefore your fine Wheat-flower, which is a little baked in the Oven before it be kneaded is the best for that purpose.

To speak then of the mixture and kneading of Pastes, you shall understand, that your Rye-paste would be kneaded onely with hot water, and a little Butter, or sweet Seam, and Rye-flower very finely sifted; and it would be made tough and stiffe, that it may stand well in the rising, for the Coffin thereof must ever be very deep; your course Wheat-crust should be kneaded with hot water, or Mutton broth, and good store of Butter, and the paste made stiffe and tough, because that Coffin mull be deep also: your fine Wheat crust must be kneaded with as much butter as water, and the paste made reasonable light and gentle, into which you must put three or four eggs or more, according to the quantity you blend together, for they will give it a sufficient stiffening.

Of Puffe pasts. Now for the making of puff-paste of the best kind, you shall take the finest Wheat flower after it hath been a little bak't [dried] in a pot in the Oven, and blend it well with eggs, whites and yelks all together, and after the paste is well kneaded, roul out a part thereof as thin as you please, and then spread cold sweet butter over the same; then upon the same butter roul another lets of the paste as before, and spread it with butter also; and thus roul leaf upon leaf with butter between ill it be as thick as you think good: and with it either cover any bak't meat, or make paste for Venison, Florentine, Tart, or what dish else you please, and so bake it. There be some that to this paste use Sugar, but it is certain, it will hinder the rising thereof, and therefore, when your puff-paste is bak't, you shall dissolve Sugar into Rose-Water, and drop it into the paste as much as it will by any means, receive, and then set it a little while in the Oven after, and it will be sweet enough.'

SHORTE PAESTE FOR TARTE – SHORTCRUST PASTRY
The Proper Newe Booke of Cookerye, c. 1557
A rich shortcrust pastry blended from flour, butter, egg yolks, saffron and a little water, which can be used with all shortcrust recipes in this book. You can make this with plain flour, but Elizabethan flour was much more coarsely ground, so to achieve something like the original texture, you can mix plain flour with coarse whole wheat flour.

'To make fhorte paeft for tarte. Take fryne floure and a curfey of fayre water and a dyfche of fwete butter and a lyttel faffron, and the yolckes of two egges and make it thynne and as tender as ye maye.'

Ingredients: 175 g plain flour; 60 g coarse whole wheat flour; 1 egg yolk; pinch of saffron threads, crumbled; 3 tbsp cold water.

Method: Whisk the egg yolk and saffron together with 1 tbsp of the water. Set aside to infuse for 10 minutes. Combine the flours in a bowl (if using two), dice the butter and add to the flour. Then rub in with your fingertips until the mixture comes together and resembles fine breadcrumbs. Add the egg yolk and saffron mix and work into the flour and butter mix. Now add the remaining cold water, a little at a time, and work together until the mixture comes together as a dough. Cover this with cling film and chill in the refrigerator for 20 minutes before rolling and using.

PAEST ROYALL – ROYAL PASTRY
The Proper Newe Booke of Cookerye, c. 1557
This was the richest pastry of the age for pies and desserts. As the flour is very fine, this would only have been used for the very best tables.

'To make Pyes …. And if you will have paest royall / take butter and yolkes of egges and so to temper the floure to make the paest.'

Ingredients: 700 g fine plain flour; 350 g salted butter; 4 lightly beaten egg yolks; 5 tbsp ice-cold water.

Method: Cut the butter into the flour in a bowl with a pair of pastry knives. Use your fingers to rub the butter into the flour until it resembles fine crumbs. Add the egg yolks and knead into the pastry. Add water a little at a time if the dough is too dry. The pastry is done when it forms a solid ball and does not stick to the sides of the bowl. Cover in cling film and refrigerate for 15 minutes before use.

SWEET PAEST ROYALL

If making sweet pastry for a dessert, add an extra 20 g of flour and 4 tbsp of honey to the above mixture.

ELIZABETHAN PIE CRUST

Traditional, an amalgam of several Elizabethan recipes

Most modern recipes for pie bases and pie tops rely upon refined modern wheat flour and often use margarine as the oil-based binding agent. Medieval flour was much coarser and butter was always used as the binding agent. The following recipe is a suitable adaptation to modern tastes.

Ingredients: 175 g plain flour; 60 g coarse whole wheat flour; 75 g unsalted butter (if using salted butter, do not add extra salt); ¼ tsp salt; twist of black pepper; 2½ tsp water. If making a sweet, rather than savoury pie, omit the black pepper and substitute 4 tbsp honey.

Method: Cut the butter into small cubes and leave to warm up. Mix the two flours together in a large bowl and add in the salt and pepper. When the butter has softened, use your fingers to rub the butter into the flour and keep rubbing until the texture resembles that of breadcrumbs. Add the water a little at a time until the mixture binds together but is not too tough. This pastry dough should be good enough to roll immediately and is enough for one 9-inch pie. If the pastry is a little tough to roll out, cover with cling film and place in the fridge for about 30 minutes before trying again.

COFFIN PASTRY

The Good Huswifes Handmaide for the Kitchin, 1594

'To make Paste, and to raise Coffins. Take fine flower, and lay it on a boord, and take a certaine of yolkes of Egges as your quantitie of flower is, then take a certaine of Butter and water, and boil them together, but ye must take heed ye put not too many yolks of Eggs, for if you doe, it will make it drie and not pleasant in eating: and ye must take heed ye put not in too much Butter for if you doe, it will make is so fine and so soft that you cannot raise, And this paste is good to raise all manner of Coffins: Likewise if ye bake Venison, bake it in the paste above named.'

COFFIN PASTRY ANOTHER WAY
The Good Huswifes Handmaide for the Kitchin, 1594
'To make fine Paste a nother way. Take Butter and Ale, and seeth them together: Then take your flower, and put thereinto three Eggs, Sugar, Saffron, and salt.'

COFFIN PASTRY IN LENT
The Good Huswifes Handmaide for the Kitchin 1594
'To make short paste in Lent. Take thick Almond milke seething hot, and so wet your flower with it: and Sallet oyl fryed, and Saffron, and so mingle your paste altogether, and that will make good paste.'

THICK PIE CRUST
In Medieval times a thick pie crust of water and flour was also made, which can be used for recipes that do not specify a specific kind of pie crust. However, this is much tougher and thicker than a standard pastry crust and is enough for a 9-inch pie dish.
Ingredients: 550 g plain white flour; 140 g coarse wholewheat flour; 300 ml water or milk; ¼ tsp salt.
Method: Place the flour and salt in a bowl and mix together. Add the water or milk a little at a time and mix into the flour with a fork. Milk gives a smoother texture. Keep on adding the liquid until the flour comes together into a solid, but pliable, dough, adding more flour or liquid as needed. Leave to rest in the fridge for about 20 minutes, then roll out on a cold, floured worktop or board. You will not be able to roll this as thinly as a standard pie dough.

TARTES OF RED CHERRIES – ROSE AND CHERRY CHEESECAKE
Epulario, or, The Italian Banquet, 1598
'To make Tartes of red Cherries. Take the reddest cherries that may bee gotten, take out the stones and stampe them in a morter, then take red Roses chopped with a knife with a little new Cheese and some old Cheese well stamped with Sinamon, Ginger, Pepper, and Sugar, and all this mired together, adde thereunto some egs according to the quantity you will make, and with a crust of paste bake it in a pan, and being baked strew it with Sugar and Rosewater.'

ROIAL SPICERIE – A ROYAL COLLECTION FOR THE VOIDE
Two Fifteenth Century Cookbooks – Harleian MS. 279 & Harl. MS. 4016, c. 1440
This is mentioned in Chaucer's *Tale of Sir Thopas*, wooing the elf-queen in *Canterbury Tales* of 1387. This 'roial spicerye' of cakes, spices, fruits and wine has all the elements of the 'Voide'.

'Bryndons. Take Wyn, and putte in a potte, an clarifyd hony, an Saunderys, pepir, Safroun, Clowes, Maces, and Quybibys,and mynced Datys, Pynys and Roysonys of Corauns, and a lytil Vynegre, and sethe it on the fyre; an sethe fygys in Wyne, and grynde hem, and draw hem thorw a straynoure, and caste ther-to, an lete hem boyle alle to-gederys; than take fayre flowre, Safroun, Sugre, and Fayre Water, and make ther-of cakys, and let hem be thinne Inow; than kyte hem y lyke lechyngys, an caste hem in fayre Oyle, and fry hem a lytil whyle; thanne take hem owt of the panne, an caste in-to a vesselle with the Syryppe, and so serue hem forth, the bryndonys an the Sirippe, in a dysshe; and let the Sirippe be rennyng, and not to styf.'

Ingredients: 2 cups flour; 2 cups sugar, half cup or more cold water; a few drops each of red and yellow food colouring; ¼ tsp salt; vegetable oil; 750 ml sweet red wine; 1½ cups honey; ½ cup red wine vinegar; 1 cup figs; 1 tsp each pepper, cloves, mace; ½ cup each chopped dates, currants, pine nuts or slivered almonds.

Method: Bring the wine and honey to the boil. Reduce heat, skimming off the scum until clean. Add the vinegar, red colouring, pepper, cloves, mace, fruits and nuts. Return to the boil and then reduce heat to a low simmer. In a separate bowl, mix together the flour, sugar and salt. Dye the water yellow with a few drops of colouring, then slowly work into the flour enough of the water to make a smooth dough, similar to pie pastry. Roll out on a floured board and then cut in strips about 1 inch wide and 4 inches long. In a deep skillet or pan, fry the strips in oil until lightly browned and very crisp. Drain. Place the cakes on a serving platter, then spoon on the fruits and nuts.

EGGES IN MONESHYNE – EGGS IN MOONLIGHT
The Proper Newe Booke of Cookerye, c. 1557
The eggs are cooked by poaching in a syrup of rose water and sugar, so that they look like moons.
Ingredients: 60 ml rose water; 100 ml water; 75 g caster sugar; 4 eggs.
Method: Combine the water, rose water and sugar in a small frying pan. Heat gently, stirring until the sugar dissolves. Bring to a simmer then crack in the eggs one by one. Ensure the eggs have enough space so that they cook without touching. Cook until the whites are cooked but the yolks are still runny.

Transfer the eggs to plates and spoon over some of the syrup. This is even better served on toast for breakfast.

A TART OF RYCE – RICE PUDDING PIE

Thomas Dawson's *The Good Huswifes Jewell*, 1585, 1594, 1596

'To make a Tart of Ryce. Boyle your Rice, and put in the yolkes of two or three Egges into the Rice, and when it is boyled, put it into a dish, and season it with Suger, Sinamon and Ginger, and butter, and the juyce of two or three Orenges, and set it on the fire againe.'

Ingredients 3 cups of rice, cooked; 3 egg yolks; ¼ cup sugar; 1 tsp cinnamon; ½ tsp ginger; 3 tbsp butter; ½ cup orange juice.

Method: Take hot, cooked rice and stir in butter and egg yolks. Add sugar, cinnamon, ginger and orange juice. Pour into tart crust and bake at 180°C until golden. Serve hot.

GYNGERBREDE – HONEY GINGERBREAD

Two Fifteenth Century Cookbooks – Harleian MS. 279 & Harl. MS. 4016, c. 1440

Gingerbread made of honey, breadcrumbs and ginger, is the ancestor of modern gingerbreads. Add a few drops of red food colouring, rather than sandalwood, when adding the spices if you wish it to have a red appearance.

'Take a quart of honey, and boil it, and skim it clean. Take saffron, pepper, and throw on. Take grated bread, and make it so thick that it can be sliced. Then take cinnamon, and strew on. Then make it square, like you would have it sliced; and when you slice it, stick in cloves. And if you would have it red, colour it with sandalwood.'

Ingredients: 900 ml honey; 450 g breadcrumbs; 1 tbsp ginger; 1 tbsp cinnamon; 1 tsp ground white pepper; whole cloves; pinch of saffron.

Method: Bring the honey to the boil and skim off any scum. Keep the saucepan over a very low heat, stirring in the breadcrumbs and spices. When the mixture is a thick, well-blended mass, remove from the heat and allow to cool slightly. (Add more breadcrumbs if it does not thicken.) Place on a flat surface and press firmly into an evenly shaped square or rectangle, about 0.6 cm thick. Allow to cool more and then cut into small squares to serve. Garnish each square by sticking a whole clove in the top centre.

ROYAL COURT LIQUORICE GINGERBREAD

Sir Hugh Plat's *Delightes for Ladies*, 1602

A rich, boiled gingerbread made at festivals such as Easter and Christmas for the royal court, stamped with patterns before serving.

'To make Gingerbread. Take three ſtale manchets and grate them, drie them, and fift them through a fine fieue then ad vnto them one ounce of ginger being beaten, and as much Cinamon, one ounce of liquerice, and annifeedes being beaten together and fearced, halfe a pound of fugar, then boile all thefe together in a pofnet, with a quart of claret wine till they come to a ftiffe pafte with often ftirring of it, and when it is stiffe, molde it on a table and fo driue it thin, and print it in your moldes; duft your moldes with Cinamon, Ginger, and liquerice, being mixed together in fine powder. This is your Gingerbread vfed at the Court, and in all gentlemens houfes at feftiuall times. It is otherwise called drie Leach.'

Ingredients: 400 g stale white bloomer loaf, finely grated and dried in a low oven; 1 tbsp finely-grated ginger; 2 tsp ground cinnamon; 1 tbsp ground liquorice root; 1 tbsp ground aniseed; 225 g sugar; 400 ml claret or full-bodied red wine; icing sugar mixed with a little ground ginger, ground cinnamon and ground liquorice.

Method: Stir the dried crumbs, ginger, cinnamon, liquorice, aniseed and sugar in a bowl. Work in a little of the claret until you have a smooth paste, then work in the remaining claret. Turn the mixture into a pan, stir constantly and bring to a gentle simmer. Continue cooking, stirring constantly, until you have a very thick paste. Remove from the heat and allow to cool until it can be handled. Turn the paste onto a cold marble slab and then roll out to about 2 cm thick. Dust the surface with a mix of icing sugar, ginger, cinnamon and ground liquorice and then cut into squares or diamonds. You can roll these shapes into moulds or you can press stamps into the surface to decorate with crests or animal patterns.

MY LADY MIDDLESEX' SYLLABUB

The Closet of the Eminently Learned Sir Kenelme Digbie Kt Opened, 1669

Syllabub was invented in the sixteenth century, and Digby's cook has copied an earlier recipe.

'My Lady Middlesex makes Syllabubs for little Glasses with spouts, thus. Take 3 pints of sweet Cream, one of quick white wine (or Rhenish), and a good wine glassful (better the ¼ of a pint) of Sack: mingle with them about three quarters of a pound of fine sugar in Powder. Beat all these together with a whisk, till all appeareth converted into froth. Then pour it into your little Syllabub-glasses, and let them stand all night. The next day the Curd will be thick and firm above, and the drink clear under it. I conceive it may do well, to put into each glass (when you pour the liquor into it) a sprig of Rosemary a little bruised, or a little Limon-peel, or some such thing to quicken the taste; or use Amber-sugar, or spirit of Cinnamon, or of Lignum-Cassiae; or Nutmegs, or Mace, or Cloves, a very little.'

Ingredients: 400 ml double cream; 100 ml dry white wine; 50 ml sack

(Madeira, Marsala, sherry or port); 50 g caster sugar; grated rind of half a lemon; ground cinnamon to decorate; caster sugar for dusting.

Method: Stir together the white wine, 'sack', caster sugar and lemon rind until all the sugar has dissolved. Stirring with a whisk, blend in the cream and then whip lightly until the mixture becomes slightly bubbly. Pour the mixture into half a dozen large wine glasses. If you wish you can decorate with a slice of lemon. Place in the refrigerator and serve cold, sprinkled with a little nutmeg and a dusting of caster sugar.

If you wish to make a classic modern lemon syllabub, substitute the juice of a whole lemon for white wine and increase the volume of 'sack' to 80 ml.

TOSTEE – GINGER SYRUP TOASTIES

The Master-Cook of Richard II, *The Forme of Cury, c.* 1390

These are a little like hot jelly upon toast, with a wonderful flavour.

'Tostee. Take wyne and hony and found it togyder and skym it clene. and seeþ it long, do þerto powdour of gyngur. peper and salt, tost brede and lay the sew þerto. kerue pecys of gyngur and flour it þerwith and messe it forth.'

Ingredients: ¼ cup red wine; ¼ cup honey; 1 tsp fresh ginger; ⅛ tsp ground ginger; pinch of salt; pinch of pepper; 2 slices toast.

Method: Peel the fresh ginger, chop very finely and set aside. Put the wine, honey, ground ginger, salt and pepper into a saucepan and bring to a boil. Reduce to medium heat and simmer until bubbles begin, or until syrup thickens. Spoon over fingers of toast, sprinkle with a little fresh ginger and serve warm.

A POTTAGE OF ROYSONS – APPLE AND RAISIN PUDDING

Two Fifteenth Century Cookbooks – Harleian MS. 279 & Harl. MS. 4016, c. 1440

A classic stew of apple and raisins in a thickened almond milk sauce.

'A potage of Roysons. Take Raysonys, and do a-way þe kyrnellys; and take a part of Applys, and do a-way þe corys, and þe pare, and bray hem in a mortere, and temper hem with Almande Mylke, and melle hem with flowre of Rys, þat it be clene chargeaunt, and straw vppe-on pouder of Galygale and of Gyngere, and serue it forth.'

Ingredients: 4–6 apples, peeled, cored, and sliced; 225 g raisins; 340 ml almond milk; 4 tbsp rice flour or unbleached white flour; 1 tbsp sugar; 1 tsp mixture of galingale or ginger.

Method: Boil the apples and raisins until the apples are very soft. Drain well, mash the fruit and place in a saucepan with the almond milk, spices and sugar. Cook over a medium heat and then add the flour, whisking rapidly to combine. Cook until thickened. Sprinkle with ginger or galingale (or a mix of both) just before serving.

SPICED HONEY CUSTARD

Thomas Dawson's *The Good Housewife's Jewel*, 1597

'To make a Custard. Breake your Egges into a bowle, and put your Creame into another bowle, and straine your egges into the creame, and put in saffron, Cloves and mace, and a little synamon and ginger, and if you will some Suger and butter, and season it with salte, and melte your butter, and stirre it with the Ladle a good while, and dubbe your custard with dates and currans.'

TRUE ENGLISH SHORT CAKES

Hannah Woolley's *The Queen-Like Closet*, 1672

Although this is later than the Tudor period, these are shortcakes or shortbreads – traditional Elizabethan biscuits made with yeast and flavoured with caraway seeds and rose water. Not until the nineteenth century did the recipes for the Scottish versions of shortbreads, using almonds, take over to become the shortbread we know today. For a less upper-class version, substitute 300 g of the flour with 300 g of ground oats. Caraway comfits may be hard to find, so you could use caraway seeds dipped in honey. However, making your own caraway comfits by dipping caraway seeds in molten sugar syrup, until they have developed a thick coating, is better.

'To make Short Cakes Take a Pint of Ale Yest, and a Pound and half of fresh Butter, melt your Butter, and let it cool a little, then take as much fine Flour as you think will serve, mingle it with the Butter and Yest, and as much Rosewater and Sugar as you think fit, and if you please, some Caraway Comfits, so bake it in little Cakes; they will last good half a year.'

Ingredients: 250 ml water; 1 sachet baker's yeast; 2–3 tsp sugar; 500 g salted butter; 1.2 kg flour; 50 ml rose water; 100 g Demerara sugar; 50 g caraway seeds encrusted in sugar; granulated sugar for dusting.

Method: Allow the butter to soften at room temperature and then cut into cubes. As the butter is softening, pour 250 ml warm water (about 37°C for optimal activation of the yeast) into a mug and stir in 2–3 tsp of sugar. Add the yeast and stir in. Cover and leave for at least half an hour, until the liquid starts to form a froth on the top, which shows that the yeast is active. Sift the flour and sugar into a bowl. Add the butter and rub between your fingers until the mixture resembles fine breadcrumbs. Add the mug of yeast mixture and the rose water, and mix in well. If the mixture is too dry add a little more water and if too wet add a little more flour. Knead the mixture well for at least five minutes and place in a bowl. Cover and leave in a warm place for at least 2 hours or until the dough has doubled in size. Tip onto a floured board and roll out into a rough circle about 2 cm thick. Spread half the caraway comfits over half of this, fold the uncovered half over and roll out again. Repeat this process with the other half of the caraway seeds. Then roll the dough out and fold over several times. Once you have finsihed, roll the dough into a ball, knead and tear small balls from this, to make small circles about 4 cm in diameter and 2 cm thick. Place these on a greased baking tray, dust with a coating of granulated sugar and cook in an oven preheated to 170°C for 35 minutes, or until the shortcakes turn golden brown.

TARTE OF PRUNES – DAMSON PIE
A Proper Newe Booke of Cookerye, c. 1545

This is a wonderful fruit tart with a nice flavor of red wine. A classic tart made from a purée of prunes and white breadcrumbs in red wine, made into a custard with eggs, and baked in a rich shortcrust pastry shell.

'To make a tarte of Prunes. Take prunes and set them upon a chafer wyth a little red wyne and putte therto a manshet and let them boyle together, then drawe them thorowe a streyner with the yolkes of foure egges and season it up wyth suger and so bake it.'

Ingredients: 12 oz pitted prunes; 3 cups red wine; 6 egg yolks; ½ cup sugar; pie crust.

Method: Cook the prunes in wine for about an hour, or until the prunes have plumped and the wine is syrupy. Put prunes through a colander with egg yolks, to remove skins. It may be necessary to also use cheesecloth to collect all the fruit pulp. Add sugar and pour into pie crust. Bake at 180°C for 45–60 minutes, until pie has thickened in the centre.

TARTE OF CHERRIES
Use the same method as above, substituting cherries, gooseberries or other handy fruit in season.

TARTE OF PROINES – PLUM PASTE TOASTIES
*Thomas Dawson's *The Good Huswifes Jewell*, 1585, 1594, 1596*

Damson plums were a favourite Elizabethan fruit, generally eaten before dinner, 'to provoke a mans appetyde'. Perhaps because they inflamed men's appetites, 'stewed prunes' were served at the many Elizabethan brothels in London and became a synonym of prostitutes. This dish was recommended by Markham as a first course, but is placed here to compare with the 'tarte of prunes' above.

'To make a tarte of proines. Put your proines into a pot, and put in red wine or claret wine, and a little faire water, stirred them now and then, and when they be boyled enough, put them into a bowle and strain them with sugar, synamon and ginger.'

Ingredients: 6 oz pitted dried plums (prunes); 2-inch stick of cinnamon; 2

tbsp extra virgin olive oil; 1 cup red wine; 2 tbsp sugar; 1 baguette; 2 tbsp julienned fresh ginger; zest of ½ lemon; salt to taste.

Method: Simmer the wine, sugar, prunes and cinnamon stick over a low heat for around 30 minutes in a non-stick saucepan, until the mixture has thickened. Remove the cinnamon and mash the prunes. Preheat the grill and cut the baguette into ¼ inch slices, placing on a baking sheet. Brush the bread with olive oil, sprinkling lightly with salt and place under the grill for around 3–5 minutes until golden brown on both sides. Spread a tablespoon of the prune paste on each toast piece and sprinkle with lemon zest and ginger.

APPLEMOYSE – APPLEMUSE (1)

A Proper Newe Booke of Cokerye, 1545

Apple-moyse is 'Any of various dishes made from stewed apples; spec. a dessert made from sieved apple pulp flavoured with saffron or other spices.' The word 'dessert' is confusing here, as the dish is medieval, but the concept of a dessert course is nineteenth century. Apple-moyse, however it is spelled, can have the form of a pottage, a pie filling, or a type of apple butter.

'Take a dosen apples and ether rooste or boyle them and drawe them thorowe a streyner, and the yolkes of three or foure egges withal, and, as ye strayne them, temper them wyth three or foure sponefull of damaske water yf ye wyll, than take and season it wyth suger and halfe a dysche of swete butter, and boyle them upon a chaffyngdysche in a platter, and caste byskettes or synamon and gynger upon them and so serve them forthe.'

Ingredients: 675 g peeled and cored cooking apples, chopped; 4 tbsp water; 3 egg yolks; 2 tbsp rose water; 50 g butter, finely chopped; 3 tbsp sugar; ground ginger and ground cinnamon to garnish.

Method: Combine the cooking apples and water in a pan. Cover with a tight-fitting lid and cook gently, stirring frequently, until the apples are very tender. Pass through a fine-meshed sieve to purée. Beat together the egg yolks, rose water and sugar in a bowl and then fold this into the apple purée, along with the butter. Place the mixture back into the saucepan and heat gently, stirring constantly, until the fruit custard thickens. Turn the mixture out into a dish, garnish with a dusting of ground ginger and cinnamon then serve. It can be topped with 'snowe', recipes as below.

APPILLINOSE – APPLEMUSE (2)

A Noble Boke off Cookry ffor a Prynce Houssolde Holkham MSS 674, 1480

'To mak an appillinose, tak appelles and sethe them and lett them kelle, then fret them throughe an heryn syff on fisshe dais take almonde mylk and oile olyf ther to. and on flesshe days tak freche brothe and whit grece and sugur and put them in a pot and boile it and colour it with saffron and cast on pouders and serue it.'

APPULMOS – **APPLEMUSE (3)**
The Master-Cook of Richard II, The Forme of Cury, c. 1390
'For To Make Appulmos. Nym appelyn and seth hem and lat hem kele and make hem thorw a clothe and on flesch dayes kast therto god fat breyt of Bef and god wyte grees and sugar and safroun and almande mylk on fysch dayes oyle de olyve and gode powdres and serve it forthe.'

APPLE MOYE – **APPLEMUSE (4)**
The Good Huswifes Handmaide for the Kitchin, 1594
'To make an Apple Moye. Take Apples, and cut them in two or foure peeces, boyle them till they be soft, and bruise them in a morter, and put thereto the yolkes of two Egs, and a little sweet butter, set them on a chafingdish of coales, and boyle them a litle, and put thereto a litle Sugar, synamon and Ginger, and so serue them in.'

TARTE OF STRAWBERRIES
The Good Huswifes Jewel, 1596
This simple dish can be served with the strawberries placed on 'snowe', recipe as below.
'To Make a tarte of Strawberries. Wash your strawberries, and put them into your Tarte, and season them with suger, cynamon and Ginger, and put in a littl red wine into them.'

A DYSSCHEFULL OF SNOWE – **APPLE PURÉE IN SNOW**
A Proper Neue Book of Cokery, c. 1575
'To make dyschefull of Snowe: Take a pottel of swete thycke creame and the whytes of eyghte egges, and beate them altogether wyth a spone, then putte them in youre creame and a saucerful of Rosewater, and a dyshe full of Suger wyth all, then take a stick and make it cleane, and than cutte it in the ende foure squsre, and therwith beate all the aforesayde thynges together, and as ever it ryseth takeit of and put it into a Collaunder, this done take one apple and set it in the myddes of it, and a thick bushe of Rosemary, and set it in the myddes of the platter, then cast your Snowe upon the Rosemary and fyll your platter therwith. And yf you have wafers cast some in wyth all and thus serve them forthe.'
Ingredients: 150 g peeled and cored cooking apples, chopped; 600 ml double

cream; 4 egg whites; 200 g caster sugar; 2 tbsp rosewater; 1 sprig of rosemary; ratafia or amaretti biscuits or wafers.

Method: Combine the apple and rose water in a pan. Cover tightly, bring to a simmer and cook gently for about 30 minutes, or until the apple is soft. Remove from the heat and purée by beating with a spoon. Set aside to cool. Put the egg whites in a dry bowl and beat until soft peaks form. Add 4 tbsp of the sugar and fold into the egg whites and then beat until stiff and glossy. Add the cream to a separate bowl and beat until soft peaks form. Fold in the remaining sugar then beat until stiff, but do not over beat. Fold the apple purée into the beaten cream then fold in the stiff egg whites. Place the mixture on a serving dish and garnish with the rosemary sprig and wafers or ratafia biscuits.

A DYSSCHEFULL OF SNOWE – STRAWBERRIES ON SNOW
A Proper Newe Book of Cokery, c. 1575

Ingredients: 8 egg whites; 1 pint whipping cream; ½ cup sugar; 1–2 tbsp rose water; 2 pints strawberries; 1 cup red wine; ¼ cup sugar; ½ tsp cinnamon; ¼ tsp ginger; ratafia or amaretti biscuits or wafers.

Method: Whip the cream and set aside. Beat egg whites until they form soft peaks. Add the egg whites to the whipped cream and whisk together. Add rose water and add a little sugar at a time, blending in smoothly. Place cleaned strawberries into a bowl. Mix red wine, sugar, cinnamon and ginger. Pour mixture over strawberries and allow to marinate for an hour or two. Serve the 'snow' with strawberries on top and with a couple of wafers or amaretti biscuits on the side.

FRUIT SNOW
Food Facts leaflet No. 284, mid-December 1945

This recipe is included to show the long-lasting tradition of 'snow'. Over 500 Second World War Ministry of Food *Food Facts* leaflets were produced, beginning in 1940 and continuing for several years after the war. The leaflets were produced to assist the housewife in her role at 'The Kitchen Front'. Rationing had begun in Britain in 1940, but did not end completely until July 1954. Restrictions were often greater in the post-war years than they had been during the war itself, as Britain diverted resources to assist the recovery of Europe, despite being heavily indebted to the USA and international bankers as a result of financing the war. The British Government in 2015 announced that it had finally paid off its World War One debts, again mainly to the USA, but it was simply a rescheduling of these debts. Alongside these war debts, Britain is still paying off its loans used for military actions in Korea, Aden, Kenya, the Falklands, Libya, Iraq, Kuwait, Afghanistan etc. As Christmas approached in 1945, the Ministry of Food produced a batch of leaflets advising about the slightly eased rations granted, and its recommendations for substituting and making-do, so that the season would still be festive.

'FESTIVE TOUCHES FOR CHRISTMAS. FRUIT SNOW: A favourite with the children. (Enough for 4.) Ingredients: ½ pint water, 1 level tablespoon sugar, 1 level tablespoon powdered gelatin, quarter pint fruit pulp, made from stewed or bottled fruit. Method: Heat the water and sugar together and pour onto the gelatin. Stir until dissolved. When cool add the fruit pulp and beat until the consistency of whipped cream. Serve in individual glasses or pile into a dish.'

SNOW LIKE A SILLIBUBBE – SNOW SYLLABUB
Mistress Sarah Longe her Receipt Book, c. 1610

Syllabub is a delicious Elizabethan creation which used to be served as a party drink, flavoured with nutmeg and decorated with clotted cream and ground nutmeg on top. In the seventeenth century, milk and ale were gradually replaced by cream and wine. According to Elizabeth David, the original syllabub was made when a milkmaid would send a stream of new, warm milk directly from a cow into a bowl of spiced cider or ale. A light curd would form on top, with whey underneath. Today's syllabub is more solid and mixes sherry and/or brandy, sugar, lemon, nutmeg and double cream into a custard-like dessert or an eggnog-like beverage, depending upon the cook. The following recipe is for a sweet, creamy dessert similar to syllabub which comes from the English housewife Sarah Longe's personal recipe book. *Sack*, a fortified white wine, is a favourite drink of Sir John Falstaff in Shakespeare's *Henry IV* plays, similar to sherry.

'To make Snow. Take a pint of thicke sweete Creame – and halfe a pint of Sack and halfe a pound of Sugar, and the white of two Eggs well beaten, and a pretty deale of limon (lemon), and mingle all this together, and put it into a pretty big earthen Pan, or Bason, and take a pretty big birchen rod, and beate it till the froth doth rise, and then take it of with a stirre, and put it into the thing you would have it goe in, (it should bee a glasse Sillibubbe pot, if you have it, if not, a white creame dish will serve: you should lett it stand a pretty while before you eate it, because it should settle with a little kinde of drinke at the bottome, like a Sillibubbe.'

TARTE OF CHESE – PROPER CHEESE PIE
The Proper Newe Booke of Cookerye, c. 1557

Ingredients: 250 g mature Cheddar, sliced; 200 ml milk; 6 raw egg yolks; 2 tbsp brown sugar; 4 tbsp butter; 1 batch short pastry.

Method: Roll out the pastry and use to line a deep pie dish of 9-inch diameter. Line with greaseproof paper, fill with baking beads and transfer to an oven preheated to 180°C. Blind bake for about 15 minutes, or until the pastry is just dry to the touch, but not browning. Remove from the oven, remove the paper and baking beads and set aside. Place the cheese slices in a shallow dish and pour over the milk, then set aside to soak for 3 hours. After this time, drain the cheese. Pound the cheese and egg yolks in a mortar, or purée in a food processor. Pass the mixture through a fine-meshed sieve and then mix with the brown sugar and butter. Pour into the prepared pie shell and transfer to an oven preheated to 180°C. Bake for about 25 minutes, or until the pastry is golden and the filling has set, and serve warm.

JOHN MURREL'S FINE SUGAR CAKE – SUGAR BISCUITS
John Murrel's *A Daily Exercise for Ladies and Gentlewomen*, 1617

'To make a fine Sugar cake. Bake a pound of fine wheat flower in a pipkin close couvered, put thereto halfe a pound of fine Sugar, foure yolkes and one white of egs, Pepper and Nutmegs, straine them with clouted creame, and with a little new Ale yeast, make it in past, as it were for a Manchet, bake it in a quicke oven with a breath fire in the ovens mouth, but beware of burning them.'

Ingredients: 1 lb flour; 2 oz softened butter; 1 oz milk; 8 oz granulated sugar; 1 tsp ground black pepper; 1 tbsp ground nutmeg; ⅛ tsp salt; 2 oz warm, flat beer; ¾ tsp yeast; 2 eggs; 1 egg yolk.

Method: Beat together the butter and milk and keep beating until well combined. Mix the flour, sugar, salt, pepper and nutmeg in a large bowl with the buttered milk. Make a well in the middle of this mixture and put in the beer and yeast, allowing to rest for 10 minutes. Add 2 eggs plus 1 egg yolk, lightly beaten. Mix into the flour mixture, then knead on a lightly-floured surface. Put into a bowl and cover, allowing to rise for 1 hour. Remove from the bowl onto a lightly-floured surface. Divide into approximately 30 one oz balls. Preheat oven to 200°C. Place balls onto greaseproof sheets. Flatten balls to about ½ inch thick and prick each several times with a knife. Allow to rise for about 30 minutes. Bake for approximately 15 minutes, then remove to a rack to cool.

WARDENS IN CONSERVE – PEARS IN RED WINE SYRUP (1)
The Proper Newe Booke of Cookrye, c. 1557

The original recipe calls for dried and powdered lemon skins, but these are replaced with zest.

Ingredients: 4 cooking pears; 250 ml red wine; 125 ml clear honey; 100 g sugar; 1 cinnamon stick, broken in half; 1 tsp ground ginger; generous pinch of ground cloves; 1 tbsp grated lemon zest.

Method: Combine the wine, honey, sugar, cinnamon, ginger, cloves and lemon zest in a saucepan. Bring to a simmer and cook, stirring constantly, until the sugar has dissolved. Bring to a boil and cook for 5 minutes, then remove from the heat. Pour the mixture through a fine-meshed sieve. Take this liquid and pour into a pan just large enough for the pears to fit. Peel the pears, but do not core and leave the stalks on. Sit these in the pan and bring to a simmer. Cover with a lid and cook gently for about 20 minutes, or until the pears are tender. Increase the time to around 40 minutes if using hard, Warden pear varieties. Baste the pears frequently with the wine syrup while they are cooking. When tender, arrange the pears in a dish, spoon over the syrup and serve.

WARDONYS IN SYRUP – PEARS OR MIXED FRUIT IN RED WINE SYRUP (2)

Two Fifteenth Century Cookbooks – Harleian MS. 279 & Harl. MS. 4016, c. 1440
This is a simpler alternative to the above recipe.

'Take wardonys, an caste on a potte, and boyle hem till they ben tindie; than take hem up and pare hem, an kytte hem in to pecys; take y-now of pawder, canel a good Quantyti an caste it on red wyne an draid it throu a straynour; caste sugar ther-to an put it in an erthern pot and let it boyle; an thane caste the preys ther-to and let boyle togetherys an when thay have boyle a whyle; take pauder of gyngere an caste ther-to, and a lytil vinegre an a lytil saffron; an loke that it be poynaunt an dowcet.'

Ingredients: 1 lb pears or mixed fruit; 1 cup cream sherry; ½ cup white sugar; ½ cup brown sugar; ½ cup wine; 1 tsp cinnamon; 1 tsp ginger; pinch of salt; 1 tbsp vinegar; pinch of saffron.

Method: Cover the fruit with water, add the cup of wine and ½ cup white sugar and simmer for about 15 minutes until tender. Take the remaining ingredients except the vinegar and saffron and boil briefly in a separate pan until slightly thickened. Then add this syrup to the fruit and simmer for about 10 minutes. Add the vinegar and saffron, and the pears or fruit can be served warm or chilled.

TARTE OF MARIGOLDS, PRIMROSES OR COWSLIPS – APPLE AND FLOWER PETAL CUSTARD PIE

The Proper Newe Booke of Cookrye, c. 1557

This is a lovely looking summer dish, a tart made from an apple purée mixed with marigold, primrose or cowslip petals and cream cheese, made into a 'custard' with eggs, before being baked in a shortcrust pastry shell.

Ingredients: 300 ml petals from borage, marigolds, primroses or cowslips (or a mixture); 1 cooking apple, peeled and cored; 200 g ricotta cheese; 4 egg yolks; 2 tbsp butter; ¼ tsp ground mace; 1 batch short pastry.

Method: Roll out the pastry and use to line a deep pie dish of 9-inch diameter. Line with greaseproof paper, fill with baking beads and transfer to an oven preheated to 180°C. Blind bake for about 15 minutes, until the pastry is just dry to the touch but not browned. Remove from the oven, take out the paper and baking beads and set aside. Combine the apple and 2 tbsp water in a small pan. Bring to a simmer and cook uncovered for about 20 minutes or until the apple has broken down. Add the flower petals to the apple along with the butter and mace. Beat with a wooden spoon until puréed. Beat the cream cheese in a bowl until soft. Add the egg yolks and beat until combined. Work in the apple and petal mix. Turn this mixture into the blind baked pastry shell and transfer to an oven preheated to 180°C. Bake for about 25 minutes, or until the pastry is golden and the custard filling has set. This can be served either hot or cold.

LEECH – TUDOR SWEET CUBES

Thomas Dawson's *The Good Housewife's Jewel*, 1596

Leech, or *leach*, was a popular sweet in the banquet course, usually made from milk, sugar and rose water, and cut into cubes. It was then displayed as a chessboard, with some of the leech left plain and other cubes gilded.

'Take a quart of milk and three ounces weight of isinglass, half a pound of beaten sugar; stir them together. Let it boil half a quarter of an hour till it be thick, stirring them all the while. Then strain it with three spoonfuls of rose water. Then put it into a platter and let it cool, and cut it in squares. Lay it fair in dishes, and lay gold upon it.'

Ingredients: 5 tsp gelatine; 4 oz sugar; 1 pt milk; 1½ tsp rose water.

Method: Sprinkle the gelatine over 4 tbsp milk in a cup. Let it stand for 5 minutes, then set the cup in hot water and stir until the gelatine is dissolved. Warm the rest of the milk and stir in the sugar and gelatine mixture. Simmer, stirring continuously, for 5 minutes. Remove from heat and stir in rose water. Pour into a shallow dish that has been rinsed in cold water. Refrigerate until set. Cut into squares or cubes.

The Tudor Kitchen

LEACH – ELIZABETHAN ALMOND PANNA COTTA

Sir Hugh Plat's *Delightes for Ladies*, 1602

Essentially this recipe is the Italian *panna cotta* (cooked cream), enriched with almond paste. Plat's version, however, is set harder than modern pannacotas and is served sliced. Isinglass was made from the dried swim bladders of sturgeon – a remarkable discovery in itself – and is replaced by gelatine below. In 1795 William Murdoch invented a cheap substitute for isinglass using cod, but isinglass is still used in fining beers.

'Seeth a pinte of Creame, and in the feething put in fome diffolued Ifinglas, ftirring it vntil it be very thicke, then take a handfull of blanched Almonds, beat them and put them in a difh with your Creame, feafoning them with fugar, and after flice it and difh it.'

Ingredients: 600 ml double cream; 100 ml full cream milk; 3 sheets of gelatine; 100 g blanched almonds; 1 tsp rose water; 4 tbsp caster sugar.

Method: Pour the cream into a medium saucepan. Bring the cream to the boil over a medium heat. As soon as the mixture comes to a boil, reduce to a simmer and cook for around 10 minutes until the cream has reduced in volume by about ⅓. Remove from the heat and set aside to cool. Soak the gelatine sheets in the milk until they are soft, then use a slotted spoon to transfer to a plate. Pour the milk into a medium saucepan and bring to a simmer. Whisk in the sugar, then add the gelatine and continue heating until completely dissolved. Add the milk mixture to the cream and combine. Then pass through a fine-meshed sieve into a bowl. Roughly grind the blanched almonds in a food processor. Place the ground almonds and rose water in a mortar and pound to a smooth paste. Scrape this paste into the still-warm cream and gelatine mix and whisk well to combine. Pour the mixture into a small loaf tin lined with cling film. Allow to cool, then transfer to the refrigerator and chill overnight to set. When ready to serve run a little hot water over the base of the dish and gently ease the *leach* away from the sides. Cut into slices and arrange these on serving plates. Garnish with some fruit and a sprig of mint then serve.

LEACH OF ALMONDS – ALMOND PUDDING

A Noble Boke off Cookry ffor a Prynce Houssolde Holkham MSS 674, 1480 and Hugh Plat's *Delights for Ladies*, 1602

A gilded *leche, leech* or *leach* was served at Henry VIII's Garter Feast at Windsor in 1520, appearing in both the first and second courses. This rose water flavoured jelly featured as a chessboard with the 'black' squares gilded. Leach continued to be a favourite dish at other Garter Feasts until the seventeenth century. Leach was closely related to 'ribband jelly', a jelly moulded in multicoloured layers, also popular in Tudor times.

'To make Leach of Almonds. Take halfe a pound of sweet Almonds, and beat them in a mortar; then strain them with a pint of sweet milke from the cow; then put to it one graine of musk, 2 spoonfuls of Rose-water, two ounces of fine sugar, the weight of 3 whole shillings of isinglass that is very white, and so boyle them; and let all run thorow a strainer: then may you slice the same, and so serve it.' (Hugh Plat)

Ingredients: 1 cup almond milk; 1½ tbsp sugar; ¼ cup cream; ½ tbsp rose water; ½ tbsp gelatine.

Method: Heat almond milk and add cream. Add sugar and rose water when it comes to simmer. When simmering again, add gelatin. When thoroughly mixed, refrigerate for about 4 hours. When the pudding sets, place in a serving bowl and sprinkle with sugar. The dish will seem a little thin comparted to our modern idea of pudding.

LENTEN LEACH (LEECH) – MILK AND WINE JELLY
Thomas Dawson's *The Good Housewife's Jewel*, 1596

By the middle of the eighteenth century, *leach* had become known as *flummery* or *blancmange*. *Leach* was often moulded into shapes using wooden moulds. Although no Tudor moulds have survived, there are records of jellies moulded into the shape of castles and animals at Henry VIII's court. In the Plantagenet period, even more elaborate jellies and leaches had been served to royalty. At Henry VI's coronation in Westminster Hall in 1429, his personal badge, 'an antelope with a crowne about his necke with a chayne of golde' was emblazoned on a white leach. There was also 'Gely party wryten and noted with Te Deum laudamus'. This modern version is of two jellies made on top of each other, but it is a lengthy dish to prepare as each part needs to set before continuing. Making the jelly only takes 15–20 minutes but the layers need to set overnight. There are milk versions but this one was a dish for Lent when the Tudors could not use dairy products, using almond milk instead.This is a high table dish for a gentry family and is served attractively, and the top half of the *leach* is coloured with red wine.

'Take a quart of almond milk and three ounces of gelatine, half a pond of beaten sugar; stir them together. Let it be thick. Then strain it with three spoonfuls of rosewater. Then put it into a platter and let it cool, and cut it in squares. Lay it fair in dishes, and lay gold upon it.'

Ingredients for the Milk Jelly: 1 pint full fat milk or almond milk; 2–3 leaves of gelatine; 2 oz sugar.

Ingredients for the Wine Jelly: ¼ pint red wine or grape juice; 1 leaf of gelatine; 5–6 rose petals or a little rose water; to decorate, a few raspberries or redcurrants.

Method for the Almond Milk: If you are using almond milk, make this the day before you make the milk jelly. About 250 g almonds and 2 tbsp rice flour with 550ml water, makes 1 pint of almond milk. Cover the ground almonds with the boiling water, stand for 15 minutes, rub through a sieve or cloth. Straining through a cloth produces a smoother milk. If it is a little thin, add rice flour and warm in a pan until it thickens. Cool and put in the fridge overnight.

Method for the Milk Jelly: Make the milk jelly first, before the wine jelly. Soak the gelatine leaves in water. Warm the milk or almond milk but do not boil. Add the gelatine and stir until dissolved. Pour into four glasses and set overnight, preferably in a refrigerator.

Method for the Wine Jelly: Soak the gelatine leaf and warm the wine. Dissolve the gelatine in the wine. Chop and add the rose petals or a teaspoon of rose water. Allow to go cold and spoon the cold wine mixture onto the set milk pudding and return to the fridge to set. Once both parts are set, decorate with a few raspberries and serve.

SHREWSBURY CAKES – SHREWSBURY SHORTBREADS
A Delightfull Daily Exercise for Ladies and Gentlewomen, 1621

As part of banquets, 'fine cakes' were served alongside hippocras, sweetmeats and other sweet delicacies. One of these 'fine cake' recipes is now known as Shrewsbury or Shropshire Cake, and they were already associated with the town of Shrewsbury by 1596. In that year there was a shortage of grain and a ban on the making of 'fine cakes' was imposed in Shrewsbury. In 1602, Lord Herbert of Cherbury wrote to his guardian, Sir George More with a pack of 'bread' or 'cake' particular to Shrewsbury: 'Lest you think this country ruder than it is, I have sent you some bread, which I am sure will be dainty, howsoever it be not pleasinge; it is a kind of cake which our country people use and made in no place in England but in Shrewsbury; if you vouchsafe to taste them, you will enworthy the country and sender. Measure not my love in substance of it, which is brittle, but the form of it, which is circular'. The description of those cakes being both 'brittle' and 'circular', suggests that they are similar to the round shortbreads of later recipes.

'Take a quart of very fine flower, eight ounces of fine sugar beaten and cersed, twelve ounces of sweet butter, a Nutmegge grated, two or three spoonfuls of Damask rose-water, worke all these together with your hands as hard as you can for the space of half an houre, then roule it in little round Cakes, about the thickness of three shillings one upon another, then take a silver Cup or glass some four inches over, and cut the cakes in them, then strowe some flower upon white papers and lay them upon them, and bake them in an Oven as hot as for Manchet.'

Ingredients: Around 4 cups of flour; 1 cup granulated sugar; 12 oz butter; 1½ tsp grated nutmeg; 3 tbsp rose water.

Method: Cream the butter and sugar, then add the rest of the ingredients. Roll out about ¼ inch thick or less. Cut with a round cutter or a glass. Bake on greaseproof paper at 200°C for 10 minutes. Poke holes in them with a fork before baking, as in some shortbread recipes, to keep them flat.

PRINCE BISKET – ROSE WATER BISCUITS

Delightes of Ladies to adorne their Persons, Tables, Closets, and distillatories with Beauties, banquets, perfumes and waters. Reade, Practise, and Censure, 1602

'Take one pound of very fine flower, and one pound of fine sugar, and eight egges, and two spoonfuls of Rose water, and one ounce of Carroway seeds, and beat it all to batter one whole houre: for the more you beat it, the better your bread is: then bake it in coffins, of white plate, being basted with a little butter before you put in your batter, and so keep it.'

Ingredients: 500 g flour; 350 g sugar; 5 eggs, beaten; 4 tsp caraway seeds; 2 tbsp rose water.

Method: Sift the flour and sugar together and add the beaten eggs, caraway seeds and rose water. Mix all the ingredients together with a wooden spoon until they form a solid dough. This may take some time as the eggs will stiffen as they are being beaten, but carry on until the eggs will stiffen no more. The dough will still be a little liquid, but this is fine. Once the dough will stiffen no more, spoon out some of the mixture onto a greased cooking sheet to form circles 2½ inches round. Place in an oven preheated to 170°C for 20 minutes. Allow the biscuits to cool and harden before transferring to a wire rack so that they can cool properly. If baked in small moulds, the biscuits can make decorative individual servings.

WAFFRES – CHEESE FRITTERS

Two Fifteenth Century Cookbooks – Harleian MS. 279 & Harl. MS. 4016, c. 1440

'Take þe Wombe of A luce, and seþe here wyl, and do it on a morter, and tender cheese þer-to, grynde hem y-fere; þan take flowre an whyte of Eyroun and bete to-gedere, þen take Sugre an pouder of Gyngere, and do al to-gerderys, and loke þat þin Eyroun ben hote, and ley þer-on of þin paste, and þan make þin waffrys, and serue yn.'

Ingredients: 10 large eggs; 700 g flour; 75 g sugar; 1 tbsp ginger; 350 g grated Cheddar cheese; ½ tsp salt.

Method: Mix together all ingredients, except the eggs and cheese, in a bowl. Beat the eggs lightly and add them to the flour mixture. Then add the cheese and mix thoroughly until the mixture resembles a thick batter. Butter a frying pan, heat it and drop a ladle-full of the batter into the middle. Cook for about five minutes, then serve. Alternatively you can use a waffle iron to cook the *waffres*.

CHAR DE CRABB – DON THOMAS AWKBAROW'S HONEY AND CRAB APPLE PIE

The Babees Book, or A 'Lytyl Reporte' of How Young People Should Behave, MS. Harl. 5086, c. 1475

'To make Crabapple Pie. Recipe: crabapples and boil them in water til they be soft, and take hony and strain the crabbs therewith through a cloth. Put to a 3rd part of clarified honey and a quantity of sandalwood, and colour it with saffron; then put thereto a quantity of powder of pepper and 2*d* worth of the flour of anise and a quantity of powder of licorice. Then take grated bread and mould it up therewith, and put it in pie shells and serve it forth, and you will go well. So says Don Thomas Awkbarow.'

Ingredients: 5 large green or Bramley apples or 15 crab apples, peeled cored and sliced; 250 ml honey; 10 saffron threads; ½ tsp ground liquorice; 1 tsp ground aniseeds; 200 g unseasoned breadcrumbs; 1 tsp white pepper; ½ tsp salt; a few drops of red food colouring; 1 pre-baked 9-inch pie shell.

Method: Boil the apples until soft, then drain. Blend in a food processor along with 200 ml of the honey to make a smooth purée. Place this purée in a large bowl and then taste for sweetness and blend in additional honey if required. Add the food colouring, saffron, salt and pepper along with the ground aniseeds and liquorice and blend in with a large spoon. Add sufficient breadcrumbs to thicken the mixture to the consistency of a heavy cake batter. Place the apple mixture in the pre-baked pie shell and place in an oven preheated to 160°C and bake for about 25 minutes, or until the filling is bubbling. Remove from the oven, allow to cool and set.

APPLE PUFS – APPLE PANCAKES

John Murrell's *A New Booke of Cookerie*, 1615

'To Make Apple Pufs. Take a pomewater or any other Apple that is not hard, or harsh in taste: mince it small woth a dozen or twenty Razins of the Sunne: wet the Apples in two Egges, beat them all together with the back of a knive of a Spoone. Season them with Nutmeg, Rosewater, Sugar, and ginger: drop them into a Frying-pan with a spoone, fry them like egges, wring or the juyce of an Orenge, or Lemmon, and serve them in.'

Ingredients: 2 peeled and cored apples, chopped; 2 tbsp raisins (about 30); 3

large or 4 small eggs; 1 tsp fresh nutmeg; 1 tsp rose water; ½ tbsp sugar; 1 tsp ginger, dried; butter for frying; orange or lemon juice to squeeze on top.

Method: Mince the apples finely, with some raisins, but retain some texture. Put the eggs in a bowl, then put the minced apples in and beat all together. After beating, add the remaining ingredients and mix together. To save time, the batter could be prepared 24 hours in advance. The batter resembles thin pancake batter with apple lumps. Melt a small amount of butter in a frying pan and drop the batter by teaspoons into hot butter. Cook over medium heat. Turn once when the apple 'puff' develops air bubbles. Remove from heat when browned on both sides and squeeze orange or lemon juice onto the pancakes.

RYS ALKERE – APPLE AND FIG RICE PUDDING
Curye on Inglysch – Diversa Servicia, 14th century

'For to make rys alkere, tak figys and reysons, and do awey þe kernelis; and a god perty of applys, and do awey þe paryng of þe applis and þe kernelis; and brey hem wel in a morter and temper hem vp wyþ almande mylk and menge hem wyþ flour of rys þat yt be wel chariand. and strew þervpon powder of galyngale and serue yt forth.'

Ingredients: 12 apples; 12 figs; 1½ cups raisins; 2.7 cups almond milk; ½ cup cream of rice; cinnamon.

Method: Peel and core the apples, dice them and the figs. Mix in the raisins. Cook with almond milk over medium heat, gradually adding cream of rice. Stir constantly until a spoon can stand up and the apples are soft. Sprinkle with cinnamon and serve.

PICE AR Y MAEN – WELSHCAKES ON THE STONE
Traditional Welsh – modern redaction

Ancient Celts baked bread on a stone, with a further refinement of placing an iron pot over the dough. This closed method of cooking, much like a modern oven, provided a way of heating the food from all angles. A bakestone is an early type of griddle, formerly the portable flat stone placed on or next to a fire, originally used to cook bread and then cakes of various kinds. It was often oval and made of slate until it was replaced with cast iron plate in the nineteenth century. The Welsh bakestone, or *planc*, is a now a flat circle of cast iron, usually with a hoop for hanging over the fire, and is essential for the preparation of many traditional recipes. Iron is much more conductive than stone and was an enormous step forward in the progress of cookery, and a well seasoned bakestone will last a lifetime. It needs very little cooking fat and will improve in performance with age. The traditional fat used is lard, but vegetable oil can be used instead.

The *planc* or *maen* is used to bake authentic regional recipes such as breads, scones, cakes, pies, pancakes, tarts and biscuits. Old bakestones or modern reproductions can be used over an open fire using a fire jack (trammel, pot-hook) to hang from, or fire dog to sit on. It can also be used on a modern gas stove, electric stove and even on a convection stove. A bakestone heats up quickly, radiates heat more evenly and can sustain that heat at a constant temperature better than anything else in the modern kitchen. When you cook on a bakestone (after seasoning it) the heat under the bakestone can be set just low to medium, as for a modern frying pan. It takes a little longer to heat up, but once it does it will sustain this temperature. Made from thick dough similar to scone dough, with currants and spices, Welshcakes are cooked on the bakestone and eaten warm, sprinkled with sugar. Brittle and crumbly, they are extremely popular. The art of a good Welshcake is to cook them quickly on both sides so that they stay moist in the centre.

Ingredients: 8 oz self-raising flour; 1 tsp mixed spice; 4 oz butter; 3 oz caster sugar; 3 oz mixed currants and sultanas; 1 large egg, beaten; zest of half a lemon.

Method: Sieve the flour and spice into a mixing bowl and rub in the butter until the mixture resembles fine breadcrumbs. Add the sugar, lemon rind and dried fruit. Pour in the beaten egg and stir to make a firm dough. On a floured board, roll or press the dough to ¼ inch thick and cut into circles with a 2-inch cutter. Bake around 15–18 cakes on a medium hot griddle if you have no bakestone, turning once until golden brown on both sides but still soft in the middle. Dust with caster sugar while still hot. Lacking a griddle, you can use a heavy based frying pan that has been lightly buttered. These cakes keep for up to 10 days and freeze well. Serve with clotted cream and jam, or just with butter.

PICE'R PREGETHWR – PREACHER'S PIKELETS TWO WAYS

Tradition Welsh – modern redaction

There were many dishes cooked upon bakestones, including *crempothau*, crumpets, and these are a type of crumpet. Dropped pikelets of flour, sugar, butter, egg and milk batter.

Ingredients 1: 225 g self-raising flour; 125 g butter, diced; 125 g caster sugar; 2 eggs; 150–300ml milk; 1 tsp vanilla extract or almond extract.

Method 1: In a bowl, rub the butter into the flour until the mixture resembles breadcrumbs, then stir in the sugar. Whisk together the eggs, 150 ml milk and the vanilla or almond extract. Work this mixture into the flour mix and add enough extra milk to give the batter about the consistency of double cream. Heat a griddle or non-stick frying pan and when hot add the batter by the tablespoon. Fry until bubbles appear on the upper surface then turn over and cook until browned on the base. Serve warm, with butter.

Ingredients 2: 4oz plain flour; 2 eggs, beaten; 3oz butter or margarine, melted; ½ pint buttermilk.

Method 2: Mix the flour, eggs, melted butter and buttermilk with a fork or a whisk, until there are no lumps. Spoon a few tablespoons of the pancake batter into a lightly greased, hot pan. When the pancakes start to bubble, turn over with a spatula. When they are cooked, place them on a plate and keep warm in the oven while you cook the remaining batter. Serve with butter, syrup or jam.

A TARTE OF CUSTARD WITH RAISINS AND DATES – ELIZABETHAN SWEET DATE CUSTARD TART

The Proper Newe Booke of Cookerye, c. 1557

'A Custarde: the coffyn must be fyrste hardened in the oven, and then take a quart of creame and fyve or syxe yolkes of egges, and beate them well together, and put them into the creame, and put in Suger and small Raysyns and Dates sliced, and put into the coffyn butter or els marrowe, but on the fyshe daies put in butter.'

Ingredients: 450 ml single cream; 3 egg yolks; 60 g sugar; 80 g raisins; 60 g stoned and chopped dates; 45 g butter; 9-inch pie crust shell.

Method: After you have made your pie crust, place in a 9-inch pie dish and add dried beans to keep the bottom flat. Blind bake in an oven at 200°C for 10 minutes. Beat the egg yolks together, adding the cream, sugar, raisins and dates. Pour this mixture into the part-baked pie crust and dot the surface with butter. Bake the tart in the oven at 170°C for 75 minutes, or until its surface turns golden brown.

PASTE OF NOUISE – SPICED CAKE

Sir Hugh Plat's *Delightes for Ladies*, 1602

'To make paſte of Nouie. Take a quarter of a pounde of Valentian almonds, otherwiſe called the ſmall almonds or Barbarie almonds, and beate them in a mortar til they come to paſte, then take ſtale Manchet beeing grated, and drie it before the fire in a diſh, then ſift it, then beat it with your almondes, put in the beating of it a little cinnamon, ginger and the iuce of a Lemmon, and when it is beaten to perfit paſte, printe it wt your moldes, and ſo dry it in an ouen after you haue drawn out your bread : this paſte will laſt all the yeare.'

Ingredients: 250 g stale manchet or white bloomer, rendered to fine crumbs and dried for 20 minutes in a low oven; 120 g blanched almonds; ½ tsp ground cinnamon; ¼ tsp ground ginger; juice of 1 lemon, strained.

Method: Grind the almonds in a blender, turn into a mortar and pound to a

CHIRESEYE – CHERRY BREAD PUDDING (1)

Curye on Inglish, Diuersa Servicia, 14th century

The Feast of St. John the Baptist was 25 June and these cherries would have been picked at this time. 'Wastel' bread was a very fine white bread.

'For to make Cherries, take cherries at the feast of Saint John the Baptist, and do away the stones. Grind them in a mortar, and after rub them well in a sieve so that the juice be well coming out; and do then in a pot and do there-in fair grease or butter and bread of wastel minced, and of sugar a good part, and a portion of wine. And when it is well cooked and dressed in dishes, stick therein clove flowers and strew thereon sugar.'

Ingredients 1: 2 cups fresh cherries, stoned; 2 cups fresh breadcrumbs; ⅓ cup sugar; ¾ cup red wine; 1 tbsp melted butter.

Method 1: In a blender, blend all ingredients except the butter, then place in a pan. Add butter and simmer, stirring constantly, for 5 minutes or until thickened. Pour into serving dish and let it cool, then chill. Serve with Crème Bastard – see below.

CHIRESEYE – CHERRY BREAD PUDDING (2)

Ingredients 2: Fresh stoned cherries; cherry juice (only to be added if you do not get enough juice from the cherries themselves); very soft butter; unseasoned breadcrumbs or finely minced white bread; sugar; semi-sweet red or white wine; edible pink flowers if available.

Method 2: Purée the cherries by using a blender. Place in a large pot and add enough cherry juice to make a very wet mixture. Blend in the butter and wine and then beat in bread, enough to thicken the cherries to a pudding-like consistency. Add sugar to taste. Bring the cherries to a low boil, then reduce to a gentle simmer and cook for several minutes, stirring often to prevent sticking. Place the pudding in serving dishes, decorate with the flowers and sprinkle sugar on top. If serving with Crème Bastard – see next recipe – add the flowers and sugar on top of the sauce.

CRÈME BASTARD to accompany Chireseye – WHITE CUSTARD SAUCE

Two Fifteenth Century Cookbooks – Harleian MS. 279 & Harl. MS. 4016, c. 1440

This is recommended as an accompaniment to 'baken mete', roast meat, which again shows the Tudor sweet and savoury taste. This is excellent poured over strawberries or raspberries, as well as cherries, and can also be baked.

'Take the white of eggs in a great heap and put it on a pan full of milk and let it boil. Then season it with salt and honey a little, then let it cool and draw it through a strainer and take faire cow milk and draw it withall, and season it with sugar and look that it be poignant and sweet; and serve it forth for a pottage, or for a good baken mete, whether that thou would.'

Ingredients: 4 egg whites, beaten until a little frothy; ¾ cup of whole milk; 2 tbsp warmed honey; 2 tsp sugar; 2 tbsp cream; pinch of salt.

Method: Place the whole milk, or half and half, in a small pan with the egg whites. Bring to a low boil, stirring constantly so as not to scorch, and cook for about 2 minutes. Add the honey and salt and simmer a little longer to properly combine. When the mixture has thickened a little, remove it from the heat and put it through a strainer to remove any bits of egg white that may have scrambled. Add the cream and sugar and whisk for about 100 strokes, before pouring into an airtight container or using immediately.

WARM BASTARD ALMOND MILK

A.W., *The Booke of Goode Cookry Very Necessary for all Such as Delight Therein*, 1584, 1591

This author has taken a liberty with the title of this dish – 'bastard' was a sweetened wine. The reader must be aware that almond milk goes off quickly, so when you make it, use it soon.

'Take blanched Almonds and bray them smal, then with faire water draw them through a strainer, and make them not too thin nor too thick, and then put them into a pot with a quarter of a pound of sugar and let them boile over the fire, and when they boyle take them from the fire, then take a manchet loaf and cut it in thin peeces, steep it in a pinte of White wine, [such] as Bastard, Tire [Tyre], or Maulmsie [Malmsey], then cast it into Almond Milk and dresse it in fair dishes, and so serve it foorth.'

TARTE OF RYCE – TUDOR RICE PUDDING

The Good Huswife's Jewell, 1596

Rice was an expensive import and was used in luxury Lenten dishes for the rich. Medieval rice pottages were made of rice boiled until soft, then mixed with almond milk or cow's milk, or both, sweetened and sometimes coloured. Recipes for baked rice puddings began to appear in the early seventeenth century and the use of nutmeg survives in modern recipes. This pudding is only mildly sweet, gaining most of its sweetness from the raisins and currants. If you prefer a sweeter pudding, add more sugar to taste.

'To make a Tart of Ryce. Boyle your Rice, and put in the yolkes of two or three Egges into the Rice, and when it is boyled, put it into a dish, and season it with Suger, Sinamon and Ginger, and butter, and the juyce of two or three Orenges, and set it on the fire againe.'

Ingredients: 2 cups uncooked rice; ¼ cup unsalted butter; 1½ cups milk; 1¼ cups thick cream; 3 egg yolks; ½ cup sugar; 1¼ tsp cinnamon; ½ tsp ginger; ½ tsp nutmeg; ¾ cup raisins; ¾ cup currants; butter for greasing dish; cinnamon sticks for garnish (optional); orange juice (optional).

Method: Preheat oven to 180°C. Steam rice until tender. While rice is cooking, place raisins and currants into a small pot and cover with hot water. Bring to the boil, then immediately remove from the heat. Let the fruit soak in the hot water to plump. After the rice has cooked, stir in the butter until melted. In a mixing bowl, whisk together milk, cream, egg yolks, sugar, cinnamon, ginger and nutmeg. Pour this mixture into the rice and stir until combined. Drain the raisins and currants, then fold them into the rice mixture. Grease a 9 x 9-inch baking dish with butter and pour the rice mixture into the dish. Place in the oven and bake uncovered for about 45 minutes until the top of the pudding turns golden brown. Serve garnished with a cinnamon stick, if desired.

PESCODS – MOCK PEAPODS

A.W., *The Booke of Goode Cookry Very Necessary for all Such as Delight Therein*, 1584, 1591

'How to make Pescods, First make short paste with yolks of egs, butter and a little sugar. Then take for the stuffe, Marow, small raisins, dates, Sinamon, Sugar and Ginger, and then frye them with sweet butter, and when you serve them, cast on Sugar and Sinamon.'

PESCODS OF MAROW – SWEET MOCK PEAPODS

The Treasurie of Commodious Conceits & Hidden Secrets, 1573

'To make Pescods of Marow. Fyrst slice your Marow in length, dry your pastry as thin as a paper leafe: then take and lay smal Raisins, Cinimon and a little ginger and Suger aboute the Marow, fashion them up lyke Pescodes, frie them in butter, cast upon them Cinimon and suger, and serve them.'

PESCODDES – FRIED MARROW HALF-MOONS

The Proper Newe Booke of Cookerye, c. 1557

A snack or dessert of deep-fried, marrow-filled, pastry half-moons.

'Pescoddes. Take marybones and pull the mary hole out of them, and cutte it in two partes, then season it with suger, synamon, ginger and a little salte and make youre paeste as fyne as ye canne, and as shorte and thyn as ye canne, then frye theym in swete suette and caste upon them a lyttle synamon and ginger and so serve them at the table.'

Ingredients: 60 g bone marrow; 2 tsp sugar; ¼ tsp cinnamon; ¼ tsp freshly-grated ginger; 2 tbsp lard for frying; salt to taste; 22 cm pie crust shell; cinnamon and ginger to sprinkle before serving.

Method: Make a standard pie crust. Mix the marrow, sugar, cinnamon and ginger to make a smooth paste, and add sugar to taste. Roll the pastry on a floured board until it becomes very thin. Using a cutter cut the pastry into as many 3-inch diameter circles as you can. Spread a thin layer of marrow mixture across the centre of each round. Wet your finger and trace it around the edge of a circle, fold these in half and seal the edges. Repeat until finished. Once you have a pile of these half-circles heat up your lard in a frying pan and brown the *pescoddes* on each side. Arrange on a plate, sprinkle with cinnamon and ginger and serve.

A SOLTETY OF MOCK ENTRAILS – BATTER-FRIED FRUIT AND NUTS MADE TO APPEAR AS ENTRAILS
Harleian MS 4016, *c.* 1450

This simple 'subtlety' was served as a sweet and can be made using four pieces of heavy string, each 18 inches long.

Ingredients: ¼ cup sliced almonds, soaked in warm water; 18 dried figs, halved; 6 oz dates, halved; ½ cup raisins; 1½ cups oil; 7 oz beer; 1 tsp sugar; ¼ tsp ground cloves; ½ tsp ground ginger; 1.3 cups flour; dash of salt.

Method: Using a sharp needle, thread the dried fruits and nuts onto the strings, alternating the fruits and nuts to achieve an uneven appearance, and set to one side. Beat together the beer, flour, salt and spices. Dip the strings of fruit and nuts in the batter to coat. Fry in oil over high heat, one string at a time. Fry each string of 'entrails' until golden and drain.

PEACH TARTE – ANY FRUIT PIE
Thomas Dawson's *The Good Huswifes Jewell*, 1585, 1594, 1596

Boiling the peaches before putting them in the pie allows the use of slightly under-ripe peaches and also reduces the baking time.

'To make all maner of fruit Tartes. You must boyle your fruite, whether it be apple, cherrie, peach, damson, peare, Mulberie, or codling, in faire water, and when they be boyled inough, put them into a bowle, and bruise them with a ladle, and when they be colde, straine them, and put in red wine or Claret wine, and so season it with suger, sinamon and ginger.'

Ingredients: 5 peeled and sliced peaches; ¼ cup red wine; ¾ cup sugar; ½ tsp cinnamon; ½ tsp ginger; ¼ tsp salt; pie crust.

Method: Parboil sliced peaches in water until just tender. Drain well and place in a pie crust. Make syrup by heating sugar, spices and wine. Pour this over peaches and cover with top crust, making a few slits in the top. Bake at 220°C for 10 minutes, then reduce heat to 180°C and bake for about 30–40 minutes more until done.

COFFYN OF GRENE APPLES – GREEN APPLE PIE
The Proper Newe Booke of Cookrye, c. 1557

This is a version of the Warden Pear pie, essentially an apple pie made with unripe apples and baked in a hot water crust made with butter, as opposed to lard. Eliza Acton, in her 1845 book, has a recipe for a very similar pastry, showing how well this recipe stood the test of time.

'Take your apples and pare them cleane and core them as ye wyll a Quince, then make youre coffyn after this namer, take a lyttle fayre water adn halfe a dyſhe of butter nad a lyttle Saffron, and ſette all this vpon a chafyngdyſhe tyll it be hoate, then temper your flower with this ſayd licour, and the whyte of two egges, and alſo make your cofyn, and ceaſon your apples with Sinemone, Gynger and Suger ynoughe. Then pute them into your coffin and laye halfe a dyſhe of butter aboue them, and ſo cloſe your coffin, and ſo bake them.'

Ingredients: 450 g plain flour; 200 ml water; 150 g butter; 2 egg whites; 500 g unripe or Bramley apples, peeled and cored; 200 g Demerara sugar; ½ tsp ground ginger; ½ tsp ground cinnamon; 1 egg, whisked in 2 tbsp water to glaze.

Method: Sift the flour into a bowl and set aside. Combine the water and butter in a saucepan and heat until just melted. Work the egg whites into the flour, then form a well and pour in the water and butter mixture. Mix with a spoon until it holds together, then turn out onto a floured work surface and knead briefly. Make the mixture into a ball and cover with cling film. Set aside until cold enough to roll out. Cut two-thirds of the dough off and roll into a round about 1 cm thick. Place a large, floured jar in the centre and shape the pastry around this. Leave for 5 minutes until set, then ease the dough away from the mould. Meanwhile, cut the apples into chunks and mix these with the sugar, ginger and cinnamon. Spoon this mixture into the dough mould. Roll the remainder of the dough out to form a lid and fix this to the pie with a little water. Trim any excess pastry neatly and pierce an air hole in the top. Transfer to a greased baking sheet and glaze with the beaten egg and water mix. Place in an oven preheated to 200°C and bake for 30 minutes, or until the pastry is golden and crisp. Serve either hot or cold.

TARTE OF DAMSONS AND PEARES
The Proper Newe Booke of Cookrye, c. 1557

'To make a tarte of damſons.Take damſons and boyle theym in wyne, eyther red or claret, and put thereto a doſen of peares, or els whyte bread too make theym ſtyffe wyth all, then drawe theym vp wyth the yolkes of ſyxe egges and ſwete butter and ſo bake it.'

Ingredients: 200 g damson plums, halved and pitted; 2 cooking pears, peeled, cored and chopped; 200 ml red wine or claret; 2 tbsp unsalted butter; 4 egg yolks; 1 batch short pastry. Gooseberries and other fruit can also be used.

Method: Roll out the pastry and use to line a deep, 9-inch wide pie dish. Line with greaseproof paper, fill with baking beads and transfer to an oven preheated to 180°C. Blind bake for about 15 minutes, or until the pastry is just dry to the touch but not browned. Remove from the oven, take out the paper and baking beads and set aside. Combine the plums, wine and pears in a saucepan. Bring to a simmer, cover and continue cooking for about 40 minutes, or until the fruit has completely broken down and the mixture is thick. Stir now and then. Pass through a fine-meshed sieve, pressing down on the mixture with the back of a spoon. Whisk the egg yolks in a bowl, then add a ladleful of the hot damson mixture to temper. Pour the resulting egg mix into the main damson mix and whisk to combine, adding the butter at this point. Pour this mixture into the blind baked pastry shell then transfer to an oven preheated to 180°C and bake for about 25 minutes, or until the pastry is golden and the custard filling has set. This can be served either hot or cold.

AN EXCELLENT CAKE FOR KENELM DIGBIE
The Closet of the Eminently Learned Sir Kenelm Digbie, Knight, Opened, 1669

'To make an Excellent Cake. To a peck of fine flour take six pounds of fresh butter, which must be tenderly melted, ten pounds of currants, of cloves and mace, ½ an ounce of each, an ounce of cinnamon, ½ an ounce of nutmegs, four ounces of sugar, one pint of sack mixed with a quart at least of thick barm of ale (as soon as it is settled to have the thick fall to the bottom, which will be when it is about two days old), half a pint of rosewater; ½ a quarter of an ounce of saffron. Then make your paste, strewing the spices, finely beaten, upon the flour: then put the melted butter (but even just melted) to it; then the barm, and other liquours: and put it into the oven well heated presently. For the better baking of it, put it in a hoop, and let it stand in the oven one hour and a half. You ice the cake with the whites of two eggs, a small quantity of rosewater, and some sugar.'

Ingredients for the cake: 450 g flour; 170 g butter; 300 g currants; 2 tsp sugar; 1 tbsp sugar; ¼ tsp each of mace and freshly-grated nutmeg; ½ tsp cinnamon;

2 tbsp sack (you can make this with sherry and 1 tsp of honey); 60 ml ale yeast; 8 saffron threads ground into 2 tbsp warm rose water with a pestle and mortar.
Ingredients for the icing: White of ¼ egg; ¼ tbsp rosewater; 2 tsp sugar.
Method: Stir 2 tsp of sugar into 60 ml of warm water (around 37°C) and add the yeast. Cover and set aside in a warm place to work. Place the butter in a pan and melt gently. Sift the flour and spices into a bowl and add the butter, mixing it in thoroughly. Add the currants and mix them in. Add all the liquid ingredients, including the yeast. Mix this to a smooth paste and pour into a lined and greased 10-inch cake tin. Place in an oven preheated to 180°C and bake for 40 minutes. Meanwhile mix the egg, sugar and rose water. Use this to thinly cover the top of the cake as soon as it emerges from the oven.

IUMBOLLS – ELIZABETHAN JUMBLED BISCUITS
Sir Hugh Platt's Delightes for Ladies to adorne their Persons, Tables, Closets, and distillatories with Beauties, banquets, perfumes and waters. Reade, Practise, and Censure, 1602

These are Elizabethan biscuits made from ground almonds and leftover shortcake, flavoured with caraway seeds. They are sometimes known as *jumbles*, from their plaited or knotted nature. Sarah Longe (1610) made *jumballs* from flour, sugar, eggs, cream, coriander and fennel seed: 'Worke all together well, then roll it into small rolls, and cast it into [ornamental] Knots'. Plat's recipe is as follows.

'Take ½ a pound of almonds being beaten to paste with a short cake being grated, and two eggs, two ounces of caraway seeds, being beaten, and the juice of a lemon: and being brought into paste, roll it into round strings: then cast it into knots, and so bake it in an oven and when they are baked, ice them with rose water and sugar, and the white of an egg being beaten together, then take a feather and gild them, then put them again into the oven, and let them stand in a little while, and they will be iced clean over with a white ice: and so box them up and you may keep them all the year.'

Ingredients: 115 g ground almonds; 115 g grated shortcake; 1 egg, beaten; 4 tsp caraway seeds; juice of ½ lemon; 8 tbsp sugar; 1 tbsp rose water; white of half an egg.
Method: Mix the ground almonds, grated shortcake, beaten egg, lemon juice and caraway seeds. Divide the mixture in three, roll into long tubes and plait them together. Place on a baking sheet and cook in the oven at 160°C for 15 minutes. While it is cooking, mix the sugar, rose water and egg white to form the icing. After 15 minutes take the cake from the oven, cover with the icing and return to the oven to cook for a further two minutes. Take out of the oven, divide into 'biscuits', allow to cool and serve.

IUMBALS – SPICED BISCUITS

Gervase Markham's *Countrey Contentments, or, The English Hus-wife*, 1615

Also called *jumbles, iumbolls* or *jumbals*, these are a sort of sweet cookie.

'To make the best Iumbals, take the whites of three egges and beat them well and take of the viell; then take a little milke and a pound of fine wheat flower and suger together finely sifted, and a few Aniseeds well rubd and dried; and then work all together as stiffe as you can work it, and so make them in what forms you please and bake them in a soft oven upon white Papers.'

MARMALADE OF ALL SORTES

Charles Butler's *The Feminine Monarchie, Or, The Historie of Bees*, 1609

This book contains many novel ideas for using honey. This recipe is for 'marmalade', which was originally a sliceable quince preserve, similar to the modern 'fruit sticks' made from dried fruit pulp and marketed as children's or energy snacks.

'Marmalade is thus made. First boile your Quinces in their skins till they be soft: then, hauing pared and strained them, mix therewith the like quantitie of clarified Honie: and boile this together till it be so thicke, that in stirring (for you must continually stirre it for feare of burning) you may see the bottom ;or, being cooled on a Trencher, it be thicke enough to slice: then take it vp and box it speedily. You may also adde a quantitie of Almonds, and Nut-kernels: also Cinamom, Ginger, Cloues and Mace, of each a like quantitie pounded small and put into the Honie with the Quinces, and in boiling to be stirred together. This is very good to comfort and strengthen the stomack. For want of Quinces you may take Wardens, Peares, or Apples, and specially the Peare-maine, Giliflower, Pipin, and Roiall.'

SIR KENELM'S MOST EXCELLENT SMALL CAKES

The Closet of the Eminently Learned Sir Kenelm Digbie, Knight, Opened, 1669

'Take three pound of very fine flower well dried by the fire, and put to it a pound and a half of loaf sugar sifted in a very fine sieve and dried; 3 pounds of currants well washed, and dried in a cloth and set by the fire; when your flour is well mixed with the sugar and currants, you must put in it a pound and a half of unmelted butter, ten spoonfuls of cream, with the yolks of three newlaid eggs beat with it, one nutmeg; and if you please, three spoonfuls of sack. When you have wrought your paste well, you must put it in a cloth, and set it in a dish before the fire, till it be through warm. Then make them up in little cakes, and prick them full of holes; you must bake them in a quick oven unclosed. Afterwards ice them over with sugar. The cakes should be about the bigness of a hand breadth and thin; of the size of the sugar cakes sold at Barnet.'

Ingredients: 600 g flour; 170 g sugar; 350 g currants; 170 g butter; 2½ tbsp cream; yolk of 1 egg; ¼ tsp freshly-ground nutmeg; 2 tbsp sack for the cake and up to 2 tbsp for the icing. If you have no sweet Madeira wine, use Marsala or add 1 tsp of honey to 2 tbsp of sherry or port.

Method: Cream the butter, sugar and the egg yolk together then add the flour to this and mix until well combined. Add the cream, currants, nutmeg and sack and fold in properly. Place butterfly casings in wells in a cake tin and spoon the mixture in. Place the tray in an oven preheated to 180°C for about 20 minutes. While the cakes are baking make an icing by adding as much sack to 75 g of sugar as is needed to make it just spreadable. As soon as you take the cakes from the oven, cover them with the icing and allow to cool before tipping out.

SHELLBREAD – SWEET MUSSEL BREAD BITES

John Murrell, *A Delightfull daily exercise for Ladies and Gentlewomen … Whereby is set foorth the secrete misteries of the purest preservings in Glasses and other Confrictionaries, as making of Breads, Pastes, Preserves, Suckets, Marmalates, Tartstuffes, rough Candies, with many other things never before in Print. Whereto is added a Booke of Cookery. By John Murrell professor thereof A Daily Exercise for Ladies and Gentlewomen*, 1621

This is a traditional Elizabethan recipe for rich breads that were flavoured with rose water and aniseed, and were traditionally baked in mussel shells. Sugar was just becoming a readily available commodity from the Canary Islands. The original recipe used mussel shells to bake these cakes but you can use butterfly cake cases which work just as well.

'Beate a quarter of a pound of double refined sugar, cearse it with two or three spoonefuls of the finest [flour], the youlkes of three new laid eggs, and the white of one, beate all this together in with two or three spoonefulls of sweete cream, a grain of muske, a thimble full of the powder of a dried Lemon, and a little Annise-seede beaten and cearsed, and a little Rose-water, then baste Muskle-shells with sweete butter, as thinne as you can lay it on with a feather, fill your shells with the batter and lay them on the gridiron or a lattise of wickers into the oven, and bake them, and take them out of the shells, and ise them with Rosewater and Sugar. It is a delicate bread, some call it the Italian Mushle, if you keepe them any long time, then alwaies in wet weather put them into your oven.'

Ingredients: 125 g caster sugar; 2 tbsp flour; 1 whole egg; 2 egg yolks; 3 tbsp double cream; grated rind of 1 lemon; 1 tsp rose water; pinch of aniseed.

Method: Put the egg yolks, sugar, cream, lemon rind and rose water in a bowl. Beat with a whisk until light and fluffy, then fold in the flour. Spoon the mixture into mussel shells or butterfly cake casings, and bake in an oven preheated to 180°C for about 20 minutes, or until the tops of the cakes begin turning a light golden. Keep for up to a week in an airtight container.

COURSE GINGER BREAD – GINGER AND LICORICE LOAF

Gervase Markham's *Countrey Contentments, or, The English Hus-wife*, 1615

'Course Ginger Bread. Take a quart of Honey clarified, and seeth it till it be brown, and if it be thick, put to it a dash of water: then take fine crumbs of white bread grated, and put to it, and stir it well, and when it is almost cold, put to it the powder of Ginger, Cloves, Cinamon, and a little Licorice and Anise seeds: then knead it, and put it into a mould and print it. Some use to put to it also a little Pepper, but that is according unto taste and pleasure.'

Ingredients: 240 ml honey; ¼ tsp powdered ginger; ⅛ tsp ground cloves; ⅛ tsp ground cinnamon; ⅛ tsp ground liquorice; 350 g dry breadcrumbs; 1 tbsp aniseeds.

Method: Heat the honey in a bain-marie and when it becomes liquid enough to stir easily, add all the powdered spices, but not the aniseeds. Stir to mix into the honey, then add the breadcrumbs and mix thoroughly. Cover and allow to cook for 15 minutes. This allows the bread to absorb the honey and the resulting mixture should be thick and moist. Tip the dough into a large sheet of greaseproof paper and fold up the sides to form a rough rectangle. Sprinkle the aniseeds on top of this, pressing them gently into the dough with the back of a wetted spoon. Transfer to the refrigerator. Allow to cool for at least two hours, to solidify the mixture and allow it to be cut into thin slices before serving. Traditionally the tops of gingerbread loaves were decorated with incised or stamped patterns. You can also dust the surface of this cake with cinnamon and caster sugar if you wish.

GYNGERBREDE – HONEY GINGERED BITES

Redacted by the Tudor chefs' feast team at Hampton Court.

Ingredients: 1 cup honey; 1 loaf wheat bread, ground into bread crumbs; ¾ tsp cinnamon; ¼ tsp black pepper; ¼ tsp ginger; cinnamon and red sandalwood (or red colouring) to coat.

Method: Bring the honey to a boil, reduce heat and allow to simmer for 5–10 minutes, skimming off any scum. Remove from the heat and add pepper, cinnamon and ginger. Add breadcrumbs, one cup at a time, kneading until the honey and breadcrumbs are thoroughly mixed. Divide the mixture into quarters and roll out on greaseproof paper. Cut into 1-inch squares and dust with mixture of one part cinnamon to two parts sandalwood.

A COVER TARTE IN THE FRENCH MANNER – LARGE CUSTARD PIE
The Proper Newe Booke of Cookerye, c. 1557

Ingredients: Batch of short pastry for a deep double-crust pie about 9 inches in diameter; 500 ml single cream; 8 egg yolks; 100 g unsalted butter, diced; 4 tbsp caster sugar.

Method: Roll out just over half the pastry and use to line a 9-inch diameter deep pie dish. Line with greaseproof paper, fill with baking beads then transfer to an oven preheated to 180°C. Blind bake for about 10 minutes, or until the pastry is just dry to the touch but not browing. Remove from the oven, take out the paper and baking beads and set aside. Whisk together the cream, egg yolks and sugar in a bowl. Pour into a saucepan, add the butter and heat gently until the butter has melted. Whisk the mixture to combine, then continue heating gently, beating constantly, until the custard thickens. Remove from the heat and allow to cool slightly, then pour into the prepared pie crust base. Take the remaining pastry and roll out until large enough to cover the top of the pie. Crimp the pastry to the base and trim off any excess. Cut a cross in the top of the pastry to allow steam to escape, then peel back the four points. Transfer to an oven preheated to 180°C and bake for about 30 minutes, or until the pastry is golden brown and the custard filling has set. Remove from the oven and allow to cool a little. It can be served warm or cold.

TARTE OF MEDLERS – MEDLAR CUSTARD PIE
The Proper Newe Booke of Cookerye, c. 1557

'To make a tarte o medlers. Take medlers when they be rotte, and bray them with the yolkes of foure egges, then ceafon it vp wyth fuger and finamon and fwete butter, and fo bake it.'

Ingredients: 200 g bletted medlars, chopped; 100 ml white wine; 4 tbsp sugar (or to taste); 2 tbsp unsalted butter; ¼ tsp ground cinnamon; 4 egg yolks for tart; 1 batch of 'short paest' as in a preceding recipe in this chapter.

Method: Roll out the pastry and use to line a deep, 9-inch diameter pie dish. Line with greaseproof paper, fill with baking beads then transfer to an oven preheated to 180°C. Blind bake for about 15 minutes, or until the pastry is just dry to the touch but not browning. Remove from the oven, take out the paper and baking beads and set aside. Combine the chopped medlars and wine in a saucepan. Bring to a simmer, cover and then continue cooking for about 40 minutes, or until the fruit has completely broken down and the mixture is thick. Pass through a fine-meshed sieve, pressing down on the mixture with the back of a spoon. Whisk the egg yolks in a bowl, then add a ladleful of the hot medlar mixture to temper. Pour the resulting egg mix into the main mix and whisk to combine, adding the sugar, butter and ground cinnamon.

Pour this mixture into the blind baked pastry shell then transfer to an oven preheated to 180°C and bake for about 25 minutes, or until the pastry is golden and the custard filling has set. Serve either hot or cold.

SIR KENELM'S SACK POSSET – MADEIRA CREAM DESSERT

Sir Kenelm Digby's *The Closet of Sir Kenelm Digby Knight Opened*, 1669

Although of the Stuart period, the book was written by an old servant of Digby, who used medieval recipes onwards. A chafing-dish is 'a vessel to hold burning charcoal or other fuel, for heating anything placed upon it; a portable grate', and the *OED* gives the first known written use in English as being in 1483, in an English Act of Parliament, but the method itself had already been in use for a long time. Traditionally *sack* was Madeira, but any fortified wine such as Marsala, sherry or port will also work.

'Sack Posset. Boil two wine-quarts of Sweet-cream in a Possnet; when it hath boiled a little, take it from the fire, and beat the yolks of nine or ten fresh Eggs, and the whites of four with it, beginning with two or three spoonfuls, and adding more till all be incorporated; then set it over the fire, to recover a good degree of heat, but not so much as to boil; and always stir it one way, least you break the consistence. In the mean time, let half a pint of Sack or White muscadin boil a very little in a bason, upon a Chafing-dish of Coals, with three quarters of a pound of Sugar, and three or four quartered Nutmegs, and as many pretty big pieces of sticks of Cinnamon. When this is well scummed, and still very hot, take it from the fire, and immediately pour into it the cream, beginning to pour neer it, but raising by degrees your hand so that it may fall down from a good height; and without anymore to be done, it will then be fit to eat. It is very good kept cold as well as eaten hot. It doth very well with it, to put into the Sack (immediately before you put in the cream) some Ambergreece, or Ambered-sugar, or Pastils. When it is made, you may put powder of Cinnamon and Sugar upon it, if you like it.'

Ingredients: 1.1 l single cream; 300 ml sack (see above); 8 egg yolks; 4 egg whites; 4 nutmeg quarters; 150 g sugar; 2–3 sticks of cinnamon; ground cinnamon to decorate; caster sugar for dusting.

Method: Place the cream in a pan along with the cinnamon sticks. Bring to the boil and simmer for a few minutes. Remove from the boil and beat the eggs together. Add the egg mixture a spoonful at a time to the cream, stirring all the while, until the eggs are all mixed in. Meanwhile bring the sack to the boil and add the sugar to dissolve it, then add the nutmeg quarters to infuse. Return the cream mixture to the heat, but do not boil. Take the cream off the heat again and allow the sack to go off the boil. Begin whisking the cream mixture and gently pour in the sugared sack, whisking all the while. Remove the cinnamon sticks and nutmeg, return to the heat to thicken, but do not boil. This custard-like dessert can be served immediately or, when cool enough, it can be poured into bowls and chilled in the fridge. Serve cold with a dollop of rhubarb or gooseberry stew placed in the centre. You can dust the surface of the sack posset with cinnamon and caster sugar before serving and add fruit if wished.

PEARES SODDEN IN ALE, BASTARD AND HONNEY – HONIED PEARS AND BASTARD PIES

A.W., *The Booke of Goode Cookry Very Necessary for all Such as Delight Therein*, 1584, 1591

'Anon, anon sir; score a pint of bastard in the halfe moone.' *Henry IV, Part 1.*
Bastard is defined by the OED as a 'sweet kind of Spanish wine, resembling *muscadel* in flavour; sometimes applied to any kind of sweetened wine', and references to it start in the late fourteenth century. In the household books of George, Duke of Clarence, there is an entry dated 9 December 1409, for a sum of twenty pounds allowed for the purchase off 'Malvesie, romenay, osay, bastard, muscadelle, and other sweete wynes.'

'Take Peares also sodden in Ale, and bray and straine them with the same Licour, and put therto Bastard and Honny, and put it into a pan and stir it on the fire til it be wel sodden, then make little coffins and set them in the Oven til they be hard, and then take them out againe, and put the foresaid licour into them and so serve them forth.'

DARYOLS – SAFFRON CUSTARD DARIOLE

The Master-Cook of Richard II, *The Forme of Cury*, c. 1390
Dariole is the French term for a small, cylindrical mould, and it never ceases to amaze this author that there are so many French words in the English language. Michel Thomas used to claim that there was 80 per cent commonality. The term also refers to the dessert baked in the mould. Classically, it is made by lining the mould with puff pastry, filling it with an almond cream and baking until golden brown. There are also savoury *darioles*, usually made with vegetable custards. When cooked as popular desserts in Tudor times, they sometimes included fruit, cheese, bone marrow or fish as fillings in the pastry. In May Byron's *How to Save Cookery* of 1915, 'Savoury Darioles' was an austerity recipe of the First World War: 'Take one breakfastcupful of soaked and drained breadscraps, and mix well with the following; one medium boiled onion finely minced or grated; one teaspoon finely-minced parsley, pepper and salt to taste, two (dried) beaten eggs, a little fat of some sort [-butter was rationed], and a little milk to moisten. Have ready some greased dariole tins;

half fill with the mixture; place in a good over for about twenty-five minutes.'
The following medieval recipe would have been used throughout the ages and
would have been a particularly expensive dessert with its use of saffron and
sugar.

Ingredients: Elizabethan pie crust as in the recipe near the start of this
chapter, omitting the black pepper and adding 4 tbsp honey; 300 ml single
cream; 2 eggs; 60 g sugar; 10 saffron threads; large pinch of salt; five violet
flowers to decorate, fresh or candied.

Method: Make the pie crust. Roll out the pastry and use to line a 9-inch pie
dish. Top the pastry with baking beads and blind bake in an oven at 180°C for
15 minutes. Mix all the other ingredients together and pour into the prepared
pie case. Bake in the oven at 180°C until the the pie contents solidify. Decorate
with violet flowers and serve.

FRENCH BISKET – CORIANDER RUSKS

Sir Hugh Plat's *Delightes for Ladies*, 1602

Biscuits made from coriander seed flavoured bread, which is sliced and baked
again until completely dry.

'To make bifket bread, otherwife called french bisket. Take halfe a pecke of fine
flowor, two ounces of Coriander feedes, one ounce of annis feedes, the whites
of foure egges, halfe a pinte of Ale yeaft, and as much water as will make it vp
into stiffe paft, your water muft be but blood warme, then bake it in a long roll
as big as your thigh, let it ftay in the ouen but one houre, and when it is a daye
olde pare it and flice it ouerthwart, thē fugar in ouer with fine poudred fugar,
and fo drie it in an ouen again, and being dry, take it out and fugar it again,
then boxe it and fo you may keepe it all the yeare.'

Ingredients: 500 g sifted plain flour; 1 tbsp lightly-crushed coriander seeds;
1½ tsp aniseeds, lightly crushed; 4 egg whites: 1 packet active, dried yeast;
pinch of sugar; lukewarm water.

Method: Dissolve the yeast and sugar in a cup of warm water. Cover and set
aside for about 15 minutes, or until bubbling. Sift the flour into a large bowl
and mix in the coriander seeds and aniseed. Work in the egg whites and
yeast mixture and then add just enough water to make a stiff dough. Knead
the dough until smooth and elastic, then cover with a cloth and set aside in
a warm place for about an hour to rise. Knock the dough back then remove
from the bowl and knead lightly. Shape into a long roll about 2 inches wide
and 1 inch high, then place on a greased baking tray. Transfer to an oven
preheated to 180°C and bake for about 35 minutes, or until lightly golden and
cooked through. Remove from the oven and allow to cool completely before
cutting into slices about 1 inch thick. Arrange these slices in a single layer on

a baking tray tray, then transfer to an oven preheated to 140°C and bake for about 60 minutes, or until crisp and completely dry. Allow to cool, and store in an airtight jar.

WHITE GELLY OF ALMONDS – CINNAMON AND ALMOND JELLY
Sir Hugh Plat's *Delightes for Ladies*, 1602

'A white gelly of Almonds. Take Rofewater, gum Dragagant diffolued, or Ifinglaffe diffolued, and fome Cinamon groffely beaten, feethe them altogether, then take a pounde of almonds, blanch and beate them fine with a little faire water, drie them in a faire cloth; and put your water aforefaid into the Almonds, feeth them together and ftir them continually, then take them, from the fire, whe- all is boiled to a fufficient height.'
4 tbsp water.

Ingredients: 100 ml rose water; 1 leaf of gelatine, ¼ tsp ground cinnamon, 300 g blanched almonds; 4 tbsp water.

Method: Gently heat the rose water and when warm, mix in a bowl with the gelatine and ground cinnamon. Set aside until the gelatine has dissolved. Grind the almonds in a food processor, then transfer to a mortar and pound with the water to a smooth paste. Scrape this paste into a double layer of muslin or cheesecloth and squeeze out all the excess moisture. Take the ground almonds and mix with the rose water and gelatine mixture. Pour into a saucepan, bring to the boil and cook for 5 minutes. Take off the heat and allow to cool slightly, then whisk to mix well before dividing between small ramekins. Allow to cool completely, cover with cling film then set aside in the refrigerator to chill until completely set. Serve slightly chilled. It can be topped with redcurrants or blackcurrants.

CRUSTARDE/CUSTARDE LUMBARDE – LOMBARD OPEN PIE (1)
The Boke of Kokery, c. 1440

Until the nineteenth century the word *custarde* had a different definition. A *custarde* was a kind of open pie containing pieces of meat or fruit and covered with a sweet and spicy egg and milk sauce. This sauce was something like today's custard. The pies were also known as *crustardes*, showing us that the word custard is closely related to the word crust, as in pastry crust. The recipe is for a traditional open pie, a dish for the wealthier, calling for figs, dates and expensive sugar. Note that the original pie shell crust would likely have been a free-standing one, not baked in a pie pan, and the bone marrow would just melt into the pie, like pieces of butter.

'Take good cream, and mix in leaves of parsley. Break the yolks and whites of eggs into the mixture. Strain through a strainer, till it is so stiff that it will support itself. Then take good marrow, and dates cut in 2 or 3 pieces, and prunes, and put them in nice coffins. Put the pies in the oven, and let them bake until they are hard. Then take them out and put the liquid into them, and put them back in the oven. Let them bake together until done, but add sugar and salt to the liquid when you put it into the coffins. And if it is in Lent, take cream of almonds and leave out the egg and the marrow.'

Ingredients: 2 cups thick cream; 3 eggs plus 2 yolks; 4 tbsp raw beef marrow, chopped; ½ cup dates, pitted and minced; ½ cup prunes, pitted and minced; 9-inch bakery shell, prebaked; 2 tbsp parsley, finely chopped.

Method: Heat the cream, but do not boil. Beat the eggs and yolks in a bowl, then pour in the hot cream, beating as you do. Arrange the marrow, dates and prunes in the pastry shell and pour in the custard. Stir in the parsley. Bake at 180°C degrees for 25 minutes.

CRUSTAD LUMBARD – LOMBARD OPEN PIE (2)
An Ordnance of Pottage Beinecke MS 163, 1460

'And on fisch days boyle wardons tendyr, or othir perys; pare hem and hole hem at the crown. Fil hem full of blaunch poudyr and turne yn the poudyr of gynger that the poudyr lefe theryn; and set hem in cofyns, and the stalkes upward. and yf thu wilte, thu may turne hem that they be hid yn bature and fry hem or thu couch hem. Let no flesch come therto. Make thy syripe of thicke mylke of almondys. Make up thy crustardys as thu dedyst on flesch days. When they be bake, yf thu wilte, thu may gylte the stalkys of the perys; and serve hem forth.'

Ingredients: Enough pears to fill a pie crust; pie crust; blaunch pouder, ½ to ¾ cup of sugar, ginger, cinnamon; 1 to 1½ cups of almond milk; ¾ cup round almonds to 1½ cups boiling water.

Method: Boil the pears until tender but not mushy. Peel them and hollow out from the bottoms, coring but leaving the tops intact. Fill with blaunch powder and set them in the pie shell, stems up. Cover the holes with a spoon and place them in the pie shell with the spoon, so the powder will not all pour out. Pour the almond milk in, and bake. Sprinkle in some blaunch powder over the top for added flavour.

CUSTAD LOMBARD (3) – THE PLUMLESS PLUM PUDDING AND THE ORIGIN OF CHRISTMAS PUD
A Noble Boke off Cookry England, 1468

Puddings were made in animal guts, so Tudor Christmas pudding was shaped like a sausage, containing meat, oatmeal and spices. It is sometimes known as plum pudding, despite having no plums, because in pre-Victorian times, 'plums' was a term for raisins. The pudding is aged for a month or even a year, with the high alcohol content preventing it from spoiling. Prior to the nineteenth century, Christmas pudding was boiled in a pudding cloth, often represented as being perfectly round. Although it took its final form in Victorian England, the Christmas pudding's origins can be traced back to the 1420s. It was not a confection or a dessert, but a way of preserving meat at the end of the season. Because of shortages of fodder, all surplus animals except sheep were usually slaughtered in the autumn. The meat was then kept in a large sealed pastry case, with dried fruits acting as a preservative. The resultant large 'mince pies' could then be used to feed many people, particularly at the festive season. Another ancestor of the pudding was pottage, the meat and vegetable dish originating in Roman times. This was prepared in a large cauldron, the ingredients being slow cooked, with dried fruits, sugar and spices added. By the fifteenth century, plum pottage was a sloppy mix of meat, vegetables and fruit, served at the beginning of a meal.

'To mak custad lombard mak a large coffyn then tak dates from the stones tak gobettes of mary and smalle birdes and parboile them in salt brothe and couche ther in then tak clowes mace and raisins of corans and pynes fryed and strawe ther on and sett them in the oven to bak and luk ye haue a coup of cowes creme yolks of eggs good pouderes saffron sanderes and salt then fill the coffins ther with, and on fishe daies boille wardens or other peres paire them and hole them at the crown then fill them full of blaunche poudur and torn them in blaunche poudur and skoche them all about that the pouder may abid ther in then set the stalks upryght and ye may mak your coup of creme of almondes and shak up your custad as ye did of flesche and when they be bak gilt the stalkes of the peres and serue them.'

CRUSTAD LUMBARD (4)
Wagstaff Miscellany, Beinecke MS 163, 1460
'Crustad lumbard. Make large cofynys take datys pyke out the skynnys and yf thu wilte thu may cut thy datys or els stop hem with blanch poudyr with yn and do ther to grete gobets of marye and couch ther yn rabets with the marye and small bryddys perboylyd well in fat broth and couch in ther to clovis macys reysons of corauns and fry pynes and strew theron and set hem yn ther own syrip of creme of cowmylke yolkes of eyron and good poudyr sygure saundres safron and salt fyl hem ther with and on fisch days boyle wardons tendyr or othir perys pare hem and hole hem at the crown fil hem full of blaunch poudyr and turne yn the pouydyr of gyngour that the poudyr lese ther yn and set hem in cofyns and the stalkes upward and yf thu wilte thu may turne hem that they be hid yn bature and fry hem or thu couch hem let

no flesch come ther to make thy syripe of thicke mylke of almondys make up
thu crustardys as thu dedyst on fisch days when they be bake yf thu wilte thy
may gylte the stalkys of the perys and syve hem forth.'

PRESERVED FRUITS IN HONEY

Charles Butler's *The Feminine Monarchie, Or, The Historie of Bees*, 1609
Instead of bottling fruit with sugar, honey sometimes gives a more delicious
result. Certainly, adding honey to vinegared pickles keeps them crunchy. The
'quodling' seems to have been a cooking apple and is remembered in the
naming of the codling moth, a pest of apples, pears and quinces.

'Preserve Fruits after this manner, The Damascens, or other Fruit, being
gathered fresh from the tree, faire,and in their prime, neither greene or sower,
nor ouer-ripe or sweet, with their stalks,but cut short; weigh them, and take
their weight in raw fine Honie: and putting to the Honie the like quantitie of
faire water, boile it some halfe quarter of an houre, or till it will yeeld no skum:
then hauing slit the amascens in the dented side for feare of breaking, boile
them in this liquor with a soft fire, continually skimming and turning them till
the meat commeth cleane from the stone, and then take them vp. If the liquor
be then too thinne, boile it more: if in the boiling it be too thick, put in more
faire water,or Rose-water if you like it. The liquor being of a fit consistence,
lay vp and preserue therein your Fruits. If they be greater Fruits, as Quinces,
Pipins, or the like; then shall it bee expedient, when you haue bored them
through the middle, or haue otherwise coared them, to put them in as soone
as the liquor is first skimmed: and then to let them boile till they be as tender
as Quodlings.'

LECHE LUMBARDE (1) – DATE BALLS (or PASTE)

Two Fifteenth Century Cookbooks – Harleian MS. 279 & Harl. MS. 4016, c. 1440
In this recipe, the spices seem to have been used as a coating instead of sugar,
but the undiluted spices may be too robust for modern tastes. However,
they could also be mixed with the sugar coating. You could also use the date
mixture as a thick paste to spread on toast, or as a filling for pies.

'Leche Lumbarde. Take datys and do away the stones; and seth hem in swete
wyne and take hem uppe, and grinde hem in a morter, and draive hem thorgh
a streynour with a litull swete wyne and sugur, and caste hem in a potte and
lete boyle til it be stiff; and then take hem uppe, and ley hem upon a borde;
and then take pouder ginger, canell and melle al togidre in thi hande and
make it so stiff that hit woll be leched and if hit be not stiff ynowe, take hard
yolkes of eyren and crème theron, or elles grated brede, and make it thik

ynough; take Clarey, cand caste thereto in manner of sirippe, whan tou shalt serue it forthwith.'

Ingredients: 8 oz packaged dates, pitted and finely chopped; 1 cup sweet red wine; 1½ cups sugar; 2–3 tbsp flour or breadcrumbs; ginger and cinnamon to taste.

Method: Cover the dates with wine or half wine and half water. Boil until it forms a thick paste. Mix with a little more wine and force through a strainer or use a blender. Add the sugar and spices and return to the saucepan. Boil until the mixture thickens enough to mould. If it needs extra thickening, add the flour. Cool completely. Form into small balls and roll in powdered sugar, or any other coating of your choice to remove the stickiness. Serve.

LECHE LUMBARDE (2) – STICKY DATE PUDDING SLICES
Two Fifteenth Century Cookbooks – Harleian MS. 279 & Harl. MS. 4016, c. 1440

Leche is derived from the Old French *lesche*, slice, and a *leche* is basically any sliced food – in this case, slabs of a sweet cake, served with a sweet syrup. Clary wine may have been either 'clarrey', or a sweet wine made from the flowers of clary sage and is replaced by sherry for the modern redaction.

Ingredients: 300 g chopped dates; 2 tsp ginger; 300 ml sherry; 1 tsp cinnamon; 650 g loaf bread; 2 tbsp sugar.

Ingredients for syrup: 100 ml sherry; 6 sage leaves.

Method: To make the *leche*, simmer the dates and sherry together for around 15–20 minutes until the dates are soft. Add the ginger, cinnamon and sugar and then blend until smooth in a blender. Wait a few minutes for the date paste to cool. Pulverise the bread to crumbs, then mix into the date paste until it is stiff and well combined. To make the syrup, simmer the sherry and sage together until the liquid is reduced by half. Just before serving, slice the *leche* into serving pieces and then pour over the syrup.

A TARTE OF APPLES AND ORENGE PILLES – APPLE AND MARMALADE TART
The Good Huswives Handmaid for Cookerie in her kitchen, 1588

The 'orenge pilles' (orange peel) preparation is substituted by orange marmalade.

'Take your orenges and lay them in water a day and a night, then seeth them in faire water and honey and let seeth till they be soft; then let them soak in the sirrop a day and a night; then take forth and cut them small and then make your tart and season your apples with suger, synamon and ginger and put in a piece of butter and by a course of apples and between the same course of apples a course of orenges, and so, course by course, and season your orenges as you seasoned your apples with somewhat more sugar; then lay on the lid and put it in the oven and when it is almost baked, take Rosewater and sugar and boyle them together till it be somewhat thick, then take out the Tart and take a feather and spread the rosewater and sugar on the lid and let it not burn.'

Ingredients for tart: 12-oz jar of sweet orange marmalade; 6 apples of around ½ lb each; ½ cup sugar; ½ tsp ground cinnamon; ¼ tsp ground ginger; 2 tbsp butter; prepared pastry crusts for a double-crust pie.

Ingredients for syrup: ½ cup water; 1 tbsp rose water concentrate; 1 tbsp sugar.

Method for tart: Preheat oven to 230°C. Soften marmalade by setting opened jar in a pan of hot water. Peel, core and thinly slice the apples. Mix sugar and spices well, sprinkle over the apples and stir gently until the slices are well coated. Line a 9-inch pie pan with the pie crust. Put in one-third of the apple slices, dot with one-third of the butter and smear over this one-third of the marmalade. Repeat this procedure twice, using up the ingredients. Cover with a pricked upper crust. Bake at 230°C for 10 minutes, then lower heat to 180°C and bake for about 60 minutes until pie is done.

Method for syrup: Boil all ingredients until reduced by ½ to ⅔. Brush thickened glaze onto pie crust about 10 minutes before the tart is completely baked.

CONDONACK – QUINCE PASTE CONFECTIONS

Thomas Dawson's *The Second Part of the Good Huswifes Jewell*, 1597

Condonacks were also spelt *codiniacs, goodinyakes, quideniock and quidony*. Quinces were made into a sort of marmalade or spread, but Portuguese traders were increasingly exporting wooden boxes of quince paste called *marmelada* to England, where it was given as a gift or served during the banquet course among the nobility. In the Dawson cookbook, as above, there is also a recipe 'To make drie Marmelat of Peches', followed by 'To make the same of Quinces, or any other thing'. These recipes are both thicker than the *condonack/cotignac* recipes and are done when your spoon stands up straight in the mixture. The sweetmeats were shaped and printed with fancy patterns, then strewn with sugar and kept by the fire to stay dry. Later it became popular to serve red and white quince pastes together and there are more recipes in Gervase Marhkam's *Country Contentments, or The English Huswife* of 1615.

'To make a condonack: Take quinces and pare them, take out the cores, and seethe them in fair water until they break, then strain them through a fine strainer, and for eight pound of the said strained quince, you must put in three pound sugar, and mingle it together in a vessel, and boil them on a fire always stirring it till it be sodden which you may perceive, for that it will no longer cleave to the vessel, but you may stay musk in powder, you may also add spice to it, as ginger, cinnamon, cloves and nutmeg, as much as you think meet, boiling the musk with a little vinegar, then with a broad slice of wood spread this confection upon a table, which must be strewed with sugar, and there make what proportion you will, and let it in the sun till it be dry, and when it hath stood a while turn it upside-down, making always a bed of sugar, both under and above, and turn them still, and dry them in the sun until they have gotten a crust. In like manner you may dress pears, peaches, damsons, and other fruits.'

A FREGESEY OF EGGES – APPLE OMELETTE FRICASSEE
John Murrel's *A New Booke of Cookerie*, 1615
'A Fregesey of Egges. Beat a dozen of Egs with Creame, Sugar, Nutmeg, Mace, Rosewater, and a Pomewater cut ouerthwart in slices: put them into the Frying-pan with sweet Butter, and the Apples first: when they be almost enough take them up, and cleanse your Pan: put in sweet Butter, and make it hot: put in halfe the Egges and Creame at one time: stirre it with a Sawcer, or such a thing. Take it out, and put it in a Dish, put in the rest of the Egges and Creame, like the former, and then put in your Apples round about the batter. Then cast on the other side on the top of it, and keepe it from burning with sweet Butter. When it is fryed on both sides enough wring on the iuyce of an Orenge, and serve it in.'
Ingredients: 6 eggs; ⅜ cup cream; 1½ tbsp sugar; 1 tsp nutmeg; ½ tsp mace; ½ tsp rosewater; 5 oz apples, peeled and sliced thin; 1 tbsp butter; 3 more tbsp butter, for omelette cooking; juice of an orange.
Method: Beat together the first six ingredients. Fry the apple in the first tablespoon of butter until almost tender. Cook half of the egg mixture in 1½ tbsp butter and remove from the pan. Cook the other half of the egg mixture in butter, add apples and top with first half of the egg mixture. Arrange on plate, and top with the juice of orange. Serve hot.

WALNUTS ARTIFICIAL – SUGAR PASTE WALNUTS
W.M., *A Queen's Delight in The Queen's Closet Open'd*, 1655
Throughout Tudor times sweetmeats were made in the form of castles, walnuts, mussels and the like. A fruitwood mould would have been used to separately make the walnut shell and its kernel for this recipe. They were often filled with caraway comfits, or mottoes written on strips of paper, the precursor of the 'fortune cookies', which are not an ancient Chinese tradition, but invented for the 1915 San Francisco World Fair.
'Take searsed sugar, and Cinnamon, of quantity alike, work it up with a little

Gum Dragon, steepe it in Rose-water, and print it in a mould made like a Walnut shell, then take white sugar plates, print it in a mould made like a Walnut kernel, so when they are both dry, close them up together with a little Gum Dragon betwixt, and they will dry as they lie.'

BUTTERED EGGS

Thomas Dawson's *The Good Housewife's Jewel*, 1597

'Take eight yolks of eggs, and put them into a pint of cream. Beat them together and strain them all into a posnet, setting upon the fire and stirring it. Let it seeth nntil it quaile, then take it and put it into a clean cloth, and let it hang so that the whey may void from it. When it is gone, beat it into a dish of rosewater and sugar with a spoon. So shall you have fine butter. This done, you may take the white of the same eggs putting it into another pint of cream, using it as the yolkes were used. And thus you may have as fine white butter as you have yellow butter.'

Ingredients: 4 eggs; 1 pint thick cream; rose water; 4 tbsp sugar, or to taste.

Method: Separate the egg yolks from the whites. Beat each with a cup of cream, then cook on very low heat until they quiver, stirring frequently. Wrap each tightly in cheesecloth and hang for several hours. Wring any remaining whey out and then mix each with 2 tbsp sugar and a dash of rose water.

LLYMRU – TRADITIONAL WELSH FLUMMERY

A Welsh dish of fine oatmeal steeped in water and buttermilk then strained to remove the starch which was boiled until almost solid. The dish spread to Cheshire and Lancashire where its name was anglicised to 'flummery'.

Ingredients: 500 g fine oatmeal; 1 l water; 1 l buttermilk; salt, to taste.

Method: Combine the water and buttermilk and warm through then pour over the oatmeal in a bowl. Cover and set aside in a warm spot to ferment for 3 days. After the 3 days the liquid is sour and strain the mixture through muslin and discard the oats. Transfer the liquid to a large pan and bring to the boil. Continue cooking, stirring all the while, until the mixture thickens almost to the point of being solid then season with salt. Ladle into bowls, allow to cool until completely cold and serve with hot milk.

FLUMMERY – OATMEAL GRUEL

Gervase Markham's *Countrey Contentments, or, The English Hus-wife*, 1615

Flummery can be defined as any of several soft, sweet, bland foods, such as custard. In Britain, Northern Europe and Russia, *flummery* is a set dish made from the starch derived from steeped grains, typically oats. The origin of the dish and the name in Britain seems to be Welsh, derived from the Welsh *llymru* or *llumruwd*, a thin porridge. It literally means 'too much sharpness' in the sense of both the sharp taste of the dish and the pain in the belly during lean times, so the name takes us back to times when *llymru* was a starvation food. There is a Welsh saying '*Llymru lled amrwd i lenwi bol, yn lle bwyd*' (Flummery; more than crude to fill the belly, in place of food). Thus the dish was not considered overly nourishing. In essence, *llymru* is a sour-grain soup made by pouring fine oatmeal into an earthenware pot and covering with a tepid mix of water and buttermilk. This was stirred and allowed to stand and ferment for at least three days until the contents soured. After this time the mixture was strained through muslin or a fine sieve. The grains were discarded and the liquid was poured into a cauldron which had to be set on a very hot fire. Another saying is: '*tân llym o dan y llymru, tan mall wna'r uwd yn well*' (a keen fire beneath the llymru, a dead fire improves the porridge). *Llymru* was then stirred constantly until it had boiled and thickened to the desired consistency. It was then served with hot milk and according to tradition it should be swallowed without chewing. A far richer version including stale bread, ginger and black treacle was also made.

'From this small Oat-meal, by oft steeping it in water and cleansing it, and then boiling it to a thick and stiff Jelly, is made that excellent dish of meat which is so esteemed in the West parts of this Kingdom, which they call Wash-brew, and in Cheshire and Lancashire they call it Flamerie or Flumerie.'
Ingredients: 150 g rolled oats; sugar, to taste.
Method: Place the oats in a broad, deep, pan and cover with water. Stir to mix, then allow to stand for 12 hours. After this time, pour off the liquid then re-cover the oats with fresh water and allow to stand for a further 12 hours. Again, decant the water then cover the oats and allow to stand for a further 12 hours. At the end of this time remove the water then pour the soaked oats into a saucepan. Add just enough water to almost cover, then heat and, stirring continually, cook until the mixture begins to bubble and thicken. Add more water, if needed to achieve a thick paste. Pour into dishes and season with sugar. Set aside to cool then turn out onto plates. Accompany with milk, buttermilk, beer or wine and honey.

LLYMRU CYFOETHOG – RICH WELSH FLUMMERY
Traditional, as above.
Ingredients: 500 g fine oatmeal; 1 l water; 1 l buttermilk; 4 thick slices of stale bread, torn into small pieces; 2 tsp ground ginger; 4 tbsp black treacle; salt, to taste.
Method: Combine the water and buttermilk and warm through, then pour over the oatmeal in a bowl. Cover and set aside in a warm spot to ferment

for 3 days. After the 3 days the liquid will be sour. Strain the mixture through muslin and discard the oats. Transfer the liquid to a large pan and bring to the boil then stir in the bread, ginger and treacle. Continue cooking, stirring all the while, until the mixture thickens almost to the point of being solid then season with salt. Ladle into bowls, allow to cool until completely cold and serve with hot milk.

MUSKADINE COMFITS
A Closet for Ladies and Gentlewomen, 1608

Musk mallow seeds are the spice component of *Abelmoschus moschatus*, the Annual Hibiscus, and have a sweet, flowery, heavy fragrance similar to that of musk. Today they are most commonly used as a flavouring additive to coffee, but can be used as a flavour base for confectionery, biscuits and cakes, as well as some savoury dishes. By late Tudor times, it was being used as a cheaper alternative to animal musk in flavouring spiced wines, such as *hypocras*.

'To Make Muskadine Comfits. Take halfe a pound of Muske suger beaten and searsed, then take Gumtragacant, steeped in Rose water, and two graines of Muske, and so beat them in an Alabaster morter, till it come to perfect Paste, then drive it verie thinne with a rowling pinne, and then cut it into small pieces like Diamonds, some cut with a rowle spoone on the sides: being thus cut, store them, and so keepe them all the yeare.'

LORD CONWAY'S AMBER PUDDING
The Queen's Closet Newly Opened, 1655

The pudding is flavoured with a blend of ambergris, musk and orange flower water. When toasted or lightly fried it looks remarkably like a sausage, but has a sweet, perfumed taste. According to W.M., the compiler of *The Queen's Closet*, the recipe was given to Lord Conway by an Italian 'for a great rarity'. Sir Edward Viscount Conway of Ragley (1564–1630) was Principal Secretary of State to Charles I. Ambergris was a popular ingredient in both confectionery and cookery in the Stuart period. Though it smells of very little in its raw state, it releases a violet-like odour when blended with other ingredients like musk and perfumed waters. In addition to ambergris puddings, some early cookery texts have recipes for ambergris cakes. Lord Conway's pudding tastes like an orange flower scented marchpane and is surprisingly delicate. Both musk and ambergris were considered to be powerful aphrodisiacs at this time.

'The Lord Conway his Lordships receipt for the making of Amber Puddings. First take the Guts of a young hog, and wash them very clean, and then take two pound of the best hogs fat, and a pound and a halfe of the best Jordan almonds the which being blancht, take one half of them, and beat them very small, and the other halfe reserve whole unbeaten then take a pound and a halfe of fine Sugar and four white Loaves, and grate the Loaves over the former composition and mingle them well together in a bason having so done, put to it halfe an ounce of Ambergreece the which must be scrapt very small over the said composition take halfe a quarter of an ounce of levant musk and bruise it in a marble morter, with a quarter of a Pint of Orange Flower water then mingle these all very well together, and having so done, fill the said Guts therwith, this Receipt was given his Lordship by an Italian for a great rariety, and has been found so to be by those Ladies of honour to whom his Lordship has imparted the said reception.'

A PLAIN QUAKING PUDDING (1)
The Closet of the Eminently Learned Sir Kenelme Digbie Kt Opened, 1669
The word 'pudding' historically refers to a food that is contained in animal gut, so as to hold it when cooking, like 'Black Pudding' or sausages. By the seventeenth century, cooks realised that they could make puddings by containing food in cloth bags or bowls and this led to more sweet puddings being made than before. For example, Quaking Pudding became a staple in recipe books from the seventeenth to the nineteenth centuries.

'Take about three Pints of new morning milk, and six or seven new laid eggs, putting away half the whites, and two spoonfuls of fine-flower, about a quarter of a nutmeg, grated, and about a quarter of a pound of sugar (more or less, according to your taste).

After all these are perfectly mingled and incorporated together, put the matter into a fit bag, and so put it into boiling water, and boil it up with a quick fire. If you boil it too long, the milk will turn to whey in the body or substance of the pudding, and there will be a slimy gelly all about the outside. But in about half an hour, it will be tenderly firm, and of a uniform consistence all over. You need not put in any butter or marrow or suet, or other spice, but the small proportion of nutmeg set down, not grated bread. For the sauce, you pour upon it thickened melted butter, beaten with a little sack, or orange-flower water, and sugar; or compounded in what manner you please, as in other such like puddings.'

Ingredients for the pudding: 3 cups full cream milk; 3 egg yolks; ½ cup sugar; 1 tsp nutmeg; 2 cups flour.
Method for the pudding: Mix ingredients thoroughly and heat in a fairly hot bain-marie, until it is 'tenderly firm'.

Ingredients for the sauce: 1 cup powdered sugar; 5 tbsp butter; 1 tbsp orange-flavoured dessert wine.

Method for the sauce: Mix ingredients on a low heat and candied orange peel, candied ginger, or cinnamon can be sprinkled on the sauce when it is poured on the pudding.

A QUAKING PUDDING (2)

Elizabeth Raffald gives two versions in her book *The Experienced English Housekeeper for the use and ease of Ladies, Housekeepers, Cooks, &c, written purely from practice*, published in 1814:

'To make a Quaking Pudding.

Boil a quart of cream, and let it stand till almost cold, then beat four eggs a full quarter of an hour, with a spoonful and a half of flour, then mix them with your cream, add sugar and nutmeg to your palate, tie it close up in a cloth well buttered, and let it boil an hour, and turn it carefully out.

To make a Quaking Pudding a second way.

Take a pint of good cream, the yolks of ten eggs and six whites, beat them very well, and run them through a fine sieve; then take two heaped spoonfuls of flour, and a spoonful or two of cream, beat it with the flour till it is smooth, and mix all together, and tie it close up in a dish or bason (sic) well rubbed with butter and dredged with flour; the water must boil when you put in the pudding. One hour will boil it; serve it up with wine sauce in a boat.'

A QUAKING PUDDING (3)

W. M., *A Queen's Delight in The Queen's Closet Open'd*, 1655

Quaking Pudding is a light sweet, gently flavoured dish that gained its name owing to the fact that it quakes and shakes like a jelly when it is served.

'Sugar, but very little flower, for it will make it sad and heavy; make a piece of puff paste as much as will cover your dish, so cut it very handesomely what fashion you please; butter the bottom of your dish, put the pudding into the dish, set it in a quick oven, not too hot as to burn it, let it bake till you think it be enough, scrape on sugar, and serve it up.'

TANZY – TANSY PUDDING

Liber Cure Cocorum, 1430

A pudding or omelette of green leaf vegetables with fillers such as breadcrumbs, flavoured with tansy. Formerly strongly associated with the spring festival, a sixteenth-century book of church music has 'Soone at Easter commeth alleluya, With butter cheese and a tansay', and the *Connoisseur* magazine could say in 1767 that 'Mince-pie … is as essential to Christmas, as… tansy to

Easter.' Tansy is a bitter plant with yellow button flowers, its tea was a spring tonic and a cure for colds, and tansy puddings and cakes were commonly eaten during spring. Tansy was also often used in vinegar sauce to accompany roast lamb. The young leaves were mixed with eggs and this favourite dish was known as a tansy. It was eaten at Easter to celebrate the end of Lent and the return of eggs to the diet. It was also supposed to purify the body of bad odours after forty days of salt fish.

'Breke egges in bassyn and swyng hem sone,

Do powder of peper þer to anone;

þen grynde tansy, þo iuse owte wrynge,

To blynde with þo egges with owte lesynge.

In pan or skelet þou shalt hit frye,

In buttur wele skymmet wyturly,

Or white grece þou make take þer to,

Geder hit on a cake, þenne hase þou do,

With platere of tre, and frye hit browne.

On brode leches serve hit þou schalle,

With fraunche mele or oþer metis with alle.'

'Tansye: Take fair Tansye, and grind in a morter; thanne take eggs, the yolks and the whyte, and strayne them thorw a strainer; and strayne also the Ius of the Tansye, and melle to-gederes; and take fair Freysche grease, and put ther-on over the fire, tylle it melte; than caste the stuf ther-on, and gadere to-gedere with a Sawcer or a dish, as thou wolt it, lasse other more, and turne it in the panne; and than serve it forth.' – *Two Fifteenth-Century Cookery Books*

Ingredients: 4 slightly-beaten eggs; 1 cup cream; ¾ cup spinach juice; 1 tbsp juice of crushed tansy; 1 tsp thyme; 1 tsp sweet marjoram; 1 tsp parsley; 1 cup breadcrumbs; ½ cup sugar; ½ tsp nutmeg.

Method: Mix eggs with cream, spinach juice and tansy juice. Shred herbs and add to the tansy. Stir in bread crumbs, sugar and nutmeg. Mix well. Fry light brown or bake in a buttered dish until firm.

TWELFTH NIGHT CAKE

Medieval and Tudor – modern redaction given

Twelfth Night, also known as Twelfth Day Eve, Epiphany and Old Christmas Eve, falls on 5 January, the twelfth day after Christmas. In medieval and Tudor times, the twelfth night after Christmas marked the end of the winter festival that started on All Hallows Eve, Halloween. On this day the King and all those who were among the upper-classes would become the peasants and vice versa, with the 'Lord of Misrule' symbolizing the world turning upside down. At the beginning of the Twelfth Night Festival, a cake that contained a bean was eaten and the person who found the bean would rule the feast. Midnight signalled the end of his rule and the world would return to normal. The common theme was that the normal order of things was reversed. This tradition dates back to pre-Christian times, to the Celtic festival of *Samhain* and the Roman feast days of *Saturnalia*. The punches called *Wassail* and *Lambs Wool* were consumed especially on Twelfth Night, but also throughout Christmas time. Shakespeare's *Twelfth Night* was actually written as a Twelfth Night entertainment. The play has many elements that are reversed, in the tradition of Twelfth Night, such as the woman Viola dressing as a man and the servant Malvolio imagining that he can become a nobleman.

By the eighteenth century, Twelfth Cake, the forerunner of today's Christmas cake, had become the centrepiece of the party and a slice was given to all members of the household. Traditionally, it now contained both a dried bean and a dried pea. The man whose slice contained the bean was elected King for the night and the Queen was found with a pea. For the rest of the evening, they ruled supreme. Even if they were normally servants, their exalted position was recognised by all, including their masters. 'Twelfth Cake' is still eaten and a toast drunk in honour and memory of Richard Baddeley, the comedian, who died in 1794. Baddeley was a pastry cook who later became an actor. Upon his death he left the sum of £100, invested at 3 per cent interest, to provide a cake, known as the 'Baddeley Cake', to be eaten annually, in his memory, by 'His Majesty's Company of Commedians'. In the day of Robert Herrick (1591–1674), 'Twelfth Cake' was similar to ordinary plum cake, but became more elaborate as time went on. Herrick described the gay seventeenth-century custom of choosing the King and Queen in *Hesperides, Twelfe Night, or King and Queene* (1648):

'Now, now the mirth comes / With the cake full of plums, / Where Beane's the King of the sport here;

Besides we must know, / The Pea also Must revel, / as Queene, in the Court here.

Begin then to chuse / This night as ye use / Who shall for the present delight here,

Be a King by the lot, / And who shall not / Be Twelfe-day Queene for the night here.

Which knowne, let us make / Joy-sops with the cake, / And let not a man be seen here,

Who unurg'd will not drinke / To the base from the brink / A health to the King and Queene here.

Next crowne the bowle full / With gentle lamb's woll; / Add sugar, nutmeg and ginger,

With store of ale too; / And this ye must do / To make the wassail a swinger.'

Ingredients: 3 cups all-purpose flour; ⅝ cup currants; ¾ cup sultanas; 1⅓ cups shredded mixed peel; ⅝ cup brown sugar; 1 tbsp molasses; 3 eggs; ¼ cup milk; ¼ tsp allspice; 1¼ tsp ground cinnamon.

Method: 'Cream together butter and sugar. Add the eggs, one at a time, beating thoroughly after each addition. Warm the molasses and milk and add them to the butter, sugar and eggs, beating briskly. Sift a little of the flour over fruits, to prevent them from falling to bottom of pan. Sift together flour and spices and mix into batter, stirring lightly. Hide a bean and a pea in it. Fold in fruits last of all. Line bread tin with waxed paper. Pour in mixture and bake in slow oven (250° F.) for approximately 2–2¼ hours.' (- Dorothy Gladys Spicer)

FYGEY – **FIGGY PUDDING**
The Master-Cook of Richard II, *The Forme of Cury*, *c.* 1390

Palm Sunday, the Sunday before Easter, is the day Jesus was said to have ridden into Jerusalem a week before his crucifixion. Followers greeted him by waving palm branches and some believe that Jesus ate figs along the way. For this reason, Palm Sunday is sometimes known as *Fig Sunday*, and fig pudding is served to celebrate. Fig pudding is the ancestor of boiled plum pudding and Christmas pudding, but is less rich and easier to make.

'Take Almande blanched; grynde hem and brawe hem up with water and wyne; quarter figs, hole raisins. Cast perto powder ginger and hony clarified; seep it wel and salt it, and seve forth.'

Ingredients: ½ cup each of water, ground blanched almonds, white wine (or Madeira for a richer taste); 1 cup each quartered dried and stoned figs, and whole raisins; 2 tbsp clear honey; ½ tsp powdered ginger (use fresh for stronger taste); ¼ tsp salt.

Method: Use some of the wine or water to make a paste with the almonds, over a medium heat. Add the rest of the wine and water, mix in and let the mixture steep for a few minutes over a low heat. Then stir in the figs, raisins, honey, ginger and salt and bring to the boil while stirring. Cook on a simmer, while stirring for around 5 minutes, or until the mixture thickens and is well blended. Serve warm. You can make this in advance, cover with foil and reheat in an oven.

10

Snacks

Many Tudor dishes can make excellent snacks today. The Tudors did not have today's 'grazing' habits, except in the cities when watching entertainments such as plays, cockfighting or bear-baiting. The poor struggled to stay alive and their meal times were generally set by the needs of their farming masters. The rich sat down formally twice a day. Some of these Tudor 'snacks' can serve as desserts, breakfast or side dishes.

PURSSES OR CREMITARIES – ELIZABETHAN SMALL BEEF PATTIES

Thomas Dawson's *The Good Huswifes Jewell*, 1585, 1594, 1596

'"A" shall answer it. Some pigeons, Davy, a couple of short-legged hens, a joint of mutton, and any pretty little tiny kickshaws, tell William cook.' *Henry IV Part II*.

A *kickshaw* was a delicacy, small snack or appetiser and *kickshaws* is the Elizabethan misspelling of *quelque choses*, 'some things'. Markham's 1615 *The English Huswife* begins: 'Now the compound Fricases, are those which consist of manie things such as Tansies, Fritters, Pancakes, and anie Quelquechose whatsoever, being things of great request and estimation in France, Spaine, and Italy, and the most curious Nations.' Dawson's kickshaw recipe is for small meat turnovers called *purses*. They were named after the wallet which hung from a man's belt. Pockets had not been invented, and 'cutpurses' stole them by cutting the cord and running away. In 1630 John Taylor, in *The Great Eater of Kent*, his poem for Nicholas Wood, describes sweets as 'Whether it bee … Fritter, or Flapiacke, or Posset, Galley-Mawfrey, Mackeroone, Kickshaw, or Tantablin.' *Kickshaws* could be so many things that in 1755, Samuel Johnson offered this definition in his *Dictionary of the English Language*: 'Kickshaw: A dish so changed by the cookery that it can scarcely be known.'

'Take a little mary, small raysons, and Dates, let the stones bee taken away, these being beaten together in a Morter, season it with Ginger, Sinemon, and Sugar, then put it in a fine paste, and bake them or fry them, so done in the serving of them cast blaunch powder upon them.'

Ingredients: 8 oz ground beef; ⅓ cup currants; 6 finely chopped pitted dates; 1 tbsp finely-chopped candied ginger; ¼ tsp each of rosemary, nutmeg and cinnamon, all ground; 2 tbsp brown sugar; ½ tsp salt; black pepper to taste; large beaten egg; pastry dough.

Method: Place all ingredients, except the egg and dough, into a mixing bowl, mix well and leave overnight, or for at least 6 hours, in a refrigerator. Remove and leave for about an hour to reach room temperature. Preheat the oven to 180°C. On a floured work surface, roll out the dough to around ⅛ inch thick. Use a 3-inch round cutter to make about 24 pie circles and place 1½ tbsp of meat mixture upon each pastry circle. Fold in half and crimp the edges to seal into small pasties, then brush them with the egg. Place the 24 'purses' on a greased baking sheet in the oven for around 15 minutes, or until they are golden brown.

CAWS POBI – WELSH RABBIT

Traditional Welsh, first mentioned by Andre Boorde in the chapter on Wales in his *Fyrst Boke of the Introduction of Knowledge*, 1542. This is the earliest known reference to the tasty savoury snack of cooked cheese being eaten in the British Isles.

'I do love cawse boby, good rosted chese;
And swyshe swash e metheglyn I take for my fees;
And yf I have my harpe, I care for no more;
It is my treasure, I do kepe it in store;
For my harpe is made of a good mares skyn,
The stringes be of horse heare, it maketh a good din;
My songe, and my voyce, and my harpe doth agree,
Muche lyke the hussyng of a homble be…'

There is a wonderful letter from Andrew Boorde to Thomas Cromwell in 1536, given by Sir Henry Ellis in his *Original Letters, Illustrative of English History, etc*. The letter is 'from leth [Leith], a myle from Edvnborowh', and Boorde calls himself Karre, so that the people might take him for 'a skotysh manes sone.' He says he was 'in skotland in a lytle vnyuerayte or study namvd Glasco, where I study and practice phvsvk.' In his *Introduction of Knowledge made by Andrew Borde, of Physyeke Doctor*, printed in 1870 by the Early English Text Society, we read: 'Trust yow no Skot! As there are many sundry Nations, so are there as many inclinations: the Russian, Polonian, German, Belgian, are excellent in the Art of Drinking; the Spaniard will Wench it;

the Italian is revengefull; the French man is for fashions; the Irish man, Usquebaugh makes him light heel'd; the Welsh mans Cowss-boby works (by infusion) to his fingers ends, and translates them into the nature of lime-twigs; and it is said, that a Scot will prove false to his Father, and dissemble with his Brother; but for an English man, he is so cleare from any of these Vices, that he is perfectly exquisite, and excellently indued with all those noble abovesaid exercises.'

Caws Pobi means baked cheese in Welsh and is a savoury dish created by serving a sauce of melted cheese and other ingredients over hot toast. When Francis Grose defined 'Welsh rabbit', in *A Classical Dictionary of the Vulgar Tongue* in 1785, he mistakenly indicated that rabbit was a corruption of rarebit. In Fowler's *A Dictionary of Modern English Usage* of 1926, we read: 'Welsh Rabbit is amusing and right. Welsh Rarebit is stupid and wrong.' The term Welsh rabbit may come from the poverty of the poor in Wales, as landlords would not allow rabbit catching, so a Welshman's substitute for rabbit was cheese. The term Welsh rarebit is now used in place of Welsh rabbit, but we use the old term here, just as there is no duck in Bombay duck or toad-in-the-hole.

In Tudor times there was some despair in London at the number of Welshmen in court after the first Tudor, Henry VII, came to the throne. *A C Merie Talys* (100 Merry Tales), was a book of jokes printed in 1526, which Shakespeare is thought to have used, and tells us that God became weary of all the Welshmen in heaven, 'which with their krakynge and babelynge trobelyd all the others'. He thus asked St Peter, the Porter of Heaven Gate, to do something about it. Peter went outside the gates and called in a loud voice 'Cause bobe, yt is as moche to say as rostyd chese'. On hearing the call, all the Welshmen ran out of heaven and when St Peter saw they were all outside, he went in and locked the gates, which is why there are no Welshmen in heaven. The 1526 compiler says he found this story 'Wryten amonge olde gestys', so the Welsh love of cheese was well known at this time. Interestingly, in the prestigious Cardiff and County Club, founded in 1866, Welsh Rarebit is a favoured dessert of the older members. There are many, many recipes, and this modern one will suffice:

Ingredients: 8 oz grated, strong Cheddar or Caerphilly cheese; 1 tbsp butter; 2 tsp Worcestershire sauce; 1 tsp mustard; 2 tsp plain flour; 4 tbsp beer or milk; freshly-ground black pepper; 4 slices bread.

Method: Mix the cheese, butter, Worcestershire sauce, mustard and flour together in a dry saucepan. Place on the heat and as the cheese begins to melt, add a dash of the beer or milk and keep stirring. Do not allow the pan to become too hot or the mixture will burn, and do not add too much liquid or it will become too wet. Continue to add small quantities of beer or milk as you are melting the ingredients, until it is paste-like but still thick. If you add too much liquid in error, add a little more flour and cheese to absorb it again. Grill the bread on one side only. Turn the slices over and spread the cheese mixture onto the un-grilled sides. Sprinkle with freshly-ground black pepper and place back under a medium grill until the cheese mixture bubbles. Under a medium heat it will take longer to cook but will melt more evenly, producing the perfect Welsh rabbit. Alternatively, the hot cheese sauce may be served in a chafing dish, like a fondue, accompanied by sliced, toasted bread.

A terrific 'update' on the recipe was given in the Perth newspaper, *The West Australian* on 9 January 1880: 'CHEESE CURRY. Grate a teacupful of rich, hard cheese, and add to it a teacupful of milk, a teaspoonful of mixed mustard and one of curry powder. Stir it over the fire till thick and smooth, and spread it over slices of buttered toast. Brown a few minutes in the oven, and serve hot.'

IRISH, SCOTCH, WELSH RABBIT AND ENGLISH RABBIT TWO WAYS
Mrs Hannah Glasse, *The Art of Cookery made Plain and Easy*, 1747

There is a variety of old recipes in which bread was steeped in beer or floated in soup. Some claim that Irish rabbit is just bread, Welsh rabbit is bread and cheese, Scottish rabbit is bread and dripping and English rabbit is actually rabbit. However, Mrs Glasse gave traditional recipes for Scotch rabbit, Welsh rabbit and two versions of English rabbit: 'To make a Scotch rabbit, toast the bread very nicely on both sides, butter it, cut a slice of cheese about as big as the bread, toast it on both sides, and lay it on the bread… To make a Welsh rabbit, toast the bread on both sides, then toast the cheese on one side, lay it on the toast, and with a hot iron brown the other side. You may rub it over with mustard… To make an English rabbit, toast the bread brown on both sides, lay it in a plate before the fire, pour a glass of red wine over it, and let it soak the wine up. Then cut some cheese very thin and lay it very thick over the bread, put it in a tin oven before the fire, and it will be toasted and browned presently. Serve it away hot… Or do it thus. Toast the bread and soak it in the wine, set it before the fire, rub butter over the bottom of a plate, lay the cheese on, pour in two or three spoonfuls of white wine, cover it with another plate, set it over a chafing-dish of hot coals for two or three minutes, then stir it till it is done and well mixed. You may stir in a little mustard; when it is enough lay it on the bread, just brown it with a hot shovel.'

BREWET OF AYRENN – SCRAMBLED CHEESY SAFFRON EGGS
The Master-Cook of Richard II, *The Forme of Cury*, c. 1390

Ingredients: 6 eggs; 200 ml water; 3 tbsp butter, chopped; 15 saffron threads ground in 2 tbsp water in a pestle and mortar; 1 tsp verjuice; 100 g grated cheese.

Method: Beat the eggs together and add the butter, water and saffron. Mix together with a whisk and add the cheese. Let it rest for 10 minutes for the saffron to infuse. Tip the egg mixture into a saucepan and add the verjuice. Cook gently, taking care not to boil, until the eggs scramble and the mixture solidifies. Serve immediately on toast.

SUGAR CAKES – ROSE BISCUITS
Mistress Sarah Longe, her Receipt Booke, c. 1610
'To make sugar cakes. Take a pound of butter, and wash it in rose-water, and half a pound of sugar, and half a douzen spoonefulls of thicke Cream, and the yelkes of 4 Eggs, and a little mace finely beaten, and as much fine flower as it will wett, and worke it well and roll them out very thin, and cut them with a glasse, and pricke them very thicke with a great pin, and lay them on plates, and bake them gently.'

Ingredients: ¼ cup rose syrup, or 1 tsp rose water mixed with 1 tbsp water and 3 tbsp honey; 2 cups pastry flour; 2 tbsp cream; 2 large egg yolks; ½ cup sugar, ½ cup butter; ⅛ tsp ground mace; 2 tbsp crushed, candied rose petals (optional).

Method: Use a food mixer to cream 2 tbsp of the rose syrup, butter, sugar and mace, until it fluffs up. Add the egg yolks one at a time, beating each in to mix thoroughly. Add the flour, a cup at a time, mixing in well to form the baking mixture. Preheat the oven to 180°C. On a buttered surface, press flower shapes into the mixture and bake for approximately 10 minutes. Brush the remaining 2 tbsp of rose syrup onto the hot biscuits and sprinkle with rose petals.

PIGGES ROLLES – SPICED SAUSAGE ROLLS
The Master-Cook of Richard II, *The Forme of Cury, c. 1390*
In essence *pigges rolles* are an early type of sausage roll. These are easily made now, whereas in Tudor times there would have been hours of work in preparing and grinding down the pork and the spices in a mortar. The rolls would have been costly and time consuming to prepare, an indicator of high status.
'To pork well ground add salt, currants, ginger, powdre fort, pepper and egg to hold it togedre. Wrap in fine pastry and coat with egg white And fry or bake though they can be boiled.'

ELIZABETHAN DRIED APPLE RINGS
Traditional medieval/Tudor snack
Dried apple rings were popular in the sixteenth century as a way of storing

fruit to last for the winter. Dried fruit could also be soaked and used in puddings and sauces as needed. These keep well and still make a healthy snack, like most dried fruit.

Ingredients: 3–4 apples; honey and cinnamon to serve (optional).

Method: Peel apples and core them. Slice apples thinly, making 6–9 rings per apple. Thread the apples onto a string and use pegs to space them, or tie knots in the string between them so they do not touch each other. Hang in a sunny spot, such as inside a window. Leave for several days until the rings are dry to the touch but still slightly springy when squeezed. They are tasty if dipped in honey spiced with cinnamon.

GINGERED BREAD

Traditional Tudor sweetmeat

This dish bridges the gap between the sticky, honeyed medieval gingered bread and the more modern cake and biscuit forms.

Ingredients: 225 g of slightly stale sliced bread; 125 g butter; 50 g clear honey; ½ tbsp ginger; ¼ tsp of crushed peppercorns.

Method: Remove the crusts and roughly crumble the bread into a bowl. Rub the bread through your fingers to make fine crumbs. Melt the butter and honey together. Pour the melted mixture into the breadcrumbs. Add the ginger and pepper and mix well to make a stiff dough. Line a tin or dish with greaseproof paper and scrape the dough into the lined dish. Leave to cool completely or cool in the refrigerator for an hour. Using the paper, lift the gingered bread from the tin and slide off onto a cutting board. Leave for around an hour in the refrigerator, then cut into 16–18 squares or shapes.

PYES OF VEAL OR MUTTON

A Newe Booke of Cookerye, 1591

'For fine Pyes of Veale or Mutton. Perboyle your meat and shredde it fine, and shred your Suet by it selfe. When your Suet is fine shred put it to your Mutton or Veale and mince them togither, put therto halfe a dozen yolkes of Egges being hard sodden and fine minced, small Corance, dates fine minced, season it with cloves and mace, Sinamon and Ginger, a very little Pepper, a handfull of Carowaies, Sugar and Vergious, and some Salt, and so put it into your paste being Chewets or Trunk pyes.'

LADY ELINOR FETTIPLACE'S MINCE PIES

Elinor Fettiplace's Receipt Book, 1604

Mince pies receive their name from the fact that the filling is chopped very finely, i.e. 'minced' small. From at least the Middle Ages these pies included a proportion of meat, generally chicken and tongue, rump steak or mutton, as well as the other ingredients that we would recognise today – suet, dried fruit, citrus peel, sugar spices and alcohol. The change from a savoury to a sweet pie is relatively recent, with recipes for Christmas mince pies in Victorian and Edwardian cookery books still often including meat. Lady Elinor's mince pies are savoury, rich and fruity but not at all sweet, and are seemingly intended to be eaten as a small handheld treat, as opposed to being eaten at the dinner table. Any leftovers from a Sunday roast are ideal for making this.

'Parboile your mutton, then take as much suet as meat, and mince it both small, then put mace and nutmegs and cinamon, and sugar and orange peels, and currance and great reasins, and a little rose water, put all these to the meat, beat your spices and orange peel very small, and mingle your fruit and spice and all together, with the meat, and so bake it, put as much currance as meat and twice as much sugar as salt, put some ginger into it, let the suet bee beef suet, for it is better than mutton suet.'

Ingredients: 8 oz lean, mutton or lamb, cooked with a chopped onion, sliced carrot, chopped stick of celery, a bay leaf and some seasoning; 8 oz beef suet, chopped small; 8 oz currants; 8 oz raisins; ¼ tsp ground ginger; ¼ tsp ground mace; ½ level tsp freshly grated nutmeg; 1 level tsp cinnamon; 1 well rounded tsp salt; 2 well rounded tsp of dark brown sugar; finely-grated zest of an orange; 6 tbsp of rose water; sweet sherry; 1½ lbs shortcrust pastry.

Method: Cover the meat halfway with water and simmer very gently for about 6 hours until very tender. Remove the bay leaf and leave everything else in the pot to cool completely. Skim off the solidified fat and keep the stock as a base for soup. Chop the meat very finely and add it to the rest of the ingredients, except the sherry and rose water. Leave in the refrigerator overnight for the flavours to develop. The following day stir the mixture, adding in the sherry and enough rose water to moisten the mixture without making it too wet. Roll out the shortcrust pastry as thinly as possible and cut rounds to the correct size for your pie tin. Fill the rounds with plenty of the lamb mixture, squeezing it down a little as it will shrink during cooking. Moisten the edges of the lids with a little cold water and place over the filling. Crimp around the tops to seal well. Prick a couple of times with a skewer and glaze well with a beaten egg. Bake in the centre of a hot oven at 220°C for about 20–25 minutes until golden and sizzling. Serve warm or cold.

RICE-CREAMED PIGEONS
Sir Hugh Plat's *Delightes for Ladies*, 1602

'To boyle Pigeons with rice. Boyle them in mutton broth, putting sweete hearbes in their bellies, then take a little Rice and boyle it in Creame, with a little whole mace, season it with sugar, lay it thick upon their breasts, wringing also the juice of a Lemmon upon them, and so serve them.'

BISKETELLO – SWEET HOLLOW BISCUITS
Sir Hugh Plat's *Delightes for Ladies*, 1602

This is a snack or biscuit of a sugar paste flavoured with musk and caraway seeds, which becomes hollow when baked. *Tragacanth* is a natural gum obtained from the dried sap of several species of Middle Eastern legumes of the genus *Astralagus*. The gum is sometimes called *shiraz gum*, *shiraz*, *gum elect* or *gum dragon*. The name derives from the Greek *tragos* and *akantha*, meaning goat thorn, and Iran is its biggest producer. *Gum tragacanth* is a viscous, odourless, tasteless, soluble mixture. It has many industrial uses, including cloth finishing, calico printing and waterproofing of fabrics. It has been used medicinally for thousands of years, dating back several centuries before the Christian era. In folk medicine it has been used for a laxative, persistent cough, diarrhoea and as an aphrodisiac. Its superior water absorbing qualities make it an excellent thickening agent. It is used in many everyday items, from cosmetics and toothpaste, to jellies and salad dressings. Only a small portion of it is soluble so it has to be soaked in water for several hours so that the soluble portion can thicken the water.

'To make another kinde of bisket, called biskettello. Take halfe an ounce of gumme Dragagant, diſſolue it in Rosewater with the iuice of a lemon and two graines of muske, then ſtraine it through a faire linen cloth with the white of an eg, then take halfe a pound of fine ſugar being beaten, and one ounce of carroway ſeedes, beeing alſo beaten and ſearced, and then beat them altogether in a mortar till they come to paſte, then rol them vp in ſmall loaues about the bignes of a ſmall egge, put vnder the bottome of euerie one, a peece of a wafer, and ſo bake them in an Ouen vpon a ſheete of paper, cut thē on the ſides as you do a manchet, and pricke them in the middeſt: when you break them vp they will bee hollow and full of eyes.'

Ingredients: 15 g gum tragacanth or ½ tsp xanthan gum; juice of 1 lemon; 1 tbsp rose water; ⅛ tsp musk; 1 egg white; 225 g caster sugar; 30 g ground caraway seeds.

Method: Combine the gum, lemon juice, rose water and musk (or other preferred flavouring) in a small bowl. Cover and set aside for at least 2 hours to allow the gum to dissolve. Pass the mixture through a fine-meshed sieve into a clean bowl and whisk in the egg white. Sift the sugar and ground caraway seeds into a bowl, then work in the gum and egg white mixture until you have a smooth paste. Take portions of the paste, about the size of an egg, and roll into balls. Arrange on a greased baking tray then place in an oven preheated to 150°C and bake for about 20 minutes, or until the coating is crispy. Allow to cool and serve.

CARNATION FLOWER SPANISH CANDY WEDGES – SWEET APPLE WEDGES

A Book of Fruits and Flowers, 1653

This is a confection of baked apples, carnation petals, verjuice and sugar that is cut into wedges and was traditionally decorated with gold leaf. They were made in Tudor times, but this is a later recipe. The best carnations are clove pinks, *Dianthus caryophyllus graandin,* which impart a wonderful red colour and a clove-like taste. In Elizabethan cookery *Manus Christi* (see recipe below) was a sugar confection and 'boyle it to the height of Manus christi' is a reference to its cooking. The sugar needs to be boiled to the 'thread stage' of sugar cookery (110–13°C), when there is 80 percent sugar concentration. When you drop a little of the syrup in water at this stage it forms a liquid thread that will not ball up. This is both the stage of sugar syrup and the stage at which sugar baskets can be 'woven'.

'Take Violets, Cowslips, or any other kinde of Flowers, pick them, and temper them with the pap of two roasted Apples, and a drop or two of Verjuice, and a graine of Muske, then take halfe a pound of fine hard Sugar, boyle it to the height of Manus christi, then mix them together, and pour on a wet Pye plate, then cut it in Wedges before it be thorough cold, gild it, and so you may box it, and keep it all the year. It is a fine sort of Banquetting stuffe, and newly used, your Manus Christi must boyle a good while, and be kept with good stirring.'

Ingredients: 100 g carnation flowers; 2 dessert apples; ½ tsp verjuice; 50 mg musk or ambergris; 225 g sugar.

Method: Core the apples, place on a baking tray, add a little butter and transfer to an oven preheated to 160°C and bake for about 40 minutes, or until very soft. Take the apples from the oven, remove the skins and beat the flesh until smooth. Remove the husks, stems and heels from the flowers then mix into the beaten apples. Add the sugar to a pan and heat gently, stirring constantly, until the sugar dissolves. Continue heating (still stirring all the time) until the sugar reaches about 112°C (the 'thread stage'). Immediately take the sugar off the heat and beat into the apple and flower mix. Turn this mixture into a buttered pie dish and spread out evenly. Just before the mixture sets completely cut into wedges. Allow to cool then separate the wedges. Traditionally these would have been gilded before eating.

HEARTSEASE FLOWER SPANISH CANDY WEDGES
A Book of Fruits and Flowers, 1653

This is an almost identical recipe to the above, a sweet of apple purée flavoured with heartsease flowers and set with sugar, cut into wedges, gilded and served. The wild pansy, *Viola tricolor*, is known as heartsease, heart's ease and heart's delight, and is a common European wild flower, the origin of today's cultivated pansies. It is also known in folklore as herba trinita, herb trinitatis, tickle-my-fancy, Jack-jump-up-and-kiss-me, cuddle me, come-and-cuddle-me, three faces in a hood, three-faces-under-a-hood, love-in-idleness, love-lies-bleeding, loving idol, love idol, cull me, call-me-to-you, meet-me-in-the-entry, kiss-her-in-the-buttery, Kit-run-in-the-fields, Kit-run-about, pink-o'-the-eye, godfathers, godmothers, stepmother, herb constancy, pink-eyed-John, bouncing Bet, flower o'luce, bird's eye and bullweed.

ENGLISH PANCAKES
Traditional

Shrove Tuesday was the day when people went to confession to be 'shriven', or 'absolved', from their sins in preparation for Lent, the 40 days of fasting before the great feast of Easter. They would spend those days commemorating Christ's 40 days of fasting in the wilderness. Shrove Tuesday became the day on which people had to use up the foods which they were forbidden to eat during Lent and these included meat, eggs and animal-derived products such as milk and cheese. Lent fell at the 'hungry period' when winter stores were running low and summer crops were yet to come. To be unable to eat food such as eggs and cheese would have been hard, so Tudor cooks used up these forbidden fats by making simple pancakes. Since 1445, a pancake race has been run in the Buckinghamshire town of Olney on Pancake Day, the day before the beginning of Lent. Tradition records that on Shrove Tuesday, the 'Shriving Bell' rang out to signal the start of the Shriving church service. On hearing the bell a local housewife, who had been busy cooking pancakes in anticipation of the beginning of Lent, ran to the church, frying pan still in hand, tossing the pancake to prevent it from burning. The women of Olney recreate this race every Shrove Tuesday (known overseas as *Mardi Gras* or Fat Tuesday) by running from the market place to the Church of St. Peter and St. Paul, a distance of 415 yards. The 'prize' is a kiss from the verger. There are various explanations for this custom, but it seems to have started when the medieval church bells rang to summon the faithful to confess their sins. Shrove Tuesday is actually forty-seven days before Easter Sunday. These seven Sundays during Lent, were not 'fast' days but 'feast' days on which you could break your fast and eat normally, from which the word 'breakfast' may have originated.

Ingredients: 150 g plain flour; 2 large eggs; 0.3 litre milk and water mixed; 25 g melted butter; more melted butter in a container for frying; cooking oil.
Method: Sift the flour and salt into a large bowl and make a well in the centre. Break the eggs into the well and then, either with an electric whisk or wooden spoon, start to whisk the flour into the egg. Continue to do this, incorporating the flour slowly, until the mixture is quite thick. Start adding the milk and water mixture slowly, beating all the time, until you have a smooth batter. Then add the melted butter and beat to incorporate it. Rest the batter for 30 minutes. Heat a frying pan until it is very hot, add a tiny drop of oil and rub the pan round with a small roll of kitchen paper dipped in the melted butter. Use a cup or ladle to pour in just enough batter to cover the pan bottom and swirl it round evenly. Cook it until the top is just set, give the pan a good shake and toss the pancake. Cook the raw side very briefly then slide it out of the pan onto a plate and keep it warm. Put more butter in the pan as before and repeat. Stack your pancakes as you cook them. Serve them hot with lemon juice and sugar.

CREMPOG – WELSH PANCAKE
Traditional Welsh – modern redaction

There are many variations of pancake type goods made from batter on a *planc* or *maen* (bakestone). The famed Breton *crepes* and *galettes* are made in a similar way, the Bretons and Welsh sharing a language and culture for 1,500 years. The ingredients are similar to English pancakes, but the difference lies in the depth and diameter and the ways in which they are served. Welsh pancakes are made in a pile, smothered in Welsh butter and then served sliced into wedges like a cake. Savoury versions are also made with herbs and onion mixed in. A popular recipe amongst the gentry of the large estates of eighteenth century Wales was a dish entitled 'the quire of paper'. Twenty paper-thin pancakes, made from a scented rich cream batter, were stacked and served sliced. Rose water and orange blossom water were used in the more affluent households for scenting desserts such as this. Traditional Welsh *crempog* are much thicker pancakes, thicker than a *crepe* and bigger than a pikelet. The *crempog* is more like the American pancake and bigger than the Scotch pancake. It is thought to be the origin of the English word crumpet and in Brittany is known as *krampouezh*. *Crempog* can be made with or without yeast, with buttermilk, oats or speckled with raisins or currants. Traditionally, they are made from flour, salt, eggs, milk and butter.
Ingredients: 2 oz butter; 15 fl oz warm buttermilk; 10 oz all purpose or plain flour; 3 oz sugar; 1 tsp bicarbonate of soda; ½ tsp salt; 1 tbsp vinegar; 2 well-beaten eggs.

Method: Stir the butter into the warmed buttermilk until melted. Gradually pour the milk and butter into the flour and beat well. Leave the mixture to stand for at least 30 minutes before stirring in the sugar, bicarbonate of soda, salt and vinegar into the beaten eggs. Pour this mixture into the flour, butter and milk mixture and beat well to form a smooth batter. Heavily grease a griddle or bakestone and heat, then drop the batter, a tablespoon at a time onto the heated griddle and cook over a moderate heat until golden brown on both sides. Keep the *crempog* warm and continue this method until all the batter is used up. Spread butter on each pancake and eat while warm.

MANUS CHRISTI – ELIZABETHAN ALMOND SWEETIES
A Closet for Ladies and Gentlewomen, 1608

Almond and sugar paste sweets bound with rose water, which can be topped with treats, sweetmeats and comfits before being served and which make excellent treats for Christmas or Easter.

'To make Manus Chrifti. Take halfe a pound of refined Suger, and fome Rofe water, and boyle them together, till it come to fuger againe, then ftirre it about while it be fomewhat cold, then take your leafe gould, and mingle with it, then caft it according to art, That is, in round gobbets, and fo keepe them.'

Ingredients: 225 g caster sugar; 60 ml rose water; gold leaf, torn (optional).

Method: Combine the sugar and rose water in a pan. Heat gently until the sugar dissolves, then bring to a boil. Continue cooking, stirring frequently, until the sugar reaches 112°C, as measured on a confectioner's thermometer. Line a baking tray with greaseproof paper. When the sugar syrup is ready, take off the heat and allow to cool slightly then stir in the gold leaf. Drop this mixture by the teaspoon onto the paper, forming it into round mounds. Set aside to cool and harden then carefully peel from the greaseproof paper. Store or serve.

POLONIAN SAWSEDGE – POLISH SAUSAGE
Sir Hugh Plat's *Delightes for Ladies*, 1602

This is possibly Plat's cook's attempt at recreating Polish *krajana* or *siekana kielbasa*. The sausages are stuffed, then cured in brine, blanched and hung up in a chimney. The recipe states they will keep for a year and will engender a mighty thirst. Ned Ward's *London Spy* (1698–9) described the Spaniards as being recognised by their smell, 'for they Stink as Strong of Garlick as a Polonian Sausage' displaying the true Englishman's active and lasting distaste for 'Johnny Foreigner.'

'To make a Polonian sawsedge. Take the fillets of an hog, chop them verie small, with a handfull of red sage, season it hot with Ginger and pepper, and then put it into a great sheepes gut, then let it lie three nights in brine, then boyle it and hang it up in a chimney where fire is usually kept, and these sawsedges will last one whole yeare. They are good for sallades, or to garnish boyled meats, or to make one relish a cup of wine.'

TROFLES FOR THE SEA – SEA TRUFFLES
Sir Hugh Plat's *Delightes for Ladies*, 1602

Basically these are sugar pills and were also used as the base for pills and pastilles. The Elizabethans blended medicines with sweet confections such as these and this version was possibly intended to be taken to sea.

'To make trofles for the sea. Firſt make paſte of ſugar and gum Dragagant mixed together, thē mixe therewith a reaſonable quātitiy of the powder of Cinamon and ginger, and if you pleaſe a little muske alſo, and make it vpp into rols of ſeuerall faſhions, gilding them heere and there. In the ſame manner you may alſo conuey any purgatiue, vomit, or other medicing into ſugar paſte.'

Ingredients: 15 g gum tragacanth (or ½ tsp xanthan gum); 60 ml water; 200 g powdered sugar; ½ tsp ground cinnamon; ½ tsp ground ginger; gold leaf and edible silver leaf (optional).

Method: Crush the gum tragacanth in a mortar and mix with the water, and set aside to infuse for at least 2 hours. Then pass the mixture through a fine-meshed sieve, covered with a double layer of muslin, to separate away the solids. Sift together the powdered sugar and spices into a bowl. Add the gum mixture, a little at a time, mixing until you have a solid but dry paste. Form this paste into small balls and set aside in a warm place over night to dry. Gild with gold leaf or edible silver.

BURSEWS – PORKY MEATBALLS
The Master-Cook of Richard II, *The Forme of Cury, c.* 1390

There is another version of *bursews* made of entrails in Chapter 12, but this is a shallow-fried pork and egg meatball intended as a snack.

'Take Pork, ſeeþ it and grynde it smale wiþ sodden ayren. do þerto gode powdours and hole spices and salt with sugur. make þerof smale balles, and cast hem in a batour of ayren. and wete hem in flour. and frye hem in grece as frytours. and ſerue hem forth.'

Ingredients: 500 g ground pork; 1 soft-boiled egg; 3 tsp powder fort (see above); 2 eggs, lightly beaten; oil; 120 g wholemeal flour.

Method: Mix the ground pork, broken-up egg and spices. When the mixture comes together, form as many walnut-sized balls as you can. Coat these with the beaten egg mix and roll in the flour. Tip olive oil into a pan until you have about 1 cm depth. Heat this until almost smoking and gently place the meatballs in the oil. Keep turning the balls until they have crisped on the outside. Drain, arrange on a plate and serve with a dipping sauce.

FRUTURS – FRITTERS
The Master-Cook of Richard II, The Forme of Cury, c. 1390, *Liber Cure Cocorum, Sloane MS.* 1486, 1430 etc.
'FOR TO MAKE FRUTURS. Nym flowre and eyryn and grynd peper and safroun and mak therto a batour and par aplyn and kyt hem to brode penys and kest hem theryn and fry hem in the batour wyth fresch grees and serve it forthe.'

LENTE FRYTOURES – SWEET APPLE FRITTERS
Two Fifteenth Century Cookbooks – Harleian MS. 279 & Harl. MS. 4016, c. 1440
'Take good flour, ale yeast, saffron and salt, and beat all together as thick as other manner fritters of flesh; and then take apples, and pare them, and cut them in manner of fritters, and wet them in the batter up and down, and fry them in oil, and cast them in a dish, and cast sugar thereon enough, and serve them forth hot.'
Ingredients: 5 apples, peeled, cored and sliced; 2.7 cups flour; 12 oz beer; 3 tsp yeast; 6 threads saffron; 2 tsp salt; oil; powdered sugar.
Method: Allow the yeast to spend 2 hours in warm water and then make the batter with the flour, beer, yeast, salt and saffron. Sprinkle powdered sugar over the apples and dip in the batter. Fry a few at a time in a deep skillet with about ¾ inches of olive oil. Serve warm, with cream or ice cream.

FRYTOR OF PASTRONAKES OF SKYRWYTS AND OF APPLES (1) – PARSNIP, SKIRRET AND APPLE FRITTERS
The Master-Cook of Richard II, *The Forme of Cury, c.* 1390
A side dish or snack of parboiled parsnips, skirrets or apples that are cubed, dipped in an ale, flour and egg batter before being deep fried until golden. Skirret (*Sium sisarum*) is a Chinese plant of the parsley family, formerly cultivated in Europe for its edible roots. Now out of favour, it is a root vegetable with a cluster of long, white roots and eaten raw tastes sweet, similar to parsnips and carrots. It can be grown as a perennial and you can subdivide the roots to both crop and grow on for next year. Also known as Crummock, Sugar Root and Water Parsnip, it was mentioned by Pliny the Elder as a favourite of Emperor Tiberius. Roasted skirret root has been a coffee substitute and its name comes from the Dutch who brought it to Europe from the Far East, *suikerwortel* meaning 'sugar root'.

'Frytor of pastronakes of skyrwyts and of apples. Take skirrets and parsnips and apples and parboil them. Make a batter of flour and eggs and add ale, saffron and salt. Dip them in the batter and fry them in oil or in lard. Add to this almond milk and serve it forth.'

Ingredients: 10 peeled skirrets, or small carrots; 4 peeled parsnips; 2 eating apples, peeled and cored; 150 g plain flour; 1 large egg; 250 ml ale; oil for deep frying; ½ tsp saffron powder; salt to taste; 200 ml thick almond milk, heated, to serve.

Method: Bring a pan of water to the boil. Add the apples, skirrets and parsnips and parboil for 10 minutes. Drain the vegetables and fruit then set aside to cool before cutting into bite-sized pieces. In the meantime, whisk together the flour, eggs and ale to make a smooth batter. Stir in the saffron to flavour, then season to taste with salt. Allow to rest for 30 minutes. Heat oil to a depth of 3cm in a large pan. When the oil is hot, dip the vegetable and apple pieces in the batter, then drop into the hot oil. Fry until golden brown and cooked through. Remove with a slotted spoon, drain and arrange in a serving dish. Pour over the almond milk and serve.

FRYTOR OF PASTRONAKES (2) – VEGGIE FRITTERS
Ingredients: 460 g plain white flour; 1 egg; 250 ml beer; 1 medium parsnip; 2 medium carrots; 6 medium cooking apples, cored.
Method: Peel the parsnip, carrots and apples and chop into small cubes. Place in a saucepan, cover with water and boil until soft. Drain the excess water and roughly mash. In a bowl mix together the flour, egg and beer to form a stiff dough. Add the mashed vegetables to this and mix together well. Pour olive oil into a deep saucepan to a depth of about 4 cm. Heat the oil and, when almost smoking, drop large spoonfuls of the batter into the oil. Fry until golden brown, drain and place on a serving dish.

SMARTARD – SWEET COTTAGE CHEESE FRITTERS
A Noble Boke off Cookry ffor a Prynce Houssolde Holkham MSS 674, 1480
'To mak smartard tak wetted cruddes er they bee pressed and put them in a clothe and grinde them well to pured flour and temper hem with eggs and cowe creme and mak ther of a good batere that it be rynynge then tak whit grece in a pan and let it be hete and tak out the batter with a saucer and let it ryn into the grece and draw your hand bakward that it may ryn abrod then fry it welle and whit and somwhat craking and serue it furthe in dishes with sugur ther on.'
Ingredients: 4 eggs; 230 ml oil for frying; 50 g cottage cheese; 4 tsp double cream; brown sugar to taste.

Method: Pass the cottage cheese through a sieve into a bowl to produce a smooth paste. Add eggs and cream to the bowl and whisk together until smooth. Heat oil in a frying pan and fry the mixture a small amount at a time, spreading it out as it is poured into the pan. Allow the fritters to cook until they start to brown around the edges, then carefully remove from the oil and drain on paper towels. Arrange on a serving dish and sprinkle with brown sugar.

FRUTURS – SPICED FRITTERS
The Babees Book, or A 'Lytyl Reporte' of How Young People Should Behave, MS. Harl. 5086, c. 1475
'Recipe þe cromys of whyte brede, and swete apyls, and 3 okkis of eggis, and bray þam wele, and temper it with wyne, and make it to sethe; and when it is thyk, do þer-to gode spyces, gynger and galingay and canyll and clows, and serve it forthe.'

FRUTURS OF FYGIS
The Babees Book, or A 'Lytyl Reporte' of How Young People Should Behave, MS. Harl. 5086, c. 1475
'Recipe and make bature of floure, ale, peper and saferon, with oþer spices; þan cast þam in to a frying pann with batur, and ole, and bake þam and serve.'

SAMACAYS – CURD CHEESE FRITTERS
An Ordinance of Pottage, Beinecke MS 163, 1460
'Take vellyd cruddys or they be pressyd; do hem yn a cloth. Wryng out the whey. Do hem in a mortar; grynd hem well with paryd floure and temyr hem with eyryn and creme of cow mylke, and make thereof a rennyng bature. Than have white grece in a panne: loke hit be hote. Take up the bature with a saucer; let hit renne in the grece; draw thy hond backward that hit may renne abrode. Then fry hem ryte well and somdell hard reschelyng and serve hit forth in disches, and strew on white sygure.'

FRITTERS OF SPINNEDGE – SPINACH FRITTERS (1)
Thomas Dawson's *The Good Housewife's Jewell*, 1596
'Take a good deale of Spinnedge, and washe it cleane, then boyle it in faire water, and when it is boyled, then take it forth and let the water runne from it, then chop it with the backe of a knife, and then put in some egges and grated Bread, and season it with suger, sinamon, ginger, and pepper, dates minced fine, and currans, and rowle them like a ball, and dippe them in Butter made of Ale and flower.'

SPYNOCHE FRUTURS – SPINACH FRITTERS (2)

John Partridge's *The Treasurie of Commodious Conceits & Hidden Secrets*, 1573

Ingredients: 225 g cooked and drained spinach; 50 g fresh white breadcrumbs; 2 beaten eggs; 1.5 ml ginger; 1.5 ml cinnamon; 50 g or more of butter; sugar to sprinkle.

Method: Chop and blend the spinach, breadcrumbs and spices, then beat in enough egg to form a soft paste. Heat a little butter in a frying pan and drop in a tablespoon of the paste, spreading it and levelling it with the back of the spoon, and shaking the pan to ensure it does not stick. Fry on both sides and remove to a hot dish, continuing until all the mixture has been used. Serve sprinkled with sugar.

TOURTELETES IN FRYTURE – HONEY-COATED FIG FRITTER PIES

Curye on Inglysch, 14th century

'Take figs and grind them small; add therein saffron and powder fort. Close them in foils of dough, and fry them in oil. Clarify honey and baste them therewith. Eat them hot or cold.'

Ingredients: 200 g figs; 7 strands saffron; 2 tsp powder forte (see recipe above); 250 g pastry dough; 200 ml oil; 100 ml honey; beaten egg.

Method: Dice the figs as finely as possible and mix them with the saffron and powder forte. Roll out the pastry and cut into medium-sized circles. Add a spoonful of the filling in the centre of each pastry circle, wet the outside with beaten egg and place a second pastry circle on top. Crimp the edges together and pierce the upper surface with a fork. Continue until all the fig mixture is used up. Fry the pies in hot oil until lightly browned and crispy, then remove from the heat and drain on kitchen paper. Heat the honey gently in a saucepan and brush onto the top of the pies.

FRYTOUR OF ERBES (1) – HERB BATTER FRITTERS IN HONEY

The Master-Cook of Richard II, *The Forme of Cury, c.* 1390

'Take gode erbys; grynde hem and medle hem with flour and water, and a lytel yest, and salt, and frye hem in oyle. And ete hem with clere hony.'

Ingredients: 120 g finely-chopped herbs such as parsley, sorrel, rosemary, tarragon, thyme, savory; 230 g flour; 180 ml water.

Method: Mix the flour and water into a batter. Add the chopped herbs and mix. Make balls and cook in a deep-fat fryer preheated to 190°C. Alternatively place about 6 cm of oil in a deep saucepan or wok and heat. Take heaped tablespoons of the batter and drop into the hot oil. Fry for about 4 minutes until brown and crispy. Take from the batter with a slotted spoon and serve drizzled with honey.

FRYTOUR OF ERBES (2) – MIXED HERB BATTER FRITTERS

Curye on Inglysch, fourteenth century

Ingredients: 3 cups flour; 2¼ cups water; ¼ tsp yeast; ⅛ tsp salt; oil; honey; mix of fresh herbs such as 2½ tsp sage; 1½ tsp thyme; 6 tbsp parsley; 1 tbsp oregano.

Method: Dissolve yeast in ½ cup warm water and add salt to flour. When yeast is bubbling, add rest of flour to water. Let it rest while herbs are chopped and ground; note that quantities of herbs are after chopping. Either divide the batter in 4, add 4 kinds of herb fritter, or add 4 times as much of any one of the herbs to the whole batter. Add ½ tbsp of the batter at a time, to fry in ¼ inch deep oil, to make about 36 fritters.

FRYTOUR BLAUNCHED – FRIED HONEYED WHITE ALMOND RAVIOLI

The Master-Cook of Richard II, *The Forme of Cury*, c. 1390

A rich egg and flour fritter filled with almonds, served as a snack or a dessert.

Ingredients: 230 g flour; 1 large egg; 6 tbsp ground almonds; 6 tbsp honey; 2 tbsp dry white wine; olive oil to moisten and fry.

Method: Place the flour in a bowl and add the egg. Add a few drops of olive oil and mix to a fairly stiff dough. If possible, pass the dough through a pasta maker several times to increase elasticity and to gain a thin sheet of dough. Otherwise roll the dough very thinly on a cold, floured surface. Cut small ravioli-sized rectangles, fill with ground almonds, fold over and seal. Pour oil into a frying pan until it coats the base evenly to a depth of about 2 mm. When the oil is hot, add the ground almond ravioli and fry until browned on both sides. Meanwhile add the honey and wine to a small saucepan, heating gently until the honey becomes liquid. Place the pastries in a bowl and pour the honey sauce over the top. Place these in an oven preheated to 190°C, cook for about 5–10 minutes and serve immediately.

FRYTOUR OF MYLKE – LEMON CURD FRITTERS

The Master-Cook of Richard II, *The Forme of Cury*, c. 1390

Ingredients: 600 ml whole milk; juice of 2 lemons; 2 egg whites; pepper to taste (optional); caster sugar and lemon juice to garnish.

Method: Place the milk in a bowl and add the lemon juice. Stir together and wait about 2 hours for the citric acid in the lemons to precipitate curds. Pour the curdled milk into a sieve and drain off the whey. Transfer the remaining curds into a bowl and add the beaten whites of two eggs. Mix these with the curds, seasoning with a little pepper if you wish. Take 2 tsp of the mixture and add to a frying pan greased with butter. Fry until golden brown and turn over to fry the other side. Transfer to a plate and keep frying fritters until all the mixture has gone. Dust with sugar, squeeze the lemon juice over and serve.

MAGNIFICENT IMPERIAL FRITTERS
Anonymous, Venetian *Libro di cucina/ Libro per cuoco*, 14th–15th century
'If you want to make Imperial fritters, take the whites of eggs and slices of fresh cheese. Beat the cheese with the white of the egg, and add a little bit of wheat flour and whole peeled pine nuts. Take a frying pan with plenty of oil and put it to heat and then make the fritters fry. When they are cooked sprinkle them with plenty of sugar and keep them hot.'

ELDERFLOWER FRITTERS
Anonymous, Venetian *Libro di cucina/ Libro per cuoco*, 14th–15th century
'Take elder flowers and put them to soak in water and let them become very soft, then take out the flowers and grind them well. Add a little bit of wheat flour and temper with eggs and with the milk in which you soaked the flowers. Then have a frying pan with enough oil inside and fry them. When they are cooked, cover with a trivet to keep in the heat and they are good.'

WHITE FRITTERS
Anonymous, Venetian *Libro di cucina/ Libro per cuoco*, 14th–15th century
'To make white fritters. Take almond milk and yeast, add flour and blend them together and leave them to raise, then make the fritters. When they are cooked, powder with sugar and they are good.'

APPLE FRITTERS FOR LENT
Anonymous, Venetian *Libro di cucina/ Libro per cuoco*, 14th–15th century
'Take apples and peel them, then cut in the way of the host [thin circular slices]. Make a batter of flour with saffron [and presumably water], and add currants, and put the apples in this batter; then fry them in sufficient oil for each. Powder with sugar when they are cooked.'

POKEROUNCE – HONEY PINE NUT TOASTIES
Two Fifteenth Century Cookbooks – Harleian MS. 279 & Harl. MS. 4016, c. 1440
'Pokerounce. Take Hony, and caste it in a potte tyl it wexe chargeaunt y-now; take and skeme it clene. Take Gyngere, Canel, and Galyngale, and caste þer-to; take whyte Brede, and kytte to trenchours, and toste ham; take þin paste whyle it is hot, and sprede it vppe-on þin trenchourys with a spone, and plante it with Pynes, and serue forth.'

Ingredients: 300 ml clear honey; ¼ tsp freshly-grated ginger; ¼ tsp ground cinnamon; ¼ tsp galingale; 1 whole loaf of wholemeal bread; large handful of pine nuts; sesame seeds (optional).

Method: Remove all the crusts from the bread, cut the remaining loaf lengthways into large slices about 1 inch thick and toast. Toast the pine nuts in a dry frying pan until they become a light golden brown then remove from the heat. Meanwhile pour the honey into a saucepan, add the spices and begin to heat gently. Every now and then skim off any scum. The honey will at first appear thin but will then start to thicken again. When it has reached this stage spread it on the bread and top with the toasted pine nuts. You can also use toasted sesame seeds if you wish.

LET LARDES – MULTICOLOURED CUSTARD FRY-UP
The Master-Cook of Richard II, *The Forme of Cury*, *c.* 1390

'Take parsley and pound it with cow milk. Mix it with eggs and diced lard. After you have done this, mix it with milk and make of it diverse colours. If you would have yellow add to this saffron, but no parsley. If you would have it white: do not add parsley nor saffron, but add to it wheat starch. If you would have it red, add to it sandalwood. If you would have it pownas [golden orange] add to it turmeric. If you would have black, add to it blood that has been boiled and fried. And set on the fire in as many dishes as you have colours and boil it well and lay the first of these colours on a cloth and sit another upon it and sit the third [on top] and then the fourth. And press it hard until all the excess liquid is extracted. And when it is cold slice it thinly, put it in a pan and fry it well. And serve it forth.'

Ingredients: 600 ml milk; 3 beaten eggs; 50 g finely-diced lard; 6 tbsp parsley, pounded to a paste in a mortar; generous pinch of saffron; 1 tsp cornflour; red food colouring; 100 ml blood (preferably black food colouring); 1 tsp turmeric; oil for frying.

Method: In a bowl, beat the eggs. Whisk in the milk then add the lard. Set aside. In the meantime, prepare the colourings. For green, pound the parsley in a mortar until you have a smooth paste, then work in 50 ml milk and turn into a cup. For yellow, pound saffron in a mortar, then work in 50 ml milk then turn into a cup. For white, whisk the cornflour with 50 ml milk until you have a smooth slurry then set aside. For red, whisk red colouring into 50 ml milk. For a golden orange colour, mix the turmeric with 50 ml milk. If you are using blood (this writer is too squeamish!), pour into a pan, bring to a boil and cook for 2 minutes, then take off the heat and set aside to cool. Once the blood has cooled, heat a little oil in a frying pan, add the boiled blood and fry briskly until black. Take off the heat and set aside to cool, then pound in a mortar.

Use about 2 tbsp of this black paste to colour some custard black. For black, work 50 ml milk into 2 tbsp of the blood mixture prepared above, or use black food colouring. Divide the egg, lard and milk mixture into five portions and mix in each the appropriate colouring of black, orange, red, yellow and green. Place these mixtures separately in small pans, heat gently until the lard melts then bring to a simmer and cook until the custard is very thick. Pour into ring moulds set on greaseproof paper and allow to cool. When the custards have almost set, but are still warm, arrange them in a stack, one colour above the other. Surround with a metal ring or card tube then press down with a weight to extract any excess moisture and bind the colours together. When you have a nice sandwich of colours that are bound together, slice thinly then fry gently until warmed though and serve.

HASTLETES OF FRUYT – ROAST EASTERN FRUIT

The Master-Cook of Richard II, *The Forme of Cury, c.* 1390

'Hastletes of Fruyt. Take quartered figs, raisins, whole dates and whole almonds. and run them on a spit and roast them until golden as pomme dorres and serve them forth.'

Ingredients: 6 fresh figs, quartered; 100 g raisins; 60 g whole, pitted, dates; 100 g blanched almonds; 2 tbsp olive oil.

Method: Place all the ingredients in a roasting pan. Drizzle the olive oil over the figs then place in an oven preheated to 160°C. Leave for about 4 minutes, until the almonds have coloured. Turn everything over and cook for a further 4 minutes and serve warm.

LECHE FRYED – SWEET CHEESE TARTS

Beinecke MS 163, An Ordinance of Potage

'Take Tendyr chese: cut hit in shiveres and do hit in hote skallyng watyr. When hit Rennyth and yeldesth togedyr, do awey the watyr as clene as thu may and do therto clarifyed buttur alhote, a grete dele, and clarifyed hony, and tyol hit well togadyr with yolkes of eyron. Have cofyns with Low brerdys as thin as thu may draw hem; put yn youre stuf that the botom be helyd, and let hem bake esyly and serve hem forth.'

Ingredients: 2 lbs mild Cheddar; ½ cup honey; 6 tbsp melted butter, cooled; 1 pie shell.

Method: Slice the cheese and add it to boiling water. Stir well and eventually the cheese will come together into a sort of a ball. Drain off the liquid. Mix the eggs, butter and honey together. Now blend with the cheese in a food processor. Fill the pie crust and cook on a baking sheet, until firm. Serve warm, as the cheese is rubbery when cold.

A LONG-LIFE PYE

Thomas Dawson's *A Booke of Cokerie*, 1620

Voyages at sea could last over a year and one way of keeping meat for a prolonged period was to bake it in a pie. One of the features of pies intended for long keeping was that they had an extremely thick, hard, rye flour pastry shell which, if it was properly sealed and did not become damp or cracked, functioned as an airtight container.

'To make a pye to keep long. First perboyle your flesh and presse it, and when it is pressed, season it with Pepper and salt wile it is hot, then larde it, make your paste of Rie flower, it must be very thick or else it will not holde, wen it is seasoned and larded, lay it in your Pye, then cast on it before you close it a good deale of Cloves and Mace beaten small, and throw upon that a good deale of Butter, and so close it up, you must leave a hole in the top of the lid, and when it hath stood two houres in the Oven you must fill it as full of Vineger as you can, then stop the hole as close as you can with paste, and then set it into the Oven again, your Oven must be very hote as at first, and then your Pyes will keepe a great while, the longer you keepe them, the better they will bee: when they be taken out of the Oven and almost cold, you must shake them betweene your hands, and set them with the bottome upward, and when you set them into the Oven, take great heede that one pye touch not another by more then one hand bredth: Remember also to let them stand in the Oven after the Vineger be in two houres and more.'

CHEWITES OF VEAL – VEAL IN WINE DUMPLINGS

The Good Huswifes Handmaide for the Kitchin, 1594

Chewite is an alternative spelling for *chewet*, 'a dish made of various kinds of meat or fish, chopped fine, mixed with spices and fruits, and baked, fried, or boiled.' *Chewets* were small, individually-sized pies. However, we would today call the boiled versions, such as in the following recipe, dumplings.

'To make Chewites of Veale. Take a leg of Veal and perboyle it, then mince it with beefe suet, take almost as much of your suet as of your Veale, and take a good quantitie of Ginger, a little Saffron to colour it. Take halfe a goblet of white wine, and two or three good handfuls of grapes, and put them all together with salt, and so put them in coffins, and let them boyle a quarter of an houre.'

PAX CAKES – PEACE BISCUITS

An almost forgotten tradition associated with Palm Sunday is the giving of pax cakes. Dating back to at least 1570, these small biscuits were handed out by vicars to their congregations as they left church on Palm Sunday and were said to represent good will and neighbourliness (*pax* being Latin for 'peace'). The rare custom of distributing these cakes after the Palm Sunday service is still observed at St Tysilio's Church, Sellack, near Ross-on-Wye in Herefordshire. Hentland and Kings Caple also observe this custom which is thought to be now unique to this small area. The cakes carry an impress of a lamb and a flag. They were originally buns, and at Sellack and Kings Caple, free ale was at one time also provided by a bequest but this was unfortunately discontinued from 1831. They are distributed with the salutation 'Peace and Good Neighbourhood'. The origins of the 'pax cakes' ceremony lie with the family of Thomas More, vicar of Sellack and Kings Caple in 1442. He died on Palm Sunday 1448, leaving a massive £20 to a local charity. He willed 'that bread and ale to the value of 6*s* 8*p* be distributed to all and singular in the aforementioned churches for the good of my soul'.

Ingredients: To make the batter, beat one egg. Then add and beat the following until smooth: 1 cup sour milk or buttermilk; 2 tablespoons salad oil; ½ cup whole wheat flour; ¼ cup wheat germ; ¼ cup white flour; 1 tbsp sugar; 1 tsp baking powder; ½ tsp soda; ½ tsp salt.

Method: Grease a heated skillet or griddle. Pour the batter onto the hot griddle in 3–5 cm diameter drops. Turn the pax cakes when bubbles show. Heat on the second side until brown. Sprinkle with powdered sugar. Cinnamon may be added if desired.

DOUCETTY (1) – PORK PIE IN HONEY CUSTARD

The Master-Cook of Richard II, *The Forme of Cury*, c. 1390

This could also be a dessert or sweetmeat, as the pork is sitting in honey custard. In the Middle Ages, custard tarts were also called *dovecettes* and *darioles*, and in 1339, Henry IV included the name 'dovecettys'.

'Take Porke and hakke it smal, and Eyroun y-melled togedrys, and a lytel milke, and melle hem to-gederys with Hony and Pepper, and bake hem in a cofyn, and serve forth.'

Ingredients: ½ to ⅔ lb of pork chops; 3 tbsp milk; pinch of pepper; 6 eggs; 2 tsp honey; 9-inch pie crust.

Method: Cook the pork in the oven or boil it for about 20 minutes. Make a pie crust, prick it and place in a 200°C oven for about 10 minutes to harden it. Mix the remaining ingredients. Cut pork into small pieces and add to mixture, place in the pie crust and bake at 180°C for about 40 minutes.

DOUCETTY (2) – PORK PIE IN HONEY CUSTARD

The Master-Cook of Richard II, *The Forme of Cury*, *c.* 1390

Ingredients: 1 lb pork; salt; ¼ lb. honey; ⅛ tsp pepper; 3 beaten eggs; 2 tbsp flour; ¼ cup milk; ⅛ tsp salt; ⅛ tsp mace; 1 prebaked pie shell.

Method: Preboil pork in salted water in a large pot for 30 minutes, until almost cooked. Remove, allow to cool and cut into ½ inch cubes, removing as much fat as possible. Mix cubes in a bowl with 1 tbsp flour. Add the following to the pork cubes, mixing in each thoroughly before the next addition: ¼ cup milk; 3 beaten eggs; 1 tbsp flour; ¼ lb honey. Pour the pork mixture into the prebaked pie shell. Bake at 190°C for 15 minutes, then lower heat to 120°C and bake for an additional 20 minutes, or until the mixture is set firm. This is an open pie, but can be covered with a pastry lid to last longer.

CHICKENS WITH DAMSONS – CHICKEN AND PLUM PIES

The Good Huswifes Handmaide for the Kitchin, 1594

'To bake Chickens with Damsons. Take your Chickens, drawe them and wash them, then breake their bones, and lay them in a platter, then take foure handfuls of fine flower, and lay it on a faire boord, put thereto twelve yolks of Egs, a dish of butter, and a litle Saffron: mingle them altogether, and make your paste therewith. Then make sixe coffins, and put in euery coffin a lumpe of butter of the bignesse of a Walnut: then season your sixe coffins with one spoonful of Cloues and Mace, two spoonfuls of Synamon, and one of Sugar, and a spoonefull of Salt. Then put your Chickens into your pies: then take Damisons and pare away the outward peele of them, and put twentie in euery of your pies, round about your chicken, then put into euerie of your coffins, a hand full of Corrans. Then close them vp, and put them into the Ouen, then let them be there three quarters of an houre.'

KING JAMES BISCUITS – TUDOR SPICED SCONE BISCUITS

Mistress Sarah Longe, her Receipt Booke, c. 1610

This is a Tudor recipe for around 24 scones and Sarah Longe wrote in her manuscript that 'King James, and his Queene [had] eaten with much liking these biscuits.'

Ingredients: 7 large egg yolks; 4 large egg whites; 3 tbsp rose water; 1 cup sugar; 5 cups pastry flour; 1 tsp each caraway and aniseed.

Method: Use a blender on high speed to beat the egg yolks, rose water and sugar for 2 minutes. Add a cup of flour and mix for another 2 minutes. Add another cup of flour and mix for 1 minute. Reduce the mixer speed to low, add a third cup of flour and mix for 2 minutes. Whip the egg whites to soft peaks in a separate bowl. Add this, the fourth cup of flour, caraway and aniseed to the dough and mix for 2 minutes. Add the fifth cup of flour, mixing until the dough is smooth and elastic. If the dough is too thick for your mixer, remove, add this fifth cup and knead by hand. Preheat the oven to 180°C. Drop the dough, 2 tbsp at a time, onto a greased baking sheet and cook for 15 minutes or until golden brown.

BANBURY CAKES

Gervase Markham's *Countrey Contentments, or, The English Hus-wife*, 1615
Banbury cakes were first mentioned in 1586. The 'barm' called for in this recipe is the yeasty froth that lies on top of beer. This recipe has been adapted from the original to allow for the use of active, dried yeast.

'To make a very good Banbury cake, take four pounds of currants, and wash and pick them very clean, and dry them in a cloth: then take three eggs and put away one yolk, and beat them, and strain them with good barm, putting thereto cloves, mace, cinnamon, and nutmegs; then take a pint of cream, and as much morning's milk and set it on the fire till the cold be taken away; then take flour and put in a good store of cold butter and sugar, the put in your eggs, barm, and meal and work them all together an hour or more: then save a part of the paste, and the rest break into pieces and work in your currants; which done, mould your cake of what quantity you please; and then with that paste which hath not any currants cover it very thin both underneath and aloft. And so bake it according to the bigness.'

Ingredients: 2 tsp active, dried, yeast; 40 g caster sugar; 1 egg; 200 ml warm milk; 200 ml warm cream; 750 g plain flour; 60 g butter; 2 tsp ground cinnamon; ½ tsp ground mace; ½ tsp freshly-grated nutmeg; 300 g currants.

Method: Combine the yeast, sugar and 100 ml of the warm milk in a bowl. Cover and set aside for 5 minutes, or until frothing. Whisk in the egg and spices then set aside. Sift the flour into a bowl. Rub in the butter with your fingertips then add the yeast mix, the remaining milk and the cream. Work together until thoroughly combined, adding more flour or milk as needed. Knead for about 10 minutes, or until smooth and elastic. Cover the dough and set aside in a warm place for 40 minutes to rise. Then knock the dough back and reserve just over one-third. Take the remaining dough and knead in the currants until evenly distributed. Take small pieces of the dough and shape into square blocks about 3 cm thick. Now take the reserved dough and roll out until quite thin. Use this to cover the top and bottom of the currant dough so you have a 'sandwich'. Transfer to a greased baking tray, then place in an oven preheated to 200°C and bake for about 25 minutes, or until golden brown. The cakes should be springy to the touch. Cool on a wire rack, but serve warm.

BLAUNCHT MANCHET – FRIED WHITE BREAD PUDDING
A New Booke of Cookerie, 1615

A vegetarian pudding. It should be golden brown, not crisp and is best served hot.

'Take halfe a dozen eggs, halfe a pint of sweet Creame, a penny manchet grated, a nutmeg grated, two spoonfuls of Rosewater, two ounces of suger: Worke all stiffe like a Pudding: then fry like a Tansey in a very little frying Pan, that it may be thicke: fry it browne, and turn it out upon a plate. Cut it in quarters and serve it like a pudding: scrape on Sugar.'

Ingredients: 2 large eggs; ⅓ cup cream; 2 cups fresh, untoasted breadcrumbs; 1 tsp rose water; ¾ tsp nutmeg, grated; 1½ tbsp sugar; ½ tsp butter for frying; sugar to sprinkle.

Method: Beat eggs lightly, then add cream, sugar, rose water and nutmeg. Mix in the breadcrumbs until well dampened. It will form a thick batter. Lightly grease a 6-inch frying pan, using ½ to 1 tsp butter. Pour the batter into the pan and it will be about 1 inch thick. Cook on the lowest heat the first side for about 5 minutes, until the bottom and side are golden brown and beginning to pull away from the sides. ½ inch from the edge should look a little darker and dryer. Carefully turn over with a spatula. Cook the second side for about 3 minutes until done. Test with a knife, which should come out dry. Turn out onto a plate, slice into sixths and sprinkle lightly with sugar or brush with butter or lemon juice.

WAFFLES QUATRE MODES – FOUR WAYS WITH WAFFLES
Le Ménagier De Paris, 1393

'Waffles are made in four ways. In the first, beat eggs in a bowl, then salt and wine, and add flour, and moisten the one with the other, and then put in two irons little by little, each time using as much batter as a slice of cheese is wide, and clap between two irons, and cook one side and then the other; and if the iron does not easily release the batter, anoint with a little cloth soaked in oil or fat. – The second way is like the first, but add cheese, that is, spread the batter as though making a tart or pie, then put slices of cheese in the middle, and cover the edges [with batter]: thus the cheese stays within the batter and thus you put it between two irons. – The third method, is for dropped waffles, called dropped only because the batter is thinner like clear soup, made as above; and throw in with it fine cheese grated; and mix it all together. – The fourth method is with flour mixed with water, salt and wine, without eggs or cheese.

Item, waffles can be used when one speaks of the "large sticks" which are made of flour mixed with eggs and powdered ginger beaten together, and made as big as and shaped like sausages; cook between two irons.'

SAVELOY – SPICED PORK, BACON AND CHEESE SAUSAGES

Das Kochbuch der Sabina Welserin (Sabina Welserin's Cookbook), 1553

The Saveloy sausage was one of the classic boiled sausages throughout Europe, including England, during the Tudor and early Stuart periods.

'*Wie man zerwúlawirstlach machen soll* (How one should make Saveloy): First take four pounds of pork from the tender area of the leg and two pounds of bacon. Let this be finely chopped and add to it three ounces of salt, one pound of grated cheese, one and one half ounces of pepper and one and one half ounces of ginger.'

Ingredients: 1.8 kg pork, taken from the leg; 900 g bacon; 90 g salt; 450 g cheese, grated; 45 g freshly-ground black pepper; 45 g ground ginger; 45 g ground cinnamon; 7.5 g ground cloves; 7.5 g freshly-grated nutmeg; 30 g brown sugar; artificial or natural sausage casings; 7 g saffron.

Method: Wash the sausage casings, place in a large pan or bowl with the saffron and cover with warm water. Set aside to soak and colour, as you prepare the filling. Mince the pork and bacon then place in a large bowl and knead in the salt, cheese, black pepper, ginger, cinnamon, cloves, nutmeg and sugar. Drain the sausage casings, reserving the saffron and soaking liquid, and fill with water to expand them. Now stuff the meat and cheese mixture into the casings and form into links. Place the saffron and casing soaking liquid in a large pot. Add more water and bring to the boil. Add the sausages and boil for 6 minutes. After this time you can freeze the sausages to store. Either fry or re-boil to use.

SOBRE SAWCE – PRUDENT SAUCE

The Master-Cook of Richard II, *The Forme of Cury*, *c.* 1390

Toasted bread drizzled with honey syrup flavoured with 'good powder'.

'Take raisins and grind them with crusts of bread and strain it up with wine. Add to this good powders and salt and boil it. Fry roaches, loaches, soles or other good fish, pour over the sauce and serve it forth.'

Ingredients: 150 g raisins; 6 tbsp bread; 300 ml white wine; 2 tsp good powder (see spices chapter); salt, to taste.

Method: Pound together the raisins and bread in a mortar, or purée in a blender. Work in the wine, then turn into a pan. Bring to the boil, reduce to a simmer and cook until thickened. It was popular as a sauce to pour over fried fish.

The Tudor Kitchen

CRUSTE ROLLE – HENRY VIII'S CRACKERS

Two Fifteenth Century Cookbooks – Harleian MS. 279 & Harl. MS. 4016, c.
1440

This is a fried cracker, a little like a tortilla chip, used like breadsticks before eating, or as a dessert if coated in sugar. Many historians believe that Henry VIII did actually go 'crackers' after a jousting fall that nearly killed him. His personality altered remarkably.

'Take fayre smal floure of whete, nym Eyroun and breke therto and coloure the past with safroun; rolle in on a borde al so thinne as parchment, round about as an oblye [a sacramental wafer used in Mass], frye them and serve forth.'

Ingredients: 2 cups flour; 3 beaten eggs or egg yolks; pinch of saffron; dash of salt; oil for frying.

Method: Mix the flour with the eggs until it is like dough. Add a little water if it is too dry, or flour if too wet. Roll out with flour several times until it is stretchy, flexible and easy to handle. Roll paper-thin – this is easier with a pasta maker – and cut in small circles or squares, about 2–3 inches in diameter. Deep-fry in hot oil for only a few seconds, until golden brown. Sprinkle with salt and a topping, such as garlic powder, herbs or sesame seeds. Eat while warm.

CROSS BUN, GOOD FRIDAY BUN, ST ALBANS BUN – HOT CROSS BUN

Hannah Glasse *The Art Of Cookery*, 1740

This is a spiced, sweet bun dating from medieval times, which became popular under the Tudors, but there appears to be no earlier recipe. The tradition of baking bread marked with a cross is linked to paganism as well as Christianity. The barbarian Saxons would bake cross buns at the beginning of spring in honour of the goddess *Eostre*, the origin of the name Easter. The cross represented the rebirth of the world after winter and the four quarters of the moon, as well as the four seasons and the wheel of life. Christians saw the Crucifixion in the cross bun and the spices came to represent those in which Jesus was embalmed and they replaced the pagan meaning with a Christian one, the resurrection of Christ at Easter. As Christianity spread, it seems that monks adopted a long-standing custom of marking loaves with a cross to make portion cutting easier, to represent Christ's cross. In many Christian countries, buns are traditionally eaten hot or toasted during Lent, beginning with the evening of Shrove Tuesday, to midday Good Friday. Under Elizabeth I, in 1592, the London Clerk of Markets issued a decree forbidding the sale of hot cross buns and other spiced breads, except at burials, on Good Friday or at Christmas. The punishment for transgressing was the forfeiture of all the forbidden product to the poor. Of course the poor could not afford spices necessary for making the buns. The decree was because they were not of a size permitted by law in relation to bread products and such restrictions continued until well into the seventeenth century.

Superstitions surround the buns, one being that buns baked and served on Good Friday will not spoil, nor grow mouldy during the subsequent year. A piece of it given to someone ill was said to help them recover. Bread baked on Good Friday was grated to be used as a medicine in later years. If taken on a sea voyage, cross buns were said to protect against shipwreck. If hung in the kitchen, they protected against fires and ensured that all breads turn out perfectly, being replaced each year. From the diary of Samuel Pepys we know that on Good Friday in 1664 he ate buns (or 'wiggs') but rather than for breakfast he had them just before he went to bed, with some ale, which he called a 'Lenten supper'. These Good Friday buns merely have the cross cut into the buns rather than piped on top with flour and water paste or rolled pastry. They used no fruit and were flavoured with spices such as caraway, nutmeg and coriander. As time passed and affluence increased, the recipes changed, adding fruit and varying the spices. They were simply called cross buns, until the first recorded reference to 'hot' cross buns in *Poor Robin's Almanac* in the early 1700s: 'Good Friday come this month, the old woman runs. / With one or two a penny hot cross buns.' This satirical rhyme was also probably the inspiration of the commonly known street vendors' cry:
'Hot cross buns, hot cross buns!
One ha'penny, two ha'penny, hot cross buns!
If you have no daughters, give them to your sons,
One ha'penny, two ha'penny, hot cross buns!'

St Alban's Cathedral is campaigning for the revival of the Alban bun, which since 1361 has been given out to the local poor on Good Friday. A denser, more cakey product than the supermarket hot cross bun, it claims to be the precursor to the modern version. It has two major differences: the cross is cut into the top of the bun, rather than piped on top, and its ingredients include grains of paradise. The Very Rev Jeffrey John, Dean of St Albans Cathedral, said: 'Recently we've lost touch with the significance of the bun, and its link to Holy Week and the Cross.' The Cathedral has persuaded the local Sainsbury's to produce the Alban bun, using the original medieval recipe, with wholemeal flour, milk, cardamom and yeast, on a commercial scale in the run up to Easter. The recipe is said to date back to 1361, when a local monk called Thomas Rockcliffe first started distributing them on Good Friday to the poor of the city. The Victorian baker Frederick Vine, in *Saleable Shop Goods* of 1898, gives us illustrated instructions on how to make a bun docker, the special tool used to cross the buns.

'TAKE two pounds of fine flour, a pint of good ale-yeast, put a little sack [sweet white wine] in the yeast, and three eggs beaten, knead all these together with a little warm milk, a little nutmeg, and a little salt; and lay it before the fire till it rises very light, then knead in a pound of fresh butter, a pound of rough carraway comfits, and bake them in a quick oven, in what shape you please, on floured paper.'

Ingredients: 4 cups all purpose flour; 1 tsp salt; 1 level tsp allspice or mixed spice; 2 oz butter; ½ cup currants, or raisins or sultanas; 1 oz yeast; ½ cup sugar; 1 cup milk.

Method: Sift the flour, salt and spice into a large bowl. Rub in the butter and then add the currants. Warm the milk. Cream the yeast and sugar together and add to the warm milk. Leave to rest for about 10 minutes until the batter is of sponge-like consistency. Add the milk mixture to the ingredients in the bowl and mix to form a dough. Leave to rise in a warm place until dough has doubled in size. Turn out onto a floured surface and knead well, then cut into 12 pieces. Flatten each piece into a circle. Using a knife, mark each bun deeply with a cross. Allow to rest again for about 10 minutes. Bake in the oven at 200°C for 20 minutes. Glaze with sugar dissolved in water.

SHROPSHIRE BISCUITS – EASTER BISCUITS

Traditional Shropshire recipe

As an easier and cheaper alternative to cross buns, many counties developed recipes for 'Easter Biscuits.' They differed from biscuits available at other times of the year only in that they were originally made with allspice, which was also used in the cross bun. Shropshire is one of the counties claiming to be the originator of Easter biscuits.

Ingredients: 2 cups all-purpose flour; 4 oz butter; 1 cup sugar; grated rind of ½ a lemon; ¼ tsp of allspice or mixed spice; ½ tsp of baking powder; 1 egg; ¼ cup of currants.

Method: Rub the butter into the flour and add the sugar, lemon rind, allspice, baking powder and currants. Make into a dough with a little of the beaten egg. Roll out the dough to a thickness of ¼ inch and cut into biscuits. Bake on a baking tray for 20 minutes at 180°C. Remove them from the oven, dust with sugar and leave to cool.

SHREWSBURY SIMNEL – SIMNEL CAKE

Traditional, dating from pre-Tudor times.

This was originally made for the middle Sunday of Lent, when the 40-day fast would be relaxed. This was known as *Laetare* Sunday, Refreshment Sunday, Mothering Sunday, Sunday of the Five Loaves and Simnel Sunday (after the cake). This was the day when the congregations of the daughter churches of a parish went to the mother church, usually an abbey, to give their offerings. In the seventeenth century, Mothering Sunday became the day when girls and boys in service were allowed a day off to go and visit their mothers. The girls might bake their mothers a Simnel cake as a gift. Simnel cakes have been baked since the Middle Ages and it is believed that the word comes from the Latin *simila*, a very fine flour made from wheat, which also gives us the word semolina. The cakes were difficult to make, but if made properly they would keep for a few weeks. Thus the baking of a simnel cake for Mothering Sunday was not only a gift from a girl to her mother, but also a test of the girl's cooking skills. The cake would not be eaten until Easter Sunday and the whole family would be anxious to see if the cake was still moist. With the demise of service after the First World War, the simnel cake began to be treated as an Easter cake in its own right. From Victorian times, the cake was decorated with eleven marzipan balls, representing Jesus' disciples, minus Judas the traitor. Originally it was also decorated with fresh flowers, but sugar flowers are often used today.

There are several different kinds of simnel cake. The Devizes simnel Cake was made with currants and lemon peel, coloured golden with saffron and always made in a star shape, 'boiled, baked and glazed'. The Bury simnel cake is a flat spiced cake and possibly the first to have the Victorian additions of marzipan balls. The best known of all is the Shrewsbury simnel with a central layer of marzipan in a rich fruit cake with saffron, boiled and baked and decorated on top with a circle of points.

Ingredients for cake: 6 oz butter; ¾ cup sugar; 2 cups plain flour; 1¼ tsp baking powder; 3 eggs; 3 cups mixed dried fruit; ½ cup chopped almonds; ½ cup cherries; ½ cup mixed peel; 2 tbsp milk; 1 tsp mixed spice.

Ingredients for almond paste: 2 cups ground almonds; 1 cup confectioners icing; sugar; ½ cup caster sugar; 1 tsp lemon juice; 2 drops almond essence; 1 beaten egg.

Method: Cream the butter and sugar together. Sieve the flour, baking powder and mixed spice together. Beat the eggs and add, one at a time, with a spoonful of the flour, into the butter and sugar mixture. Add all the other ingredients and fold in carefully. Make the almond paste by mixing almonds, icing sugar and sugar together. Add the lemon juice, almond essence and enough egg to form a fairly dry paste. Cut the almond paste in two and roll out one half to the size of an 8-inch diameter cake tin. Put half the cake mixture into the greased tin, then place the almond paste layer on top before adding the rest of the cake mixture. Bake in oven at 150°C for 2 to 2 ½ hours. It is difficult to test with a fork to see if the cake is cooked, as the almond paste is sticky when hot. Press the cake with a finger and it should be firm. Allow to cool in the tin for a short while before turning out. When cool, decorate with the remaining almond paste.

BARA CEIRCH (1) – WELSH OATCAKES
Traditional medieval Celtic – similar to Scottish bannocks

Oatcakes are a popular bakestone treat, traditionally eaten on May Day. Oatcakes have been a staple in all Celtic countries since ancient times, but the method of preparation is different depending on the region. Always use a warm bakestone or a wide, flat pancake pan, but any heavy, non-stick pan will do. Oatcakes must be pressed and rolled out as quickly as possible. It is not advisable to mix too many at the same time.

Ingredients: 1½ tsp bacon dripping; 110 ml tepid water; 450 g oatmeal.

Method: Combine the dripping and the water and mix well. Place the oatmeal in a bowl and add the liquid gradually, using just enough to form a dough that holds together well but is not sticky. Mould the dough into a ball then flatten into a circle. Roll out carefully, playing close attention to keeping an even edge. Roll until the cake is about 3 mm thick and about the size of the bakestone or pan. Transfer to the hot bakestone, or a heavy, dry frying pan, and cook for around 4 minutes on each side until golden brown. Remove from the heat and leave to harden in a warm place before serving.

BARA CEIRCH (2) – WELSH OATCAKES
Traditional medieval Celtic – similar to Scottish bannocks

Ingredients: 3 tbsp hot water; 4 tbsp oatmeal; ½ tbsp bacon fat; pinch of salt; flour; cheese (optional).

Method: In a saucepan, melt the bacon fat in hot water, then sprinkle in oatmeal. Knead for several minutes, then roll out onto a floured board. Roll thin. Cut the dough into large or small rounds. Cook on a medium–hot griddle, warmed bakestone or cast iron frying pan for about 10 minutes. Remove from heat and allow to harden. Perhaps serve with slices of cheese.

11

Preserves, Spices and Sauces

Apothecaries as well as spice merchants sold two main spice combinations ready prepared – *powdre (poudre) douce* and *powdre (poudre) forte*. *Powdre douce* means sweet spice, not unlike the mixed cake spice mixture available today and including fennel, aniseed and sugar. Strong spice, or *powdre forte* included a variety of early peppers – cubebs, grains of paradise and peppercorns, ground together with cloves, mace, cinnamon and ginger, to give quite a kick.

POUDRE DOUCE – SWEET POWDER TWO WAYS

There exist many different recipes for this sweet spice mix, used to season desserts and fruit. The fourteenth-century manuscript *Le Menagier de Paris* suggested a mix of grains of paradise, ginger, cinnamon, nutmeg, sugar and galingal/galingale. There is a related mixed spice, *poudre-forte*, 'strong powder'. The following are easy modern versions which will keep for several months in an airtight jar.

Ingredients 1: 1 tbsp ground hyssop; 1 tbsp aniseed; 1 tbsp fennel seeds; 4 tbsp sugar.

Ingredients 2: 3 tbsp ginger; 1 ½ tbsp cinnamon; 1 tsp cloves; 1 tsp nutmeg; 2 tbsp sugar.

Method: Grind all the ingredients together in a pestle and mortar and use immediately and/or store.

POUDRE FORTE – STRONG POWDER

Anonymous, Venetian *Libro di cucina/ Libro per cuoco*, fourteenth to fifteenth century

This again is one of the spice blends prominent in medieval and Tudor cuisine, but each cook might personalize the blend to his/her own taste or to the nature of the dish. The two common ingredients that make the blend 'strong' are pepper and either ginger or cinnamon.

'Fine spices for all things. Take one ounce of pepper, one of cinnamon, one of ginger, half a quarter of cloves, and a quarter of saffron.'

Ingredients: ¼ cup powdered ginger; ¼ cup long pepper, ground; 1½ tsp cloves, ground; ¼ cup ground cinnamon; ¼ cup ground black pepper.

Method: Combine all ingredients together and place in an airtight jar.

BLACK AND STRONG SPICES

Anonymous, Venetian *Libro di cucina/ Libro per cuoco*, 14th–15th century

'Black and strong spices to make sauces. Take half a quarter of an ounce of cloves, two ounces of pepper and an equal quantity of long pepper and nutmeg and do as all spices [grind].'

POUDRE FINE – FINE POWDER

Le Ménagier de Paris, 1393

'Fine powder of spices. Take an ounce and a drachma of white ginger, a quarter-ounce of hand-picked cinnamon, half a quarter-ounce each of grains and cloves, and a quarter-ounce of rock sugar, and grind to powder.'

Ingredients: 3 tbsp ginger; 2 tbsp sugar; 1½ tbsp cinnamon; 1 tsp cloves; 1 tsp grains of paradise.

Method: Grind fine and store in airtight container.

GODE POWDER – GOOD POWDER

As with the above strong, sweet and fine powders, each cook had his/her own preference and this recipe comes from a number of medieval and Tudor sources as a composite, all-purpose spice mix, used to season sweet dishes.

Ingredients: 1 tbsp ground cinnamon; 1½ tbsp ground mace; ½ tbsp ground pepper; 2 tbsp ground galingale; 1 tbsp crushed cardamom.

Method: Grind all ingredients together in a pestle and mortar and store in an airtight jar. This will keep for several months.

A SAWCE FOR A ROSTED RABBIT: TO KING HENRY THE EIGHTH

John Partridge's *The Treasurie of Commodious Conceits & Hidden Secrets*, 1573

A chafing dish (French *chauffer*, to make warm) was a portable grate raised on a tripod, heated with charcoal in a brazier and used for foods which require gentle cooking, away from the stronger heat of direct flames. It could be used at table, or provided with a cover for keeping food warm on a buffet.

'A Sawce for a rosted Rabbet: to King Henry the eight. Take an handful of washed percelye, mince it small, boyle it with Butter and verjuce upon a

---

chaffing dish, season it with sugre and a little Pepper gross beaten, when it is redi: put in a few fine Crumes of white bread, put it in amongst the other, let it boyle agayne till it be standing, the lay it in a Platter, lyke the breadth of three fingers, lay of each side one rosted Conye (or more) and so serve them.'

VINEGRE ROSET – TO MAKE VINEGAR OF ROSES, VIOLETS OR ELDER FLOWERS

John Partridge's *The Treasurie of Commodious Conceits & Hidden Secrets*, 1573

'In Sommer time when Roses blowe, gather them ere they be full spred or blowne out, and in dry wether: plucke the leaves, let them lye halfe a day upon a fayre borde, then have a vessel with Vineger of one or two gallons (if you wyll make so much roset,) put therein a great quantity of the sayd leaves, stop the vessell close after that you have styrred them wel together, let it stand a day and a night, then devide your Vineger and Rose leaves together in two parts put the in two great Glasses and put in Rose leaves ynoughe, stop the Glasses close, set them upon a Shelfe under a wall syde, on the Southside wtout your house where the Sonne may come to them the most parte of the daye, let them stande there all the whole Somer longe: and then strayne the vineger from the Roses, and keepe the vinegre. If you shall once in .x. dayes, take and strain out Rose leaves, and put in newe leaves of halfe a dayes gatheryng, the vyneger wyll haue the more flavor and odour of the Rose. You may use in steede of Vinegre, wyne: that it may wexe eygre, and receive ye vertue of the Roses, both at once. Moreover, you may make your vineger of wine white, red, or claret, but the red doth most binde the bellie, and white doth most lose. Also the Damaske Rose is not so great a binder as the red Rose, and the white Rose loose the most of all: wereof you may make vinegre roset. Thus also, you may make Uinegre of Uiolets, or of Elder flowers: but you must first gather and vse your flowers of Eldern, as shal be shewed hereafter, when we speake of makyng Conserve of Elderne flowers.'

THE VERTUE OF THE CONSERVE OF ELDER FLOWRES

John Partridge's *The Treasurie of Commodious Conceits & Hidden Secrets*, 1573

'Conserve of the flowres of Elder is good agaynst the morphewe, it clenseth the stomack, and ye whol body from scabbs. Gather the clusters, or bunches whereon ye flowres grow when they are newe blowne and spreade: lay them vpon a fayre sheete abrode in a Chamber a daye or two tyll ye shal perceve ye flowre wyll shake off and fall awaye, then pyke thm cleane, and make therof conserve, as ye do of other flowres. And whereas it is more holsome then pleasant, therfore put some other conserve (suche as ye luste) amongst it, when ye wyl occupy it.'

SAUSE FOR ROST CAPON – CITRUS FRUIT SAUCE FOR CHICKEN

Gervase Markham's *Countrey Contentments, or, The English Hus-wife*, 1615

'To make an excellent sause for a rost Capon, you shall take Onions, and having sliced and peeled them, boyle them in fair water with Pepper, Salt, and a few bread crummes: then put unto it a spoonfull or two of claret Wine, the juyce of an Orenge, and three or four slices of Lemmon peel: all these shred together, and so pour it upon the Capon being broke up.'

Ingredients: 400 g finely-chopped onion; ¼ tsp minced lemon peel; 330 ml orange juice with 1 tbsp lemon juice added; 2 tbsp dry red or white wine; 2 tbsp breadcrumbs; salt and pepper to taste.

Method: Place the onion in the bottom of a saucepan and add just enough water to cover. Bring this to the boil and season with salt and pepper. Leave to simmer for about 15 minutes, and then add the remaining ingredients. Bring the liquid back to the boil and simmer until it thickens. Serve over baked chicken breasts.

CAPON SAUCE

A.W., *The Booke of Goode Cookry Very Necessary for all Such as Delight Therein*, 1584, 1591

'To make sauce for a capon another way. Take Claret Wine, Rosewater, sliced Orenges, Sinamon and ginger, and lay it upon Sops, and lay your Capon upon it.'

CANDIED GOOS-BERRIES – GOOSEBERRY CONSERVE

A Closet for Ladies and Gentlewomen. Or, The Art of Preseruing, Conseruing, and Candying, 1602–08

Though the date of the book puts it in the Stuart period, it was actually registered with the London Company of Stationers on 1 September 1602 and not published until 1608, which makes it a late Elizabethan book.

'To Candy Goos-berries. Take of your faireſt Berries, but they muſt not bee two ripe, for then they will not bee ſo good, and with a linen cloth wipe them verie cleane, and picke off all the ſtaulkes from them, and weigh them, and to euery ounce of Berries, you muſt take two ounces of ſuger, and halfe an ounce of Sugercandy, and diſſolue them in an ounce or two of Roſe water, and ſo boyle them vp to the height of Manus Chriſti, and when it is come to his perfect height, let it coole and put in your Berries, for if you put them in hot, they will ſhrinke, and ſo ſtirre them round with a wooden ſpatter, till they bee candied: and thus put them vp and keepe them.'

Ingredients: 500 g gooseberries (not too ripe), topped, tailed and washed; 1 kg sugar; 225 g candied sugar; 75 ml rose water.

Method: For candied sugar (sugar candy), take the weight of the candied sugar asked for, and dissolve it in half as much water, i.e. 115 g. Bring it to the boil, add a splash of lemon juice and boil for several minutes until it caramelizes into an amber, candied sugar. Combine the sugars and rose water in a saucepan. Heat gently until the sugar has dissolved, then bring to the boil. Continue cooking, stirring frequently, until the sugar reaches 112°C, as measured on a confectioner's thermometer. Remove from the heat and allow to cool slightly then add your gooseberries. Stir the gooseberries into the syrup with a wooden spoon until they are completely covered. Spoon the coated gooseberries into jars that have been sterilized and warmed in the oven. Top up with the syrup, seal with the lid and set aside to cool. Store in a cool, dark, cupboard. Alternatively, line baking trays with greaseproof paper and when the gooseberries are nicely coated in sugar arrange on the paper, allow to harden and serve as sweetmeats.

CANDIE OF ORENGE PILLES – ELIZABETHAN ORANGE SWEETMEATS

Delightes of Ladies to adorne their Persons, Closets, and distillatories with Beauties, banquets, perfumes and waters. Reade, Practise and Censure, 1602

'To candie Orenge pilles. Take your Orenge pilles after they be preferued, then take fine fugar and Rofewater, and boile it to the height of Manus Chrifti, then drawe through your fugar, then lay them on the bottome of a fieue, and dry them in an ouen after you haue drawne bread, and thy will be candied.'

Ingredients: Peel from 4 thick-skinned oranges; juice of the oranges; 400 g caster sugar; 400 ml water; 2 tbsp rose water.

Method: Peel the oranges then squeeze the juice and reserve. Slice the orange peels into pieces about 3 cm wide. Set these aside to soak in the orange juice. Combine the 200 g caster sugar and 400 ml water in a pan. Bring to a simmer. When the sugar has dissolved, add the strips of orange peel and the orange juice. Return to a simmer and cook gently for about 20 minutes, or until the orange peels are tender. Remove from the heat and set aside to cool for 1 hour. After this time, return the mixture to the heat, bring back to a simmer and cook for 20 minutes more. Take off the heat and set aside to soak in the syrup over night. The following day, remove the cooked orange peels from the syrup. Combine the second portion of caster sugar and rose water in a small pan. Heat until the sugar dissolves and then bring to the boil and cook until the sugar reaches 110–13°C as measured on a confectioner's thermometer. Add the orange peel strips and stir into the syrup. Take off the heat and allow to cool very slightly. Using a fork, remove the orange peel pieces and arrange them in a single layer on a baking tray covered with greaseproof paper.

Transfer to an oven preheated to 140°C and leave them in the oven for about 1 hour, or until the sugar coating has set. Allow to cool and store in an airtight jar until needed. These can be eaten as sweetmeats or they can be used as ingredients for cakes and cake decorations.

KEEPING POMGRANATES – STORED POMEGRANATES
Sir Hugh Plat's *Delightes for Ladies*, 1602

'Keeping of Pomgranats. Make choice of such Pomgranates as are sound and not prickt as they tearme it, lap them over thinly with wax, hang them upon naales, where they may touch nothing, in some cupboard or closet in your bedchamber, wher you keep a continual fire, and every 3 or 4 daies turn the undersides uppermost, and therefore you must so hang them in packthread, that they may have a bowe knot at either end. This way Pomgranates have been kept fresh till whitsontide.'

CHERIES FRUT LETHER – CHERRY, PLUM, PRUNE OR DAMSON FRUIT LEATHER
Delightes of Ladies to adorne their Persons, Closets, and distillatories with Beauties, banquets, perfumes and waters. Reade, Practise and Censure, 1602

Cherry, plum, prune or damson pulp is boiled until almost dry and then dried in an oven. Essentially this is a recipe for preserving fruit for winter. Modern leathers would probably have 2 tbsp honey and 1 tbsp lemon juice added per 500 ml of fruit pulp. This Elizabethan version is far more acid and, unusually for the period, contains no sweeteners.

'Cheries Frut Lether. How to keepe the drie pulpe of cheries, Prunes, Damsons. all the yeare. Take the kinde of cherries which are sharp in taste (Quære if the common black and redde cherrie will not also serue, hauing in the ende of the decoction a little oyle of Vitrioll or Sulphur, or some veriuice of soure grapes, or iuice of Lemmons mixed therewith, to giue a sufficient tartnesse) pull of their stalks and boile them by themselues without the addition of any liquor in a caldron or pipken, and when they begin once to boile in their own iuice, stir them hard at the bottom with a spattle, least they burn to the pans bottom. They haue boyled sufficiently, when thy haue caste off all their skins, and that the pulp and substance of the cherries is grown to a thicke pap: then take it from the fire, and let it coole, then diuide the stones and skins, by passing the pulpe onely through the bottome of a strainer reuersed as they vse in caffia fistula, then take this pulpe and spread it thin vpon glazed stones or dishes, and so let it drie in the sunne, or else in an ouen presently after you haue drawne your breade, then loose it from the stone or dish, and keepe it to prouoke the appetite, and to coole the stomacke in feuers, and all other hote diseases. Proue the fame in all manner of fruit. If you feare aduſtion in this worke, you may finiſh it in hote balneo.'

Ingredients: 500 g pitted cherries, or similar fruit; 2 tbsp verjuice or lemon juice.

Method: Place the fruit in a large pan with a tight-fitting lid. Heat gently until the fruit begins to break down, then bring to the boil and continue boiling, stirring constantly, until the cherries have completely broken down and the mixture is thick. Remove from the heat and pass through a fine-meshed sieve, pressing down with the back of a spoon to extract as much pulp as possible. Stir the lemon juice into the pulp then set aside to cool. Line a baking tray with heatproof cling film. The average baking tray of about 30 cm x 42 cm will hold about 500 ml of purée. Add the purée to the covered baking tray and spread evenly with a spatula to a depth of about 4 mm. Place the tray in an oven preheated to 140°C. However, leave the door ajar to let the steam escape and dry the leather. Cook for about 6 hours, or until the fruit leather is very dry. The exact drying time will depend on the sugar levels, the more sugar the longer it will take to dry. The leather must be completely dry, or it will not keep. To ensure the leather is dry simply try to pull it away from the cling film. If it comes away easily and holds its shape then it is dry. To store, cover the fruit leather in cling film and roll loosely. Place in a clean, dry airtight container. It will keep in the store cupboard for between 4 and 12 months or you can refrigerate and keep it even longer.

THE BEST CARMELINE SAUCE

Anonymous, Venetian *Libro di cucina/ Libro per cuoco*, 14th–15th century

'To make the best carmeline sauce, take peeled almonds, grind and strain them [to produce almond milk]. Take currants, cinnamon, cloves and a little bit of bread crumb, and mix everything together, temper with verjuice and it is done.'

CAMELINE SAUCE – VINEGAR AND CINNAMON SAUCE

Le Viandier de Guillaume Tirel dit Taillevent, c. 1440

'Cameline: To Make Cameline Sauce. Grind ginger, a great deal of cinnamon, cloves, grains of paradise, mace, and if you wish, long pepper; strain bread that has been moistened in vinegar, strain everything together and salt as necessary.'

Ingredients: 1 cup each cider vinegar and water; ½ tsp cinnamon; ¼ tsp each of ginger, cloves, mace, grains of paradise, pepper and salt.

Method: Combine liquids, add spices and mix thoroughly with a wire whisk.

Taste for seasonings and adjust accordingly. Use immediately or refrigerate for later use.

ELIZABETHAN MUSTARD – GINGER AND HORSERADISH MUSTARD
The Closet of the Eminently Learned Sir Kenelme Digbie Kt Opened, 1669

'The best way of making Mustard is this: Take of the best Mustard-seed (which is black) for example, a quart. Dry it gently in an Oven, and beat it to a subtle powder, and searse it. Then mingle well strong Wine-vinegar with it, so much that it be pretty liquid, for it will dry with keeping. Put to this a little Pepper beaten small (white is the best) at discretion, as about a good pugil, and put a good spoonful of Sugar to it (which is not to make it taste sweet, but rather quick, and to help the fermentation) lay a good Onion in the bottom, quartered if you will, and a race of Ginger scraped and bruised; and stir it often with an Horseradish root cleansed, which let always lie in the pot till it have lost its virtue, then take a new one. This will keep long, and grow better for a while. It is not good till after a month, that it hath fermented a while. Some think it will be the quicker, if the seed be ground with fair water [clear spring water], instead of Vinegar, putting store of Onions in it.'

Ingredients: 450 g brown or black mustard seeds; ½ large white onion; ½ hand of ginger, peeled; ½ horseradish root about 6 inches long, peeled; 1 tsp white pepper; ½ tsp sugar; cider vinegar.

Method: Toast the mustard seed in a pan until it begins to colour and you can smell the aroma. Grind the mustard as fine as you can in a blender. Purée the onion, ginger and horseradish in a blender. Add the pepper and sugar to the purée and pour this over the ground mustard. Mix well and cover the bowl with a towel. Leave over night. The following day add a little cider vinegar to form a smooth but stiff paste. If you want a smoother mustard, place in a blender and blend a little more. Place in a bottle or sterilised jar and leave for two weeks for the flavour to develop before consuming. Store in a refrigerator once opened.

BROOM CAPERS IN VERJUICE
Delightes of Ladies to adorne their Persons, Closets, and distillatories with Beauties, banquets, perfumes and waters. Reade, Practise and Censure, 1602

Broom capers are the flower buds of the broom plant. Unlike many flower buds these are available most of the year, though most common in spring and early summer. Nasturtium flower buds, nasturtium seed pods and gorse flower buds can be preserved in the same manner. Mediterranean capers are quite expensive, so these make an excellent, and cheap, substitute. These can

The Tudor Kitchen

be used to garnish salads and make an unusual substitute for capers in fish sauces.

'To preferue broome capers all the yeare. Boyle a quart of Veriuice and an handfull of baye falte, and therein you may keepe them all the yeare.'

Ingredients: 500 ml verjuice or white wine vinegar; 5 tbsp fine sea salt; 400 ml freshly-picked broom buds, washed and drained dry in a colander.

Method: Combine the verjuice and salt in a saucepan. Bring to a boil and cook until the salt has dissolved. Add the broom buds and cook for 1 minute, then take off the heat. Strain out the broom buds and pack into jars that have been washed, sterilized and dried in the oven. Pour the hot pickle into the jars, cover with vinegar-proof lids and set aside to cool. Set aside to mature for at least 3 weeks before using.

PRESERVED COWCUMBER – TUDOR GHERKINS

Sir Hugh Plat, *Delightes for Ladies to adorne their Persons, Closets, and distillatories with Beauties, banquets, perfumes and waters. Reade, Practise and Censure*, 1602

This is the recipe for 'dill pickles' that are still used today. A 'pottle' is an Elizabethan unit of measurement of half a gallon, approximately 2.25 litres. If using tap water, boil and set aside to cool before use to remove any chlorine.

'To preferue Cowcumbers all the yeere. Take a galon of faire water, and a pottle of veriuice, and a pint of bay falt, and a handfull of green fennell or Dill: boyle it a little, and when it is cold put it into a barrel, and then put your Cowcumbers into that pickle, and you fhal keep them all the yeere.'

Ingredients: 500 ml water; 250 ml verjuice or white wine vinegar; 2½ tbsp sea salt; 500 ml baby cucumbers (gherkins); a few sprigs of dill or fennel fronds.

Method: Combine the water, verjuice and salt in pan. Bring to a boil and cook for a few minutes. Remove from the heat and allow to cool slightly. Wash and pat the baby cucumbers dry. Pack into a large jar with the dill or fennel. Pour the hot, but not boiling, brine over them and seal securely with a vinegar-proof lid. Allow to cool, label and set aside for at least two weeks to mature before opening. Once opened store in a refrigerator.

AGLIATA – ROASTED GARLIC SAUCE

Anonymous, Venetian *Libro di cucina/ Libro per cuoco*, 14th–15th century

'Agliata to serve with every meat. Take a bulb of garlic and roast it under the coals. Grind the roasted garlic and mix with ground raw garlic, bread crumbs and sweet spices. Mix with broth, put into a pan and let it boil a little before serving warm.'

CONSERVE OF STRAWBERIES – ELIZABETHAN STRAWBERRY JAM

Delightes of Ladies to adorne their Persons, Closets, and distillatories with Beauties, banquets, perfumes and waters. Reade, Practise and Censure, 1602

This is a classic method of preserving strawberries by boiling with white wine and sugar until the setting point is reached.

'To make conferue of ftrawberies. Firft feeth them in water, and then caft away the water, and ftraine them, then boyle them in white wine, and work as before in damfons, or elfe ftraine them being ripe, then boyle them in wine and fugar till they be ftiffe.'

Ingredients: 1 kg strawberries; 1 kg sugar; 100 ml dry white wine.

Method: Pick over the strawberries, remove any stalks, wash and dry thoroughly. Bring a pan of water to the boil, drop in the strawberries and cook for about 5 minutes, or until just tender but still whole. Drain the fruit in a colander then turn into a clean pan and mash with a potato masher. Add the wine and bring to a simmer. Allow the fruit and wine mix to cook for 20 minutes or until the fruit is tender and the juices are running freely. Remove the pan from the heat, then add the sugar, stirring until completely dissolved. Return to the heat, bring to the boil and cook rapidly for about 15–20 minutes. Skim the surface then ladle into sterilized jars that have been warmed in an oven set to 100°C for 5 minutes. Allow 1 cm of head space then secure the lid, allow to cool and store.

APRICOCKE PRESERVE

A Closet for Ladies and Gentlewomen. Or, The Art of Preseruing, Conseruing, and Candying, 1602–08

'To preferue Apricockes. Take a pound of Apricockes, and a pound of fugar, and claryfie your fugar with a pint of water, and when your fugar is made perfect, put it into a Preferuing-pan, and put your Apricockes into it and fo let them boyle gently, and when they bee boyled ynough and your Syrope thicke, pot them and fo keepe them. In like maner may you preferue a Pear-plum.'

Ingredients: 500 g apricots; 500 g granulated sugar; 500 ml water.

Method: Combine the sugar and water in a pan. Heat gently until the sugar dissolves, then bring to a simmer and continue thickening until the sugar has caramelised and the syrup has thickened. Halve the apricots and remove the stones. Place the apricot flesh in the syrup and cook gently for about 15 minutes, or until the apricots are tender and a pin will easily pass through them. Remove from the heat, spoon the apricot halves into jars that have been sterilized and warmed in the oven. Top up with the hot syrup then secure a lid, allow to cool, label and store.

PRESERVE OF CHERRIES

A Closet for Ladies and Gentlewomen. Or, The Art of Preseruing, Conseruing, and Candying, 1608

'To preferue Cherries. Take of the beft and fayreft Cherries fome two pound, and with a paire of fheeres clippe of the ftalkes by the midft, then wafh them cleane, and beware you bruise them not, then take of fine barbarie fugar, and fet it ouer the fire with a quart of faire water in the brodeft veffell you can get, and let it feeth til it be fomewhat thicke, then put in your Cherries, and ftirre them together with a filuer fpoone and fo let them boyle, alwayes fcumming, and turning them very gently, that the one fide may be like the other, vntill they be ynough, the which to know, you muft take vp fome of the fyrope with one Cherrie, and fo let it coole, and if it will fcarce run out it is ynough, and thus being cold, you may put them vp, and keepe them all the yeare.

Ingredients: 1 kg cherries; 1 l water; 1 kg sugar.

Method: Combine the sugar and water in a large pan. Heat gently until the sugar has melted, then bring to the boil and cook until the syrup has thickened slightly. Use a pair of scissors to cut the cherries off their bunches, so that a small portion of the stalk remains. Wash them carefully then dry in a cloth. Place the cherries in the syrup and cook, turning frequently with a slotted spoon, until they are tender. Spoon the cooked cherries into jars that have been sterilised and warmed in the oven. Top up with the syrup, seal with the lid and set aside to cool. Label the jars and store in a cool, dark cupboard.

DRIED PEARES

John Partridge's *The Widdowes Treasure*, 1586

'To make drie Peares. Take faire [spring] water and Rosewater according to the quantitie of your Peares, then take Honey as muche as you thinke good and put in your Peares, then let them seethe very softly that thei breake not, then take them out and put them in a Collander, and let them dreaine, then when you drawe your bread put them into the Oven in some earthen panne, and if they be not drie at the first, put them in againe until they be drie, then barrel them.'

HONEY-PRESERVED VENISON

John Partridge's *The Widdowes Treasure*, 1586

'To keepe Venison freshed long tyme. Presse out the bloud cleane, and put it into an earthen pot, and fill it with clarified Honey two fingers above the fleshe, and binde a leather cloase about the mouth that mo ayre enter.'

CONSERVE OF ROSES IN THE ITALIAN MANNER
The Queen's Closet Opened, 1655

This is a highly-scented preserve and for best effect use deep red, heavily-scented damask roses. Choose those that are not completely open.

'Conserve of Roses in the Italian Manner. Take fresh red Roses not quite ripe, beat them in a stone Mortar, mix them with double their weight of Sugar, and put them in a glass close stopped, being not full, let them remain before you use them three moneths, stirring of them once a day … The Vertue. The Stomach, Heart, and Bowels it cooleth, and hindereth vapours, the spiting of blood and corruption for the most part (being cold) it helpeth. It will keep many years.'

Ingredients: 200 g roses; 400 g caster sugar.

Method: Trim the bases and any green bits from the roses, then pound in a mortar or chop in a food processor. Add the sugar and pound into the roses, then pack into a clean and sterilized jar. Seal the lid tightly and set aside for three months in a cool, dry, cupboard before use.

SIRUP OF ROSES – ROSE JAM
Sir Hugh Plat's *Delightes for Ladies*, 1602

John Gerard's *Generall Historie of Plantes* was first published in 1597 and devotes twelve pages to the description and virtues of roses, far more than it gives to any other herb. Sir Hugh Plat has sixteen recipes for preserving roses in various forms in this book.

'A Singular manner of making the sirup of Roses. Fill a silver Basin three quarters full of rain-water or Rose-water: put therein a conveient proportion of Rose-leaves: cover the basin and set it upon a pot of hot water (as we usually bake a custard) in 3 quarters of an houre, or one whole houre at most, you shal purchase the whole strength and tincture of the rose: then take out those leaves, wringing out their liquor gently, and steepe more fresh leaves in the same water: continue this iteration seven time, then make it up in a sirup: and this sirup worketh more kindly than that which is made meerly of the juice of the Rose.'

SEROP OF ROSES – ROSE JAM
Elinor Fettiplace's Receipt Book, 1604

At the base of each petal is a small white patch, called the 'nailes', by John Gerard, and the 'whights', by Lady Elinor. It should be removed using a pair of small, sharp scissors, as it will add a bitter taste to the final product. Also, the petals should be rinsed thoroughly with cool running water and allowed to air dry, before being cooked.

'To Make A Serop Of Roses … Take damask rose buds six handsfulls, and cut of the tops, and take a quart of faire running water, and put the roses therein, and put them in a basin and set them over the fire, that the water may be warm one day and night, then in the morning squise the roses hard between your hands out of the water, and put in as many fresh, and let them stand still on the fire, this doe nine times, then take out your roses, cleane out of the water, and put in as much sugar as will make it sweet, and boyle it till it come to a serop; you must put to everie pinte a pound of sugar.'

CONSERVES OF ROSES
The Feminine Monarchie, or the Historie of Bees, 1623
'Conserves of Roses is thus to be made. Take of the juice of fresh Red Roses one ounce, of fine Honie clarified tenne ounces, boile this together; then it beginneth to boile, adde of the leaves of fresh Red Roses clipt with Scisoors in little pieces four ounces, boile them up to the consumption of the juice, and presently put up the Conserves into some earthen vessell. Keepe it long therein, for in time it waxeth better and better.'

CONSERVE OF PRUNES OR DAMSONS
Sir Hugh Plat's *Delightes for Ladies*, 1602
This is termed a conserve, but is more like today's jam.
'Conſerue of prunes or Damſons made another way. Take a pottle of damſons, prick them and put them into a pot; putting thereto a pinte of Roſewater or wine, and couer your pot, let them boile well, then incorporate them by ſtirringe, and when they be tender let them coole, and ſtraine them with the liquor alſo, then take the pulpe and ſet it ouer the fire, and put thereto a ſufficient quantitie of ſugar, and boile them to their height or conſiſtencie, and put it vp in gallypots, or iarre glaſſes.'
Ingredients: 1.5 kg damson plums (or prunes); 600 ml rose water or dry white wine; 500 g caster sugar per 500 g fruit pulp.
Method: Wash the fruit well then place in a large pan with the rose water or wine. Bring to a simmer and cook for about 10 minutes, or until the fruit has softened, then increase to a gentle boil and cook for about 15 minutes more, or until the fruit has broken down. Take off the heat and allow to cool slightly then turn into a fine-meshed sieve. Press the fruit pulp through into a bowl using the back of a spoon. Measure the weight of the pulp then scrape into a saucepan along with 500 g sugar per 500 g of fruit pulp. Return to the heat, bring to the boil and cook for about 15 minutes. Skim the surface then ladle into sterilized jars that have been warmed in an oven set to 100°C for 5 minutes. Allow 1 cm of head space then secure the lid, allow to cool and store.

MARMELADE OF QUINCES OR DAMSONS
Sir Hugh Plat's *Delightes for Ladies*, 1602

'To make marmelade of Quinces or Damſons. When you haue boyled your Quinces or Damſons ſufficiently, ſtraine them; then dry the pulpe in a pan on the fire, and when you ſee there is no water in it, but that it begineth to bee ſtiffe, then mixe two pounds of ſugar with 3. poūd of pulp, this marmelade will be white marmelade: and if you will haue it looke with an high colour, put your ſugar and your pulpe together, ſo ſoone as your pulpe is drawne, and let them both boile together, and ſo it will looke of the colour of ordinarie marmelade, like vnto a ſtewed warden, but if you dry your pulpe firſt, it will looke white and take leſſe ſugar: you ſhall know when it is thicke enough, by putting a little into a ſawcer, letting it coole before you box it.'

Ingredients: 2 kg quinces or damson plums; 500 g sugar per 1 kg of fruit pulp.
Method: Coarsely chop the fruit, place in a pan with a few tablespoons of water, bring to a simmer, cover the pan tightly and cook for about 30 minutes for the plums and 50 minutes for the quinces, or until the fruit is soft and has broken down to the consistency of apple sauce. Take off the heat, turn into a fine-meshed sieve and press the fruit pulp through into a clean pan. Place this pan on the heat and cook gently, stirring constantly, until the pulp is thick. Now weigh the pulp and for every 1kg of fruit add 500 g caster sugar. Place back on the heat and cook until the sugar has dissolved. Bring to a boil and cook for 2 minutes, then take off the heat and spoon into cleaned and sterilized jars that have been warmed in the oven. Seal securely, allow to cool then label and store. If you want a darker, more marmalade-like preserve, then when you add the sugar to the fruit, boil it for 5–10 minutes to caramelize the sugar before potting.

MARMELADE OF LEMMONS OR ORENGES
Sir Hugh Plat's *Delightes for Ladies*, 1602

Oranges and lemons were exotic fruits in Elizabethan times. As a result, every part of them was used and when making conserves they were bulked out with other fruit, such as the apples in this example. A marmalade was generally any conserve that was boiled sufficiently long enough for the sugar to caramelize and give a dark colour. Hence, you could make a marmalade of any fruit.

'To make Marmelade of Lemmons or Orenges. Take ten lemmons or orenges and boyle them with half a dozen pippins, and ſo draw them through a ſtrainer, then take ſo much ſugar as the pulp doth wey, and boyle it as you doe Marmelade of Quinces, and then box it vp.'

Ingredients: 10 large lemons or oranges; 6 apples; 500 g caster sugar per 500 g of fruit pulp.

Method: Quarter the fruit, place in a pan with 4 tbsp water, bring to a simmer then cover with a tight-fitting lid and cook for about 40 minutes, or until the fruit has broken down into a pulp. Pass the fruit pulp through a fine-meshed sieve using the back of a spoon. Weigh the pulp and to every 500 g of fruit pulp mix in 500 g caster sugar. Place in a pan, bring to a simmer and cook until the sugar has dissolved. Bring the mixture to a boil and continue boiling for 5 minutes. At this point, test the marmalade for setting. Once you have reached the setting point, you can pot your marmalade. Spoon the finished marmalade into cleaned and sterilised jars that have been warmed in the oven. Seal securely, allow to cool then label and store.

ELIZABETHAN BÉCHAMEL SAUCE
Le Quisinier Françoise (The French Chef), Francois Pierre de la Varenne, 1651
This is one of the truly classic white sauce recipes and tales of its origins differ, ranging from its creation during the fourteenth century by the chefs of Catherine de Medici, to its invention in the sixteenth century by the gastronome, Duke Philippe De Mornay of Samur (1549–1623). Béchamel sauce was used for centuries in Tuscan and Emilian cuisine and was imported into France by the chefs of Marie de' Medici, wife of Henri IV of France (1553–1610). The recipe will have passed to Elizabethan England during Henry's reign. The sauce became a main ingredient of the French Court's cuisine and was later renamed from its original Italian name of *Balsamella* after the Marquis de Béchamel, steward to Louis XIV. Although based on de la Varenne's recipe, the sauce given below is a modern version. Elizabethans were generally fearful of milk-based sauces as there was no refrigeration and many milk sellers adulterated their product or sold rancid milk.
Ingredients: 2 tbsp butter; 2 tbsp plain flour; 50 ml cold milk; 150 ml warmed milk; salt; freshly grated nutmeg; white pepper.
Method: Melt the butter in the bottom of a saucepan on a medium heat, add the flour and stir until the resulting roux is well blended. Stir this with a whisk and add the cold milk. Once this has warmed, slowly pour in the warm milk, stirring all the time. Keep stirring continuously until the sauce just begins to boil, then add the pepper, salt and nutmeg and turn the heat down to a simmer. Keep simmering for about 5 minutes to make sure that the flour has cooked. This sauce is converted into *Mornay* sauce by the simple addition of about 100 g of grated cheese and ¼ tsp mustard powder. For a spiced version of the *Béchamel* sauce, add a small onion studded with cloves into the milk as you are warming in a saucepan. For a *velouté* sauce, simply substitute chicken, beef or vegetable stock for the milk.

PIGGESAUCE – SAUCE FOR PORK
The Good Hous-wives Treasurie, 1588

'Ripe as a pome-water, who now hangeth as a jewel in the ear of Coelo, the sky' *Love's Labours Lost*, 1597

'Piggesauce. Take halfe Vineger, and halfe Vergis [verjuice], a handful of percelly [parsley] and Sage chopte very small, a Pomewater [an extinct type of apple, see cider in drinks chapter] shredde very small, then take the gravie of the Pigge, with Suger and Pepper and boyle them together.'

SAUCES FOR GOOCE AND CAPON
The Good Hous-wives Treasurie, 1588

'Sauce for a Gooce. Take Vineger and appells shred very small, two spoonfuls of musterd a little Pepper and Salte: and take Suger sufficient to sweeten it, then boyle it well together.'

'Capon sauce. Take water, Onions, pepper, and some of the gravie and salte, and boyle together.'

SYRIP FOR A CAPON OR FAYSANT
Arundel MS 334 (second quarter of the 15th century, in *Antiquitates Culinariae*, 1791)

'Syrip for a Capon or Faysant. Take almonds and pound them [in a mortar] and temper them up with wine and make this into a good thick [almond] milk and colour it with saffron. Cook it in a possenet and add to it plenty of pine nuts and raisins and season with ginger, cloves and galingale and cinnamon. Bring it to a boil and season with sugar. And when the capons or pheasants are roasted take and pour the syrup over them and serve them forth.'

Ingredients: 350 ml almond milk made with red wine; 110 g seedless currants; 75 g pine nuts; 1 tbsp sugar; ½ tsp powdered ginger; ¼ tsp each of cinnamon and galingale; pinch each of cloves and saffron.

Method: Place the almond milk in a saucepan and add all the other ingredients. Bring to the boil over a medium heat, then reduce the heat and simmer for about 5 minutes, stirring continuously, until the sauce starts to thicken. If the sauce becomes too thick add a little more wine. Serve poured over slices of roast fowl. It also goes well with cold ham or cold slices of goose.

BLAWNCHE PERRY – WHITE LEEK SAUCE (TWO WAYS)
Two Fifteenth Century Cookbooks – Harleian MS. 279 & Harl. MS. 4016, c. 1440

'For to make Blawnche Perrye. Take the Whyte of the lekys, an sethe hem in a potte, an presse hem vp, an hacke hem smal on a bord. An nym gode almaunde_mylke, an a lytil of Rys, an do alle thes to-gederys, an sethe an stere it wyl, an do ther-to Sugre or hony, an dresse it yn; thanne take powderd Elys, an sethe hem in fayre Water, and broyle hem, an kytte hem in long pecys. And ley or in a dysshe, and putte thin perrey in a-nother dysshe, an serue the to dysshys to-gederys as Venysoun with Furmenty.'

'Blanche porrey. Take blanche almondes, And grinde hem, and drawe hem with sugur water thorg a streynour into a good stuff mylke into a potte; and then take the white of lekes, and hew hem small, and grynde hem in a morter wit brede; and then cast al to the mylke into the potte, and caste therto sugur and salt, and lete boyle; And set feyre poudrid eles in faire water ynowe, and broile hem on a gredren; and kut hem in faire longe peces, and ley two or thre in a diss togidre as ye do veneson with ffurmenty, And serue it forthe.'

PUR VERDE SAWCE – GREEN SAUCE

A Noble Boke off Cookry ffor a Prynce Houssolde Holkham MSS 674, 1480

Now unfashionable, green was a very popular colour in medieval cooking and this author has had some superb green sauce dishes at Adolf Wagner's *Apfelwein* (scrumpy cider) restaurant in Sachsenhausen, Frankfurt. This sauce was the preferred shade of green, tinted with yellow, sometimes called *vertgay*. If the flavour is a little sharp, replace some or all of the vinegar with more white wine. Basically almost any herbs were used, according to season. Green sauce appears in recipes across Europe from the twelfth century and was often favoured with fish dishes.

'To mak vert sauce tak parslye mynte sorell cyves and sauce alone then tak bred and step it in venygar do ther to peper and salt and grind them and temper them upe and serue it.'

Ingredients: 4 slices bread; ½ cup fresh mint; 1 cup fresh parsley; ¼ cup vinegar; 1 cup white wine; ¼ tsp salt; ½ tsp ginger; ¼ tsp pepper; pinch of saffron.

Method: Grind the mint and parsley well, adding a little of the wine if necessary. Place in a bowl with the rest of the wine, vinegar and bread. Allow to steep for 10–15 minutes, until the bread has turned mushy. Strain into a saucepan, pressing out as much of the liquid as possible, and discard the solids. If the colour is not as green as you would like, grind more parsley and mint with wine and strain into the pan. Add remaining spices and bring to a low boil. Reduce heat and simmer until it thickens.

GREEN SAUCE FOR KID AND OTHER BOILED MEATS

Anonymous, Venetian *Libro di cucina/ Libro per cuoco*, 14th–15th century

'Take parsley, ginger, cloves and cinnamon flowers and a little salt, grind everything together and mix with good vinegar, make it temperate [i.e. keep vinegar moderate] and they will not want to wait to taste this.'

GREEN SAUCE
Traditional, modern variant

Green sauce is today the name of several ancient sauces containing mainly herbs: *salsa verde* in Italy and Spain; *sauce verte* in France; and in Germany *Grüne Soße* or Frankfurter *Grie Soß*. The basic recipe is probably from the Near East, brought by Roman legionaries to Europe. Italian *salsa verde* is a cold rustic sauce, including parsley, capers, garlic, onion, anchovies, olive oil, vinegar and sometimes mustard. The Frankfurt sauce is made from hard-boiled eggs, oil, vinegar, salt, sour cream and generous amounts of seven fresh, local herbs: salad burnet, parsley, chives, chervil, garden cress, sorrel and borage. Variants owing to seasonal availability include spinach, lemon balm, shallots and lovage. Dandelion and daisy leaves have been used in the past. This particular Frankfurt *grüne sosse* is most often mixed with a combination of sour cream, yoghurt or crème fraiche, a little oil, vinegar, mustard, salt and pepper and then served over boiled potatoes with a couple of hard-boiled eggs. The best sauce is made by chopping the herbs with a knife and not with a blender or food processor as it changes the taste of it. Frankfurt restaurants may offer it with tender, boiled beef or as a schnitzel topped with the sauce, but it can be a full meal with just the potatoes. You may also find it on the menu at Adolf Wagner's in Frankfurt served with fried fish, cold chicken or salad. However, at Adolf's they use oil instead of yoghurt in the preparation. The sauce is traditionally made in the springtime when the herbs are at their most fragrant. Although you can get the herbs all year round, the traditional season is from Green Thursday (the day before Good Friday) until the first frost. Frankfurt has a *Grüne Sosse* festival for a week in the middle of May each year. At times you can buy ready-made green sauces, or bunches of the seven herbs, in local markets. Although this particular sauce was only written down in the eighteenth century, it is a derivant of all the medieval green sauces and superbly savoury.

Ingredients: Large bunch of mixed parsley, chives, cress, sorrel, chervil, borage and salad burnet; 3 medium eggs; 1 tbsp medium–hot mustard; 2–3 tbsp white wine vinegar; 6 tbsp sunflower oil; 1 cup crème fraiche; 2 finely-chopped shallots; salt and pepper; sugar to taste.

Method: Hard boil the eggs, peel them and separate the yolks from the whites. Press the yolks with a sieve into a large bowl and mix in the vinegar, sunflower oil, salt, pepper and sugar. Finely chop the egg white and add them to the creamy egg yolk mix. Fold in the crème fraiche and add the shallots. Wash the herbs and pat off the water before chopping finely with a sharp knife (not a processor), and add them to the mixture. Mix in well and taste. If too sharp add more sugar and if too sweet add a little vinegar. If you want it smooth, mix it in a blender before leaving to settle. Leave at least an hour before serving to let the flavour develop.

SOBRE SAWCE – A SAUCE FOR FRESHWATER FISH
Libre del Coch Spain, 1520
This is a very simple recipe for a sauce that is thickened with bread and it is unusual to find a recipe with red wine for fish.
Ingredients: 2 cups red wine; 1 cup raisins; 2 slices bread; ½ tsp powder fine (see above); ¼ tsp salt.
Method: Tear bread into small pieces and place in a bowl with red wine. Grind raisins into a paste, adding water as necessary. Add to bread and wine and mix well. Allow to soak for about 10 minutes and then strain into a saucepan, reserving liquid and discarding solids. Add remaining ingredients and bring to a boil. Simmer for about 10 minutes until the sauce thickens slightly.

PIKYLL POUR LE MALLARD – DUCK PICKLE SAUCE
Two Fifteenth Century Cookbooks – Harleian MS. 279 & Harl. MS. 4016, c. 1440
One was tempted to name this 'Quick-Quack Pickle', but resisted.
'Pickle for the Mallard. Take onions, and chop them small. Fry them in fresh grease, and cast them into a pot, [Add] fresh broth of beef, wine and ground pepper, cinnamon, and drippings of the mallard. Let them boil together for a while. Take it from the fire, and add a little mustard to it, and ginger powder. Let it boil no more, and salt it. Serve it with the Mallard.'

12

Dishes You May Not Wish to Cook (or Eat) (or See)

Even today in the Philippines a great culinary delicacy is *balut,* a boiled fertilised and half-developed duck or chicken embryo. It is complete with recognisable beak, eyes and feathers along with some remaining yolk. Lest we Europeans think we are above such things, in France, there is pressure to bring back the eating of ortolan, President Mitterand's favourite dish. Four leading French chefs, including Alain Ducasse, who has 18 Michelin stars to his name, have called for a partial reversal of the ban on killing and selling these small songbirds. Ducasse told a French food magazine that the prohibition 'undermines centuries of tradition, customs, and promotes a black market with exorbitant prices'. A single ortolan is no bigger than a baby's fist and weighs less than an ounce, but they are sold for as much as £100. Hunters catch the birds using traps set in fields during their migratory season and the birds are then kept in covered cages, encouraging them to gorge on grain in order to double their size. It is said that Roman Emperors stabbed out ortolans' eyes in order to make the birds think it was night, making them eat even more.

The birds are then thrown alive into a vat of Armagnac to marinade. They are cooked for eight minutes and served with their heads still attached. A napkin is placed over the diner's head to trap the aroma and the ortolan is popped in its entirety into the diner's mouth, who then proceeds to eat everything including the head and bones. Jeremy Clarkson ate one during his *Meet the Neighbours* TV series in 2002, and said 'It's really good. It is fantastic, fantastic.' The American chef Anthony Bourdain says the experience is close to ecstasy: 'With every bite, as the thin bones and layers of fat, meat, skin and organs compact in on themselves, there are sublime dribbles of varied and wondrous ancient flavours: figs, Armagnac, dark flesh slightly infused with the salty taste of my own blood as my mouth is pricked by the sharp bones.'

And of course, we still have the continued production of *foie gras*, the liver of a goose or duck which has been force-fed corn boiled with fat, to facilitate ingestion. This deposits large amounts of fat in the liver, thereby producing the buttery consistency sought by some of the less civilized amongst us. Some more tender-minded readers may wish to avert their eyes for the rest of this chapter.

LIVE BLACKBIRD, RABBIT, FROG, DOG OR DWARF PIE

Epulario, or The Italian Banquet, 1598 translation of 1516 edition

'Sing a song of six-pence, a pocket full of rye

Four and twenty blackbirds, baked in a pie

When the pie was opened, the birds began to sing.

Now wasn't that a tasty dish to set before the king!'

A sixteenth century court amusement was to place live birds in a pie, as a form of entremets. The way Tudors made pie crusts was a little different in that the thick crust could be baked first and would rise forming a pot, hence the term 'pot pie.' The lid would be removed from the pie and birds would then be set inside, the lid put back on and then this entertaining dish placed before the host of the party. Thus the birds were not actually cooked in the pie. The Stuart cook Robert May filled such a pie with live frogs to 'make the ladies skip and shreek.'

Not only were birds baked into pies, but rabbits, frogs, dogs and people of restricted growth, would pop out and recite poetry. At one time a whole little musical group emerged to the delight of the diners. Today, the bankers, criminals and Premier League footballers amongst us have strippers popping out of cakes. The experimental celebrity chef Heston Blumenthal attempted to recreate the dish for an episode of his television series *Heston's Medieval Feast*. Discovering that blackbirds are a protected species he altered the recipe to pigeon. The pie and pie lid were cooked separately and allowed to cool and live pigeons inserted only moments before presentation. Initial attempts resulted in the pigeons refusing to fly out, but this was solved by using trained homing pigeons to fly to their cages suspended in the ceiling.

'To make Pies that the Birds may be alive in them, and flie out when it is cut up. Take the coffin of a great pie or pastry, in the bottome thereof make a hole as big as your fist, or bigger if you will, let the sides of the coffin bee somewhat higher then ordinary pies, which done put it full of flower and bake it, and being baked, open the hole in the bottome, and take out the flower. Then having a pie of the bigness of the hole in the bottome of the coffin aforesaid, you shal put it into the coffin, withall put into the said coffin round about the aforesaid pie as many small live birds as the empty coffin will hold, besides the pie aforesaid. And this is to be done at such time as you send the pie to the table, and set before the guests: where uncovering or cutting up the lid of the great pie, all the birds will flie out, which is to delight and pleasure shew to the company. And because they shall not bee altogether mocked, you shall cut open the small pie, and in this sort you may make many others, the like you may do with a tart.'

A GOOSE ROASTED ALIVE
Giambatissta della Porta's *Magia Naturalis*,1558
First published in Naples in 1558, the book sold out in five Latin editions across Europe in just ten years, with translations into Italian, French and Dutch. One of its more horrible recipes reads thus:
'A Goose Roasted Alive. A little before our times, a Goose was wont to be brought to the table of the King of Aragon, that was roasted alive, as I have heard by old men of credit. And when I went to try it, my company were so hasty, that we ate him up before he was quite roasted. He was alive, and the upper part of him, on the outside, was excellent well roasted. The rule to do it is thus.

Take a Duck, or a Goose, or some such lusty creature, but the Goose is best for this purpose. Pull all the Feathers from his body, leaving his head and his neck. Then make a circle of fire round about him, not too narrow, lest the smoke choke him, or the fire should roast him too soon. Set the fire not too wide, lest he escape unroasted. Inside the fire boundary, set everywhere little pots full of water, and put Salt and Meum [our wild herb baldmoney, *Meum anthamanticum*] in them. Let the Goose be smeared all over with Suet, and well Larded, that he may be the better meat, and roast the better. Light the fire about the goose, but do not let it burn in haste. When the Goose begins to roast, he will walk about, and cannot get forth, for the fire stops him.

When he is weary, he quenches his thirst by drinking the water, by cooling his heart, and the rest of his internal parts. The force of the Medicament loosens and cleans his belly, so that he grows empty. And when he his very hot, it roasts his inner parts. Continually moisten his head and heart with a Sponge. But when you see him run mad up and down, and to stumble (his heart then wants moisture), wherefore you take him away, and set him on the table to your guests, who will cry as you pull off his parts. And you shall eat him up before he is dead.'

The recipe was repeated with some relish by Dr. John Wecker in 1661 in his *Eighteen Books Of the Secrets Of Art & Nature*: 'Let it be a Duck or Goose, or some such lively Creature, but a Goose is best of all for this purpose, leaving his neck, pull of all the Feather from his body, then make a fire round about him, not too wide, for that will not rost him: within the place set here and there small pots full of water, with Salt and Honey mixed therewith, and let there be dishes set full of rosted Apples, and cut in pieces in the dish, and let the Goose be basted with Butter all over, and Larded to make him better meat, and he may rost the better, put fire to it; do not make too much haste, when he begins to rost, walking about, and striving to fly away, the fire stops him in, and he will fall to drink water to quench his thirst; this will cool his heart and the other parts of his body, and by this medicament he loosneth his belly, and grows empty. And when he rosteth and consumes inwardly, alwayes wet his head and heart with a wet Sponge: but when you see him run madding and stumble, his heart wants moysture, take him away, set him before your Guests, and he will cry as you cut off any part from him and will be almost eaten up before he be dead, it is very pleasant to behold.'

ENTIRE LUNGS OF KID IN CAUL
Anonymous, Venetian *Libro di cucina/ Libro per cuoco*, 14th–15th century
'And if you want to cook entire lungs of kid, take the lungs and boil them. Then beat them with a mallet. Then take good herbs and beaten egg yolks and fry them in lard and put them into the [beaten] lungs, and grind everything together. Add half a fresh cheese and fine spices and three eggs, and mix everything together. Then one encloses it well in a caul [membrane of a newborn animal] or net and then puts this thing into a pan to fry and it is good.'

STUFFED PIGLET
Le Ménagier De Paris, 1393
'Stuffed Piglet. Have the piglet killed and its throat cut and let it be scalded in boiling water, then skinned: then take some lean pork, and remove the fat and innards of the piglet and put it on to cook in water, and take twenty eggs and cook them hard, and some sweet chestnuts cooked in water and peeled: then take the egg yolks, sweet chestnuts, fine old cheese, and the cooked meat of a leg of pork, and chop it up, then grind with saffron and a large amount of powdered ginger mixed in with the meat; and if your meat is too hard, mix in egg yolks. And do not split open your piglet's stomach but cut the smallest hole possible: then put it on the spit, and then push your Stuffing inside, and sew it up with a large needle; and it should be eaten either with yellow pepper if it is winter, or with a cameline sauce if it is summer. Note that I have often seen larded piglet, and it is very good. And thus they do it now and pigeons too.'

FRIED CODSHEAD

A.W., *The Booke of Goode Cookry Very Necessary for all Such as Delight Therein*, 1584, 1591

'To fry a Codshead. First cleve it in peeces and washe it clean and fry it in Butter or Oyle. Then cut Onions in rundels and so frye them, that doon put them in a vessell, and put to them red wine or vinagre, salt, ginger, sinamon, cloves and mace, and boile all these well togither, and then serve it upon your cods head.'

While this sounds unappealing to modern tastes, there is a recipe for baked cod's head in May Byron's *How to Save Cookery Book* of 1915, full of World War One austerity recipes: 'Wash and clean a large cod's head and shoulders. Place it in a baking tin, and sprinkle well with bits of dripping [- butter was rationed]. Bake for about an hour; frequent basting will be needed. Remove fish to hot dish, strain liquor into a small pan, add one tablespoon of chopped parsley, two tablespoonfuls of vinegar, pepper and salt to taste. Let heat thoroughly, and serve as sauce with the fish.'

PIES OF COCKS' COMBS WITH WHOLE TESTICLES

The Neapolitan recipe collection, 15th century, trans. T. Scully

'Get combs and cut them into three, and livers into four, and leave the testicles whole; get a little lardo and cut it very small and do not pound it; get three ounces of veal fat and pound it well-veal or beef marrow would be better; then get thirty dry sour cherries, cinnamon, ginger and plenty of sugar, and mix all that together; make a good pie and bake it in the oven – and make its crust as is used in pies; alternatively, put it into a pan; when it is cooked, get an egg yolk, verjuice and saffron and, mixed together, put all that into the pie and heat it again, then take it out.'

Epulario, or The Italian Banquet of 1598 has a similar dish: '"To make Pies of the Combes of Cockes and Hennes, with their stones, and livers", the other ingredients being cherries, cinnamon, ginger, saffron, and verjuice.'

POTATON TARTE THAT IS A COURAGE TO MAN OR WOMAN –
APHRODISIAC SWEET POTATO PIE WITH COCK SPARROW BRAINS

Thomas Dawson's *The Good Housewife's Jewell*, 1587

Today's potatoes, from the New World, did not arrive in Britain until the 1580s and were small and not used in cooking for some time. This is the earliest published recipe written in English for potatoes, but these are sweet potatoes, which were first brought from the Americas a century earlier by the Spanish and Portuguese. The early explorers and settlers of Virginia, when they used the word potato, were referring to the sweet potato. In his wonderful

1597 *Herball*, John Gerard called the white potato the 'Virginia potato' and described the sweet potato: 'The Potato roots are among the Spaniards, Italians, Indians, [from India] and many other nations common and ordinarie meate.' John Parkinson called it the 'Spanish kinde' in *Paradisi in Sol* (1629). Dawson's 1587 recipe points to the 'Potaton' as an aphrodisiac.

'To make a tarte that is a courage to a man or woman. Take twoo Quinces, and twoo or three Burre rootes, and a potaton, and pare your Potaton, and scrape your rootes and put them into a quart of wine, and let them boyle till they bee tender, and put in an ounce of Dates, and when they be boyled tender, Drawe them through a strainer, wine and all, and then put in the yolkes of eight Egges, and the braynes of three or foure cocke Sparrowes, and straine them intothe other, and a little Rose Water, and seeth them all with suger, Cinamon and Gynger, and Cloues and mace, and put in a little sweet butter, and set it vpon a Chafingdish of coles betweene two platters, and so let it boyle till it be something bigge.'

PYES OF CALVES FEET

A.W., *The Booke of Goode Cookry Very Necessary for all Such as Delight Therein*, 1584, 1591

'How to bake pyes of Calves feet. Take Calves feet and wash them, boyle and blanch the haire of them, season them with cloves and mace, and a little pepper, vergious and sugar, dates, prunes, corance, and sweet butter, then make your paste of fine flower with yolkes of Egges, and raise the Coffin square, when it if halfe baked, then take it out and put in Vergious and sugar with the yolks of hard Egs strained.'

HOW TO DRESSE NEATSTUNGS – OX TONGUES IN HERB SAUCE

A.W., *The Booke of Goode Cookry Very Necessary for all Such as Delight Therein*, 1584, 1591

'First boile them till the be very tender, then make tostes of bread, and toste them till they be very black, and wash the same tostes in faire water, and put them in a faire earthen Vessell, and then put to them flesh broth, Vinagre, red Wine, Sinamon and Ginger, and straine these altogither, so that it be not too thick, and put therto Sugar and salt, and boyle all these togither, then cut your tungs in faire leshes, and so frye them in sweet Butter, and that doone, put the Leshes into your sauce, and then let them boile well togither, and so serve them with the same sauce.'

A BROTH FOR A NEATSUNG – OX TONGUE BROTH

A.W., *The Booke of Goode Cookry Very Necessary for all Such as Delight Therein*, 1584, 1591

'Take Claret wine, grated Bread, Corance, sweete Butter, Sugar, and Sinamon, boyle them altogither. Then take the Neats tung and slice it and so lay it in your dish with sippets and serve it in.'

HARDTACK – SHIPS BISCUITS

Traditional

These iron-hard biscuits were stored on ships during and beyond the Tudor period and were a staple part of the diet. They were made from a simple unleavened mixture of flour, water and salt, rolled out thinly and baked slowly until very hard and dry. Milk instead of water has been added to the recipe and a little butter, to make them more edible. If cooked slowly, these biscuits are a challenge for even the healthiest of teeth. The sailors must have softened them in some liquid to be able to eat them. Cooked properly, they are hard not brittle.

These biscuits baked in a hot oven, also called sea biscuits, were taken on long voyages as they resisted spoilage. There were none of the staple carbohydrates necessary at sea, as bread would not keep on long voyages, so biscuits were made with flour and the minimum of water or milk, moulded into flat cakes and packed tightly into canvas bags. The hard tack would last for up to a year after being baked. The biscuits quickly became infested with a type of black-headed weevil (called 'bargemen'). As a result, before any seaman ate a biscuit, he tapped it on the table to knock the weevils out of it. As voyages progressed, the food would become infested with worms, maggots and other creatures. Ferdinand Columbus, describing one of his father's voyages, wrote: 'Food had become so wormy that sailors waited to dark to eat… so they could not see the maggots.'

'Ships biscuits' also became a seaman's expression of apology when he burped in public – any belch could be blamed on the poor quality of 'ship's biscuits'. My father-in-law always used this expression from his merchant navy days before the war. Dried peas also kept for a long time at sea and so were sometimes the only other source of food when boiled. Also known as 'teeth dullers' and 'sheet iron', hard tack was still issued to troops in World War One and if the French got hold of some of these British rations they used them as firelighters.

Ingredients: 1 lb flour; ½ pint water; ½ tbsp sea salt. These were the original ingredients if you want 'firelighters' and broken teeth, but to make a modern, almost edible version, add 2 oz butter and use ½ pint skimmed milk instead of water.

Method: Put the flour in a mixing bowl. Measure out the milk and butter and place in a saucepan. Melt the butter in the milk over a very low heat. Add the sea salt to the flour and mix. Add the milk and butter then the flour and mix until you have a dough, kneading the dough until all the flour is absorbed. It should be a thick, shiny, stiff mix. Roll the dough out until fairly thin. Cut the biscuit shapes using a cup rim. Place on a baking tray and prick all over to let out any air when cooking. Bake for 30–40 minutes at a moderate heat until golden brown. The biscuits should be dry right through or they might go mouldy when you take them to sea. Do not handle but leave to cool. Store in a dry place until needed.

HOG OFFAL
Le Ménagier De Paris, 1393

'HOG OFFAL, actually using the entrails, which should be emptied in the river, then washed twice in warm water, and put them in a pan and rub thoroughly in salt and water, then wash again in warm water. Some wash them in salt and vinegar, and when they are thoroughly washed be it with vinegar or without vinegar, cut them up, and put on spits and roast on the grill and eat with grain verjuice. And if you want to make soup, you must put them to cook whole in a clay pot and set them to drain on a dish, then cut up in small pieces, and fry in bacon fat; then grind up first bread, then mace, galingale, saffron, ginger, clove, grain, cinnamon: moisten with stock and set to one side; then grind toasted breadcrumbs, and mix with offal and put through a sieve and put in meat stock or stock from the offal itself, or half of one and half of the other, and boil all together with red wine, verjuice and vinegar. In winter it must be brown and served as above, and in summer clearer and more yellow; and have grain verjuice cooked in water in a cloth, or gooseberries, and when you prepare your bowls, put six or eight morsels of the offal, then the soup over, and then six or eight grains of verjuice, or gooseberries on each bowl. And some make the soup with spices and milk as above and call it "cretonne". Note that the salt and vinegar remove the freshness. And what I call offal for eating in July, and for the kebabs which are made in December, includes all the parts such as liver, lung and other parts of the offal, and this is what the poor cook in washbasins along the roadsides.'

HOG BLACK PUDDING
Le Ménagier De Paris, 1393

This is a lesson in biology as much as a recipe and pigs were an invaluable source of protein for centuries, with every part being used.
'Item, to make black pudding, have the pig blood collected in a fair basin or pan, and when you intend to see your pig destroyed, have the lights washed

very well and put on to cook, and as soon as it is cooked, take from the bottom of the pan the sticky lumps of blood and take them out; and then, have onions peeled and chopped to the amount of half the blood, with the amount of half the suet which is among the guts, which is called the "entrecercle" of the guts, chopped as small as dice, together with a little ground salt, and throw it in the blood. Then, have ginger, clove, and a little pepper, and grind it all together. Then, have the small guts well washed, turned inside out and all blood removed in a running river, and to remove the dampness, have them placed in a pan on the fire, and stir; then, add salt; and do this a second time, and yet a third time: and then wash, and turn inside out and wash them, then place to dry on a towel; and squeeze and wring them to dry. (They say the 'entrecercle' and these are the large guts which have suet inside which you get out with a knife). After you have added and adjusted by the right amounts and quantities, so that you have half as much onions as blood, and a quarter as much suet as blood, and then when your black puddings are filled with this, put them to cook in a pan in the water from the lights, and prick with a pin when they swell, or otherwise they will burst.

Note that the blood keeps well for two days, in truth for three, since the spices are inside. And some for spices, have pennyroyal, great savory, hyssop, marjoram, gathered when they are in flower and then dried, ground, for spices. And as for the lights, put in a copper pot to cook on the fire, complete and without salt, and put the length of the groove (throat) outside the pot, so that the liquid may be skimmed; and when it is cooked, take it out and consider it for making soup.

To make black puddings with liver, take two pieces of liver, two pieces of lung, a piece of suet, and place in a gut with blood: and with the remainder as above. Note that you can make nice black puddings from a goose, but it will be thin, and because of the thinness the guts are bigger than the suet. One may ask how the guts may be turned inside out for washing; I reply: with a linen thread and a piece of brass wire as long as a gauge-rod. Here follow all the special names for the offal of a pig, which are sold at the triper's for seven blancs. First when the pig is prepared, the blood and the guts come out first, and are made into black puddings if wanted. Item, first the lights and the upper abdomen, the short-ribs and then the lower abdomen. The upper abdomen is that part which is between the guts and the short-ribs. The lights, these are the liver, the lungs, the heart and the tongue. The short-ribs is the spleen and to this belongs half the liver and the kidneys; and the other half of the liver goes with the lights, between the heart and the lungs. The lower abdomen is the bowels called the "entrecercle", and are also the small bowels with which one makes black puddings and sausages, and here also is the pancreas.'

TO BOILE SPARROWES OR LARKS – SPARROWS IN MUTTON BROTH
Sir Hugh Plat's *Delightes for Ladies*, 1602

In Britain, the humble sparrow was used as a source of food until at least the nineteenth century. Enterprising householders would hang wooden, then ceramic, 'sparrow pots' from roof eaves to attract the birds which like to nest in family groups. Once the babies had hatched, people would reach in, harvest the offspring, stew the sparrow chicks and serve them on toast. Any small birds can be used in this sweet and sour herby mutton broth, but house sparrows are becoming rarer with the lack of crevices for nesting sites in houses and the rise in population of the domestic cat. Thus partridges are used in this modern version. At a recent 'shooters' dinner, I saw dozens of woodcock and snipe being served. They are such difficult birds to spot that they are often illegally shot using 'lamping' at night.

'To boile Sparrowes or Larks: Take two ladles full of mutton broth, a little whole mace, put into it a peece of fweet butter a handful of Parfly being picked, feafon it with fugar, veriuice, and a little pepper.'

Ingredients: 4 partridges or other small birds; 500 ml mutton broth; 2 blades of mace; 2 tbsp butter; 1 generous handful of parsley, shredded; 1 tbsp brown sugar; 2 tbsp verjuice; freshly-ground black pepper, to taste.

Method: Sit the birds in a heavy-bottomed pan then add the mutton broth, mace, butter, parsley, sugar, verjuice and black pepper. Bring to the boil, reduce to a simmer, cover the pan and cook for about 30 minutes, or until the birds are tender. Remove the birds from the pan and set aside to keep warm, bring the stock to a boil and continue boiling for about 15 minutes, or until reduced. Strain the stock and serve to accompany the birds.

BURSEU – A DISH OF MINCED PIG ENTRAILS
The Master-Cook of Richard II, *The Forme of Cury*, c. 1390

'Take the white parts of leeks, slice lengthways and shred finely. Take swine entrails and parboil them in broth and wine. Remove and slice then cook the leeks in the broth. Boil and add in the entrails. Make an admixture of bread and blood with vinegar and add to the broth. Boil onions, mince them and add to the broth. In the same manner, you can make this with a pig.'

Ingredients: White parts only of 4 leeks, sliced lengthways and finely shredded; 400 g pork intestines, thoroughly cleaned (or pork cut into serving pieces); 200 ml red wine; 300 ml 'gode broth' made without breadcrumbs; 200 g bread, diced; 60 ml pig's blood; 2 tbsp red wine vinegar; 2 onions, boiled for 20 minutes in water and minced fine.

Method: Placed the pig's intestines (or pork pieces) in a pan and cover with the red wine and broth. Bring to the boil, cover the pan, reduce to a simmer and cook for about 50 minutes or until the intestines are tender. Remove from the broth with a slotted spoon, chop finely and set aside. Add the leeks to the remaining broth, bring to a boil and cook for about 10 minutes, or until tender. Return the pork intestines to the pan and bring back to a simmer. Mix together the bread, blood and red wine vinegar and then stir in to the broth. Bring back to a simmer and cook for 20 minutes then add the minced onions. Allow to heat through to thicken, then serve.

GARBAGE – BROTH OF CHICKEN HEADS, FEET AND LIVERS
A Boke of Kokery, c. 1440
'Take good giblets (garbage): chickens' heads, feet, livers, and gizzards, and wash them clean. Throw them into a nice pot, and add fresh beef broth, powdered pepper, cinnamon, cloves, mace, parsley and sage chopped small. Then take bread, steep it in the same broth, draw it through a strainer, add and let boil till done. Add powdered ginger, verjuice (sour grape or apple juice), salt, and a little saffron, and serve it forth.'

HART ROWS – PIG STOMACH LEGLESS HEDGEHOGS
The Master-Cook of Richard II, *The Forme of Cury, c.* 1390
Pigs' stomachs stuffed with pork, eggs and breadcrumbs, decorated with pastry spines to look like hedgehogs.
'Make slivers of dough in the form of hedgehogs' spines, and fry them lightly in fat or oil. Take the stomachs of six or seven pigs, one larger than the rest. Stuff the stomachs with a mixture of ground pork, eggs, powder fort (likely including pepper and cloves), saffron, salt, and currants. Sew the stomachs securely and parboil them. Stick them full of the bits of fried dough so that they look like hedgehogs without legs. Roast on a spit until done, colouring them with saffron in a thin batter. Serve it forth.'

HOW TO UNROLL A HEDGEHOG
Le Ménagier De Paris, 1393
'Hedgehog should have its throat cut, be singed and gutted, then trussed like a pullet, then pressed in a towel until very dry; and then roast it and eat with cameline sauce, or in pastry with wild duck sauce. Note that if the hedgehog refuses to unroll, put it in hot water, and then it will straighten itself.'

HEDGEHOGS FOR LEPERS AND HEDGEHOG INTESTINE POWDER FOR URINARY RELIEF
Das Kochbuch des Meisters Eberhard, fifteenth century
This tells us of the health benefits of hedgehogs: 'The meat of a hedgehog is

good for lepers. Those who dry its intestines and grind them to a powder and eat a little of that are made to piss, even if they can not do so otherwise.'

SQUIRREL PIES
Le Ménagier De Paris, 1393
Do not use red squirrels in this dish.
'Squirrels are singed, gutted, trussed like rabbits, roasted or put in pastry. Eat with cameline sauce or in pastry with wild duck sauce.'

ROAST CAT AS YOU WOULD WISH TO EAT IT
Libre del Coch, 1520
If the Royal Society for the Protection of Birds should ever publish a cookery book, the following is recommended.
'Roast Cat as You Wish to Eat It. You will take a cat that is fat, and decapitate it. And after it is dead, cut off the head and throw it away because it is not for eating, for they say that eating the brains will cause him who eats them to lose his senses and judgment. Then flay it very cleanly, and open it and clean it well, and then wrap it in a cloth of clean linen. And bury it beneath the ground where it must be for a day and a night; and then take it out of there and set it to roast on a spit. And roast it over the fire. And when beginning to roast it, grease it with good garlic and oil. And when you finish greasing it, whip it well with a green twig, and this must be done before it is well-roasted, greasing it and whipping it. And when it is roasted, cut it as if it were a rabbit or a kid and put it on a big plate; and take garlic and oil blended with good broth in such a manner that it is well-thinned. And cast it over the cat. And you may eat of it because it is very good food.'

PAINSWICK PUPPY DOG PIE
After a cat dish, we have to have dog, but despite the Advertising Standards Authority's best intents, it is not a real dog. I am unsure of the antiquity of the following dish, but it is associated with the ancient Clypping Ceremony in the Cotswold village of Painswick. Before the advent of leavening agents, such as baking powder, a 'cake' was essentially a sweetened and often befruited, loaf of bread, or sometimes a meat and fruit pie. Nowadays, Painswick Dog Pie, also known as a Painswick Bun, Puppy Dog Pie, or 'Bow-Wow Cake' does not contain dog meat, but merely a china dog in recognition of a long-standing local traditional tale. Several stories account for its origin, based on rivalry between Painswick and the neighbouring town of Stroud. The story goes that a landlord of the sixteenth-century Royal Oak, running out of meat, used the meat of local stray dogs instead and fed these to a group of visitors to

Stroud, a deception that once discovered, led to a riot. Another version is that a Painswick man, having promised venison for some visitors from Stroud, on being unable to source the game, substituted with dog meat. Naturally, the deceit, when discovered, caused normal parish rivalry to escalate into name-calling and open hostility.

The first written record about the baking of a pie was by a Mrs Gomme in 1897. She discovered that it was a general custom to eat a pie in which the china figure of a dog had been baked. The pies were made at home and could contain either meat or fruit; what was necessary was that it should contain a china dog. Each year on the Sunday after the feast of the nativity the children of Painswick encircle the church of St. Mary and dance around it singing their Clypping Hymn before the Clypping Service. 'Clypping' is derived from an Old English term meaning encirclement.The service takes place outdoors beginning with a procession of the celebrantswith flowers around the churchyard accompanied by a band, crosses and banners. Well known hymns are sung in addition to the special Clypping Hymn. At this point the congregation join hands and dance back and forward towards the building in a motion described as 'rather like the hokey-cokey'. The guest preacher receives a basket of two Clypping Buns and after the service children receive a bun and a coin in the church hall.

Many churches formerly celebrated in a similar way but their customs died out. At Painswick it was revived in Victorian times but no one knows when it first began. Puppy Dog Pie is served before the service but these days the puppies are made of beef. In 2010 the Royal Oak Inn landlord had to take down his 'Lost Puppy' posters from around the village and issued an open apology. He stressed no pets were harmed in the making of the pie. He said 'The pies have been very popular – we tell people if they are not local, they can't have the tails, or that we have run out of dog, so they will have to have cat instead.' This author has unwittingly eaten curried Alsatian several times at the Plaza Indian restaurant near Manchester University from 1965–8. A 'meat curry for two' was 3*s* 9*d*, complete with two poppadoms and a pickle tray. I knew it was too good to be true...

CONYNGES IN CYNEE – RABBITS IN BLOOD, VINEGAR AND ONION BROTH

The Master-Cook of Richard II, *The Forme of Cury*, *c.* 1390

'Rabbits in Blood and Vinegar Broth with Onion. Take rabbits and chop into pieces and boil them in good broth. Mince onions and fry them in lard and add good broth to them. Make a thickening of bread, blood, vinegar and broth and add to them with powder fort.'

SEA-PIG – SEVERAL WAYS WITH A PORPOISE

Le Ménagier De Paris, 1393

Porpoise was considered a 'fish' by the church and so the mammal was suitable for eating on fish days. However, all porpoises, dolphins, whales and sturgeon are accounted as 'royal fish' and therefore owned by the queen. If catching any of the former three, you could argue the case in court that they are mammals and that the royal family needs to be brought up to speed on biology, but your chances are slim of convincing a High Court judge of this fact.

'SEA-PIG, PORPOISE (and another name also meaning porpoise) are all the same, and the whole fish must be split up the belly like a pig; and with the liver and pluck [intestines] make broth and soup as with a pig. Item, you cut it up and split it like a pig, along the back, and sometimes roast it on the spit in its skin, and then eat with a hot sauce such as sauce brule in winter. Also it is cooked in water and wine added, then powdered spices and saffron, and put in a dish in its cooking liquid like venison. Then grind ginger, cinnamon, grains, long pepper and saffron, and soak in your bouillon, and take one part out of the mortar. Item, grind bread, soak in the liquid from your fish and strain through a sieve, and put it all together to boil, and it will be clear; then serve like venison. Or grind up black pepper, and let your fish, without washing, be cooked in half water half wine, and put on a dish: and throw on your sauce such as sauce galantine, and serve. And when you want to eat it, take a little of the cooled sauce, and add either charcoal-water, or its own liquid, or vinegar and so on, and put on the fire to warm.'

FRUMENTE YN LENTYN – LENTEN PORPOISE AND FRUMENTY

An Ordinance of Pottage, Beinecke MS 163, 1460

'Frumente yn Lentyn. Take clean picked wheat. Pound it in a mortar, and remove the hull, and boil it until it cracks. Then grind blanched almonds in a mortar; make an almond milk. Add the wheat to the almond milk and boil until reasonably thick; make sure the wheat is tender. Colour it with saffron. Cut your porpoise after it has boiled, then set it in dishes with nothing else, and serve it with frumenty. Stir together all the ingredients. Bring to a boil, stirring occasionally to prevent sticking, then reduce heat to low, cover and cook for approximately 45 minutes, or until the bulgar is tender and the mixture becomes thick. Be careful not to scorch. Serve as a soup or as a sauce for meat.'

FURMENTE WITH PORPEYS

The Master-Cook of Richard II, *The Forme of Cury*, c. 1390

One website succinctly and accurately translates the following nobleman's dish as 'boil some wheat with almond milk and bung a porpoise in it.'

'Furmente With Porpeys. Take clene whete and bete it small in a morter and fanne out clene the doust, þenne waisthe it clene and boile it tyl it be tendre and broun. þanne take the secunde mylk of Almaundes and do þerto. boile hem togidur til it be stondyng, and take þe first mylke and alye it up wiþ a penne. take up the porpays out of the Furmente and leshe hem in a dishe with hoot water. and do safroun to þe furmente. and if the porpays be salt. seeþ it by hym self, and serue it forth.'

PUDDYNG OF PURPAYSE – STUFFED PORPOISE STOMACH

Two Fifteenth Century Cookbooks – Harleian MS. 279 & Harl. MS. 4016, with extracts from *Ashmole MS. 1429, Laud MS. 553, & Douce MS 55*

This recipe is essentially a porpoise haggis, similar to the traditional Scottish haggis of a boiled sheep stomach with an oatmeal stuffing.

'Puddyng of Purpayse. Take the Blood of him, and the grease of him self, and Oatmeal, and Salt, Pepper, and Ginger, and mix these together well, and then put this in the Gut of the porpoise, and then let it boil easily, and not hard, a good while; and then take him up, and broil him a little, and then serve forth.'

Ingredients: Porpoise stomach; porpoise blood; porpoise grease; oatmeal; salt; pepper; ginger.

Method: Combine the porpoise blood, porpoise grease and oatmeal and season it with salt, pepper and ginger to make a stuffing. Stuff the porpoise stomach about half full, as the stuffing will swell during cooking. Sew up the stomach tightly or secure each end with string and prick it all over with a large needle to avoid bursting. Put an upturned plate in the base of a pot of boiling water, stand the stomach on this and bring back to the boil. Boil steadily for 3 to 4 hours until done. Drain well and place in a broiler and cook for several minutes on both sides to slightly crisp the skin, then serve.

LAMPREY IN BLOOD SAUCE WITH A DEEP-FRIED LAMPREY SPINAL CORD; AND TORTURED LAMPREY FRYED, BOYLD, AND ROSTED AT THE SAME TIME

Despite its unappetising appearance and behaviour, eating lamprey was the height of culinary sophistication. An earlier fifteenth-century recipe for lamprey pie sees the fish placed in a crust and baked in a sauce of wine, vinegar, cinnamon and its own blood. The lamprey is then removed and served separately, while a syrup of sweet wine, sugar and ginger was added to the crust, along with manchet. Heston Blumenthal recently took a less traditional approach to preparing the fish. His Channel 4 series *Heston's Feast* saw him dish up lamprey 'served with blood sauce on a bed of fake sand with a side of sea foam and finished off with deep-fried lamprey spinal cord.'

In *Eighteen Books Of the Secrets Of Art & Nature*, 1661, by Dr John Wecker, we read: 'First torturing the Lamprey with rubbing him with a sharp Cloath, thrust a Spit through him; and wrap all the parts boyld and fryed, three or four times in Linnen Rags, strewing Pepper with Wine, and upon the boyled Lamprey, Parsley, Saffron, Mints, Fennel, bruised with sweet Wine, and make them wet with water and Salt, or Broth, command the fryed parts to be wrapt in Oyl at the fire, always moystning it, with a bunch of Origanum sprinkling it, when part is torrefied, take it up it will be excellent meat, set it before your company.'

SQUASHED CALVES' HEADS – MOCK STURGEON
Le Ménagier De Paris, 1393

The queen owns all the sturgeon, so if you have the heads of six calves handy, you may avoid prosecution by forging the fish.

'Veal Disguised as Sturgeon for Six Platters. The evening before, or early in the morning, take six calves' heads without skinning, and scald them in hot water like a pig, and cook them in wine. Add a half-litre of vinegar and some salt, and let it boil until the meat comes off the bone. Then let the heads cool and remove the bones. Then take a piece of good coarse cloth, and put it all in it, that is to say, one on top of the other in the smallest space you can, then sew with good strong thread, like a square pillow. Then put it between two strong planks and press very hard, and leave overnight in the cellar. Then slice it up with the skin on the outside like venison, and add parsley and venison, and only put two slices on each dish. Item, if you cannot find enough heads, it can be done with a skinned calf.'

HAGIS – CALF-ENTRAILS IN SHEEP-STOMACH HAGGIS
Mistress Sarah Longe her Receipt Book, c. 1610

'To Make a Hagis. Take a chalves Chadarne [calf's entrails], and parboyle it, when it is cold mingle it fine, with a pound of Beefe suet, a penny-lofe grated, some rosemary, time, winter-savery, and penyriall, of all a small handfull, a little Cloves, mace, nutmegge, and Cinamon, one quarter of a pound of Currence, a little sugar, a little salt, rose-water, all these mixt together, wett with 16 yolkes of Eggs, put in a Sheeps panch, and boyle it.'

RABBETES SOUKER ROST – ROAST FOETAL RABBITS
Coronation Menu of Richard III, 6 July 1483

Rabbits were bred on a large scale in medieval monasteries, which is probably related to their role on the table during periods of fasting. It is alleged that Pope Gregory I, in the year 600 allowed foetal rabbit to be eaten during Lent, by declaring them to be aquatic animals on account of the watery environment of the mother's womb. Foetal or newborn rabbits were a delicacy for nobles and royalty, served at coronations. Bitterns, cranes and egrets were then common birds, with the latter two only relatively recently returning to breed in Britain. At Richard III's coronation feast, venison, peacock, swan, pigeon, roast cygnet, roast crane, roast heron, roast bittern, roast egret, sturgeon, carp and pike were all served along with foetal rabbits. The magnificent banquet lasted from 4 p.m. to 9 p.m., and Richard's meal was served on a golden plate, while his wife Anne's was on a gilt plate. The meal began with frumenty and venison and ended with baked quinces. 3,000 people were fed at the coronation banquet, the greatest ever witnessed at Westminster Abbey, which occurred just two weeks after Richard's nephew Edward V was scheduled to be crowned. Analysis of Richard III's remains show that he suffered from stomach troubles caused by roundworms, an intestinal parasite. Researchers also found that he must have suffered severe tooth decay.

STUFFED SUFFOCATED CHICKS
Le Ménagier De Paris, 1393
'A chick should be suffocated while it is still alive, and it is suffocated at the neck; then bind its neck and let it die: then scald, pluck, gut, put it back together and stuff. Item, or else, when it is all ready to put on the spit, at the hole where it was gutted, you can separate with your finger the skin from the flesh, then stuff it using the end of your finger, then sew it back up with a whip-stitch, at the hole, sewing the skin with the flesh, and put it on the spit. And note that the stuffing is made of parsley and a little sage with hard-cooked eggs and butter, all chopped up together, and powdered spices too. For each chick you need three eggs, whites and all.'

A REALISTIC PEACOCK – FEATHERED PEACOCK WITH A GILDED BEAK
Two Fifteenth Century Cookbooks – Harleian MS. 279 & Harl. MS. 4016, c. 1440
To prevent contamination from the skin onto the cooked bird, in today's re-enactments, a chicken wire frame is made for the bird, which is presented to the table and returned to the kitchen, before the meat is brought in.
Ingredients: 1 unplucked, undrawn peacock; 3–4 beaten egg yolks; ground cumin; piece of gold leaf.
Method: Place the peacock on its back and cut around the skin at the top of each leg. Make a cut from the top of one leg to the other and pull the skin

from the lower half of the peacock, cutting off the root of the tail internally, so it stays attached to the removed skin. Now remove the skin from the top half of the bird, cutting off the last joint of the wings so that they come away with the skin. Next, peel the skin from the neck by pulling it inside out towards the head and cut through the neck. Turn the skin completely inside out to re-dress the bird when it is cooked. Draw the giblets from the bird and thickly dust its flesh with cumin. Truss the legs close to the body, as if it was sitting on a perch, and insert a long skewer down the full length of its neck. The bird was cooked upon a spit, but you can brush it with egg yolks and cook on a grid or in a roasting tin at 200°C for 20 minutes per pound, plus a further 20 minutes. Then let the bird rest for a little, while the neck sets in position. Replace the feathered skin and gild the beak just before serving. Serve with ginger sauce or ground ginger.

FLOURED, FRIED FROGS
Le Ménagier De Paris, 1393

Both frogs and snails were eaten in Tudor times, by the poor for valuable protein and by the nobility to emulate their continental couterparts.

'Frogs. To take them, have a line and a hook and bait of meat or red cloth, and having taken the frogs, cut them across the body near the thighs and empty out what is near the back end, and take the two thighs of these same frogs, cut off the feet, and skin the thighs raw, then have cold water and wash them; and if the thighs stay overnight in cold water, they will be better and more tender. And after thus rinsing them, they should be washed in warm water, then take and dry in a cloth; the thighs, thus washed and dried, should be rolled in flour, that is floured, and then fried in oil, fat or other liquid, and put in a bowl and powdered spices on them.'

SNAILS KNOWN AS ESCARGOTS
Le Ménagier De Paris, 1393

'Snails known as escargots should be taken in the morning. Take young, small snails, with dark shells, among the vines and shrubs, then wash them in plenty of water until there is no more scum. Then wash them once in salt and vinegar and put them on to cook, in water. Then you should drag the snails out of their shells with the end of a pin or needle, and then you should remove their tails, which are black, because that is their excrement. Then wash, and cook and boil in water. Then take them out and put them on a dish or in a bowl, to be eaten with bread. And also some say that they are better fried in oil and onion or other liquid after they have been cooked as above, and are eaten with powdered spices, and are for rich people.'

PODYNG OF A NOX OR OF A SHEPE – COLD BEEF OR LAMB BLOOD SAUSAGES
Gentyll Manly Cokere, MS Pepys 1047, c. 1490
'To make a pudding of an ox or a sheep. Take the blood and beat it with your hand and throw away the lumps that come. Then take the ox or sheep suet and mince it small and put it into the blood. Also put in plenty of oat grits and fill up the guts with the same and boil them, and after broil them. When they are cold serve them forth.'

COCKENTRICE – ROYAL HALF-COCKED HALF-PIG
Harleian MS.279, A Forme of Cury Douce MS.55, 1450
One of the more fanciful and imaginative dishes of the Middle Ages was the *cockentrice*, made by combining a pig and a capon into one creature, thus creating a new animal that would not only feed people but amuse them as well. *Cockentrice* is just one among many spellings of the name of this dish; originally the beast was also known as a *cokagrys* or *cotagres*, from cock (a capon) and *grys* (a pig). A *gryse* or *grys* was a suckling pig. Other period spellings include *koketris, cocagres, cokyntryche, cockyntryce* and *cokantrice*. *Cockentrice* were common entries at great dinners, and a *cokyntryche* is listed among the many feast items at a festival given by John Stafford, Bishop of Bath and Wells, on 16 September 1425.
'Cokyntryce. Take a capon, scald it, drain it clean, then cut it in half at the waist. Take a pig, scald it, drain it as the capon, and also cut it in half at the waist. Take needle and thread and sew the front part of the capon to the back part of the pig. And sew the front part of the pig to the back part of the capon. Then stuff it as you would stuff a pig. Put it on a spit, and roast it. When it is done, gild it on the outside with egg yolks, ginger, saffron, and parsley juice. Serve it forth for a royal meat.'

TO BAKE AN OXE TOUNG – SLICED COW TONGUE PIE
John Partridge's *The Treasurie of Commodious Conceits & Hidden Secrets*, 1573
'Seeth the toung till it be tender, then slyce it on a boorde in fayre peeces: and take a good quantity of Marow slyced smal, cast it into the bottome of the pye. Lay the slices of the toung upon it: and betwixte every one some marow, and a little salt upon them. Bake it the space of an howre, then tost halfe a manchet a little at the fyre, and put the tostes into halfe a pynte of Redde-wine with a little vinegar. Straine them out together. Then take cloves, Mace, Sinimon and Suger, seeth them in ye liquor tyll it waxe somewhat thick. Make a hole in ye cover of the Pye, put it in, set the Pye agayne into the Oven for a quarter of an howre, and serve it.'

HERON ROST – SPIT-ROASTED HERON
Douce MS. 55, c. 1450

'Heron rost. Take an heron and lete hym blode in the mouth as an crane, and scalde hym and draw hym att the vent as a crane. Cutt awey the boon of the necke, and folde the necke a-boute the spite [spit]. Putt the hede ynne att the golet [gullet] as a crane. Breke awey the boon fro the knee to the fote, and lete the skyn be stille, and cutt the wyng att the Joynte next the body, and putt hem on a spite. And bynde hys legges to the spyte with the skynne of the legges, and lete rost, and reyse the legges and the wynges as of a crane, and sauce hym with vynegre, and mustard, and pouudre of gyngeuere, and sett hym forth.'

CHAUDYNN FOR SWANNS – SWAN WITH BLOOD AND ENTRAIL SAUCE
The Master-Cook of Richard II, *The Forme of Cury, c.* 1390

The sauce is made from the blood, intestines and offal of the swan. As the queen owns all of the swans, use a goose.

'Take the liver and the offal of the swan and put to boil in good broth. Remove the giblets, take out the bones and chop the meat finely. Make a liaison of bread crusts and of the swan's blood, boiled and add to this ground cloves and pepper and wine and salt and boil it and add to it the chopped meats and serve it to accompany the Swan.'

MANY WAYS WITH A SWAN
Le Ménagier De Paris, 1393

As above, the queen owns the swans – unless you wish to use roadkill.

'SWAN. Pluck like a chicken or goose, scald, or boil; spit, skewer in four places, and roast with all its feet and beak, and leave the head unplucked; and eat with yellow pepper.

Item, if you wish, it may be gilded.

Item, when you kill it, you should split its head down to the shoulders.

Item, sometimes they are skinned and reclothed.

RECLOTHED SWAN in its skin with all the feathers. Take it and split it between the shoulders, and cut it along the stomach: then take off the skin from the neck cut at the shoulders, holding the body by the feet; then put it on the spit, and skewer it and gild it. And when it is cooked, it must be reclothed in its skin, and let the neck be nice and straight or flat; and let it be eaten with yellow pepper.'

SILVER GILDED SWAN WITH A CRIMSON CLOAK ON A GREEN GRASSY MEADOW

Le Ménagier De Paris, 1393

This was not a poor man's dish.

'Take a swan and prepare it and put it on to roast until it is all cooked. Then make a paste of eggs, as clear as paper, and pour it on the said swan while turning the spit so that the paste cooks on it, and be careful that no wings or thighs be broken. Put the swan's neck as though it were swimming in water, and to keep it in this position, you must put a skewer in its head which will rest between the two wings, passing all other, until it holds the neck firm, and another skewer below the wings, and another between the thighs, and another close to the feet and at each foot three to spread the foot. And when it is well cooked and well gilded with the paste, take out the skewers, except that in the neck, then make a terrace of whole-wheat pastry, which should be thick and strong, and which is one fist thick, made with nice fluting all around, and let it be two feet long, and a foot and a half broad, or a little more, then cook it without boiling. Have it painted green like a grassy meadow, and gild your swan with a skin of silver, except for about two fingers width around the neck, which is not gilded, and the beak and the feet. Then have a flying cloak, which should be of crimson sendal on the inside, and emblazon the top of said cloak with whatever arms you wish, and around the swan have banners, the sticks two and a half feet long with banners of sandal. Emblazon with whatever arms you wish, and put all in a dish the size and shape of the terrace, and present it to whomever you wish.'

HOW TO BAKE LAMPREYE, PORPOS OR PUFFINS

A.W., *The Booke of Goode Cookry Very Necessary for all Such as Delight Therein*, 1584, 1591

'How to bake a Lamprey. When you have fleied and washed it clean, season it with Pepper, and salt, and make a light Gallandine and put to it good store of butter, and after this sort you must make your gallandine. Take white bread tostes and lay them in steep in Claret wine, or else in vergious, and so strain them with vinagre, and make it somewhat thin, and put sugar, Sinamon and ginger, and boyle it on a Chafing dish of coles, this Galandine being not too thicke, put it into your pye of Lampreye, and after this sort shall you bake Porpos or Puffins.'

BAKED HOLYBUT HEAD – HALIBUT HEAD IN VERJUICE

A.W., *The Booke of Goode Cookry Very Necessary for all Such as Delight Therein*, 1584, 1591

'First water it till it be fresh then cut it in small peeces like Culpines of an Eele, and season it with pepper and Saffron, cloves and mace, small raisins and great, and meddle al these wel togither, and also put therto a good messe of vergious, and so bake the same Fish.'

SINGING CHICKEN, GOSLING OR PIGLET

The Vivendier mid-fifteenth century, north-eastern France

Of course, quicksilver (mercury) is poisonous and must never be handled, let alone used in cooking.

'To Make that Chicken Sing when it is dead and roasted, whether on the spit or in the platter. Take the neck of your chicken and bind it at one end and fill it with quicksilver and ground sulphur, filling until it is roughly half full; then bind the other end, not too tightly. When it is quite hot, and when the mixture heats up, the air that is trying to escape will make the chicken's sound. The same can be done with a gosling, with a piglet and with any other birds. And if it does not cry loudly enough, tie the two ends more tightly.'

PRETEND LIVING CHICKEN OR ANY OTHER BIRD

Le Viandier de Guillaume Tirel dit Taillevent, c. 1440

This calls for plucking a live chicken, rotating it until it becomes unconscious, painting it to appear roasted and serving it on a platter. When it wakes it will obviously move, to the 'delight' of diners.

'To make a Chicken be Served Roasted. Get a chicken or any other bird you want, and pluck it alive cleanly in hot water. Then get the yolks of 2 or 3 eggs. They should be beaten with powdered saffron and wheat flour, and distempered with fat broth or with the grease that drips under a roast into the dripping pan. By means of a feather glaze and paint your pullet carefully with this mixture so that its colour looks like roast meat. With this done, and when it is about to be served to the table, put the chicken's head under its wing, and turn it in your hands, rotating it until it is fast asleep. Then set it down on your platter with the other roast meat. When it is about to be carved it will wake up and make off down the table upsetting jugs, goblets and whatnot.'

COW'S UDDERS IN MUSTARD SAUCE

Le Ménagier De Paris, 1393

'Cow's Udders. Cooked with meat and eaten like meat. Item, salted with mustard sauce. Item, sometimes cut in strips and roasted on the grill, cooked fresh.'

BOILED VIPERS

Professor Richard Bradley, *The Country Housewife and Lady's Director in the Management of a House, and the Delights and Profits of a Farm*, 1736

The recipe is later than Tudor times, but snakes were eaten in those times by the poor and deserve inclusion, especially for the reference to their hearts. Who ever thought that snakes had hearts?

'Take Vipers, alive and cut off their Heads; then cut them in pieces, about two Inches in length, and boil them, with their Hearts. Garnish with slices of Lemon.'

BOILED BADGER

Professor Richard Bradley, *The Country Housewife and Lady's Director in the Management of a House, and the Delights and Profits of a Farm*, 1736

Another recipe from Professor Bradley's cookbook tells us that badger was traditionally considered a delicacy in some rural areas, and could be a culinary use for roadkill today – unless the queen owns them along with her swans, sturgeon, dolphins, porpoises and whales.

'The Badger is one of the cleanest Creatures, in its Food, of any in the World. When a Badger is killed, cut off the Gammons, and strip them; then lay them in a Brine of Salt and Water for a Week or ten Days; then boil it for four or five Hours, and then roast it. Serve it hot with some Lemon in slices.'

REDRESSED PEACOCKS WHICH SEEM LIVING; AND HOW TO MAKE THEM BREATH FIRE THROUGH THEIR MOUTH

Cuoco Napoletano: *The Neapolitan Recipe Collection*, late fifteenth century

'You should first kill the peacock with a feather, driving it upon its head, or else drain its blood from under its throat as with a pig; but it is better to take out its tongue and then to slice it under its body – that is, from the top of its breast to its tail – slicing only the skin and removing it gently so that it is not damaged; when you have skinned it, pull the skin back right up to the head, then cut away the head, which will remain attached to the skin; do the same with the legs, and likewise the tail, taking out the leg bones so that the iron will make the peacock stand up will not be seen; then take the skinned carcass and set it to roast stuck with lardoons, or else baste it with grease often enough that it will not burn, and stick it with whole cloves, and fill it with the Piglet stuffing but without garlic; cook it gently so its neck does not burn; if the neck should get too much heat, cover it with a damp cloth; when it is cooked, take it down and redress it in its skin, whose inside you have coated with spices, salt and cinnamon.

Then, when you have put its skin back on, get an apparatus of iron driven into a large cutting board and shove this iron through its feet and legs so it cannot be seen; in this way the peacock will be standing so that it will seem to be alive.

And to make it breathe fire through its mouth, get a little camphor with a little fine cotton-wool around it and put this into the peacock's beak and soak it with a little aqua vita or else with a little fumey old wine that is volatile; when you want to serve it, set fire to the cotton-wool: in this way it will breathe fire for a long time. To make it more magnificent you can cover the peacock with gold leaf and then cover it with its skin. The same can be done with pheasants, cranes, geese and other birds.'

A SEEMINGLY ALIVE BOILED PEACOCK, BREATHING FIRE

Giambatissta della Porta's *Magia Naturalis*, 1558

Another version of the old favourite immediately above.

'A boiled Peacock may seem to be alive. Kill a Peacock, either by thrusting a Quill into his brain from above, or else cut his throat, as you do for young Kids, that the blood may come forth. Then cut his skin gently from his throat unto his tail, and being cut, pull it off with his feathers from his whole body to his head. Cut off that with the skin, and legs, and keep it. Roast the Peacock on a spit. His body being stuffed with spices and sweet Herbs, sticking first on his breast Cloves, and wrapping his neck in a white Linen cloth. Wet it always with water, that it may never dry. When the Peacock is roasted, and taken from the spit, put him into his own skin again, and that he may seem to stand upon his feet, you shall thrust small Iron wires, made on purpose, through his legs, and set fast on a board, that they may not be discerned, and through his body to his head and tail. Some put Camphire in his mouth, and when he is set upon the table, they cast in fire. Platina shows that the same may be done with Pheasants, Geese, Capons, and other birds. And we observe these things among our guests.'

GILDED PEACOCK

Dr. John Wecker, *Eighteen Books Of the Secrets Of Art & Nature*, 1661

Dr. Wecker rewrote the above dish in his work, but added gilding: 'Kill the Peacock, either thrusting a Feather from above into his brain, or cut his throat as you do a young Kids, and let the blood run forth of his throat; then divide his skin gently as far as his tail, and being divided pull it off from his head all over his body Feathers and all ; keep this with the skin cutoff, and hang the Peacock by the heels upon a Spit, having stuffed him with sweet Herbs and Spices, and roast him, first sticking Cloves all along his brest, and wrapping his neck in a white Linnen Cloath, always wetting it, that it dry not. When the Peacock is rosted, take him off from the Spit, and put his own skin upon, him, and that he may seem to stand upon his feet, make some Rods of Iron fastned into a Board, made with leggs, that it may not be discerned, and drive these through his body as far as his head. Some to make sport and laughter, put Wool with Camphir into his mouth, and they cast in fire when he comes to the Table. Also you may gild a rosted Peacock, strewed With Spices, and covered with leaves of Gold for your recreation, and for magnificence. The same may be done with Pheasants, Crains, Geese, Capons, and other Birds.'

FRIED AND ROASTED MAGPIES, CROWS, JACKDAWS, STARLINGS, SKYLARKS AND TURTLE DOVES
Le Ménagier De Paris, 1393

'Magpies, Crows, Jackdaws. These are killed with crossbow-bolts with broad unsharpened points, and with light crossbows you can take crows which are perched on branches, but for those in the nest you need to draw large bolts to knock down nest and all. They should be singed, then parboiled with bacon, then cut in pieces, and fry with eggs like mincemeat.

Starlings. They are plucked dry, gutted, then cut off the heads and feet, then sew up, put in pastry with two strips of bacon on them: or cut the parts in pieces like a chick, and treat like mincemeat, that is to say that you cut the thigh into three parts, and leave the bones in each piece: the wings also, and the rest the same, and then fry in the skillet with eggs like mincemeat (hamburger: Trans.) It seems to be a good idea to half cook them before frying.

Roast Skylarks. Pluck them dry, then cut off the heads, and do not gut them. They are sewn back up, and the legs are not cut off, and they are spitted crossways between two slices of bacon. Item, in pastry, you do cut off the heads and legs, and gut them, and put in the hole fine cheese, and eat them with salt.

Turtledoves are good roasted and in pastry, and are in season in September, from August on. Always when roasted they smell marvellous; and if you have plenty of them and wish to feed and keep them, you should clip or pluck their tails, otherwise they will fly and maim themselves and thus die.'

SHEEP'S HEAD
Le Ménagier De Paris, 1393

'Sheep's Head should be very well cooked, then remove the bones, and chop the remainder very fine, and throw powdered herbs on it.'

PUDDYNG OF PURPAYSSE – **PORPOISE BLOOD PUDDING**

Two Fifteenth Century Cookbooks – Harleian MS. 279 & Harl. MS. 4016, c. 1440

'Pudding of porpoise. Take the Blood of him, and the grease of himself, and Oatmeal, and Salt, and Pepper, and Ginger, and mix these together well, and then put this in the Gut of the porpoise, and then let it boil easily, and not hard, a good while; and then take him up, and broil him a little, and then serve forth.'

13

Drinks

Macduff: What three things doth drink especially provoke?
Porter: Drink sir, is a great provoker of three things… nose painting, sleep
and urine. Lechery, sir, it provokes, and unprovokes; it provokes the desire
but takes away the performance. Therefore, much drink may be said to be an
equivocator with lechery: it makes him, and it mars him; it sets him on, and
it takes him off; it persuades him, and disheartens him; makes him stand to,
and not stand to; in conclusion, equivocates him in a sleep, and, giving him
the lie, leaves him.

Macbeth, Act 2, Scene 3

As noted earlier in this book, water was not recommended for consumption,
especially in towns and cities. There are plenty of home brewing recipes in
books and on the net, so it is not proposed to give many in this section.

CIDER

Cider and apples were widely regarded as having health-giving properties.
In his 1597 *Herbal*, Gerard advises that: 'There is an ointment made with the
pulp of apples and swine's grease and rose water, which is used to beautify the
face, and to take away the roughness of the skin, called in shops *pomatum* of
the apples whereof it is made.' The ointment was used to soften the skin and
fade freckles. Cider drinking was also supposed to promote longevity in this
chorus from a Devonshire cider drinking song:
'I were brought up on cider
And I be a hundred and two
But still that be 'nuthin when you come to think
Me father and mother be still in the pink
And they were brought up on cider

Of the rare old Tavistock brew
And me Granfer drinks quarts
For he's one of the sports
That were brought up on cider too'

TO CURE STRANGURY USING CIDER
The Physicians of Myddfai – medieval

The author's new translation of the thousand medieval cures in *The Physicians of Myddfai* notes several uses for cider in folk medicine. For *strangury*, a condition marked by slow, painful urination, caused by muscular spasms of the urethra and bladder, one was advised to 'seek some mouse chickweed (*Cerastium vulgatum,* Mouse-ear Chickweed) and wild sage (*Salvia verbenica,* Wild Clary), as much of the one as of the other. Then make into a powder and mix with drink. Cider is best, or else old mead, if no cider can be obtained.' An ointment for 'external inflammation' asks one to: 'Take the cream of cows' milk, and white wine or strong apple cider, or else strong old mead. Boil well together, equal quantities of each, until it becomes thick, stirring it continually. When cold, keep in a bladder or box, and when needful anoint the part therewith.' Animal bladders, from time immemorial, were useful liquid storage containers.

ANOTHER MEDICINE FOR PNEUMONIA USING CIDER
The Physicians of Myddfai – medieval

'Take white horehound [Common Horehound, *Marrubium vulgare*] and pound well. Then add some pure water, letting it stand for three hours. Strain well through a fine cloth. Add a good deal of honey to the strained liquor, and put on a slow fire to warm. Take half a draught of this every three hours, and let your diet be the best wheaten bread and milk. When thirsty, take an apple, and cover it with good old cider, eat the apple. In an hour drink the cider, and let this be your only diet.' Cider was also used for 'exathematous contamination of the humors', a skin eruption accompanying an infection: 'Take the roots and seed of nettles. Pound well, then boil in good cider which is half-a-year or a year old. Let this be your only drink. The best cider is that made with good sour winter apples.'

TO MAKE CYDER
The Whole Duty of a Woman, 1737

One of the ingredients in the *piggesauce* recipe in the chapter on preserves and sauces is a *pomewater*, 'a large, juicy, sharp-tasting variety of apple.' It was enormously popular for cooking and cider-making for several hundred years, but now appears to have disappeared. Its botanical name was *Malus carbonaria*, and it was described by John Parkinson in *Theatrum Botanicum* (1640): 'The Pomewater is an excellent, good, and great whitish Apple, full of sap or moisture, somewhat pleasant sharp, but a little bitter withall; it will not last long, the winter frosts soon causing it to rot and perish.' Incidentally, it is a rural myth that a dead rat was placed in a vat of cider to improve it. Rats were endemic in the country and probably one fell in somewhere, the cider was unaffected and so the legend spread.

'To make Cyder. Take Apples so thoroughly ripe that they will easily fall by shaking the Tree. The Apples proper are Pippins, Pomewaters, Harveys or other Apples of a watery Juice, either grind or pound them, and squeeze them in a Hair Bag, put the Juice up into a seasoned Cask. The Cask is to be seasoned with a Rag dip'd in Brimstone ty'd to the End of a Stick, and put in burning into the Bung-hole of the Cask, and when the Smoke is gone, wash it with a little warm Liquor that has run thro' a second Straining of the Mure or Husk of the Apples. Put into the Cask, when the Cyder is in, a Bit of Paste made up of Flower, and ty'd up in a thin Rag; let it stand for a Week, and then draw it off from the Lees into another season'd Cask. Some advise to put three or four pounds of Raisins into a Hogshead, and two pounds of Sugar to make it work the better.

The best Way to fine it is to rack it off often, and always into small Vessels, keeping them close bung'd, and only a small Vent-hole, and if it should work after racking, you may put some Raisins into the Vessel for it to feed upon, and to bottle it off in March, or if you bottle it up. After it has stood but a Week or thereabouts, you must not stop the Bottles for twenty-four Hours; nor must they be filled within an Inch of the Cork or more, lest it should burst; and when you have cork'd them, it will be convenient to open them once a Day for some time. If you bottle it for present Drinking, put in a Lump of Loaf Sugar. In order to keep it in the Winter, set it in a warm Place in cold Weather.'

HENRY VII'S MULLED APPLE CIDER

A modern redaction of a warmed, spiced cider, excellent after winter walks.
Ingredients: 8 pints cider; ¼ tsp freshly-chopped thyme; freshly-ground nutmeg; 1tsp ground ginger; cinnamon to taste.
Method: Place all the ingredients, except the cinnamon, into a large pot and simmer very gently for a few minutes. Boiling will evaporate the alcohol. Swirl in cinnamon to taste and allow to cool a little before serving in warmed mugs.

MULLED CHRISTMAS APPLEJACK

Calvados is Norman apple brandy and is perfect, but you can use any cheaper brandy. Brandy is traditionally used in Christmas cuisine and this is an ideal Christmas party drink. You could make it with cheaper Spanish brandy, which is distilled from sherry and so is heavier and sweeter than French brandy, which is based on wine. English apple brandy used to be known as *applejack* and the term was kept by the early American settlers.

Ingredients: 1 bottle Ludlow apple brandy, *Calvados* or cheap brandy; 6 pints cider; 1½ tsp whole cloves; 1½ tsp whole allspice; 6 sticks of cinnamon; 1½ cups brown sugar.

Method: Tie the spices in a cheesecloth and add to the cider and sugar in a large saucepan. Gently bring to the boil, stirring gently to dissolve the sugar and very gently simmer for 10 minutes to blend flavours. Do not boil. Add brandy and simmer for a minute. Discard the spices and serve in warmed mugs.

WASSAIL
Elizabethan Recipe – modernised

Many traditions are associated with cider, most notably the Wassail. Farmers and farm workers would salute apple trees in a ceremony known as wassailing. Men carried jugs of cider into the orchards and drank a health to the trees and the anticipated next year's crop, pouring cider around the tree roots. During the ceremonies, a great deal of noise was created by banging pots and pans. Wheat flour cakes were eaten at these ceremonies and small pieces of the cake were dipped in cider and placed in the forks of the trees as a thanksgiving to the spirit of the tree. The Old Norse is *ves heill*, meaning to be in good health, and wassail comes from the Old English *Wass Hal*, 'Be Thou of Good Health'. The time of the wassail lasted from Christmas Eve to Twelfth Night. There was often a large wooden bowl (later earthenware), dressed with festive ribbons, which was not only the serving bowl but also the drinking bowl, as it was passed between participants. Wassail was also sometimes served from a special bowl called a Loving Cup, seemingly used to woo ladies.

'Thou shalt have Possets, Wassails fine,

Not made of Ale, but spiced Wine;

To make thy Maids and selfe free mirth,

All sitting neer the glitt'ring Hearth.

Thou shalt have Ribbands, Roses, Rings,

Gloves, Garters, Stockings, Shooes, and Strings

Of winning Colours, that shall move

Others to Lust, but me to Love.

These (nay) and more, thine own shal be,

If thou wilt love, and live with me.' Robert Herrick (1591–1674)

Ingredients: 2 litres cheap cider; 6 cored eating apples; 6 tsp brown sugar; 100 ml water; 1 orange, studded with around 12 cloves; 1 inch cinnamon stick; 6 allspice berries; 1 wine glass of cheap brandy; 1 wine glass of cheap sherry.

Method: Place the apples on a baking tray, put a teaspoon of sugar in the hole left by the core of each and pour the water into the tray. Place into an oven preheated to 170°C. Bake for around 20 minutes until the apples are soft, but not collapsing. Meanwhile, place the cider, orange with cloves, cinnamon stick and allspice in a large pan. Bring to a gentle simmer for around 20 minutes, then taste to check that the spices have infused. Do not boil. If they have infused, add the apples with their cooking juice, the brandy and the sherry. At this stage you could add a pint of higher quality cider to improve the taste. Simmer for another 5 minutes, then serve in warmed mugs or glasses. Serve with slices of pork pie, sausages and cheese.

PERRY – PEAR CIDER

Pear cultivation was centred around the Worcestershire, Gloucestershire and Herefordshire regions and the majority of traditional perry comes from the same area today. Perry pears are unlike the cultivated pear we see in shops and contain varying amounts of the natural sweetener *sorbitol*, which does not ferment to alcohol. *Sorbitol* can have a laxative action, with some people being more susceptible than others. This property has given rise to the saying 'Perry goes down like velvet, round like thunder and out like lightning.' You have been warned.

Several writers in the sixteenth century maintained that pears were poisonous to eat, as testified in the following quotation from a manuscript written by monks in Worcestershire: 'Peres causeth ye colyck passion in ye bowlles, wyld peres stoppeth and noyeth ye stomake, but ye grete tame peres byn better usid in meates than the lyttle, and the uice of both usid before dyner stopeth ye bely, and usid after dyner layeth ye bely.' Like apples, pears were imported from France from Norman times, and for many years French varieties dominated English orchards. Sometime before 1388 the first important English pear variety, the Wardon (later Warden), was introduced by Cistercian Monks at Wardon in Bedfordshire. It was widely used for pies, which became known as Warden Pies. The fruiterer to Henry VIII introduced pears from France and the Low Countries in 1533 for planting at Teynham in Kent and William Turner mentions the revival of pear orchards and the introduction of new varieties in his *Herbal* of 1568.

In Worcestershire the importance of the pear was recognised by the incorporation in the city arms of 'three pears sable' at the direction of Queen Elizabeth I when she visited the city in 1575. In 1580, Harrison wrote that *pirrie* (from the Saxon word *pirige*, meaning pear) was made from pears along with cider, in Worcestershire, Sussex, Kent and other counties. Gerard wrote in 1597: 'Wine made of the iuce of Peares, called in English Perry, is soluble, purgeth those that are not accustomed to drink thereof; notwithstanding it is as wholesome a drinke being taken in small quantities as wine; it comforteth and warmeth the stomacke, and causeth a good digestion'. Gerard also showed that the number of pear varieties had increased since the beginning of the century and claimed that one friend of his had sixty high quality varieties in his orchard and perhaps as many again of lesser quality ones. He illustrated eight pears, the Jenneting; the Pear Royall; the Quince Pear; the Katherine; the Saint James; the Burgomet; the Bishops; and the Winter Pear. Gerard also mentioned wild or hedge pears including the Great Choke, the Small Choke, the Wild Hedge Pear, the Lowsie wild and the Crow pear. He said that many of these pears were harsh and bitter and others of such a choking taste that they could not be eaten. These 'choking pears' were often instead used for making perry. Before the end of the Tudor period, new varieties were being constantly introduced from Europe.

Parkinson, in 1629, referred to the 'Choke pear' which in his time applied to any wild, very astringent type of pear: 'The Perry made of Choke Pears, notwithstanding the harshness and evill taste, both of the fruit and juice, after a few months, becomes as milde and pleasante as wine'. There are at least 120 remaining perry pear varieties, many so local that they were only ever propagated on one or two adjacent farms. Some of the great names include the descriptive Dead Boy, Mumblehead and Merrylegs. The best perry pears, as designated by Dr. Robert Hogg in his *Fruit Manual* of 1884, were the Arlingham Squash, Cheat-boy, Aylton Red, Coppy Pear, Barland Holmer, Black Huff-cap, Longland, Butt Pear, Moorcroft, Chaseley Green, Oldfield, Parsonage, Thurston Red, Pine Pear, White Longland, Red Pear, White Squash, Rock Pear, Winnal's Longland, Taynton Squash, Yellow Huff-cap, Thorn Pear and Yoking House. The perry pear trees of Monmouthshire are localised, with often just a single example of a variety remaining. The Monmouthshire Burgundy and Monmouth Potato pears have just been rediscovered at a number of locations, and the latter does indeed resemble a potato. The *Berllanderi* Green, Early St. Brides and Chapman's Orange are other Welsh varieties. Traditional perry is served completely flat and may well be cloudy. It is far more difficult than cider to brew at home.

GILLIAN'S FIRST PERRY

Gillian Grafton, on her excellent website perryandcider.co.uk.

Ingredients: 50 lbs (approximately) of unknown variety pears; Yeastlab British Ale Yeast (A04).

Method: 'I picked the pears and left them to stand for one week in a cool well aired area. I did not wash them or cut out any diseased parts. I did discard obviously rotten fruit. I cut the pears into small slices and ran them through my fruit juicer. This machine was made to cope with the odd orange at breakfast, not such a volume of pears! It coped well enough but took hours. I'll never do it that way again, next time I'll make, buy or hire a cider/fruit press. The pears yielded approximately 2½ gallons of juice to which I added 3 crushed Campden tablets, 3 tsp of pectolase, and 3 tsp of yeast nutrient. I covered the juice and let it stand for 24 hours. The pH was 3.6 – perfect, and the O.G. 1065. I pitched the yeast and left the juice to get on and ferment. I racked after 4 weeks at which time the gravity was 1010. 4 weeks after that I bottled the perry and started drinking it just a few weeks after bottling. I should have left the perry to mature for a few months so it could undergo a malo-lactic fermentation. It was a little sharp because I didn't do this. However, having said that, it was one of the best perries I've ever drunk, even if I do say so myself. I have no idea what variety pears they were I used, however the tree is very old (200–300 years) and I strongly suspect it is an old perry variety. Sadly the tree is dying, but I'm determined to get some grafts before its demise – a pear like that can't be wasted.'

MEDIEVAL LAMB'S WOOL

Traditional medieval, a variant of Wassail

A warm, spiced drink made from mixing hot cider, sherry or ale, apples and spices. One version of its odd name is that the mixture was sometimes heated until it 'exploded' and formed a white 'woolly' head. However, it may be derived from the Irish Gaelic *la mas nbhal*, pronounced 'lamass-ool', made for the feast of apple gathering known as All Hallows Eve or Lammastide. Each guest would take a piece of apple and eat it, toasting his or her fellows.

Ingredients: 3 litres ale or stout; 12 small apples; 3 tbsp honey; ¼ tsp freshly-ground nutmeg; ¼ tsp powdered cinnamon; 2 tsp freshly-grated ginger.

Method: Bake the apples in a hot oven until they begin to split. Divide the ale between two pots. Each pot will need to be big enough to easily take all the ingredients, i.e. 3 litres and 12 apples. Place about three-quarters of the ale in one pot and heat very gently until warm. Place the remaining ale in the second pot, add the apples, honey and spices to this and bring to the boil. Immediately pour the warmed ale into this and turn off the heat. Keep pouring the heated ale between the two pots until a large amount of froth has accumulated on the top. This is the 'Lamb's Wool'. Pour into a heated punch bowl and you can ladle out, or guests can dip their cups in.

ELIZABETHAN LAMB'S WOOL

Traditional Elizabethan

You can use apple juice for a non-alcoholic version. The verse from Shakespeare's *Twelfth Night* refers to both *wassail* and *Lamb's Wool*:

'Next crown the bowl full

With gentle Lamb's Wool

Add sugar, nutmeg, and ginger,

With store of Ale too,

And thus ye must doe

To make the Wassail a swinger.'

Ingredients: 4 pints of ale or cider; 6 cored and sliced apples; 6 tbsp brown sugar; ¼ tsp cinnamon; ¼ tsp ginger; ⅛ tsp ground nutmeg.

Method: Roast the apples for around 40 minutes, until the pieces turn soft and fluffy. Heat the ale or cider, dissolving the sugar slowly in it, stirring and adding in the spices. Do not boil but simmer gently for around 15–30 minutes, then pour over the apple pieces in a punch bowl and serve.

MEAD – HONEY WINE

Many types of mead were drunk in Tudor times, with honey and wild yeasts causing fermentation. Said to be at least 9,000 years old, mead is considered our oldest intentionally fermented beverage. Around 550, the bard Taliesin wrote the *Kanu y Med*, 'Song to Mead', and this honey wine has been known in Britain since this time. This famous drink was associated with warrior bravado, especially in Taliesin's fabulous poem *Y Gododdin*, and with poetic inspiration. Along with being about mead, the bardic song refers to the legend where the young Taliesin has to free his patron and foster father Elffin from Maelgwn Gwynedd's prison.

'… May Maelgwn of Mona be affected with mead, and affect us,

From the foaming mead-horns, with the choicest pure liquor,

Which the bees collect, and do not enjoy.

Mead distilled sparkling, its praise is everywhere.

The multitude of creatures which the earth nourishes,

God made for man to enrich him.

Some fierce, some mute, he enjoys them.

Some wild, some tame, the Lord makes them.

Their coverings become clothing.

For food, for drink, till doom they will continue.
I will implore the Ruler, sovereign of the country of peace,
To liberate Elffin from banishment.
The man who gave me wine and ale and mead.
And the great princely steeds, beautiful their appearance,
May he yet give me bounty to the end.
By the will of God, he will give in honour,
Five five-hundred festivals in the way of peace.
Elffinian knight of mead, late be thy time of rest.'

Today's brewers can make either 'small mead', fermented quickly, with a high CO_2 content and more of the characteristics of a beer than a wine; or 'strong mead', far more wine-like with a high alcohol content, as much as 18 per cent by volume. Like wine, the latter can be sweet or dry, depending on the yeast strain used.

METHEGLIN – SPICED OR HERBED MEAD

Metheglin or *metheglyn* (the Welsh source word) is traditional mead with herbs and/or spices added. Some common *metheglins* are ginger, orange peel, coriander, cinnamon, nutmeg, cloves, chamomile, lavender or vanilla. The name indicates that many *metheglins* were originally employed in folk medicine in Wales. The Welsh for mead is *medd*, and *metheglin* derives from *meddyglyn*, a compound of *meddyg*, healing, and *llyn* meaning water from a lake or spring. 'Cordial' flowers are those that 'cheer the heart': 'All four of the cardinal flowers go into metheglin, the traditional drink of Wales. The rose "take of sweet-bryar and great handful", violet flowers, violet leaves, bugloss and borage. Added to these are rosemary and strawberry leaves, and a great many other herbs and spices, including a trace of ginger. The herbs are boiled in water which is then strained; a quantity of honey is added, and the mixture is fermented with ale-barm (a sort of yeast). They say it is heady stuff, and I am sure that it will warm the heart.' – Elizabeth Lawrence *Through the Garden Gate*, 1957.

MELOMEL – FRUIT MEAD

A mead with added fruit such as raspberry, blackberry or strawberry, in fact any fruit except grapes or apples. The Tudors used wild strawberries in the absence of cultivated and larger varieties.

PYMENT – GRAPE MEAD

Mead fermented with a blend of honey, grape juice and water, making a light honey-flavoured wine for summer.

CYSER – CIDER MEAD
Mead fermented with apple cider. This is a strong drink dating from Biblical times. Both the honey and the cider will ferment to a clean dry wine and can make an excellent sparkling wine when primed with corn sugar or honey when bottled. Leeners.com has recipes for all the mead-based drinks above.

BRAGGOT – ALE AND HONEY
Also called *bracket* or *brackett*, *braggot* is often associated historically with medieval Britain, with *bragawd* being its Welsh origin word. Consumed widely, it could either be ale with fermented with honey, ale blended with fully fermented mead or ale laced with honey and spices. Often it was blended on the spot in one way or another according to taste and what was available. As hops gained acceptance in later Tudor times, they were also used in *braggot*. Like other drinks, it was taken by the early colonists to America, and one can easily buy *braggot* in bottles in the USA, but it seems scarce in the UK.

ALE
A song apparently written 1471–85 warns of the dangers of ale:
'Ale mak many a man to styke at a brere [get caught in briars or brambles];
Ale mak many a mane to ly in the myere; [lie in the mire]
And ale mak many a mane to slep by the fyere; [sleep by the fire]
With doll. CHORUS
Doll thi ale, dol, dol thi ale, dole,
Ale mak many a mane to have a doty poll. [hurting head]
Ale mak many a mane to stombyl at a stone;
Ale mak many a man to go dronken home;
And ale mak many a mane to brek hys tone;
With doll. CHORUS
Ale mak many a mane to draw hys knyfe;
Ale mak many a mane to mak gret stryfe;
And ale mak many a mane to bet hys wyf;
With dole. CHORUS
Ale mak many a mane to wet hys chekes;
Ale mak many a man to ly in the stretes;
And ale mak many a man to wet hys shetes; [wet his bed]
With doll. CHORUS
Ale mak many a mane to stombyll at the blokkes;
Ale mak many a mane to make his hed have knokkes;
And ale mak many a man to syt in the stokkes;
With doll. CHORUS

Ale mak many a mane to ryne over the falows;
Ale mak many a mane to swere by God and alhalows;
And ale make many a mane to hang upon the galows;
With doll. CHORUS
Doll thi ale, dol, dol thi ale, dole,
Ale mak many a mane to have a doty poll.'

BARLEY WINE/STRONG ALE

This is ale made from the first mash. Being the first drink made from the malted barley this was by far the strongest and best and was reserved for the upper classes. The practice of hopping grains to make beer only started around 1000 in Germany and did not reach Britain until 1545 at the earliest.

STANDARD ALE

This is made from the second steeping of the mash. This was less alcoholic than the strong ale made from the first steeping and was reserved for the peasantry. It would have been stronger than modern ales, around 6–7% alcohol by volume.

SMALL BEER

Low alcohol ale was typically served to children, made from a secondary mashing. The low sugar content would only yield about 2.5% alcohol by volume. After about 1860, bottled beer became available, but tea became the national drink, even among the working class. Again, the boiling of water made the beverage safer. From the medieval *The Physicians of Myddfai* we read of an unpleasant medical use for small beer:

'The Following is the Treatment Employed by Rhiwallon Feddyg for the Relief of Constipation.

Remedy 769. Take small beer, unsalted butter, and wheat bran. Boil them well and strain. Pour into a bladder, into which insert a quill, firmly binding the bladder about it. This pipe should be passed into the patient's rectum, his head being as low, and his pelvis as high as can conveniently be. The bladder should then be compressed, and the fluid forced into the body.'

COCK ALE

The Closet of the Eminently Learned Sir Kenelme Digbie Kt Opened, 1669
The drink was known in Tudor times, but this is the earliest recipe I could find.

'Take eight Gallons of Ale; take a Cock and boil him well; then take four pounds of Raisins of the Sun well stoned, two or three Nutmegs, three or four flakes of Mace, half a pound of Dates; beat these all in a Mortar, and put to them two quarts of the best Sack; and when the Ale hath done working, put these in, and stop it close six or seven days, and then bottle it, and a month after you may drink.'

GILLY-FLOWER WINE – CLOVED SHERRY CORDIAL
W.M., *The Queen's Closet Opened*, 1655
This is an Elizabethan wine-based cordial, using clove pinks (small scented carnations), for which I give a later recipe. Gillyflower could also be the scented stock or wallflower.
'Take two ounces of dried Gilly-flowers, and put them into a bottle of Sack, and beat three ounces of Sugar-candy, or fine Sugar, and grinde some Ambergreese, and put it in the bottle and shake it oft, then run it through a gelly bag, and give it for a great Cordial after a weeks standing or more. You may make Lavender Wine as you do this.'
Ingredients: 60 g dried clove pinks; 750 ml sherry; 90 g powdered sugar; a little ambergris ground to a powder (omit if not available).
Method: Remove the husks, stems and bitter heels from the flowers, then combine all ingredients in a large jar and set aside for a week in a dark place, inverting the bottle perhaps 2–3 times a day. After this time pour through a fine-meshed sieve lined with a double layer of muslin or cheesecloth. Then pour into a bottle, stopper well and use as a cordial.

TO MAKE WINE OF WATER – MOCK WINE
Epulario, Or, The Italian Banquet, 1516, translated into English 1598
'To make wine of water. Take the grapes of a wild vine and drye them in the son then beat them into powder, and put them into water and it will have the tast and colour of wine, and if the grape be white it will have the same colour, if red the like.'

STEPONY – RAISIN WINE
The Compleat City and Country Cook: Or, Accomplish'd House-wife, 1732
A 'stean' was a vessel for liquids, or, in later use, for bread, meat, fish, etc. It was a pot or pitcher usually made of clay, with two handles or ears and is from the same source as the word used for a type of beer mug, a German *stein*. The *Oxford English Dictionary* defines *stepony* as 'a kind of raisin-wine, made from raisins with lemon-juice and sugar added.' Again, this is a later recipe for a wine that the Tudors knew – there were very few recipes for drinks until Stuart and later times as the cooks of the household were generally not responsible for brewing and distilling.

'Stepony or Raisin Wine. Take six pounds of Raisins of the Sun shred, three pounds of good Powder Sugar, the Juice of six Lemons, and the Peel of three whole. Boil them half an Hour in six gallons of Spring-Water, then take it off the Fire and pour it into a Stean, cover it close for three or four Days, stir it twice a Day, put in a little Spice, Sugar and Rose-water; afterwards strain it out, bottle it up, and it will be fit to drink in a Fortnight or three Weeks. There may be added to it Cowslips or Clove Gilliflowers, according to the Season of the Year.'

CLARREY – HONEY-MULLED SPICED WHITE WINE

The Master-Cook of Richard II, *The Forme of Cury*, *c.* 1390

'Claret. Take cinnamon and galingale, grains of paradise, and a little pepper, and make powder, and mix it with good white wine and the third part honey and run it through a cloth.'

Ingredients: 750 ml sweet white wine; 400 ml honey; 1 tbsp cinnamon; 1 tbsp galingale; 1 tbsp ground cardamom; 1 tsp grains of paradise; 1 tsp white pepper; cheesecloth.

Method: Add the wine and 300 ml honey to a saucepan and then bring gently to a simmer. Skim off the scum as it rises, taste for sweetness and add more honey as necessary. Remove from the heat and stir in the spices. Leave covered for 24 hours, during which time the spices will form a residue in the bottom of the pan. Use a ladle to pass the wine into another container, through a strainer lined with 2 or 3 layers of cheesecloth to remove the spices. Bottle and allow to stand for at least a month before serving. It is even better if you allow it to age for a year, so make after Christmas for the following festive season.

CAUDELL (1) – TUDOR ADVOCAAT

An Ordinance of Pottage, Beinecke MS 163, 1460

'Caudle. Beat egg yolks with wine or ale, so that it is runny. Add sugar, saffron, but no salt. Beat well together and set it on the fire on clean coals. Stir the bottom well, and the sides until just scalding hot. Then take it and stir away fast, and if you need, add more wine. If it rises too quickly, put it in cold water to the middle of the outside of the pot, and stir it away fast. Serve it forth.'

Ingredients: 5 egg yolks; 170 ml white wine or real ale; sugar to taste; pinch of saffron.

Method: In a saucepan, beat together the egg yolks, wine, sugar and saffron. Heat the mixture over a medium heat, stirring continually, until the caudle is hot and thick and fluffy. Be careful to not let it burn or stick to the saucepan. Serve at once, in small glasses as a drink, or as sauce with desserts.

CAUDELE (2)

Two Fifteenth-Century Cookery-Books – Laud MS. 553, c. 1420

'Caudele. Nym eyren [eggs], and sweng wel to-gedere / chauf ale and do therto / lie it with amydon [wheat starch], do therto a porcion of sugur, or a perty of hony, and a perti of safron; boille hit, and ʒif [serve] hit forth.'

CAUDLE TO COMFORT THE STOMACKE – OLD MAN'S CAUDLE

Thomas Dawson's The Good Huswifes Jewell, 1585, 1594, 1596

'To make a Caudle to comfort the stomacke, good for an old man. Take a pinte of good Muscadine, and as much of good stale ale, mingle them to-gether, then take the yolkes of twelue or thirteene Egges newe laide, beat well the Egges firste by themselves, with the wine and ale, and so boyle it together, and put thereto a quarterne of Suger, and a fewe whole Mace, and so stirre it well, til it seeth a good while, and when it is well sod, put therin a few slices of bread if you will, and so let it soke a while, and it will be right good and wholesome.'

TUDOR POSSET – ALCOHOLIC CURDLED CREAM

A.W., The Booke of Goode Cookry Very Necessary for all Such as Delight Therein, 1584, 1591

'I was so blinded with sack posset I could not see my deliverers' – Edward Ravenscroft, *Mamamouchi, or The citizen turn'd gentleman*, 1675

'Take a posnet full of creame and séethe it and put Suger and Sinamon in it, then take halfe Ale and halfe Sacke and put Suger and Sinamon in it.' A.W, 1584

Ingredients: 1 glass single cream; 1 glass rose water; ½ glass ale; ½ glass sherry; ½ glass brandy; 4 tsp brown sugar; 1 tsp cinnamon; 1 tsp nutmeg; ½ tsp allspice; 2 tbsp chopped angelica (fresh or candied); 4 egg yolks, beaten.

Method: Heat but do not boil all of the ingredients together for 2 minutes, whisking well with a fork, and pour into cups.

EGGNOG – AN ALCOHOLIC'S CUSTARD

Eggnog, or 'egg milk punch', was generally only enjoyed by the upper classes, as dairy and egg products were expensive and difficult to keep fresh. It seems to be derived from Tudor *posset*. It was also called an 'egg flip' from the practice of 'flipping', rapidly pouring the mixture between two pitchers to mix it. Egg flip was made from beer, brandy or rum, eggs, sugar, spices and milk poured together and heated with a hot poker which caused a frothing effect. The term 'nog' may have originated from the term 'noggin', a wooden drinking cup commonly used for alcohol. Eggnog was popular at court and the first recorded eggnog made and consumed in the Americas was by Captain John Smith's 1607 Jamestown settlement. In honour of the good old USA, bourbon is added to this recipe, which is more of a custard than a punch.

Ingredients: 8 large eggs; 4 egg yolks; 1 cup normal sugar; 5 cups whole milk; 1½ cups brandy or rum; 1 cup bourbon; 1 tbsp pure vanilla extract; ½ tsp ground nutmeg; 2 cups whipping cream; 2 tbsp instantly dissolving sugar.

Method: Mix eggs, yolks and normal sugar together. Pour the mixture into a saucepan and heat slowly, gradually stirring in the milk. Gently heat and stir steadily until the mixture forms a custard. Pour the custard into a large bowl and stir in vanilla, rum, bourbon and nutmeg. Let the mixture cool, then cover and refrigerate for several hours, or until the next day. 30 minutes before serving, whip the cream and instantly dissolving superfine sugar until it forms soft peaks. Fold into the chilled mixture until completely mixed. Serve in chilled glasses, garnished with ground nutmeg.

BUTTERED BEERE

The Good Huswifes Handmaide for the Kitchin, 1594, 1597 (and 1588)

This possibly evolved from *caudel* and is a splendidly warming winter drink. You can add warmed milk to the final product, if desired.

'To make Buttered Beere. Take three pintes of Beer, put five yolkes of Egges to it, straine them together, and set it in a pewter pot to the fyre, and put to it halfe a pound of Sugar, one penniworth of Nutmegs beaten, one penniworth of Cloves beaten, and halfepenniworth of Ginger beaten, and when it is all in, take another pewter pot and brewe them together, and set it to the fire againe, and when it is readie to boyle, take it from the fire, and put a dish of sweet butter into it, and brewe them together out of one pot into an other.'

Ingredients: 3 pints of good quality ale or beer; ¼ tsp ground ginger; ½ tsp ground cloves; ½ tsp ground nutmeg; 200 g Demerara sugar, adjusting to taste; 5 egg yolks; 120 g diced unsalted butter.

Method: Carefully pour the ale into a saucepan, without exciting it too much, and stir in the ground ginger, cloves and nutmeg. Gently heat this mixture to almost boiling, then turn down the heat and simmer. The frothy ale will now clear. Whisk the egg yolks and sugar in a bowl, until light and creamy. If it seems too sweet when you drink it, use less sugar next time. Remove the saucepan from the heat and add the egg yolk and sugar mixture, stirring constantly and returning to a low heat. Keep stirring constantly until the liquid starts to thicken slightly. Be careful not to let the saucepan become too hot or the egg yolks will scramble and the sugar will burn on the bottom before dissolving. Simmer this at a very low heat for 3 minutes. Take the pan from the heat and stir in the diced butter until it melts. Then froth the mixture with a hand whisk until it appears like frothy, milky tea. Otherwise you can copy the Tudors and 'flip', pouring from serving jug to serving jug, to froth it up. Allow to cool to a warm drinkable temperature, pour into small tankards and serve immediately.

BUTTERED BEERE ANOTHER WAY

Thomas Dawson's *The Good Huswifes Jewell*, 1585, 1594, 1596

Ingredients: 12 oz beer; 1 egg yolk; ¼ cup sugar; ¹⁄₁₆ tsp nutmeg; ¹⁄₁₆ tsp cloves; ¹⁄₁₆ tsp ginger; 2 tbsp butter.

Method: Put the egg yolk into a saucepan and slowly whisk in the beer. Add sugar and spices and heat over medium–high heat until the mixture just starts to come to a boil. Immediately remove from the heat, add butter and whisk until mixed. Serve hot.

YPOCRAS – HIPPOCRAS (1) – TUDOR SPICED MULLED WINE

Wynkin de Worde's *The Boke of Kervynge*, 1508, derived from recipes in John Russell's *The Boke of Nurture*, contains a hippocras recipe in verse.

Oriental spices were so expensive that only the aristocracy could afford them. *Turnsole* is the botanical source of the mauve coloured rags used for colouring hippocras and jellies and was a popular food colouring. Many different directions for preparation still exist for this aperitif, served either warm or cold with wafers, sweetmeats and comfits just before the main meal. Red wine gives you a pungent mixture, but a lighter *hippocras* can be made using a dry white wine. It is the ancestor of modern mulled wines.

'Take ginger, pepper, long pepper, grains of paradise, cassia, cinnamon, sugar and turnsole. See that you have five or six bags for your hippocras to run through, and a perch that your runners [straining bags] may hang on. Then you must have 6 pewter basins to stand under your bags. Then see your spice is ready and your ginger well pared or beat to powder. Then see your cinnamon sticks are well coloured and sweet cassia is not too gentle in operation. Cinnamon is hot or dry; grains of paradise are hot and moist; ginger, long pepper and sugar are hot and dry. Turnsole is wholesome and red wine for colouring. Now know the proportions of your Hippocras then beat your powders each by themselves and put them in bladders and hang your bags [making] sure they do not touch each other, but let each basin touch. Let the first basin hold a gallon and each of the other [basins] hold a pottle [4 pints]. Then put in your basin a gallon of red wine and into this your powders and stir them well. Then put them into the first bag and let it run. Then put them into the second bag. Then take a piece in your hand and test if it is strong of ginger, and season [or flavour] with cinnamon. If it is strong of cinnamon, season it with sugar and see that you let it run though six runners [or straining cloths]. Your Hippocras shall be the finer. Then put your Hippocras into a closed vessel and keep the receipt, for it will serve for sewes. Then serve your sovereign with wafers and Hippocras. Also see your compost be fair and clean, and your ale [is] five days old.'

Ingredients: 1 bottle of a cheap red or white wine; 1–2 cups honey, or 1–1½ cups sugar; 1 tbsp each of ginger, cinnamon, cardamom, white pepper, clove, nutmeg, caraway seed; cheesecloth.

Method: Bring the wine, honey or sugar to a simmer while stirring. If using honey, skim off the scum as it rises. Taste for sweetness and add honey or sugar as necessary. Remove from the heat, stir in spices, cover and allow to stand for 24 hours. The spices will form a thick residue which will settle to the bottom. Using a ladle, pass the wine into another container through a strainer lined with 2 or 3 layers of cheesecloth, to remove the spices, being careful to leave as much of the spice residue in the pot as possible. Make at least one month before serving, as it improves with age.

HIPPOCRAS (2) – TUDOR SPICED MULLED WINE
Le Ménagier De Paris, 1393

There is a memorable image of how to properly serve the drink at 'The Feast of the Pheasant' held at Lille in 1454. We thus read in the *Memoires d'Olivier de La Marche*: 'The dishes were such that they had to be served on trolleys, and seemed infinite in number… The figure of a girl, quite naked, stood against the pillar. Hippocras sprayed from her right breast and she was guarded by a live lion who sat near her on a table in front of my lord the duke… My lord the duke was served at table by a two-headed horse… next came a white stag ridden by a young boy who sang marvellously, while the stag accompanied him with the tenor part … Then two knights of the Order of the Golden Fleece brought in two damsels, together with a pheasant, which had a golden collar around its neck decorated with rubies and fine large pearls…'

'To make powdered hippocras, take a quarter-ounce of very fine cinnamon, hand-picked by tasting it, an ounce of very fine meche ginger and an ounce of grains of paradise, a sixth of an ounce of nutmeg and galingale together, and pound it all together. And when you want to make hippocras, take a good half-ounce or more of this powder and two quarter-ounces of sugar, and mix them together, and a quart of wine as measured in Paris.'

ENDNOTE

One cannot write a book such as this without coming up to date with the role of beer in relatively modern life. The colonies have in fact contributed strongly to the development of British cuisine, and the following Christmas dinner served just behind the lines in the First World War summarises all that was good about the British Empire. This was the wonderful Christmas dinner menu enjoyed by 'a body of Australian soldiers in France' in 1915, italics courtesy of this author.

COO-EE

17th (Australian) Ammunition Sub-Park.

Somewhere in France.

CHRISTMAS DINNER.

Patron: Major Hamilton

Committee: Lieut. Harvey, Sergeant-Major Campbell, Staff-Seageant Bird, Staff Sergeant Jackson, Corpl. Chapman, Driver J.B. Kelly, and Driver M. Williams. Catering under the direction of Staff-Sergeant Jackson, Electric Light by C. Worshop.

MENU.

HORS D'OEUVRES.

A Little Beer

SOUP.

Chicken Broth

Beer

ENTRÉE.

Giblet Pie

Some Beer

JOINT.

Roast Sirloin

Boiled Ham

Still more Beer

POULTRY.

Roast Turkey and Sausage

Roast Goose

Roast Duck and Apple Sauce

Roast Chicken and Ham

Still Beer

VEGETABLES

Brussels Sprouts

Boiled and Baked Potatoes.

Mashed Turnips

SWEETS.

Christmas Puddings

Again Beer

Crackers and Cheese

Smokes and Beer

TOAST – GOD SAVE THE KING.

Beer finis – by the Committee if necessary

Sick Parade 11 a.m., 26 December 1915

14

Tudor, Medieval and Stuart Recipe Books

PRIMARY SOURCES

Over fifty medieval recipe manuscripts remain in existence, not including the manuscripts of medical recipes, many of which contain culinary recipes. Fortunately, nearly all the early major recipe books have been digitised and are freely available on the internet. The first British-printed cookery book was published in 1500 under the title *This is the Boke of Cokery*. Eight years later *Boke of Kervynge* was printed, which gave detailed instructions for carving meats at a feast. These early British cookbooks were aimed at noble houses and formalised dining customs. Towards the end of the Tudor age, British cookbook publishing moved away from other European traditions and became predominated by literature aimed at female rather than male cooks, as demonstrated in books such as Thomas Dawson's *The Good Huswifes Jewell* (1585), Sir Hugh Plat's *Delights for Ladies* (1600) and Gervase Markham's *The English Housewife* (1615). All of these were based on earlier manuscript collections. These printed British cookbooks were unique in that they tend to be compiled directly from domestic receipt (recipe) books, hand-written manuscripts bound into book form, from upper class society.

Only the higher echelons of society would have had regular access to expensive ingredients such as sugar, spices, hothouse-grown fruits or plentiful livestock. Thomas Dawson, for example, took many of his recipes from the long-established practices of courtly kitchens and a number of his and Markham's recipes are directly attributed to noblemen and women. The majority of people, the poor, ate a bland and boring diet, so of course we are mainly left with recipes for the literate rich. The late sixteenth century was the first time that cookery books began to be published and acquired with any sort of regularity. Although many recipes are from an earlier age, these dishes were common in Tudor times. Equally, some dishes from early Stuart receipt books were dishes from the Tudor age, so there are inclusions from before and after the Tudor age. The most important primary sources for research are detailed below.

c. 1390: THE FORME OF CURY: By the Chief Master-Cooks of King Richard II (1377–99). *The Forme of Cury* (cookery) was the name given by the Reverend Samuel Pegge (1704–96) to a vellum scroll of cookery written by the Master Cooks of Richard II. Pegge transcribed it in 1791 from late Middle English. It is easily the most well known medieval guide to cooking, with around 196–205 recipes. The exact number of recipes varies slightly between different versions, but it was available and used throughout the Tudor reign. *The Forme of Cury* is the first English text to mention olive oil, cloves, mace and gourds in relation to British food. We also witness what were then luxurious spices: caraway, nutmeg, cardamom, ginger and pepper and there are recipes for cooking whales, cranes, curlews, herons, seals and porpoises.

1393: LE MÉNAGIER DE PARIS, often abbreviated as *Le Ménagier,* is a guide on a woman's proper behaviour in marriage and running a household. Like the other books, its many recipes include information on ingredients and preparation methods, but omit quantifying ingredients and do not specify the amount of heat and time of cooking. Many of the recipes are provided as remedies for common complaints. This is due to the crossover, in medieval works, between herbalism, medicine and cooking. Indeed, there often appears to be no real difference between them, as books for cooking will include information on herbalism and medicine and vice versa. *Le Ménagier* includes a variety of different types of recipes such as soups, preparations for meats, eggs, fish, sauces, beverages, pastry, tarts and so on.

c. 1390 onwards: CURYE ON INGLYSCH is the heading given to *English Culinary Manuscripts of the Fourteenth-Century (Including the Forme of Cury)*, published by The Early English Text Society in 1985. It has been compiled from more than twenty medieval manuscripts, including *Utilis Coquinario*. The recipes date from the fourteenth century and it appears that many of them found only on the menus of the upper classes, remained virtually unchanged until the sixteenth century. The menus include the all-important order of serving, that strict etiquette that ruled medieval mealtimes and which meant that most members of a household were only entitled to the first course and that the more delicate dishes were served only to the higher ranks.

c. 1430: LIBER CURE COCORUM copied and edited from *Sloane MS.* 1986 by Richard Morris, published for the Philological Society in Berlin in 1862. *Liber Cure Cocorum* is a cookery book in verse dating from northwest Lancashire, found as an appendix of the *Boke of Curtayse*. It is written in a northern English dialect and is titled *The Slyghtes of Cure* (The Art of Cookery). The poem gives a great variety of dishes under the headings of potages, broths, roasted meats, baked meats, sauces and *petecure*, including the earliest references to haggis, humble pie and other dishes.

c. 1430–40: POTAGE DYVERS. This book is divided into three parts: the first is headed *Kalendare de Potages dyuers* (directory of diverse dishes); the second part is *Kalendare de Leche Metys* (guide to sliced meats); and the third part is *Dyuerse bake metis* (diverse baked meats). Menus for a number of extravagant banquets are included. The books contain some detailed instructions, such as how to grind, chop, boil, strain or scald ingredients.

c. 1440: A BOKE OF KOKERY contains 182 recipes and gives detailed directions to show the cook how to hew (chop), mele (mix), powdr (salt) and strain. It also tells cooks how to flavour, how to alter techniques for old or young meat and how to adjust recipes for Lent.

c. 1440: TWO FIFTEENTH CENTURY COOK BOOKS – *Harleian MS. 279* (*c.* 1430), & *Harl. MS. 4016* (*c.* 1450), with extracts from *Ashmolean MS. 1439, Laud MS. 553, & Douce MS.* Transcriptions carried out in 1888 by Thomas Austin of two manuscripts in the Harleian Collection, plus related culinary items from other medieval sources.

c. 1440: LE VIANDIER *de Guillaume Tirel dit Taillevent*, ed. Jerome Pichon 1892. A newer edition is by Terence Scully, titled *The Vivendier*, Prospect Books, 1997. It draws upon the same sources as *Le Ménagier* and is attributed to a cook in the French royal kitchens at about the same time as *The Forme of Cury*.

c. 1450: THE BOKE OF NURTUR. John Russell (*fl.* 1450), was usher-in-chamber and marshal-in-hall to Humphrey, Duke of Gloucester. He made his experience serve as the basis of a handbook of contemporary manners and domestic management. It paints a picture of the household life of a noble from a servant's point of view; setting out the duties of a butler, the way to lay a table, the art of carving and other particulars. Parts of Russell's works are found in Wynkin de Worde's *Boke of Keruynge*, printed in 1513.

1460: AN ORDINANCE OF POTTAGE – *Beinecke MS 163. An Ordinance of Pottage. An Edition of the Fifteenth Century Culinary Recipes in Yale University's MS Beinecke 163*, edited by Constance B. Hieatt was published in London in 1988 and contains almost 200 recipes, adapted recipes and a commentary.

1480: A NOBLE BOKE OFF COOKRY FFOR A PRYNCE HOUSSOLDE OR ENY OTHER ESTATELY HOUSSOLDE – *Holkham MSS 674*. The text of this anonymous manuscript from Holkham Hall was prepared for publication by Mrs Alexander Napier, and was printed in 1882.

c. 1490: GENTYLL MANLY COKERE AND COPYD OF THE SERGENT TO THE KYNG – *MS Pepys 1047*. This is the opening line of the section *Miscell. of Receipt's/M.S.S. Temp. R. Ed. 4*, which includes culinary recipes. The manuscript was written during the reign of Edward IV and was probably compiled by the time of Henry VII. It entered the collection of Samuel Pepys, in 1700, three years before his death. Recipes can be found in *Stere Hit Well*, 1972.

1500: THIS IS THE BOKE OF COKERY – *Here beginneth a noble boke of festes royalle and Cokery a boke for a pryncis housholde or any other estates* – This work gives the reader recipes for use at feasts or in an aristocratic household and details many royal feasts that allow us to know exactly what was served to Plantagenet kings. This work was the first of its kind in the English vernacular.

1508: HERE BEGYNNETH THE BOKE OF KERVYNGE … The colophon is 'Here endeth the boke of servyce and kervynge and sewynge and all maner of offyce in his kynde unto a prynce or ony other estate and all the feestes in the yere. Emprynted by Wynkyn de Worde at London in the Fletestrete at the sygne of the sonne. The yere of our lorde, M,CCCCC,VIII.' It was reprinted in 1513 and later.

1539: THE CASTEL OF HELTHE, *gathered, and made by Sir Thomas Elyot knight...* This is not a cookery book, but contains advice as to the uses and physical effects of different articles of diet.

1545: A PROPER NEWE BOOKE OF COKERYE, *declarynge what maner of meates be beste in season, for al times in the yere, and how they ought to be dressed, and served at the table, both for fleshe dayes, and fyshe dayes...* Anonymous, a transcription of a cookbook in the possession of Matthew Parker, Archbishop of Canterbury from 1559 until 1575. The first book was used by Margaret Parker, wife of Matthew Parker, in running her household and was first published in 1557.

1558: THE SECRETES OF THE REVERENDE MAISTER ALEXIS OF PIEMONT *Containyng excellente remedies against divers diseases, woundes, and other accidents...* Translated from French into English, by Wynkin de Worde, it contains recipes for making Hippocras, confitures, etc.

1562: HERE FOLOWETH A COMPENDYOUS REGIMENTE OR DYETARY OF HEALTH *made in Mount pyllor: compyled by Andrewe Boorde, of physycke doctor.*

Also *The Breuyary of Health*, written also by 1542, though no edition is known till 1547. Like Elyot's *Castle of Health*, this is not a cookery book, but gives advice as to the use of food.

1573: THE TREASURIE OF COMMODIOUS CONCEITS & HIDDEN SECRETS, AND MAY BE CALLED, THE HUSWIVES CLOSET OF HEALTHFULL PROVISION – John Partridge. Three of Partridge's works are small books of recipes for cookery, confectionery, remedies and medicines. All these books were reprinted, revised and enlarged over the next century with varied titles. It was later published as *The Treasury of Hidden Secrets*. His books were reprinted many times.

1583: THE SCHOOLEMASTER, *or Teacher of Table Philosophie*. 'The first Booke of Table Philosophie treateth of the nature and qualitie of all manner meates, drinkes, and Sauces that are used at meales...' This was written by Thomas Twyne, a doctor of Lewes, or Thomas Turswell, a Canon of St. Paul's.

1584: A BOOK OF COOKRYE *Very Necessary for all such as delight therin.* Gathered by A. W.

1585, 1594, 1596, 1597: THE GOOD HUSWIFES JEWELL *Wherein is to be found most excellent and rare Devises for conceites in Cookery, found out by the practise of Thomas Dawson*

1586: THE OLDE MANS DIETARIE. This is not a cookery book, but gives advice as to the use of foods.

1582, 1586: THE WIDDOWES TREASURE, John Partridge.

1588: THE GOOD HOUS-WIVES TREASURIE. *Beeing a verye necessarie Booke instructing to the dressing of Meates.*

1591: *A BOOK OF COOKRYE Very Necessary for all such as delight therin.* Gathered by A.W.

1594 (and 1588): THE GOOD HUSWIFES HANDMAIDE FOR THE KITCHIN. *Containing manie principall pointes of Cookerie, as well how to dresse meates, after sundrie the best fashions used in England and other Countries,* Thomas Dawson. The headline is *A New Booke of Cookerie.* Cookery book writers now begin to provide practical instructions of the kind we would recognise in recipe books of today. For example, quantities are given in quarts, spoonfuls, handfuls, pints, gallons, pounds and ounces.

1594 and 1597: THE GOOD HUSWIVES HANDMAID, FOR COOKERIE *in her Kitchin, &c.,* Thomas Dawson.

1595, 1631, 1639: THE WIDDOWES TREASURE.

1597: A BOOKE OF COOKERIE, *otherwise called: The good Huswives Handmaid for the kitchen,* Thomas Dawson. This is the same book as 1594 with a new title. The headline is 'A New Booke of Cookerie'.

1597: THE BOOKE OF CARVING AND SEWING, Thomas Dawson.

1598: EPULARIO, *or The Italian Banquet.* A translation of a 1516 book by Giovanne de Rosselli.

1599: DYETS DRY DINNER: *Consisting of eight severall Courses: Fruites. Whitmeats. Hearbes. Spice. Flesh. Sauce. Fish. Tabacco. All served in after the order of Time universall. By Henry Buttes, Maister of Artes.* Henry Buttes was elected master of the Corpus Christi in 1626 and vice chancellor in 1629. 'He being to preach before the university as vice-chancellor on Easter-day, April i. 1632, was found hanging in his garters in his own chamber.'

1604: ELINOR FETTIPLACE'S RECEIPT BOOK: *Elizabethan Country House Cooking,* edited and with commentary by Hilary Spurling, 1986. Elinor (1570–1647) was the wife of Sir Richard Fettiplace of Appleton Manor and her book includes many recipes we now think of as standard English fare, for example orange marmalade, rabbit pie, bread and butter pudding. These recipes offer an amazing insight into the culinary delights of late Elizabethan/ early Jacobean society.

1608: A CLOSET FOR LADIES AND GENTLEWOMEN, *or, The Art of preserving. Conserving, and Candyng.* It resembles *Delightes for Ladies* by Hugh Plat, to whom the book is attributed, but it may be a rival work. It was actually registered with the London Company of Stationers on 1 September 1602 but not published until 1608, which makes this a late Elizabethan book.

1609: THE ARTE OF PRESERVING, CONSERVING, CANDYING by Hugh Plat. Plat was the son of a brewer, and wrote extensively on 'ladies concerns', domestic economy, as well as on his inventions of assorted new methods of iron-founding and making synthetic fuels.

c. 1610: MISTRESS SARAH LONGE, HER RECEIPT BOOKE. There are sections on 'preserves & conserves', 'Cokery' and 'Physicke & Chirurgery.' Alongside recipes for gooseberry foole and rice pudding are instructions to stop bleeding and remedies for miscarriage.

1615: A NEW BOOKE OF COOKERIE. *Wherein is set forth the newest and most commendable Fashion for Dressing or Sowcing, eyther Flesh, Fish, or Fowle. Together with making of all sorts of Iellyes, and other made-Dishes for seruice; both to beautifie and adorne eyther Nobleman or Gentlemans Table. Hereunto also is added the most exquisite London Cookerie. All set forth according to the now, new, English and French fashion. Set forth by the obseruation of a Traueller*, John Murrel.

1615: COUNTREY CONTENTMENTS, OR, THE ENGLISH HUS-WIFE by Gervase Markham. *The Hus-Wife* was a companion volume to his book *The English Husbandman*, on farming techniques. Gervase (or Jervis) Markham (*c.* 1568–1637) Markham may have been a soldier and is reputed to have imported the first Arab horse into England.

1615: THE ENGLISH HUSWIFE, *Containing the Inward and Outward Virtues Which Ought to Be in a Complete Woman* – as above, printed with different titles.

1620: A BOOKE OF COOKERIE. *And the order of Meates to bee served to the Table, both for Flesh and Fish days*, Thomas Dawson.

1669: THE CLOSET OF THE EMINENTLY LEARNED SIR KENELME DIGBIE KT. OPENED, PUBLISHED BY HIS SON'S CONSENT. This contains many sixteenth-century recipes and is notable for the culinary tastes of various lords and ladies.

SECONDARY SOURCES

Aikin, Lucy, *Memoirs of the court of Queen Elizabeth* (Longman, 1828)

Anon, *The Booke of the Household of Queene Elizabeth ... in the 43rd Yeare of her Reigne* [1601] which appears in *A Collection of Ordinances and Regulations for the Government of the Royal Household, made in Divers Reigns from King Edward III to King William and Queen Mary, published for the Society of Antiquaries* (1787)

Anon, *A Collection of Old English Customs: And Curious Bequests and Charities, Extracted from the Reports Made by the Commissioners for Enquiring Into Charities in England and Wales* (1842)

Anon, *The Whole Duty of a Woman, or, An Infallible Guide to the Fair Sex. Containing Rules, Directions, and Observations, for Their Conduct and Behavior Through All Ages and Circumstances of Life, as Virgins, Wives, Or Widows. With Direction, how to obtain all Useful and Fashionable Accomplishments suitable to the Sex. In which are comprised al Parts of Good Housewifry, particularly Rules and Receipts in Every Kind of Cookery* (1737)

Anon, *Household Books of the third and fourth Earls of Derby*, as published by The Chetham Society in 1853

Austin, Thomas, *Two Fifteenth Century Cookbooks. Harleian MS. 279 & Harl. MS. 4016, with extracts from Ashmole MS. 1429, Laud MS. 553, & Douce MS 55,* The Early English Text Society (London 1888)

Brears, Peter, *All the King's Cooks: The Tudor Kitchens of King Henry VIII at Hampton Court Palace* (Souvenir Press, 1999, 2011)

Breverton, Terry, *Breverton's Complete Herbal – A Book of Remarkable Plants* (Quercus, 2011)

Breverton, Terry, *Wales, a Historical Companion* (Amberley, 2009)

Breverton, Terry, *The Physicians of Myddfai: Cures and Remedies of the Medieval World* (Cambria, 2012)

Breverton, Terry, *Breverton's First World War Curiosities* (Amberley, 2014)

Breverton, Terry, *Breverton's Nautical Curiosities – A Book of the Sea* (Quercus, 2010)

Breverton, Terry, *Everything You Wanted to Know about the Tudors but were Afraid to Ask* (Amberley, 2014)

Butler, Charles, *The Feminine Monarchie, Or the Historie of Bees: Shewing Their Admirable Nature, and Properties, Their Generation, and Colonies, Their Government, Loyaltie, Art, Industrie, Enemies, Warres, Magnamimitie, &c. Together with the Right Ordering of Them from Time to Time: and the Sweet Profit Arising Thereof* (Oxford 1609, London 1623)

Carter, Charles, *The Compleat City and Country Cook: Or, Accomplish'd House-wife. Containing, Several Hundred of the Most Approv'd Receipts in Cookery, Confectionary, Cordials [etc.] … Illustrated with Forty-nine Large Copper Plates, Directing the Regular Placing the Various Dishes on the Table … Also, Bills of Fare According to the Several Seasons for Every Month of the Year* (1732)

Chetham Society, *Household Books of the third and fourth Earls of Derby* (1853)

Davidson, Alan, *Oxford Companion to Food* (Oxford University Press, USA 1999)

Dyer, Christopher, *Everyday Life in Medieval England* (Cambridge University Press, 2000)

Ellis, William, *The Country Housewife's Family Companion* (1750)

Furnivall, Frederick James, *The Babees Book, or a 'Lytyl Reporte' of how Young People should Behave, MS. Harl. 5086, c. 1475, The bokes of nurture of Hugh Rhodes and John Russell, Wynkyn de Worde's Boke of keruynge, The booke of demeanor, The boke of curtasye, Seager's Schoole of vertue, &c. &c.*

Hansen, Marianne, 'And Thus You Have a Lordly Dish: Fancy and Showpiece Cookery in an Augsberg Patrician Kitchen.' *Medieval Food and Drink, Acta, vol. xxi.* (State University of New York Press, 1995) The proceedings of the 1994 Acta conference. This is the first English translation of some recipes from the manuscript written in 1553 by Sabina Welser of Augsburg.

Haviland, Iohn, *The Feminine Monarchie, Or the Historie of Bees: Shewing Their Admirable Nature, and Properties, Their Generation, and Colonies, Their Government, Loyaltie, Art, Industrie, Enemies, Warres, Magnamimitie, &c. Together with the Right Ordering of Them from Time to Time: and the Sweet Profit Arising Thereof* (1623)

Hazlitt, William Carew, *Old Cookery Books and Ancient Cuisine* (1902)

Hentzner, Paul, *A Description of Elizabeth I & her Court at Greenwich, from Journey into England* – Hentzner wrote *Of the Manners of the English* in 1598, in his *Itinerarium Germaniae, Galliae, Angliae, Italiae, cum Indice Locorum, Rerum atque Verborum* (published 1612)

Hieatt, Constance B., and Butler, Sharon, *Pleyn Delit: Medieval Cookery for Modern Cooks* (University of Toronto Press, 1976)

Hieatt, Constance B., and Jones, Robin F., *Two Anglo-Normal Culinary*

Collections Edited from British Library Manuscripts Additional 32085 and Royal 12.C.xii, *Speculum* 1986. (The first manuscript was bound some time after 1600 by William Kin).

Hodgett, Gerald A. J., *Stere Hitt Well. A book of medieval refinements, recipes and remedies from a manuscript in Samuel Pepys' library* (Cornmarket Reprints, 1972)

Holme, Randle, *Academy of Armory: The Description of the Seven Cardinal Vertues.*

The Academy of Armory, or, a Storehouse of Armory and Blazon containing the several variety of created beings, and how born in Coats of Arms, both Foreign and Domestick c. 1640 (Although heraldry and weaponry are the major subjects of the book, many other topics are covered too – including food and cookery).

Lady, A, *The lady's companion: or, an infallible guide to the fair sex Containing, rules, directions, and observations, for their conduct and behaviour through … of life, as virgins, wives* (1743)

Loades, David, *The Tudor Court* (Headstart, 1992)

Lodge, Rev. Barton, *Palladius On husbondrie. From the unique ms. of about 1420 A.D. in Colchester castle* (London 1879) Translated from the Latin.

Kiple, Kenneth F. and Ornelas, Kriemhild Conee, *The Cambridge World History of Food* (Cambridge University Press, 2000)

Pennant, Thomas, *Some Account of London* (1790)

Plat, Hugh, *Certaine Philosophical Preparations of Foode and Beverage for Sea-men, in their long voyages; with some necessary, approoved, and Hermeticall medicines and Antidotes, fit to be had in readinesse, at sea, for prevention and cure of divers diseases* (1607)

Plat, Hugh, *Sundrie new and Artificiall remedies against Famine* (1595)

Raffald, Elizabeth *The Experienced English Housekeeper* (1769)

Sandford, Francis and King, Gregory, *A Way to Get Wealth: Containing Six Principal Vocations and Callings* (1687)

Meltonville, Marc, *The Taste of the Fire, The Story of the Tudor Kitchens at Hampton Court Palace* (Historic Royal Palaces, 2007)

Mortimer, Ian, *How the Tudors invented breakfast, BBC History Magazine* (April 2013)

Sambrook, Pamela, *Country House Brewing in England, 1500–1900* (Bloomsbury, 1996)

Scully, Terence, *Cuoco Napoletano. The Neapolitan Recipe Collection late fifteenth century: A Critical Edition and English Translation* (University of Michigan Press, 2000)

Sim, Alison, *Food and Feast in Tudor England* (The History Press 1997, 2011)

Spicer, Dorothy Gladys, *An English Oven* (The Women's Press, 1948)

Spurling, Hilary, *Elinor Fettiplace's Receipt Book* (Penguin, 1986)

Trager, James, *The Food Chronology* (Henry Holt and Company, Inc., New York, 1995)

Tusser, Thomas, *Five Hundred Points of Good Husbandry* (1557)

Vaughan, William, *Approved Directions for Health, both Natural and Artificial: derived from the best physitians as well moderne as auncient* (1612)

Vaughan, William, *Certaine Philosophical Preparations of Foode and Beverage for Sea-men* (1607 and 1595)

Warner, Richard *Antiquitates Culinariae Or Curious Tracts Relating to the Culinary Affairs of the Old English* (1791)

Woolley, Hannah (1622–75), *The Queen-like Closet OR RICH CABINET Scored with all manner of RARE RECEIPTS FOR Preserving, Candying and Cookery* (1672)

Wecker, John, Dr. in Physick, *Eighteen Books Of the Secrets Of Art & Nature* (1661)

Wright, Thomas, *Songs and Carols Now First Printed, from a Manuscript of the Fifteenth Century* (The Percy Society, London 1847)

USEFUL WEBSITES

Nearly all of the manuscripts and books mentioned in the text have been digitised to be easily downloadable. Of particular excellence and endeavour are the *godecookery* and *celtnet* sites.

celtnet.org.uk (Dyfed Lloyd Evans' brilliant website for online food with 19,300 recipes, 10 free historic cookery books and 180 wild foods);

godecookery.com – the superb website of James L. Matterer;

medievalcookery.com;

oldcook.com;

foodsofengland.co.uk;

perryandcider.co.uk (Gillian Grafton's website);

thousandeggs.com (Cindy Renfrow's website);

florilegium.org takes you to Stefan's Florilegium, the website of Mark S. Harris (aka Stefan);

coquinaria.nl/english/recipes.

List of Illustrations